MW00586463

Get ready to be warriored-up and do battle! This book will arm you with actionable intelligence so you can take your spiritual warfare to the next level.

Lt. David Kemp, twenty-eight-year veteran police officer and SWAT commander

On Spiritual Warfare is the sequel to the bestseller *On Spiritual Combat*. This new book is the most effective apologetics and personal faith guide available today. It is poetic, motivating, doctrinally sound, and full of Scripture. It will keep you reading page after page. Lt. Col. Dave Grossman and Sgt. Chris Pascoe have done a masterful job of explaining the undeniable connection between evil, violence, and crime in the world and the spiritual warfare required to defeat it. This book is a reminder that "evildoers…will go from bad to worse" (2 Timothy 3:13), but the righteous have a duty to stand and fight in the face of evil. *On Spiritual Warfare* reveals that our law enforcement officers are more than just "cops"; they are soldiers of light, commissioned and powered by God to fight injustice and evil.

Sgt. Jeff Wolf (Ret.), author of the bestseller *Blue Lies: The War on Justice*

Now more than ever, those who serve and protect us are under assault. In order to do their job properly, they need to understand that while they may have been trained to combat *physical* threats, *spiritual* threats can also destroy lives. *On Spiritual Warfare* will help guide them toward an effectual engagement in that spiritual conflict.

Joe Giorgione, founder and CEO, 1776 Training and Consulting LLC; emergency medical service and fire instructor for over twenty-five years

My copy of *On Spiritual Combat* is dog-eared, highlighted, and full of notes. It occupies the space on my bookshelf next to *The Westminster Catechism*. The current book, *On Spiritual Warfare: 22 Warning Orders for Virtuous Warriors*, is the next step, delivering an instructional handbook for Christian warriors engaged in both spiritual and physical combat. Authors Lt. Col. Dave Grossman and Sgt. Chris Pascoe have created a treasure trove of verse, hymns, prayers, and commentary that is both inspirational in its message and practical in its application. I especially recommend this book for members of church security teams who must confront evil in the physical realm as they defend their flocks from violent attack.

Mike Smock, CEO, Distributed Security, Inc.

Since 1998, I've served in various military and law enforcement capacities. In these vocations, we are absolutely engaged in spiritual warfare. I wish I'd had *On Spiritual Warfare* years ago to help guide me as I walked this path, and I am thankful to have it now. This is no ordinary devotional. It is truly a modern adaptation of Erasmus' *Manual of a Christian Knight*, full of warnings and guidance on how to navigate our perilous times successfully. I believe that embracing the disciplines that are spelled out in this book will help you fully realize and dwell within the freedom that Christ has bought for us, and help you truly thrive in your role as protector and servant. God is on the move, and he is calling warriors to step out in faith. *On Spiritual Warfare* is going to have a powerful ministry and effect on and through those warriors. It has truly been written for such a time as this!

Andy Bowell, police officer

Do you want to be triumphant in spiritual warfare against the forces of evil? If so, then you have found a special gem containing generations of value. The authors of *On Spiritual Warfare* have been on their sheep-dog journey for a long time compared to most of us, and in their book they offer a bag *full* of treasures they've collected. If you think of the Bible as a five-thousand-piece puzzle, then *On Spiritual Warfare* and the previous book, *On Spiritual Combat*, are like the lid to the puzzle box with a beautiful full-color photo: the clarity they provide is amazing! Let *On Spiritual Warfare* be the guide on your path to becoming one of God's special ops warriors.

Miss Sequoia Palmquist

On Spiritual Warfare is neither a traditional devotional nor a theoretical treatise on the Bible's teachings on spiritual warfare. It is a timely, insightful, morale-boosting manual on effectively engaging the spiritual dangers in our world today. We can and must engage evil on both physical and spiritual fronts, and authors Dave Grossman and Chris Pascoe have knowledge and experience with both. Their book leads us in becoming the warriors that God needs us to be rather than falling as mere casualties or, even worse, as pawns or combatants for the other side. *On Spiritual Warfare* is the guidebook we all need.

William D. Watkins, writer, editor, teacher, and speaker; author of numerous publications, including *The New Absolutes* and *The Transforming Habits of a Growing Christian*

On ✝ Spiritual Warfare

22
Warning Orders for Virtuous Warriors

Lt. Col. Dave Grossman and Sgt. Chris Pascoe

BroadStreet
PUBLISHING

BroadStreet Publishing® Group, LLC
Savage, Minnesota, USA
BroadStreetPublishing.com

On Spiritual Warfare: 22 Warning Orders for Virtuous Warriors
Copyright © 2023 by David A. Grossman and Christopher L. Pascoe

9781424566228 (faux leather)
9781424566235 (ebook)

All italics in quotations are those of the authors put there for emphasis.

Stock or custom editions of BroadStreet Publishing titles may be purchased in bulk for educational, business, ministry, fundraising, or sales promotional use. For information, please email orders@broadstreetpublishing.com.

Cover and interior by Garborg Design Works | garborgdesign.com

Printed in China

23 24 25 26 27 5 4 3 2 1

To soldiers, sailors, airmen, marines,
To all first responders,
To everyone who moves toward danger.

To teachers and healthcare workers,
To social workers, clergy, and parents,
To all those who protect and defend.

And let us dedicate ourselves to serving Jesus Christ,
Who died so that everyone may live,
Who came to destroy the works of the devil.

Oh Lord, forgive us our sins,
Lead us in the battle against evil.
Through the power of the Holy Spirit,
Make us your obedient, faithful sheepdogs.
Amen.

Author's Note

This book is a joint endeavor between Chris Pascoe and me, Dave Grossman, and, we pray, the Holy Spirit.

Chris had a hand in every aspect of creating this book. Indeed, Chris deserves full credit for the initial research and concept development concerning Erasmus, Luther, and the twenty-two orders and warnings derived from their writings. Chris established the initial foundation upon the works of these men, also drawing from his own decades of police experience and godly scholarship.

I, Dave, have contributed from my personal perspective, drawing from my experiences, teaching, and presentations, and continue to build upon themes found in my book *On Spiritual Combat*. When the first-person voice (I, me, my, mine) is used in this book, the voice is mine.

Chris, however, deserves much credit and appreciation for his many contributions to and inspiration in writing this book.

And we both give God all the glory!

Contents

Foreword

A few years back, someone I consider a mentor, a dear brother in Christ, and a friend, Dave Grossman, suggested we write a book to spiritually parallel his work *On Combat*. It was a daunting task in my eyes, but one I was not afraid to tackle. The intimidation came in doing the work justice.

Over the years we have heard from many of you about how *On Spiritual Combat* has affected your lives in positive ways.

There are many things we can do in this life, many good and noble deeds. But, my friends, the things that matter the most are those things of eternal value.

We encourage you to read *On Spiritual Combat*, but the book now in front of you can stand on its own. *On Spiritual Warfare* is concerned with *advanced* spiritual warfare. It is intended for truly hungry Christian warriors seeking the strong meat of Bible doctrine (Hebrews 5:14). For them it will be a welcome and vital dish served in the foxholes of battle in this life. And all of it will be for God's glory.

As you navigate through this book, I want to personally challenge you to be a dangerous and courageous believer. In the book of Revelation, cowards are placed in the same category as the sexually immoral, idolaters, liars, and those who practice magic arts (21:8). None of them, including cowards, inherit the kingdom of God. This is not a time in history for cowardly men and women. And there is no such thing as a cowardly Christian.

So equip yourself for battle! Prepare to advance against the enemy of our souls. Prepare to advance against the kingdom of darkness and deliver a taste of heaven to those living in hell on earth. Fight with everything you have because hell is fighting to destroy everything that you love.

Adam Davis

Author/coauthor of *On Spiritual Combat: 30 Missions for Victorious Warfare, Bulletproof Marriage: A 90-Day Devotional, Behind the Badge: 365 Day Devotional for Law Enforcement, Prayers and Promises for First Responders,* and *Behind the Lines: 365 Daily Challenges for Military Personnel;* www.TheAdamDavis.com

Sheepdogs:
The Mission Continues

The artist Albrecht Dürer dedicated the wood carving
"Knight, Death, and the Devil" (1513) to his friend Erasmus

Have faith, Christ has overcome the world…
and by him we shall overcome death and the devil.
—DESIDERIUS ERASMUS

The theologian Desiderius Erasmus (ca. 1466–1536) inspired the artist Albrecht Dürer (1471–1528), who created this wood carving of a knight, death, and the devil. It symbolizes a knight (in this case, Erasmus) who is strengthened by faith as he overcomes his two unwelcome companions, death and the devil. Chris Pascoe and I (Dave Grossman) both love this image. In particular, the faithful dog, so downcast yet determined, following at his master's feet calls to the "sheepdog" in us.

"I'm Not Your Dog"

In my book *On Combat,* I introduced the concept of "sheepdog as a protector."[1] In *On Spiritual Combat*, this model went a step further, introducing the concept of "sheepdogs under the authority of the Great Shepherd." That metaphor is a model that has helped me understand my relationship with God. I know that we are adopted into the family of God as his beloved children. But most days, it is all I can do to think of myself as God's faithful dog.

My dog (a chocolate lab whose specialty is finding and lab testing chocolate anywhere in the house) runs into the neighbor's yard whenever she is off the leash. And she will roll in something stinky and filthy as soon as she gets the chance. But I understand that this is part of her nature, and I still love her. In the same way, God knows my every sin, my every failing, but he still loves me. (Oh, and one other important point about this relationship. I understand God about as well as my dog understands everything about me.) This is how God feels

1   I received a US government trademark for this phrase.

about us! We may roll around in some bad stuff, but we always come back to the Lord, who cleanses us and loves us.

All we ask of our dogs is their devotion to us. And the only way our dogs can survive in a world they cannot comprehend—a world of dangerous streets and unforgiving laws—is to trust us and obey us. In the same way, it is not our place to put expectations on the Creator of the universe. We have no rational right or reasonable expectation to do so. But it is absolutely right and appropriate for God to put expectations on us. And what he asks of us is to trust him, to obey him, and to be devoted to him.

We are the hounds of heaven! We are God's faithful, loving, obedient sheepdogs, dedicated to protecting the flock. We love our master, the Great Shepherd. And this love encompasses everything else in our relationship to him and spills out in our relationship to others (Matthew 22:36–40). It is the essence of all he asks of us. And that's good because it is all we have to give.

We are God's loving sheepdogs. We belong to him. He is our Master—no one else.

American humorist Will Rogers said, "If you get to thinking you're a person of some influence, try ordering somebody else's dog around." When you do that, the dog will look at you scornfully, and if he could talk, he would say, "I'm just a dog. I don't know much. But I know this: I'm not *your* dog."

So when the evil one comes for you and yours, look him in the eye and tell him he has no power over you. Just say, "Hey, I'm not your dog!"

Remember Why We're Here

Now, as we begin this pilgrimage, this spiritual journey, let us build upon *On Spiritual Combat* and take this opportunity to review our over-arching mission. Never lose your focus on this as you read, ponder, pray, and apply. This is our purpose in life. This is why we are here.

- To love the Lord God with all your heart, with all your soul, with all your mind, and with all your strength (Luke 10:27).
- To love others as yourself (v. 27).
- To fulfill the "Great Commission" because if we truly love people and if we love and obey God, then we will strive with all our heart to carry out the Great Commission and bring others to the knowledge of salvation (Matthew 28:19).
- To be powerful, living witnesses, bringing others to Christ by doing good deeds and never growing weary of doing good (Galatians 6:9).
- To give the honor and glory to God, and reap love, joy, and peace for ourselves (Galatians 5:22).
- And finally, to dwell in heaven forever with our loving Father (Psalm 23:6).

Thus, dear brothers and sisters in Christ, beloved fellow sheepdogs under the authority of the Great Shepherd, we fervently pray that you will read and enjoy *On Spiritual Warfare* and through it grow in faith and become more powerful Christian spiritual warriors.

Proclaim it now throughout the land: I am a sheepdog under the authority of the Great Shepherd! He who is in me is far greater than he who is in the world! I am a child of the one true King! I am a sheepdog under the authority of the Great Shepherd, and this is as far as the minions of hell are going!

> Now unto him that is able to keep you from falling, and to present you faultless before the presence of his glory with exceeding joy, to the only wise God our Saviour, be glory and majesty, dominion and power, both now and ever. Amen. (Jude 1:24–25 KJV)

Mission Prep

My country, 'tis of thee,
  Sweet land of liberty,
Of thee I sing:
  Land where my fathers died,
  Land of the pilgrim's pride,
  From every mountain side
Let freedom ring.

My native country, thee,
  Land of the noble free,
Thy name I love;
  I love thy rocks and rills,

Thy woods and templed hills.
My heart with rapture thrills
Like that above.

Our fathers' God, to thee,
Author of liberty,
To thee we sing;
Long may our land be bright
With freedom's holy light;
Protect us by thy might,
Great God, our King!

—"My Country, 'Tis of Thee," by Samuel Francis Smith;
the de facto US national anthem until 1931

This book, *On Spiritual Warfare*, builds upon the first volume, *On Spiritual Combat: 30 Missions for Victorious Warfare*. While *On Spiritual Warfare* can stand on its own, it builds on that first book as the next step in advanced spiritual warfare. *On Spiritual Combat* provides basic training, equipment issue, and preparation for frontline operations in spiritual combat. *On Spiritual Warfare* goes beyond basic training and provides what you need for longevity in the war against humanity's greatest threats: sin, death, and Satan and his demons. We give you twenty-two warnings, what to guard against, and link each warning with a corresponding order, what you can do to effectively live and thereby counter the threat. Together, these twenty-two warnings and orders give you a powerful strategy to rise as victors in our war "against the rulers, against the authorities, against the powers of this dark world and against the spiritual forces of evil in the heavenly realms" (Ephesians 6:12).

We begin every chapter with a hymn or poem (always colored blue). This beautiful and powerful old "Christian midrash" will establish a foundation for the concepts to follow. We encourage you to read these poems aloud because poetry is meant to be spoken, and much of the majesty and power of these words are lost if you don't bring them alive with your voice and spirit and let them bless, inspire, and empower you. If you know the tune of the hymn, then sing it to yourself and before God. If you are in a public place, then feel free to whisper these words or quietly hum the tune. No matter how you recite them, consider how these wise, strong, and virtuous words have blessed our ancestors across the centuries. They still have that power.

Consider the song at the beginning of this chapter, "My Country, 'Tis of Thee." Did you know that this was the "de facto" United States National Anthem until 1931?

Did you know that this song was originally a pledge of allegiance to the king of England? But Samuel Francis Smith changed the lyrics while he was a seminary student to make it America's pledge of allegiance to the true and rightful King, God Almighty.

Did you realize that this hymn is also a *prayer*? It is a prayer, a *plea* to God to bless and protect America. Psalm 33:12 tells us that "Blessed is the nation whose God is the Lord."

There is great power in such words! Think of the noble, godly individual who wrote this and all those people since who have sung it across the centuries. Think of them looking over your shoulder with pleasure. And *know* that their objective with that song is also ours.

Belief Is a Choice

Belief is a choice. We choose to believe that there is a loving God who empowers us in an epic and glorious battle against the forces of evil. And we believe that God can and will bless the nation that calls to him. As the hymn says, "Long may our land be bright, With freedom's holy light. Protect us with thy might, Great God our King!" Amen! (More about the power in that word *amen* later.)

Furthermore, we hold that the evidence and logical arguments for our beliefs about God and his activity in the world are overwhelming. We also know that *if* we were proven wrong (something we have good reason to believe will never be done), we would still lose nothing of value, and we would still gain some wonderful blessings in this life and in our nation. But knowing we are not wrong but right, we gain *everything*! All that is true, good, and beautiful is ours, and not just for now but for eternity.

On Spiritual Combat and *On Spiritual Warfare* establish a framework, an outline of what is held in common across the three great Christian traditions—Roman Catholicism, Eastern Orthodoxy, and Protestantism. A 2020 estimate by the Pew Research Center tells us that there are 2.38 *billion* Christians in the world today, making Christianity by far the world's largest religion, representing 31.4 percent of the world's population.

Our two books are humble endeavors to describe what these individuals have in common, what C. S. Lewis called "mere Christianity." Furthermore, and more specifically, our books are designed to show how our loving God intends for us to engage in spiritual combat against the forces of evil in this world.

Since God exists, we can logically agree that God should be able to give guidance, dominion, blessings, and continuity to his believers. Such a God should have been able to make his message clear across the millennia, with continuity from prehistory until modern times; with blessings, prosperity, and dominion to his believers across time; with his houses of worship in every nation; and his Word translated in myriad languages and available even in hotel rooms around the world.

If you see a god who has only a tiny minority of believers. *If* he is known only to a few. *If* he is a "johnny come lately" to the game. *If* his worshipers have not been blessed with dominion and prosperity across the millennia. *Then*, we respectfully submit, maybe that god is not much of a god if he cannot communicate his will and extend blessings to vast numbers of people across the span of thousands and thousands of years.

One more thing. If you agree that there might be a God, but you are angry or displeased with him because of things that have happened in your life, then we say, "Please don't curse God when your prayers are not answered the way you think they should be."

In the end, we will all die. God's greatest achievement is not to give us wealth or comfort or a few more days in this fallen world. God's greatest gift, his most awesome, miraculous achievement, is to save our souls and to pay the price for our sin with the blood of Jesus so that we can be adopted children in his family for eternity. And the most important thing we can ever pray for is not that our loved ones will live a little longer, not that they will have comfort or ease in this world. The greatest thing we can pray for, work for, and strive for is that they will come to the knowledge of God's salvation and embrace it as their own.

Life Is Hard, Then You Die?

The world says, "Life is hard. Then you die."

God says, "To live is Christ, and to die is gain" (Philippians 1:21 KJV). Think about that. "To live" is to be "in Christ," which is an amazing life of love, joy, and peace. And "to die" is even better because death is the final step into the presence and glory of God. This does not mean that we should be suicidal. God's Word is clear that self-murder is a sin. Think of it in terms of our overriding mission, our purpose in life: to love God and love people (Mark 12:30–31). I have lost a brother and two nephews to suicide. I can tell you from personal experience that taking your own life will cause enormous pain to your loved ones. For the rest of my life, when I hear the name of that beloved relative who took his life, I will feel remorse, regret, and sorrow. God loves us vastly more than any person can, and the pain and anguish one gives to God by taking their own life is even greater. As Christians, when our time comes, we can approach death with a peace that others can barely comprehend, and that may be the single most powerful, soul-saving, life-affirming act in our short stay here on this fallen world.

Study those two options and decide now which one you would choose. "Life is hard. Then you die"? Or "To live is Christ, and to die is gain"? Which would you choose for your loved ones and for the whole world? Remember, belief is a choice, and you can ask for more faith. You can pray, as did one man in the Bible, "I do believe; help me overcome my unbelief!" (Mark 9:24).

In "normal" battle we win, in large part, by killing people. In *spiritual* battle, we win by saving them. And that is the glorious endeavor that a loving Father has equipped us for and commanded us to engage in. If you truly comprehend the magnitude of this task, then you understand that we must get this right. It is the single most important thing anyone can ever do.

Thus, while *On Spiritual Combat* established a solid foundation for basic spiritual combat, *On Spiritual Warfare* prepares us for advanced spiritual warfare. This book is a call to a life of self-sacrifice and selfless service to God.

On Spiritual Warfare is also about "embracing the suck"—that is, about getting our heads and hearts pointed to the hard work of suffering so that we might be equipped for "Spec Ops Spiritual Combat." Spiritual warfare is not only about protecting ourselves from the evil one and telling friends and neighbors about Christ's saving work. It is also about pushing back the gates of hell and assaulting the Normandy beaches of Satan's evil empire.

As you read this book, if you find yourself saying, "I've been through this part before," then we say, "It's called the 'training cycle,' soldier!" But every old soldier knows that it is not truly a cycle but rather a spiral staircase with each repetition taking you higher and higher. Our goal is to get more out of each repetition, becoming better, wiser, and stronger Christian warriors with each cycle.

"Advanced skills are just the basics mastered" is a truth you will hear in every world-class combat training center. Over the years from elementary school through high school and even into the first couple of years of college, you went through the same cycle, learning the basics of reading, writing, and 'rithmetic. But every year you learned each subject at a higher level. The same thing is true with spiritual growth.

And remember: this war is for real. This is not a game. Not just mortal lives but also eternity and the salvation or destruction of all that we love are hanging in the balance.

Spiritual Warfare—At Every Level

Mighty spiritual warriors have gone before us. With sacrifice and toil and faith, with blood and sweat and prayers, many of these warriors established a firm godly foundation for the nation that became the United States of America. "For no one can lay any foundation other than the one already laid, which is Jesus Christ" (1 Corinthians 3:11). With their National Anthem, they called out to God, raising their voices in a vast chorus, an anthem of communal prayer, a nation singing, crying out, beseeching their heavenly Father.

My country, 'tis of thee,
   Sweet land of liberty,
Of thee I sing:
   Land where my fathers died,
   Land of the pilgrim's pride,
   From every mountain side
Let freedom ring.

Foremost among those who established this firm foundation for America were the Puritans and Pilgrims. It was their steadfast conviction, their unwavering, unflinching belief, that they had a moral obligation to use their authority as citizens and as leaders to move their nation toward righteousness.

These godly founders understood a critical, essential fact. In a democracy or a republic, we the people are the rulers. In America, through our votes and our influence upon our elected leaders and fellow citizens, *we* are the ones who rule this nation. *We* are the kings! And if we do not use every bit of influence and authority that we have to move our nation toward righteousness, then we are like the evil kings of old.

Look at the curses that God inflicted upon wicked kings in the Old Testament as punishment for their evil stewardship. That same judgment is upon each of us and our nation if we do not strive to move our nation toward righteousness. As God warns us: "'I am your enemy!' says the LORD Almighty. 'I will burn up your chariots. Your soldiers will be killed in war, and I will take away everything that you took from others.

The demands of your envoys will no longer be heard'" (Nahum 2:13 GNT).

Now, as we learned in *On Spiritual Combat*, our salvation is never in doubt if we have accepted Jesus as our Savior. But God will judge us each, individually, for the Christian stewardship of our nation. This judgment will not change the fact of our salvation, but it can affect our relationship to God and to others.

The governance side of American citizenship is a profound responsibility. It is inherent within our nation's form of government. If you do not want to accept that solemn sacred responsibility, then your only option is to renounce your American citizenship and flee to a nation where such an obligation is not intrinsic to citizenship.

America's Founding Fathers understood the inherent sinfulness of men and women, but they did not surrender to it. Instead, they established the philosophical foundation for the US Constitution with its many checks and balances and sought to add to God's kingdom on earth, as best they could, always praying, always working.

Spiritual warfare means fighting at every level. From the personal, to the congregational, to the national: at *every* level we bring the battle straight into the teeth of evil and the very gates of hell. Jesus has promised us victory in this fight. As he said, "Upon this rock I will build my church; and the gates of hell shall not prevail against it" (Matthew 16:18 KJV).

Spiritual warfare, in the power of God through our Lord Jesus Christ, says "Never surrender!" Never surrender one soul nor one city nor one nation to evil. *Never* say it cannot be done when Jesus tells us that "with God all things are possible" (19:26).

On the Shoulders of Spiritual Giants

In *On Spiritual Combat*, we introduced the concept of Christian midrash. In the Jewish faith, midrash is basically a set of commentary that surrounds God's Word, established and sustained across the generations to give us a deeper understanding of Scripture.

In this current book, *On Spiritual Warfare*, we will take you through some of the most powerful and important Christian midrash that has ever blessed our world: Luther and Erasmus. The insight we pass on here is truly midrash of the highest order—ancient wisdom virtually lost to our times. And we will introduce the timeless, triumphant spiritual warfare concept of "saved by grace, serving by faith."

In my book *On Combat*, I included the 22 Rules (or Orders) from *The Enchiridion Militis Christiani* (meaning *The Handbook of the Christian Knight*) written in 1501 and published in 1503. The 22 Rules/Orders were brilliantly summarized by Sgt. Chris Pascoe of the Michigan State Police.

The *Enchiridion* (or *Handbook*) was written by the Dutch theologian Desiderius Erasmus (1466–1536), one of the leading theologians of his time. Five centuries after Erasmus passed from this world, his 22 Rules proved to be popular with all those amazing sheepdogs, under the authority of the Great Shepherd, who read *On Combat*. In fact, a search on the internet will reveal several websites that have emulated our summary of the 22 Rules in *On Combat* to help spread the message of sheepdog service. God bless this sharing of truth and ethos.

The 22 Rules/Orders, as summarized by Sgt. Chris Pascoe, were used again in the *Sheepdogs: Meet Our Nation's Warriors* children's book that I wrote with Stephanie Rogish to inspire and influence the lives of many young sheepdogs. *The Handbook of the Christian Knight* was also very popular in its day. In fact, historians say the *Enchiridion* was second only to the Bible in that era. Many scholars believe it to be the first published book specifically dedicated to spiritual warfare.

The book was originally in Latin, and the Latin word translated as "handbook" literally means "dagger." Author Diarmaid MacCulloch, in his book *Christianity: The First Three Thousand Years*, wrote that the dagger, in this sense, is the "spiritual equivalent of the modern Swiss Army knife." To which we say, amen!

This Book's Mission

Thy word is a lamp unto my feet,
and a light unto my path. (Psalm 119:105 KJV)

The American author Nelson DeMille said, "We're all pilgrims on the same journey—but some pilgrims have better road maps." We hope and pray that the lessons, hymns, and prayers in this book will be a roadmap for you—ye pilgrim peacekeepers, our fellow sheepdogs—for a life of victorious spiritual warfare. Especially to the young pilgrim peacekeepers, we hope this book passes along lessons that we old timers, and our wise forefathers, took many years to figure out.

Historians say that Erasmus' *Handbook of the Christian Knight* influenced many, including the Augustinian monk Martin Luther (1483–1546), who became the founder and father of the Lutheran branch of Protestantism.

In Chris Pascoe's studies, he has collected 22 warnings from the writings of Martin Luther to accompany Erasmus' work. Thus, our book is organized into "22 Warnings" (inspired by Luther to help you recognize evil), combined with the "22 Rules/Orders" of Erasmus (to help you remain victorious and virtuous as you confront evil). You can consider Luther's "22 Warnings" as your guide to confession and repentance and consider Erasmus' "22 Orders" as your guide to service and sanctification.

Luther *warns* us of sin and the devil's schemes and asks us to recite the Sinner's Prayer daily. Only by confessing our sins and giving ourselves entirely to Jesus Christ can we be saved by God's forgiving grace.

Erasmus *orders* us, as servants of the Lord, to complete the missions that God assigns us. God's forgiveness is completed by service.

What is your mission? Overall, your mission is the same as ours: Follow God's commandments and rescue your brothers and sisters through triumphant spiritual warfare. Your specific calling and ours may differ, but our mission as God's followers is one that we all share.

WARNORDs: Sacred Warning Orders

We have combined Luther's "Warnings" and Erasmus' "Orders" and used the modern military concept of a "Warning Order" or "WARNORD." We believe that this "coincidence" allowing us to combine the five-hundred-year-old works and terminology of these two individuals into a modern military term is not a coincidence at all.

In *On Spiritual Combat*, we organized the book into "30 Missions." Many readers said that they felt compelled to complete those scriptural missions in a way that no chapter in any book had ever inspired them to do. Our hope is that the uniqueness of putting together Erasmus' and Luther's counsel into WARNORDs will inspire you as well.

A WARNORD is a warning of a pending mission, combined with essential information to prep for the mission. A WARNORD will usually be followed by a full, five-paragraph Operations Order (OPORD), but ideally all currently available information will be in the WARNORD. So there should be enough information in the WARNORD to accomplish the mission if a full OPORD is not present.

Luther inspires the *warning*: Repent of your sins and be saved! This is the strategic level of spiritual warfare.

Erasmus inspires the *order*: Serve the Lord and be sanctified! This is the tactical level of spiritual warfare—victory through virtue! We are talking about applied theology.

On these two precepts, all Christians can agree. The strategic (repentance) precedes the tactical (service). And if you refuse to repent and serve God, then you are serving Satan. There is no in-between. Thus, the mission of this book is literally a WARNORD. And if you find this book to be powerful and helpful, it is because the Holy Spirit had a hand in it. All honor and glory to God!

> Not unto us, O LORD, not unto us,
> but unto thy name give glory,
> for thy mercy, and for thy truth's sake.
> (Psalm 115:1 KJV)

Lone Survivor

This manual is fashioned after the prayer books that soldiers have carried in countless wars to guide their petitions, thoughts, and actions. In fact, you can think of *On Spiritual Combat* and now *On Spiritual Warfare* as a kind of spiritual *Ranger Handbook* (which is not *just* for Rangers since it is used as a standard reference for many warriors worldwide). In the *Ranger Handbook*, you will find the US Army "Ranger Creed," which concludes with a solemn vow to "fight on to the Ranger objective and complete the mission, though I be the lone survivor." Likewise, a good WARNORD should be enough to fulfill that solemn, sacred responsibility.

Even the cover of this book is designed to follow this theme. Black and gold are the Army Ranger colors and my personal favorites. Crossed gold arrows are the US Army spec ops branch symbol; crossed gold rifles: infantry branch; crossed sabers: cavalry; cannons: artillery. And crossed "crusader swords" are now the spiritual warfare symbol!

Thus, brother and sister spiritual warriors, fellow sheepdogs under the authority of the Great Shepherd, embrace these 22 WARNORDs, established by our noble forebearers five hundred years ago. And with the help of the Father, Son, and Holy Spirit, go forth to accomplish your noble and sacred mission: to defeat evil and save immortal souls in epic, supernatural, spiritual warfare.

Now, time for our Ephesians Chapter 6 spiritual warfare checklist:

✓   Buckle on your belt of truth? Check!

✓   Lace up your boots of the gospel of peace? Check!

✓   Tighten the straps on your breastplate of righteousness and your helmet of salvation? Check!

✓   Take your sword in hand? (Your Father's +4, Lightening Casting, Vorpal Sword of the Spirit that we studied in *On Spiritual Combat*.) Check!

✓   Do a quick "commo check" on the awesome radio of prayer? Check!

"Charlie Mike!" Continue the mission! Always seeking higher ground! Though you be the lone survivor. We must follow the model of the apostle Paul, who said, "I press on toward the goal to win the prize for which God has called me heavenward in Christ Jesus" (Philippians 3:14).

INTRODUCTION: *Next Level Battle Prep*

> ➢   What are the parts of a WARNORD?
> ➢   What is the purpose of a WARNORD?
> ➢   How can a sheepdog apply a WARNORD?

FIRST WARNING

THE WICKED HAVE NO FAITH

The greatest wickedness is denying
the Most High God.

(Luther)

WARNORD #1

FIRST ORDER

**INCREASE YOUR FAITH BY
ACCEPTING GOD'S GRACE**

Even if the entire world appears mad.

(Erasmus)

FIRST WARNING

THE WICKED HAVE NO FAITH

The greatest wickedness is denying the Most High God.

(Luther)

Pray that we may be delivered from wicked and evil people,
for not everyone has faith.
—2 Thessalonians 3:2

Once to ev'ry man and nation
   Comes the moment to decide,
In the strife of truth and falsehood,
   For the good or evil side.

Some great cause, some great decision,
   Off 'ring each the bloom or blight,

And the choice goes by forever
    'Twixt that darkness and that light.

Then to side with truth is noble,
    When we share her wretched crust,
Ere her cause bring fame and profit,
    And 'tis prosperous to be just;

Then it is the brave man chooses,
    While the coward stands aside.
Till the multitude make virtue,
    Of the faith they had denied.

By the light of burning martyrs,
    Christ, Thy bleeding feet we track,
Toiling up new Calvaries ever
    With the cross that turns not back.
        —"Once to Every Man and
        Nation," James R. Lowell
        (1819–1891)

Why is there so much wickedness? Child molesters, rapists, fraudsters, murderers, terrorists. The news is full of crime reports and tragic events around the globe. As Erasmus said, "The world does appear mad." And Luther said, "The fool hath said in his heart, God is nothing."

Unfortunately, we are in a war between the *faithful* and the *faithless*. This is a war that started in the spiritual realm and spread to the natural world and humanity. It is much bigger than believing or not believing in God because the Bible says that even demons believe in him (James 2:19).

Beware the Faithless

A faithless person may not believe in God, or he or she may faintly believe that God exists but, like the devil and his demons, does not worship God or seek to please him. Because the faithless do not serve God, they will serve their own evil nature and the temptations of the devil.

The Bible prophesied that some people would turn their backs on God (Proverbs 14:34). The apostle Paul describes faithless people: "They have become filled with every kind of wickedness, evil, greed and depravity. They are full of envy, murder, strife, deceit and malice. They are gossips, slanderers, God-haters, insolent, arrogant and boastful; they invent ways of doing evil...they have...no love, no mercy" (Romans 1:29–31).

Thus, the faithless pose a great danger to others, including to the faithful. This is one reason that the Bible urges us to "pray that we may be delivered from wicked and evil people, for not everyone has faith" (2 Thessalonians 3:2).

The Conflict between Infinites and Finites

The faithful believe in God and the connectedness of all living things. They see our current life as preparation for the eternal life to come. The faithful can be thought of as *infinites*. Infinites can be symbolized by the Celtic Knot. This knot consists of a loop with no start or finish (like the symbol for infinity only more complex). It represents connectedness and eternity.

So those of us who believe that Jesus is God's Son and trust in him are infinites. We have his life, which is eternal life. As Jesus said, "For this is the will of my Father, that everyone who looks on the Son and believes in him should have eternal life, and I will raise him up on the last day" (John 6:40 ESV).

The goal of infinites is to maintain the unity of the knot, seeking always the good of the whole and eternal salvation. As "The Hymn of Joy" says, "Father love is reigning o'er us, Brother love binds man to man." This is what infinites affirm. This is how they see their life in this world. And the together life of infinites is summed up by Paul: "So we, being many, are one body in Christ" (Romans 12:5 KJV).

In contrast, the faithless doubt the existence of God and see no reason to worry about life after death. The faithless see our current life as a competition, not as a brotherhood, and they live as if survival favors the most ruthless. The faithless can be thought of as *finites*.

We can symbolize finites using the Midgard Serpent from Norse mythology. It is sometimes depicted as two serpents consuming each other from their tail ends, eventually destroying each other. Finites seek their own desires at the expense of others. The Bible says that finites will "reap the whirlwind" of their own destruction (Hosea 8:7). And none of us can hide from God: "Can a man hide himself in secret places so that I cannot see him? declares the LORD. Do I not fill heaven and earth? declares the LORD" (Jeremiah 23:24 ESV).

We can see that the infinites are quite different than the finites. The infinites work to save humanity from the devil and prepare for eternity with our Lord. But the finites are selfish and create only chaos that leads to destruction; they unwittingly serve the devil and his desire to corrupt our salvation. If it were not for the peacekeeping efforts of the infinites, the finites would destroy the world. The infinites serve God and do his work. "Blessed are the peacemakers: for they shall be called the children of God" (Matthew 5:9 KJV).

These finites, the wicked faithless that Luther warned us about, are like a scourge. They prey not only on the helpless but have also learned to attack and undermine the peacekeepers. But the Bible assures us: "The wicked are punished in place of the godly, and traitors in place of the honest" (Proverbs 21:18 NLT).

The psychological disparity between faithful versus faithless people was demonstrated in a study conducted by Michael Prinzing, a PhD candidate at the University of North Carolina at Chapel Hill. Prinzing found that people who are more religious tend to see their lives as being "more meaningful" compared to people who are less religious. Religious people scored higher on scales of Social Mattering: "My life matters to other people"; and Cosmic Mattering: "My life matters in the grand scheme of the universe." Prinzing said that religious subjects often said things like, "If God didn't exist, there would be no significance to anything we do." Indicating that faithfulness is a motive for infinite thinking as well as for doing good things in life and for other people because it has a positive effect on the universe.

Now here is the terrifying part: there is no in-between. You are either a finite (faithless) or an infinite (faithful). Andrew Bowell, of the Westfield (Indiana) Police Department, states the situation accurately and bluntly: "We are slaves either of Christ (whose yoke is easy), or to the devil…serving our sinful nature and desires. Hence, if you are *not* of God…you are, in essence, a ticking time bomb…destined to fail, or worse, destined for destruction."

But God is merciful and wants to save every sinner. Reverend Jeff Wolf, a retired police sergeant and revivalist, says we should consider the story of Abraham pleading with God to spare Sodom and how God responded by saying, "If I find fifty righteous people in the city of Sodom, I will spare the whole place for their sake" (Genesis 18:26). Abraham continued to plead with God until God said in verse 32, "For the sake of ten, I will not destroy it." This is proof that God will spare a nation for the sake of just a few righteous people. This is yet another reason to "hang in there" in spiritual combat, "though the whole world be mad" and even "though I be the lone survivor."

Today, we desperately need more people of faith to become protectors of righteousness and teachers of the way or else the faithless will be lost like Sodom. "Let him know, that he which converteth the sinner from the error of his way shall save a soul from death" (James 5:20 KJV). We need to be like Isaiah, who, when he "heard the voice of the Lord saying, 'Whom shall I send? And who will go for us?,'" responded, "Here am I. Send me!" (Isaiah 6:8). This is the Master's call to his sheepdogs and the answer we should have ready in our hearts.

This Is "The Way"

Early Jewish Christians referred to themselves as "The Way" (τῆς ὁδοῦ), probably because "the way" is how Jesus referred to himself: "I am the way and the truth and the life. No one comes to the Father except through me" (John 14:6). During his trial, the apostle Paul said, "I admit that I worship the God of our ancestors as a follower of the Way" (Acts 24:14). The apostle Peter refers to Christianity as "the way of truth" (2 Peter 2:2). And the writer of Hebrews says that the sacrifice of Jesus Christ on the cross is the "new and living way" for us to enter the Most Holy Place (Hebrews 10:19–20).

The Bible speaks of the Way numerous times, and it truly is an ethos worth living for, dying for, and teaching to all so that they may be saved. Here are just a few passages:

- "And they shall keep *the way* of the Lord, to do justice and judgment" (Genesis 18:19 KJV).
- "Behold, I send an Angel before thee, to keep thee in *the way*" (Exodus 23:20 KJV).
- "They have turned aside quickly out of *the way* which I commanded them" (32:8 KJV).
- "Cursed be he that maketh the blind to wander out of *the way*" (Deuteronomy 27:18 KJV).
- "Good and upright is the Lord: therefore will he teach sinners in *the way*" (Psalm 25:8 KJV).
- "Blessed are the undefiled in *the way,* who walk in the law of the Lord" (119:1 KJV).
- "I have rejoiced in *the way* of thy testimonies, as much as in all riches" (v. 14 KJV).
- "Teach me, O Lord, *the way* of thy statutes; and I shall keep it unto the end" (v. 33 KJV).
- "See if there be any wicked way in me, and lead me in *the way* everlasting" (139:24 KJV).
- "*The way* of the Lord is strength to the upright: but destruction shall be to the workers of iniquity" (Proverbs 10:29 KJV).

- "Thus saith the LORD, thy Redeemer, the Holy One of Israel; I am the LORD thy God...which leadeth thee by *the way* that thou shouldest go" (Isaiah 48:17 KJV).

- "Thus saith the LORD; Behold, I set before you *the way* of life, and *the way* of death" (Jeremiah 21:8 KJV).

- "Narrow is *the way,* which leadeth unto life, and few there be that find it" (Matthew 7:14 KJV).

As you read through this book, remember this about the WARNORDs:

- ○ The WARNING is the "Wrong Way."
- ○ The ORDER is "God's Way."

Keep the Way and You *Shall* Win the Battle

In distant lands or on the home front, evil has no boundaries. We see the works of evil in this world daily. Many of you have already encountered evil in your own journey while others have yet to face it. As a sheepdog, first responder, active military (or veteran), or simply one who follows the warrior or protector path, it is inevitable that you must stare into the face of evil.

Evil. What else can you call it when helplessly bound victims have their heads cut off, when people are burned to death in cages, and when airliners full of men, women, and children are slammed into buildings to murder thousands of other terrified civilians. This is the hideous face of monstrous evil, and you must understand that you are a living shield of flesh and blood, standing between evil and the precious innocent lives at home. This is true physically, and you must believe that it is true spiritually.

It was in our book *Prayers and Promises for First Responders*, under the subject of "Evil" that I was able to first speak on the concept of faith. If you believe in a force of evil in this world—and who can deny it—then you are doomed in your battle if you do not believe in a superior force for good and apply that force for good in your daily life. If you lack in faith, you will be intimidated by evil. You will be like Prime Minister Neville Chamberlain prior to the start of World War II, who kept appeasing Hitler's demands, giving in to evil because he was afraid to stand up to it. Finally, Winston Churchill stepped in and said, "We will never surrender" to this evil! This is what strong faith looks like.

Faith is one of the "Pillars of Resiliency" in military training across the globe. And around the world, we are seeking resiliency for our military and first responders. But for your faith to fully empower you and make you resilient, it must be strong. A strong faith is one that is rational and sound. It is based in logic. It is a faith that you can see triumphant in the world every day. And as we have said before, only the God of mainstream Christianity meets the standard that any reasonable person would expect of an omnipotent God.

Evil: The Opposite of Love

The opposite of love is not hate but evil. Indeed, the presence of evil is solid proof of God and his holy forces of good. Consider what happens when the sun is eclipsed by the moon. We cannot bear to look directly at the sun, but the darkness of the eclipse proves the presence of light. So, too, does the darkness of evil prove the presence of good. Evil is the absence of love just as darkness is the absence of light. And God *is* love! All love emanates from him. He loves you with a love that is "to infinity and beyond" any earthly love that we can comprehend.

As you follow the sheepdog path and place your mind and body in peril daily, you must understand that no one does this just for the money. At the moment of truth, *love* is what motivates us: love for your nation, love for your way of life, love for your comrades, love for your family, and love for your God.

And love is what motivates God. Satan strives to manipulate, coerce, and compel humans into his stronghold. Satan would turn us into his puppets. But this is not how divine love works. We are not God's puppets. God has given us free will. God is more like a lover wooing us, persuading us, seeking to change our minds and hearts but without intimidating us or coercing us. Divine love wants us to come freely, not by coercion.

We say, "I wish I had solid proof! Just show yourself to me, God!" But that would not be faith. What kind of loving parent would raise a beloved child with overwhelming fear, constant coercion, and relentless threats? That is not the action of a loving parent, and it most certainly would not inspire love from a child.

We have heard it said that if you truly love something, set it free. If it comes back, it is yours. The author of that quote is unknown, but it captures the essence of God's love. God loves us so much that he gave us *true* freedom. He doesn't use a draft to force us into his army. The faith-based army of spiritual warriors God is raising up today is an all-volunteer force.

There is a mighty, awe-inspiring force for good in this universe. He loves you. He wants you not just to survive but to thrive! And he will give you all that you need to triumph in this battle. But you must accept God's grace. He will not inflict it or force it on you. That would not be love.

Many people see hate as a bad thing. But the God of love also hates: he hates evil deeds, such as theft (Isaiah 61:8), hypocritical worship (1:13–15), idolatry (Deuteronomy 16:22), lying, murder, arrogance, and deception (Proverbs 6:16–19). And the same God tells us that there are things in this world that we should hate. Amos 5:15 affirms this in six of the most powerful words in the Bible: "Hate evil, love good; maintain justice." Boom. Spiritual warfare in six words.

The Merriam-Webster Dictionary defines hate as "intense hostility and aversion usually deriving from fear, anger, or sense of injury." We need not fear evil, for we are strengthened by God's love, and we are told that "perfect love drives out fear" (1 John 4:18). But we *should* have hostility and aversion toward evil. We *should* also have a sense of anger toward evil. And we do indeed have the feeling that we have suffered injury, for we fully comprehend the great, grievous injury that evil would inflict upon all that we love.

In *On Spiritual Combat,* we describe this mighty, epic, global battle against evil.

You can think of this like the United States during World War II. The entire nation was focused on winning that war. The farmer in the field and the clerk in the store were striving, working in their jobs with victory in mind. They bought war bonds. The students in school wrote letters to our troops, collected scrap metal, and bought "war saving stamps." Every other citizen, everyone in between, accepted war rationing, and they all worked together for victory, leading ultimately to the troops in the front lines. All of them were part of a concerted effort to defend our nation and defeat our enemy.

In the same way, every believer in Christ is part of a similar, vast endeavor, striving toward a single goal. In World War II we won, in large part, by killing the enemy. In this war, we win by saving lives!

Furthermore, in World War II, troops in the front lines did the fighting, and everyone else was in support. In this war, everyone is in the fight. There are no rear lines. A grandmother praying in Chicago can turn the tide of battle on the other side of the planet. A gesture of kindness and love from a child—or to a child!—can change the world: "As ye have done it unto one of the least of these...ye have done it unto me" (Matthew 25:40).

Jesus said, "The greatest love you can have for your friends is to give your life for them" (John 15:13 GNT). When we mention that verse, we think of Jesus who died for us, and we apply it to our military who give their lives in battle. But there are many ways to *give* your life.

One additional similarity between World War II and our war is that many of our troops in that war enlisted for the duration. Then they deployed to a war zone without any idea how long they would be there. In spiritual warfare, always remember that this is not our home. We are warriors deployed to a "war zone" (this world) for the duration. For us that means until we die or until Jesus returns, whichever comes first. *Then* our "tour of duty" is over, and we finally will get to go home!

Our goal in this war is to save lives, and you can think of saving lives spiritually and eternally, like this:

In the physical realm, one "ultimate evil" can undo a lifetime of good. No matter how many good deeds and wonderful works you have done, if you commit murder (if you unlawfully, willingly, directly take the life of a single innocent person), then you will spend the rest of your life in prison or possibly even face execution. This one ultimate bad of murder will undo all the good in your life. And the world often holds in high esteem those who hunt down murderers. That is just the way the universe works.

In the spiritual realm, one perfect good can undo a lifetime of human bad. The ultimate good of Jesus' sacrifice upon the cross to pay the price for our salvation saves us spiritually, eternally. That one perfect good undoes a lifetime of our bad. Think about that: every bad act in our lives—past, present, and future—is forgiven if we believe and accept the price that Jesus paid upon the cross. And God holds in highest esteem those who save lives by bringing the gospel, the good news of salvation through Jesus, to others. That is simply the way that the just and righteous God who made the universe works (Genesis 9:5–6; Romans 13:3–4).

WARNING #1: Next Level Battle Prep

- ➤ Describe the difference between finites and infinites.
- ➤ What does the Midgard Serpent represent?
- ➤ Describe the origin and meaning of "The Way."
- ➤ What is the opposite of evil?
- ➤ How must we fight the war against evil?

FIRST ORDER

INCREASE YOUR FAITH BY ACCEPTING GOD'S GRACE
Even if the entire world appears mad.
(Erasmus)

The Lord is faithful, and he will strengthen you
and protect you from the evil one.
—2 Thessalonians 3:3

The Lord has the power to arm us in this battle against wickedness. The source of our strength is faith. We must accept God's grace and let him increase our faith. It all starts with the Sinner's Prayer, also known as the Salvation Prayer. The biblical foundation for that prayer can be found in Acts 2:38: "Repent and be baptized, every one of you, in the name of Jesus Christ for the forgiveness of your sins. And you will receive the gift of the Holy Spirit."

Here is Reverend Billy Graham's Salvation Prayer:

Dear Lord Jesus, I know that I am a sinner, and I ask for your forgiveness. I believe you died for my sins and rose from the dead. I turn from my sins and invite you to come into my heart and life. I want to trust and follow you as my Lord and Savior. In your name. Amen.

Now is a good time to stop reading and consider your relationship with God. Have you entered into a saving relationship with him? If not, please do that now. Don't put it off.

Are you now his disciple, seeking to follow him no matter what? If not, you will never have victory in the spiritual war he wants to prepare you to face fully and confidently.

Jesus Christ is our foundation for justification (salvation from the penalty of sin), sanctification (salvation from the power of sin), and glorification (salvation from the very presence of sin). And he is the one who leads us forward into the war against evil, a war that he has ensured his church will be won fully and completely and finally.

Repentance is the humble acceptance of God's saving grace, his forgiveness, offered free as a gift, paid for by Christ's obedience even unto death on the cross.

Faith is a gift that comes with receiving the Holy Spirit. Faith is involved in all three stages of salvation named above:

justification, sanctification, and glorification. The Spirit is also involved at each salvation stage and even before, as he convicts the world of sin, righteousness, and judgment (John 16:8). Now obedience, too, is part of every salvation stage. I come to God his way, not mine, which involves my obedience. I pursue God's way in sanctification, which also involves my obedience. And when I finally remain in God's presence forever, fully glorified, I live in his presence with unhindered and delightful obedience.

So faith involves justification and sanctification: coming to Christ and living in Christ. Faith is not just a get-out-of-hell-free card. It is signing up to obey the WARNORDs and OPORDs of the Lord, to the very best of our ability "though I be the lone survivor" and "even if the entire world appears mad."

The Faith Journey

While Jesus Christ died on a cross as payment for all sin, it is *essential* for each of us to respond to him by faith for the remedy to be effective. Confess your sinfulness and ask Jesus Christ to become your Savior and Lord (John 1:12; Romans 10:9–10; Revelation 3:20). Once you do, praise be to God! The angels in heaven rejoice (Luke 15:7)! Jesus will forever be a part of your life, and he will begin to make you a new person from the inside out (2 Corinthians 5:17).

The Salvation Prayer is part of repentance, and it is personal; you may express it with groans and pleas (Romans 8:26) when the Holy Spirit enters your heart. Many Christians will use the Salvation Prayer to ask God for more faith in times of trial or temptation because, as Paul wrote: "I am convinced that nothing can ever separate us from God's love. Neither death nor life, neither angels nor demons, neither our fears for today nor our worries about tomorrow—not even the powers of hell can separate us from God's love" (v. 38 NLT).

"The apostles said to the Lord: 'Increase our faith!'" (Luke 17:5). It really is okay to ask for more faith. Salvation comes through faith, and through it we receive life and healing: "LORD my God, I called to you for help, and you healed me" (Psalm 30:2). Faith bolsters and defends you: "The Lord is faithful, and he will strengthen you and protect you from the evil one" (2 Thessalonians 3:3).

We must form a loving, serving relationship with God so that we can know him personally through his Son, Jesus Christ (John 17:3). Then we will receive the power of the Holy Spirit and be victorious in the battle against evil (15:26). Luther said, "Without the mercy of God the [human] will is ineffective."

Become a Warrior Priest

Throughout history, in all cultures and religions, a select group of soldier priests have been recorded. Warrior priests were considered the elite of all peacekeepers due to the honor and integrity they brought to an otherwise dangerous occupation.

In ancient Israel, the *Levites* were a devout group of warrior priests who were entrusted to carry and protect the ark of the covenant, which held the stone tablet remnants of the Ten Commandments given to Moses by God on Mount Sinai. As the Bible tells us, the Levite warriors needed to consecrate themselves before God would allow them to carry the ark: "The Levites consecrated themselves to bring up the Ark of the LORD, the God of Israel. And the Levites carried the ark of God on their shoulders with the poles, as Moses had commanded according to the word of the LORD" (1 Chronicles 15:14–15 ESV). To *consecrate* means to "make worthy" or to separate oneself from things that are unclean and devote oneself irrevocably to the worship and service of God. This is what these warriors did in order to carry out their mission in carrying the ark.

The power of the ark was legendary, and it protected the Jews as long as they remained faithful to God's law. The Ten Commandments, hidden inside the ark, were more than guidance created by God. They were heavenly derived orders with great spiritual ramifications: "You must faithfully keep all my commands by putting them into practice, for I am the LORD" (Leviticus 22:31 NLT).

Jeremiah was a Levite from the tribe of Benjamin and was chosen by God to prophecy. It is not always popular to tell people of God's will and guidance in their lives and in their nation. We can see this constant struggle in the powerful old hymn at the beginning of this WARNORD. It concludes with these words:

> Then it is the brave man chooses,
>   While the coward stands aside
> Till the multitude make virtue,
>   Of the faith they had denied.

Are we cowards who will stand aside? Or are we courageous sheepdogs who will follow the Great Shepherd in an epic battle between good and evil?

Jeremiah was unpopular with the people, due to his warnings and rebukes about pagan worship as he tried to stop the downfall of his country, but he was no coward! In many ways, his story is an inspiration to us today. Jeremiah also prophesied about a new covenant and a new Israel that would be eternally obedient to God. Indeed, one of the most amazing things about the Bible is the constant foretelling of a coming Messiah in the Old Testament and the fulfillment of every single one of those prophesies through Jesus Christ in the New Testament. Our God didn't show up just in the last one thousand years or two thousand years or even four thousand years. Our God has been active from the beginning, with a clear plan for his will on earth and clear guidance for how we should fulfill his plan and his will.

Knights of Chivalry

The Catholic Church, in feudal Europe, recreated chivalric military orders along the lines of the Levites, such as the Knights Templar, the Knights Hospitaller, the Teutonic Knights, and many others. Like the Levites, individuals had to fulfill certain requirements before they could be consecrated as knights to ensure they were worthy to be peacekeepers. A lengthy training period to achieve knighthood was necessary due to the complex combat skills they needed to develop, but even more important was the spiritual training required for the calling.

Likewise, the Puritans viewed themselves as having knightly responsibilities to serve the kingdom of God. In the "Red Cross Knight," chief hero of the epic poem *The Faerie Queene*, Edmund Spenser (1590) designed a character to be the very image of Puritan virtue. The "Red Cross Knight" is the retelling of St. George, who slew a dragon that was terrorizing a village. In the poem, the knight was twice mortally wounded by the dragon but miraculously healed by God to continue fighting. The "Red Cross," which the knight bore on his shield, became a symbol to identify armed forces medical services.

Becoming a Christian knight takes a faith that has been tested and strengthened so that it can resist evil and do good works in the field of spiritual combat. The Bible says, "The weapons we fight with are not the weapons of the world. On the contrary, they have divine power to demolish strongholds" (2 Corinthians 10:4). How long this learning takes is different for each believer, but let us examine the history of this righteous endeavor. Remember, the Christian path is a lifelong endeavor, filled with hills and valleys, but no matter the struggles, all warriors can move forward knowing that "to live is Christ, and to die is gain" (Philippians 1:21 KJV).

Fourteen Years of Training

During the Middle Ages, starting at age seven, a boy from a good family could start training as a page, then eventually become a squire. At about age twenty-one, the young man having proven his mastery of the skills of combat and honor of chivalry, a ceremony granting knighthood (consecration) could be held. In the Middle Ages, a knight who had "won his spurs" had attained knighthood by performing an act of unselfish bravery. A king or lord presented the spurs and belt to the knight, and from then on, people referred to such an individual as "a belted knight." This is a direct reference of the "belt of truth" outlined in the full armor of God passage contained in Ephesians 6 and covered in detail in *On Spiritual Combat*.

Fourteen Weeks of Training

Today, police cadets receive a minimum of fourteen weeks of training before they are sworn in as probationary police officers. Due to the enormous responsibilities entrusted to them, screening and background checks are essential to finding quality candidates who are worthy of consecration as police officers.

As a recognizable symbol of sacrifice, duty, and service, the newly certified officer receives the police badge, which represents the profession's honor and authority. This badge, usually in the shape of a shield and always worn on the left side over the heart, is a direct reference to the knight's shield. We can also see it as a reference to the "shield of faith" in Ephesians 6. (Even the badge in the shape of a star, varying with anything from five to nine points, simply represents the sun gleaming off the shield, and basically has the same meaning.)

The term *officer* indicates a select individual who is "commissioned" and "entrusted" with authority. Therefore, being "commissioned" is, in essence, comparable to being consecrated like the knights of old. Commissioning the wrong person significantly jeopardizes the entire mission in both military and law enforcement operations.

A formal commission usually involves a mission and the authority to execute that mission. In the US military, officers receive a commission with a mission as outlined in their oath and their authority to fulfill the mission from the president of the United States.

In the Great Commission given to disciples by Jesus Christ, we recognize our ultimate mission, affirmed by the highest possible authority. Our mission is to "make disciples of all nations," saving souls and giving them the gift of eternal life, and we do so with the authority "of the Father and of the Son and of the Holy Spirit" (Matthew 28:19).

Can you fully grasp the magnitude of this amazing quest, this worthy endeavor? Are you prepared to accept the ultimate mission, backed by the greatest possible authority? What greater quest, what more noble battle could any knight ever aspire to?

God's Commissioning Guidance

What character traits and qualities are background investigators looking for to commission someone as a police officer? Or for any other commission, including the Great Commission, which Jesus commanded all believers to fulfill? The Bible describes several worthy qualities:

- **Honesty** – An officer should be incorruptible, having high moral character or integrity. "Select capable men from all the people—men who fear God, trustworthy men who hate dishonest gain—and appoint them as officials over thousands, hundreds, fifties and tens" (Exodus 18:21).

- **Calmness** – Officers should be capable of self-regulating and intentionally responding rather than just reacting, and they should be able to carry out the hazardous and stressful tasks of their calling while remaining in control of their emotions. "Do not repay anyone evil for evil. Be careful to do what is right in the eyes of everyone. If it is possible, as far as it depends on you, live at peace with everyone" (Romans 12:17–18).

- **Consideration** – An officer should have empathy for victims of crime and be respectful of the rights of the accused. "If one of you wants to be great, you must be the servant of the rest" (Matthew 20:26 GNT).

- **Bravery** – An officer should have the courage to protect those who are in danger and the fortitude to uphold the high standards of the military or law enforcement. "Be on your guard; stand firm in the faith; be courageous; be strong" (1 Corinthians 16:13).

The opposite traits pose grave character issues:

- **Deceitfulness** – Beware hiring those with a history of lying, stealing, and other forms of deception. "For the LORD your God detests anyone who does these things, anyone who deals dishonestly" (Deuteronomy 25:16).

- **Impulsivity** – Beware hiring those with no self-control: a history of anger problems, overly aggressive tactics, or reckless behaviors. "An angry person stirs up conflict, and a hot-tempered person commits many sins" (Proverbs 29:22).

- **Disrespectful** – Beware hiring those who are argumentative and discourteous. "The heart of the righteous weighs its answers, but the mouth of the wicked gushes evil" (15:28).

- **Timidity** – Beware hiring those who lack moral conviction or think only of their own welfare. "For the Spirit God gave us does not make us timid, but gives us power, love and self-discipline" (2 Timothy 1:7).

"Our challenge is not economics. Our challenge is not finance. Our challenge is faith. People have lost their faith," said New York Mayor Eric Adams in 2023. "You take the heart out of the body, the body dies," he said, referring to the vital role of faith as the "heart" of our nation.

Moreover (as reported by Aaron Kliegman on FoxNews.com), Adams called on faith leaders and clergy to be part of a "major recruitment campaign" to get young people to become police officers. Mayor Adams, a retired NYPD captain, understands that policing is built around an ethos, and men and women with strong religious convictions can make a profound positive contribution to virtuous professional law enforcement.

To consecrate or commission a person of bad character is like placing in authority over the flock a wolf who will "kill people to make unjust gain" (Ezekiel 22:27).

The Bible instructs that only the worthy shepherd should be consecrated.

> Shepherd the flock of God that is among you,
> exercising oversight, not under compulsion,
> but willingly, as God would have you; not for
> shameful gain, but eagerly; not domineering
> over those in your charge, but being examples to
> the flock. (1 Peter 5:2–3 ESV)

If you feel that you may not measure up to this standard, have faith that God can provide these things to you. If you ask for them and strive for them, then God will provide.

WARNORD Recap

Thus we have the first step on this path. The first Warning tells us of an evil and unsaved world, and the first Order tells us God's answer to that challenge.

Luther warns us that "the wicked have no faith," and Erasmus says to "increase your faith" by accepting God's grace and to follow God's path and his will and his Great Commission, "even if the entire world appears mad." This is an impossible task without God, but he makes it possible as the omnipotent, loving Father who wants us to be triumphant in the face of a world gone mad.

Once to ev'ry man and nation
    Comes the moment to decide,
In the strife of truth and falsehood,
    For the good or evil side.

*Almighty God, and most merciful father, who
didst command the children of Israel to offer a
daily sacrifice to thee, that thereby they might
glorify and praise thee for thy protection both
night and day, receive, O Lord, my morning
sacrifice which I now offer up to thee.*

*I yield thee humble and hearty thanks that thou
has preserved me from the danger of the night
past, and brought me to the light of the day, and
the comforts thereof, a day which is consecrated
to thine own service and for thine own honor...*

*Bless my family, kindred, friends and country, be
our God and guide this day and for ever for his
sake, who lay down in the Grave and arose again
for us, Jesus Christ our Lord, Amen.*

> —George Washington, passage from his
> "Sunday Morning Prayer"
> (date unknown)

ORDER #1: Next Level Battle Prep

➢   What is your faith journey?

➢   Who are (or were) the warrior priests in your life?

➢   Who are you helping along the faith journey?

➢   What qualities are necessary in order to be commissioned as a spiritual warrior?

➢   What next steps do you need to take to "increase your faith by accepting God's grace?" List them.

➢   What next steps do you need to take to help others? List them.

SECOND WARNING

THE WICKED DOUBT THE LORD

He who is not at one with God doubts and worries; they give up, thinking that God has forsaken them and has even become their enemy; they lay the blame for their ills on other men and become vindictive.

(Luther)

WARNORD #2

SECOND ORDER

ACT ON YOUR GOD-GIVEN FAITH

Even if you must undergo the loss of everything.

(Erasmus)

SECOND WARNING

THE WICKED DOUBT THE LORD

He who is not at one with God doubts and worries; they give up, thinking that God has forsaken them and has even become their enemy; they lay the blame for their ills on other men and become vindictive.

(Luther)

In the pride of his face the wicked does not seek him;
all his thoughts are, "There is no God."
—Psalm 10:4 ESV

Thou art the Way: to Thee alone
From sin and death we flee;

And he who would the Father seek
  Must seek Him, Lord, by Thee.

Thou art the Truth: Thy word alone
  True wisdom can impart;
Thou only canst instruct the mind,
  And purify the heart.

Thou art the Life: the rending tomb
  Proclaims Thy conquering arm;
And those who put their trust in Thee
  Nor death nor hell shall harm.

Thou art the Way, the Truth, the Life:
  Grant us that Way to know:
That Truth to keep; that Life to win,
  Whose joys eternal flow.
    —"Thou Art the Way, to Thee
Alone," George Washington Doane
      (1799–1859)

On July 12, 2016, a funeral was held for five Dallas police officers: DPD Senior Cpl. Lorne Ahrens, DPD Officer Michael Krol, DPD Sgt. Michael Smith, DART Officer Brent Thompson, and DPD Officer Patricio "Patrick" Zamarripa. These five officers had been guarding a group of Black Lives Matter protesters on July 7, 2016, when a sniper ambushed and murdered them. It was the largest mass murder of law enforcement officers in a single incident in US history, with the exception of the 9/11 terrorist attacks. No one can deny that this was an evil act.

But it was not only an attack on police officers. It represents a greater spiritual challenge to authority, to our society, and to our way of life.

President Obama spoke at the funeral and called the incident "a vicious, calculated, and despicable attack." He went on to say that the fallen officers had "answered the call" [from God] to serve, and "these five heroes knew better than most, we cannot take the blessings of this nation for granted." Then the president tried to make sense of the loss and our suffering.

> We ask the police to do too much, and we ask too little of ourselves…we tell the police, "You're a social worker, you're the parent, you're the teacher, you're the drug counselor." We tell them to keep those neighborhoods in check at all costs, and do so without causing any political blowback or inconvenience. Don't make a mistake that might disturb our own peace of mind. And then we feign surprise when, periodically, the tensions boil over. We know those things to be true. They've been true for a long time.

Police: God's Servants or Society's Scapegoats?

In Romans 13:3–4, the Bible tells us that the police officer is "God's servant."

> For rulers hold no terror for those who do right, but for those who do wrong. Do you want to be

free from fear of the one in authority? Then do
what is right and you will be commended.

For the one in authority is God's servant
for your good. But if you do wrong, be afraid,
for rulers do not bear the sword for no reason.
They are God's servants, agents of wrath to bring
punishment on the wrongdoer.

And yet, some people in society have become so vindictive toward our peacekeepers that they have persuaded themselves to hate the police and even attack them. Worse, conflicting and paradoxical political demands on our peacekeepers have become so irrational as to drive some officers into depression and even suicide.

In 2017, the Ruderman Foundation reported the first year where more police officers committed suicide (140) than were killed in the line of duty (129). Likewise, more firefighters committed suicide (103) than were killed in the line of duty (93). There is something seriously wrong when those who have been chosen to protect society are instead choosing to end their own lives.

Through God, the public and the police can work together to establish law and order in a free society. If all sectors of society work together toward a common godly goal to address the root cause of crime, then we can truly achieve miracles.

Without God, we are doomed.

Alexis de Tocqueville was an early French observer of the United States who published in 1840 a two-volume work called *Democracy in America*. He stated that religion was an essential ingredient in a successful democracy. After years of observation and research, he concluded that "Despotism may govern without faith, but Liberty cannot."

The Wicked Become Vindictive, Vicious, and Violent

In 2016, the same year in which those five officers were murdered, we saw an explosion of homicides across the US. This mass murder of police officers in Dallas was surely an act of pure evil, but it is also a graphic and tragic symptom of a far greater evil. It's a manifestation of Martin Luther's "Second Warning." The "wicked" have no confidence in God. They do not think that God can solve our problems. They blame others for their failures and therefore become vindictive, vicious, and violent.

And the situation is even worse—far worse—than it looks. To truly grasp the deterioration of society, we must understand the impact medical technology has had on holding down the murder rate. In 2002, Anthony Harris and a team of scholars from the University of Massachusetts and Harvard University published their landmark research in the journal *Homicide Studies*. They concluded that advances in medical technology between 1960 and 1999 cut the murder rate to a third or a quarter of what it would otherwise be. Victims were saved from certain death. And the leaps and bounds of life-saving technology in the decades since then have saved the lives of even more victims of violence, thus preventing many more successful murders.

Everyone understands the concept of "inflation adjusted dollars." When we finally start reporting "medically adjusted murders," then we will begin to appreciate just how desperate and tragically bad the situation has become. For every murder we report, there are ever increasing numbers of our citizens physically maimed and scarred and emotionally crippled and traumatized by violence.

Thus, you must multiply homicides in the 1960s by a factor of about 3.5 to compare with the 1990s. And a similar dynamic is in play between the 1990s and the 2020s. (Some medical experts believe that tourniquets alone may have cut the murder rate in half in just the last decade.) Take that into consideration when you reflect upon the fact that the annual increase of homicides in 2020 was almost 30 percent.

The worst annual increase in homicides we have ever seen was a 12.5 percent annual increase in the 1960s. But that comparison between 2020 and the 1960s completely breaks down. The year 2020 was not "almost three-times worse" than anything we have seen before. It was ten to twenty times worse than we have ever seen!

News headlines say that "Homicides Are Back to 1990s Levels." But now we understand that is completely wrong. After adjusting the numbers for medical improvements, the murder rate is far worse than that. What happened in 2020 is orders of magnitude worse than anything we have ever seen before. And

2021 was even worse, "compound interest" stacking a huge annual homicide increase on top of 2020.

Heather MacDonald, author of the excellent book *The War on Cops*, along with many other experts in the field, believes that the explosion of violence in 2016 (and those five murdered cops in Dallas) was "the Ferguson Effect," referring to the anti-police riots and biased media coverage emerging from the tragic death of Michael Brown at the hands of a police officer in Ferguson, Missouri. Writing in the *Wall Street Journal* on January 24, 2021, MacDonald stated that the explosion of homicides in 2020 and 2021 in the United States was not related to the COVID-19 pandemic (for a similar increase in violence did not occur on the same scale during the pandemic in any other nation around the globe) but was instead "tied to the street violence unleashed by the death of George Floyd in Minneapolis on May 25, 2020. The political and media response to Floyd's death amplified the existing narrative that policing was lethally racist."

There is another important dynamic that we must consider. A monstrous mass murder by a single individual can create more psychosocial trauma than countless deaths by natural causes such as disease, cancer, tornados, hurricanes, or floods. And with modern mass media, even one murder is often amplified to devastating psychosocial effect. Think about that. Less than fifty years ago, many reported incidents remained truly local news, but now because of the internet, everything is global.

In its section on PTSD, the *DSM-5* (considered to be the Bible of psychology and psychiatry) tells us that, whenever the cause of trauma is "human in nature" (such as assault, torture, or rape), the degree of trauma is "more severe and long lasting." Millions die from disease and other natural causes every day, and it has little impact on our behavior, but one serial killer or serial rapist can paralyze a city. Thus, the overall societal harm of violent crime can be far greater than the harm caused by disease or any other factor. And we now understand that for every murder, there is an ever-increasing number of citizens physically maimed and emotionally crippled by violence.

We Didn't Get Here Overnight

How did we arrive at this dark and tragic place? Well, it didn't happen overnight. Comparing murder rates across the decades without allowing for improvements in medical technology is like comparing minimum wage without allowing for inflation. And when we take medical technology into consideration, we can see that violent crime has increased almost every year since the late 1960s.[2]

Up until the 1960s, Hollywood and the TV industry operated by a voluntary set of guidelines called the Hayes

---

2   There is a temptation to use data such as the "aggravated assault rate" to measure the problem over the years, but it is too easy to fudge that data. Where do you draw that magic line between "aggravated assault" and "simple assault"? Most cops will tell you that they can make the aggravated assault rate say whatever they want it to say. But dead is dead, and murder is a far better measure of the problem *if* we allow for medical technology.

Code. The entertainment industry basically said (paraphrasing here) that "We know the stories we tell will have an impact on our society. And we know we have a responsibility to tell stories that will have a positive impact." A good part of the Hayes Code could be condensed into three words, "Crime doesn't pay." This is a paraphrasing and simplification, but it truly addresses the heart of the matter.

In general, under the Hayes Code, movies and TV shows would not depict law enforcement officers in a negative manner, and they would not present crime and criminals in a positive manner. Hollywood and the television industry accepted responsibility for their actions and their impact on our society. Then in the late 1960s, and getting worse and worse decade after decade since then, the entertainment industry turned this code on its head. They refused to accept any social responsibility for the endless hours glorifying crime and criminals and vilifying law enforcement while simultaneously claiming that the few seconds of commercials or "product placement" would change the behavior of millions of people.[3]

But there is one thing that does reduce crime, and that is religion. In the study "Religious Involvement and Adult Mortality in the United States" published in the *Southern Medical Journal* (2004), researchers found that metropolitan

---

3   Much more information about media violence and its impact on our nation can be found in *Assassination Generation: Video Games, Aggression, and the Psychology of Killing*, by Lt. Col. Dave Grossman and Kristine Paulsen, with Katie Miserany (New York: Little, Brown and Co., 2016).

areas with high rates of congregational membership had lower crime rates (especially homicide and suicide rates) than metropolitan areas with low church attendance. In fact, according to the study "Escaping from the Crime of Inner Cities: Church Attendance and Religious Salience among Disadvantaged Youth" in *Justice Quarterly* (2000), religious attendance resulted in a 57 percent *decrease* in the likelihood that inner-city young people would end up dealing drugs and a 39 percent *decrease* in likelihood that youths would commit other crimes when they attended religious services regularly. Clearly churches play an important role in helping to keep people from hurting themselves or others through criminal activities.

The Lord Will Give You a New Heart

At the funeral for those five murdered officers in Dallas, President Obama concluded with a dire warning that was chillingly prophetic. He said that both the police and the public must not let recent events divide them, knowing that hearts could harden against each other. That is exactly what Satan wants, for police and the public to turn against each other. President Obama warned everyone that we must "reject such despair" caused by the trauma. Sadly, since the funeral, we have seen the president's warning come to fruition as violence against police has escalated, and police suicides continue to rise.

He concluded by quoting Scripture that tells us we could stop Satan in his tracks by turning to God: "I will give you a new heart and put a new spirit in you; I will remove from you your heart of stone and give you a heart of flesh" (Ezekiel 36:26).

But if we exclude God, as the devil wants, then Psalm 127:1 (NKJV) is prophetic: "Unless the LORD guards the city, the watchman stays awake in vain."

How can spiritual warriors (sheepdogs, peacekeepers, and others) unite to successfully overcome this tragic and heartbreaking challenge? Luther gave us the "Warning" and Erasmus gave us the "Order." But always remember, God gives us the answer.

WARNING #2: Next Level Battle Prep

➤ How do people blame and scapegoat each other?

➤ What acts of vindictiveness have occurred in your community? In your country? In our world?

➤ How does religion affect vindictiveness and the crime rate?

SECOND ORDER

ACT ON YOUR GOD-GIVEN FAITH
Even if you must undergo the loss of everything. (Erasmus)

Be strong, do not fear; your God will come…with vengeance;
with divine retribution he will come to save you.
—Isaiah 35:4

What does it mean to serve the Lord? How do we act on faith and do good works?

The burdens and sacrifices required of peacekeepers are truly immense, and lacking political and public support makes it much worse. It's like fighting with one hand tied behind your back. Our society's peacekeepers must be wondering, "Who do I turn to? What do I do?"

The Bible commands us to "put on the full armor of God, so that you can take your stand against the devil's schemes"

(Ephesians 6:11). We don't hear much today about how to do this and why it matters. Instead, we hear too much preaching of God's forgiveness without including the requirement to change your ways and do the right thing. If you go to church and pray for forgiveness and then go back to practicing your usual dishonorable conduct, you are operating on the basis of cheap grace. Jesus cautioned us about this when he said, "Why do you call me, 'Lord, Lord,' and do not do what I say?" (Luke 6:46). Faith without obedience is like faith without works: dead! It's worthless. This is why so many people fail as spiritual warriors; they are a one-sided coin full of cheap grace. They want forgiveness without responsibility, a viable faith without doing good, repentance without authentic change. (If you feel a little guilty or uncomfortable reading about this other side of the faith coin, good! That's a sign of growth.) The power of the Holy Spirit is costly. Dietrich Bonhoeffer rightly said, "What has cost God much cannot be cheap for us."

First, Clothe Yourself with His Virtues

Martin Luther explained, "First, we may clothe ourselves with His virtues…Put on Christ, the Armor of Light." You cannot obey God if you do not know his laws and expectations. Those who have given their lives to Christ must learn about his love, his justice, his mercy, and his plan. Pastor Steven Sipes says, "Living a life of virtue, striving to make small, daily, virtuous choices, sets a person on the path to godly virtue."

You can start to build spiritual armor by studying Scripture and attending church. The apostle Paul said, "All

Scripture is inspired by God and is useful to teach us what is true and to make us realize what is wrong in our lives. It corrects us when we are wrong and teaches us to do what is right" (2 Timothy 3:16 NLT).

Second, Obey His Word

After accepting Christ as our Savior by God's grace, we are eager to serve. We will often pray, "Lord, tell me what to do, and then I will obey you," but the Lord answers, "First obey me, and then I will tell you what to do." You see, it is quite natural to put the cart before the horse, but obedience always precedes service. Reverend Billy Graham once said, "God does communicate with those who are willing to obey him." It is best to pray as David did.

> Teach me, O Lord, the way of your statutes;
> and I will keep it to the end. Give me under-
> standing, that I may keep your law and observe
> it with my whole heart. Lead me in the path of
> your commandments, for I delight in it. Incline
> my heart to your testimonies, and not to selfish
> gain! (Psalm 119:33–36 ESV)

Third, Act on Your Faith

Upon successful completion of their physical and spiritual training, peacekeepers must take action to protect society from evil. Pastor John Rasicci, author of the books *Grace* and

Baptism of the Holy Spirit, summarizes Titus 2:13–15 as meaning "the grace that saves will put you to work."

There are those who walk in darkness, and these faithless souls pose a great threat to others. We must continually pray that lost souls find God (Matthew 5:43–45), but realistically, peacekeepers must take action. This call to action can be found in the action verbs found in our call to duty: *serve* the Lord, *protect* the people, and *defend* the truth.

Martin Luther warned that spiritual warfare is tough: "It is no easy thing to stand always in battle array during the whole of life." The Great Shepherd's sheepdogs are always alert for danger to the flock. All of God's peacekeepers are never off duty. They wear God's badge in their heart!

The devil is our archenemy and especially hates a faithful peacekeeper because a peacekeeper under God's authority is a "beacon of light" unto others, and their good works "give glory" to God the Father in heaven (v. 16). When the devil sees a peacekeeper trying to right a wrong, when the evil one sees a sheepdog protecting the innocent from the faithless, that is when Satan will make a full-scale attack.

Fourth, Do Not Be Dismayed

While it is intimidating to know that such a powerful and evil force opposes the faithful, the Bible says

Do not be dismayed, for I am your God. I will strengthen you. (Isaiah 41:10)

Be strong; fear not! Behold, your God will come
with vengeance, with the recompense of God.
He will come and save you. (35:4 ESV)

There is only one way to win in this battle. You must
sustain your faith in God. Erasmus said, "Thou lacks nothing
as long as thou possesses Christ in whom is all things!"

Jesus' sacrifice on the cross defeated the devil in relation to our eternal destiny (giving us eternal salvation). In his
goodness, the Lord has also given us spiritual weapons for
victorious battle with the devil (Ephesians 6:10–18). If you are
a peacekeeper, if you have joined God's army to protect the
faithful from the faithless, then you can do your duty, in all
humility, through the power of the Holy Spirit.

God promises us that "if my people, who are called
by my name, will humble themselves and pray and seek my
face and turn from their wicked ways, then I will hear from
heaven, and I will forgive their sin and will heal their land" (2
Chronicles 7:14). *This* is God's solution and his answer.

But there is also another answer. A deeper, more profound, and important answer. Even if God does not heal our
nation, he is still God, and he will save our souls for eternity.
Consider the hymn by George Washington Doane at the
beginning of this WARNORD.

Thou art the Life: the rending tomb
    Proclaims Thy conquering arm;

And those who put their trust in Thee
Nor death nor hell shall harm.

"Nor death nor hell shall harm"? Well, we are all going to die, so that is demonstrably false, right? Wrong! God and the hymnist are both talking about eternal life. About preserving our souls through and after death.

Even the most optimistic patriot must conclude that sometime in the future, every nation will pass away. Will it last a hundred more years? Perhaps a thousand or even five thousand? Only God knows. But in comparison to eternity, those numbers are miniscule. They amount to nothing in light of life everlasting.

You see, God's greatest achievement and his highest goal is not to save our lives or to save our nation but to save our souls. We must never lose track of that eternal perspective.

America's Puritan forefathers desired to build a country that ensures the safety and protects the freedoms of all people who seek, find, and serve God. This is surely a peacekeeper's mission that is worth fighting for. Likewise, Chris Pascoe and I have worked for a lifetime, and will continue to strive with all our hearts, to sustain the nation to which we swore a solemn oath. You may have sworn that oath, too, even in your youth. It goes like this:

I pledge allegiance to the Flag of the United
States of America, and to the Republic for which

it stands, one Nation under God, indivisible,
with liberty and justice for all.

But even if we see our nation go down as another foot-note in history, we can rest in our faith and in the knowledge that God holds the future.

WARNORD Recap

We must never lose track of the eternal perspective that God provides for us. Never forget: terrible, tragic, horrific things will happen on this earth. But God can use those terrible things to bring people to salvation, and that is what is truly most important.

> All the nations are as nothing before him, they are accounted by him as less than nothing and emptiness.
>
> …But they who wait for the LORD shall renew their strength; they shall mount up with wings like eagles; they shall run and not be weary; they shall walk and not faint. (Isaiah 40:17, 31 ESV)

We will all die physically. Every nation will fall eventually. Our planet will die and so will our sun. The greatest of all possible goals in our short time in this world is for mankind to serve God as he saves our sorry souls and brings us to everlasting life, thanks to the price that Jesus paid for our sins on the cross: "These are written that you may believe that Jesus is the

Messiah, the Son of God, and that by believing you may have life in his name" (John 20:31).

This is the lesson we must never forget: have faith, ask God for more faith, and then act upon that faith.

Prayer for Protection

> *O GOD, who art the author of peace*
> > *and lover of concord,*
> *In knowledge of whom standeth*
> > *our eternal life,*
> *Whose service is perfect freedom;*
> *Defend us, thy humble servants,*
> > *In all assaults of our enemies;*
> *That we, surely trusting in thy defense,*
> *May not fear the power of any adversaries,*
> *Through the might of Jesus Christ our Lord.*
>
> *Amen.*

—Unknown author, *Soldier's Prayer Book* (ca. 1863)

ORDER #2: Next Level Battle Prep

- ➤ How can you clothe yourself in God's virtues?
- ➤ How can you obey God's Word?
- ➤ How can you act on God-given faith?

➤ What actions can you take to sharpen your sword and reinforce your physical and spiritual armor?

➤ How can you help others do the same?

THIRD WARNING

THE WICKED ARE SELF-CENTERED

The wicked…seek not God, nor care for the things of God; they seek their own riches, their own glory…their own power, and, in a word, their own kingdom.

(Luther)

WARNORD #3

THIRD ORDER

ANALYZE YOUR DESIRES

Seek first the Kingdom of God and what God wants, then all your other needs will be met as well.

(Erasmus)

THIRD WARNING

THE WICKED ARE SELF-CENTERED

The wicked…seek not God, nor care for the things of God; they seek their own riches, their own glory…their own power, and, in a word, their own kingdom.

(Luther)

For the mind that is set on the flesh is hostile to God,
for it does not submit to God's law; indeed, it cannot.
—Romans 8:7 ESV

Amazing grace! How sweet the sound
    That saved a wretch like me!
I once was lost, but now am found;
    Was blind, but now I see…

The Lord has promised good to me,
 His Word my hope secures;
He will my Shield and Portion be,
 As long as life endures.

Yea, when this flesh and heart shall fail,
 And mortal life shall cease,

I shall possess, within the veil,
 A life of joy and peace.

The earth shall soon dissolve like snow,
 The sun forbear to shine;
But God, who called me here below,
 Will be forever mine.

—"Amazing Grace," by John Newton (1725–1807)

Desiderius Erasmus and Martin Luther concurred: there is spiritual warfare raging around us, and we are all targets! Many people are blind to the combat, and it's that blindness that makes them even more vulnerable.

The combat is so fierce that Erasmus went so far as to say, "A Christian man should never cease from war."

When God first created humanity, we did not know sin, but Adam and Eve did have the freedom of choice. Then that serpent, Satan, deceived them, and Adam and Eve chose to know good and evil (Genesis 2:4–3:24). From that point on, as Luther explains it, free will has no longer been free but the bond-slave of evil.

The Lᴏʀᴅ God commanded the man, saying,
"You may surely eat of every tree of the garden,
but of the tree of the knowledge of good and evil
you shall not eat, for in the day that you eat of it
you shall surely die." (2:16–17 ᴇꜱᴠ)

The serpent said to the woman, "You will not
surely die. For God knows that when you eat of
it your eyes will be opened, and you will be like
God, knowing good and evil." (3:4–5 ᴇꜱᴠ)

Only through Jesus' sacrifice on the cross and accepting
him as our Savior can we be set free from that bondage of evil.

The Devil Is a Liar and a Murderer

Who is Satan, and why would he do this to human-
ity? The Bible tells us that the devil was an angel, with all the
knowledge of God's goodness that came with being in heaven.
But the devil and his followers coveted God's power and
attempted a *coup d'état*. They failed. The angel Michael and his
army soundly defeated them and banished them from heaven
(Revelation 12:7–12).

Jesus said, "I saw Satan fall like lightning from heaven"
(Luke 10:18). Jesus also identified the devil as evil, a liar, and a
murderer from the beginning (John 8:44).

In retaliation for his defeat, the devil seeks to devour as
many humans as he can, just like a raging lion (1 Peter 5:8).
While God wants to save humanity from its original sin, the

devil has the power to hurt us. In Jesus' explanation of the parable of the seeds, he talked about Satan's destructive work: "Now the parable is this: The seed is the word of God. The ones along the path are those who have heard; then the devil comes and takes away the word from their hearts, so that they may not believe and be saved" (Luke 8:11–12 ESV).

Why does God allow the devil to exist? We know that God is all good, and God cannot do evil (James 1:13). If he allows the devil to exist, it must be for a reason. We know from the book of Job that God allowed the devil to test Job. The devil plagued Job with great hardship, but Job prevailed by submitting himself to God: "I repent, sitting on dust and ashes" (Job 42:6 NASB). Although the devil sought to turn Job from God, the Lord did not give Satan free reign (1:8–12; 2:3–6). He placed limits on what the devil could do to Job. This is still true today. God allows Satan to tempt people within limits they can bear (1 Corinthians 10:13) to test and strengthen our faith. "The LORD is faithful, and he will strengthen you and protect you from the evil one" (2 Thessalonians 3:3).

But Satan is not our only problem. In one of his sermons, Martin Luther said: "For these three powerful enemies, the *devil*, the *world*, and the *flesh*, unceasingly oppose us day and night. Hence, Job (ch 7, 1) regards the life of man on earth as a life of trial and warfare." Since the world and humanity (flesh) have fallen into sin, much of the evil on earth can be blamed on ourselves, with the help of the devil tempting us. But for our salvation, Jesus Christ was crucified, and if we follow him, we can defeat sin and death (Luke 24:46–47; Romans 8:1).

We Are Not God's Puppets

You must understand that we are not God's puppets, with him manipulating us to do as he wants. People jump from saying there is no God to saying, "Well, if there is a God, why does he permit all these terrible things to happen?" The answer is that God has given us free will, and people make bad choices, and bad things can and will happen.

The right question is not "How could God permit this to happen?" Rather, we must accept responsibility for our choices and ask, "How could *we* permit such things to happen?" And, most importantly, "How can we be saved?"

God is the Alpha and Omega, the beginning and the end. He knew that humans would make a mess of free will and the knowledge of good and evil. So he planned a way to save humanity, a path to salvation that relied on Jesus Christ paying for our sins as the only worthy sacrifice. And with Jesus (God the Son) having completed his part, we can now be saved by *his* faith, which also entails *serving* by his faith.

And in response to our plea for assistance? When we cry out to God, "Do something!" his answer is, "I did. I sent you." We should be filled with joy to know that there is a loving God who gives us, first, a vital mission to accomplish here on earth; and, second (and oh so infinitely more important than anything that could happen here on earth), the path to eternal life. And we praise God that we are not his puppets!

Satan's Heart of Darkness

Father Dwight Longenecker, a theologian and author of *Immortal Combat: Confronting the Heart of Darkness*, says we can learn more about the enemies that Luther identified (the devil, the world, and the flesh) in the "attempted" temptations of Jesus Christ (Matthew 4:1–11). After Jesus was baptized by John the Baptist, Jesus went into the Judean desert to test his faith. He fasted for forty days and forty nights. Then that great tempter the devil came to him to tempt him to sin.

The Flesh

"If thou be the Son of God, command that these stones be made bread" (v. 3 KJV). The devil first tried to tempt Jesus with something simple, desires of the flesh, symbolized by the bread. Remember, Jesus was fasting, and his body was desperately yearning for food. For Jesus, however, turning stones into bread meant more than satisfying his need for food; it symbolized surrendering to all human desires, good and bad. John the Evangelist calls this "lust of the body," while psychologists refer to the uncontrollable desire for pleasure as "hedonism." At its extreme, it can be profoundly pathological. And the devil is the most sadistic of all psychopaths.

The World

"Then the devil taketh him up into the holy city, and setteth him on a pinnacle of the temple, and saith unto him, If thou be the Son of God, cast thyself down: for it is written,

He shall give his angels charge concerning thee: and in their hands they shall bear thee up, lest at any time thou dash thy foot against a stone" (vv. 5–6 KJV). The devil next tried to tempt Jesus with pride. The devil challenged Jesus to demonstrate his power by throwing himself from the temple and then saving himself. The devil was trying to goad Jesus into misusing God's power for a show of superiority. John the Evangelist calls this in-the-world desire for self-importance as the "pride of life," while psychologists refer to it as "narcissism." And the devil is the most arrogant narcissist.

The Devil

"Again, the devil taketh him up into an exceeding high mountain, and sheweth him all the kingdoms of the world, and the glory of them; and saith unto him, All these things will I give thee, if thou wilt fall down and worship me'" (vv. 8–9 KJV). The devil's final temptation was power, but the price for power was renouncing God and serving Satan. For the devil, the ends justify the means. John the Evangelist calls this ruthless desire for power the "lust of the eyes," while psychologists call this "Machiavellianism." And the devil is, indeed, the most cunning and manipulative Machiavellian.

Niccolò Machiavelli was a politician in the same era as Luther and Erasmus, but Niccolò was such a manipulative liar that many denounced him as an apostle of the devil. The term "Old Nick" is now used as a nickname for both Niccolò and Satan.

Machiavelli wrote a book called *The Prince*, which advises leaders that morals are unimportant and that it is acceptable to use whatever means necessary to pursue personal ambition—especially deceiving, bribing, pretending to be religious to gain trust, and inflicting injury to intimidate others. *The Prince* was considered so evil that the church banned it, and Erasmus wrote an opposing book called *Institutio Principis Christiani*, or *Education of a Christian Prince*. It is a sad reflection upon our world today that Machiavelli's book is widely known and studied while Erasmus' vastly superior and godly book has slipped into obscurity.

Despite Satan's best efforts, Jesus withstood his every attempt to seduce him into sin (Luke 4:1–13).

Satan's Three Temptations and the Dark Triad

Sequoia Palmquist (one of our alpha readers) points out that all three temptations—the flesh, the world, and the devil—are the result of breaking the first commandment: "Thou shalt love the LORD thy God with all thy heart, and with all thy soul, and with all thy mind" (Matthew 22:37 KJV). Giving in to any of the three temptations requires putting something before God. Remember, all three temptations totally failed against Jesus, who did not entertain even one thought about betraying God our Father.

Psychologists Delroy Paulhus and Kevin Williams, in their 2002 research published in the *Journal of Research in Personality*, coined the phrase "dark triad" to describe the unethical behavioral traits of psychopathy (lust), narcissism (pride), and Machiavellianism (manipulation). These traits precisely describe Satan, our ruthless enemy.

Satan offers all of us the same three temptations, the dark triad he tried on Jesus Christ: lust, pride, and manipulation. Only with the Lord's help can we resist the sins of lust, the lure of pride, and the desire to manipulate others. Those who do not seek the Lord's help will fail in this test and become servants of the devil. Erasmus tells us, when we see the pathological behaviors of the dark triad, "the world appears mad" because we are looking into the eyes of true insanity.

Satan's Dark Energy

A study called "The Light vs. Dark Triad of Personality" found that people with dark triad traits have a kind of dark energy that is destructive to both themselves and others. People with dark triad traits "showed stronger linkages to selfish, exploitative, aggressive, and socially aversive outcomes." Not surprisingly, studies of prison inmates found they were high in these traits.

Another study published in *Military Psychology* called "A Latent Core of Dark Traits" found that Machiavellianism, narcissism, and psychopathy all had a common core, referred to as the "core of darkness." These researchers studied military service members, and they found that those soldiers involved in severe acts of violence tended to have latent or preexisting "dark triad" traits. Those soldiers with a heart of darkness had negative views of human rights and poor relations with fellow soldiers. These individuals displayed a negative attitude toward military ethics and the code of conduct. Researchers believe the *core of darkness* is preexisting before military experience. Those soldiers who showed behaviors "such as terrorizing civilians, torturing prisoners of war, or mutilating bodies of enemies or civilians, were predicted by disruptive behavior before the age of fifteen." Research also found that soldiers associated with unethical warzone behavior scored higher on an anger measure.

The Bible identifies these dark triad behaviors as spiritual defects from man's fall into sin. Jesus described such sins as arising from evil hearts: "For from within, out of the heart of man, come evil thoughts, sexual immorality, theft, murder, adultery, coveting, wickedness, deceit, sensuality, envy, slander, pride, foolishness" (Mark 7:21–22 ESV).

The apostle Paul identified those with dark hearts as being premeditated and deliberate in their actions: "Though they know God's righteous decree that those who practice such things deserve to die, they not only do them but give approval to those who practice them" (Romans 1:32 ESV).

What is the source of this dark energy? Why would people so oppose the laws of God? We know it has something to do with the devil. (You will find more information on the "core of darkness" in WARNORD #18.)

WARNING #3: Next Level Battle Prep

➢   Describe the three evils we must conquer:

- ○   The Flesh (psychopathy)
- ○   The World (narcissism)
- ○   The Devil (Machiavellianism)

➢ What is the cause of all this "dark energy"?

➢ Which among the dark triad does your heart most resemble?

THIRD ORDER

ANALYZE YOUR DESIRES

Seek first the Kingdom of God and what God wants, then all your other needs will be met as well.

(Erasmus)

Seek ye first the kingdom of God, and his righteousness;
and all these things shall be added unto you.
—Matthew 6:33 KJV

Father Dwight Longenecker says the way for the faithful to counter this dark triad or unholy attack by the devil is to "appeal to the Holy Trinity" consisting of the Father, the Son, and the Holy Spirit.

The Heart of Light

The Opposite of Psychopathy Is Obedience to God

The Father

For the first temptation, the devil tries to tempt Jesus with things of the flesh, symbolized by bread. Jesus replies, "It is written, 'Man shall not live by bread alone, but by every word that proceeds from the mouth of God'" (Matthew 4:4 NKJV). Jesus said in John 8:44, the devil is a liar and a murderer from the beginning. The devil wants humanity to disobey God and destroy itself, just as the devil himself betrayed God. Jesus, however, is our model for obedience to God, even giving to the Father the ultimate sacrifice: "Being found in appearance as a man, he humbled himself by becoming obedient to death—even death on a cross!" (Philippians 2:8).

The Opposite of Narcissism Is Empathy

The Son

For the second temptation, the devil tries to appeal to worldly pride, by challenging Jesus to demonstrate his power. Jesus replies, "You shall not put the LORD your God to the test" (Matthew 4:7 ESV). The way of the world is narcissism or self-ishness, the way that puts "me" first.

It was because of God's empathy for us that Jesus Christ—who is one with the Father—made the ultimate sacri-fice on the cross. After the Last Supper, Jesus told his disciples, "A new command I give you: Love one another. As I have loved you, so you must love one another. By this everyone will know that you are my disciples, if you love one another" (John 13:34–35). Love. Empathy. These are the traits that define Jesus, and they should define us. It is a straight-out command, a direct order from Jesus, our Commander in Chief.

The Opposite of Machiavellianism Is Service
The Holy Spirit

For the third temptation, the devil offers Jesus authority over the world in exchange for Jesus serving the devil. Jesus replies, "Be gone, Satan! For it is written, 'You shall worship the LORD your God and him only shall you serve'" (Matthew 4:10 ESV). Jesus told his disciples, "For even the Son of Man did not come to be served, but to serve, and to give his life as a ransom for many" (Mark 10:45). Always remember, the devil's promises and temptations are counterfeit; they are all deception and lies designed to manipulate you.

Once you accept Jesus as your Savior, you will be set apart for service. The Holy Spirit will prepare you and direct you to serve in God's holy army. When we ask Jesus to enter our life, we will gradually become more and more like him: obedient to God's laws, compassionate to others, and willing to serve the Lord in the battle against evil. But if we sin and push God out of our lives, we become more and more like the devil: psychopathic, narcissistic, and Machiavellian.

Praise God for his amazing grace in taking away our dark hearts and saving us from the devil!

WARNORD Recap

Our third warning gives us insight into Satan's dark triad of selfish psychopathy, self-centered narcissism, and manipulative Machiavellianism—a triad that equates to insanity. It is also a description of the innate nature of the wicked. And it is the paradox of mental illness that, in seeking each of these things, people only bring about the opposite: the diminishment and destruction of themselves. Satan is a liar. His every word and his every promise are lies, resulting in the opposite of what he offers.

Satan is an evil, psychopathic deceiver, and Christ's mission on earth is to defeat him: "The reason the Son of God appeared was to destroy the works of the devil" (1 John 3:8 ESV). And we are called to contribute to Christ's holy mission as his loyal spiritual warriors, his faithful sheepdogs.

Thus, the third order: Seek God and the kingdom of God (Matthew 6:33) and you will be given a spirit of obedience, empathy, and service toward others. It is the paradox of the Christian life that if we dedicate our lives to serving others and placing them first, then we have the most fulfilling and joyful life—a life in which true love is triumphant, great joy is abundant, and perfect peace is possible.

Read again the powerful words of the hymn at the beginning of this WARNORD, and fully embrace the glorious fact that they are true:

The Lord has promised good to me,
     His Word my hope secures;
He will my Shield and Portion be,
     As long as life endures.

Yea, when this flesh and heart shall fail,
     And mortal life shall cease,
I shall possess, within the veil,
     A life of joy and peace.

"The Lord's Prayer"
(Matthew 6:7–13 NLT/KJV)

Jesus said, "Pray like this:
     Our Father, which art in heaven,
hallowed be thy name,
     Thy kingdom come,
     Thy will be done,
on earth as it is in heaven.
     Give us this day our daily bread.
     And forgive us our debts,
As we forgive our debtors.
     And lead us not into temptation,
but deliver us from evil:
     For thine is the kingdom,
and the power, and the glory,
     For ever. Amen."

ORDER #3: Next Level Battle Prep

➤ How has the dark triad in others affected you?

➤ What are some ways you can identify the dark triad?

➤ How can you respond when you find the dark triad has become entwined in your life?

- Reflect on how you have been *obedient* to God.
- Reflect on how you have demonstrated *empathy* to others.
- Reflect on how you have been of *service* to others.

FOURTH WARNING

THE WICKED RESIST THE LORD

The uncircumcised in heart and ears
will always resist the Holy Spirit.

(Luther)

WARNORD #4

FOURTH ORDER

**MAKE CHRIST THE ONLY GUIDE
AND GOAL OF YOUR LIFE**

Dedicate all your enthusiasm, all your effort,
your leisure as well as your business.

(Erasmus)

FOURTH WARNING

THE WICKED RESIST THE LORD

The uncircumcised in heart and ears will always resist the Holy Spirit.

(Luther)

The natural person does not accept the things of the Spirit
of God, for they are folly to him, and he is not able to
understand them because they are spiritually discerned.
—1 Corinthians 2:14 ESV

A mighty fortress is our God,
 a bulwark never failing;
our helper he, amid the flood
 of mortal ills prevailing.
For still our ancient foe
does seek to work us woe;

his craft and power are great,
   and armed with cruel hate,
on earth is not his equal.

Did we in our own strength confide,
   our striving would be losing,
were not the right Man on our side,
   the Man of God's own choosing.
You ask who that may be?
Christ Jesus, it is he;
   Lord Sabaoth his name,
   from age to age the same;
and he must win the battle…

That Word above all earthly powers
   no thanks to them abideth;
the Spirit and the gifts are ours
   through him who with us sideth.
Let goods and kindred go,
this mortal life also;
   the body they may kill:
   God's truth abideth still;
his kingdom is forever!

—"A Mighty Fortress Is Our God," by Martin Luther
(1483–1546)

When a police officer arrests a criminal, the offender may deny their crime or attempt to excuse their sinful acts. Too often criminals show no remorse. Many are repeat offenders. It is all too easy to justify sin, and we are no different. The Bible warns: "Wide is the gate and broad is the road that leads to destruction, and many enter through it. But small is the gate and narrow the road that leads to life, and only a few find it" (Matthew 7:13–14).

Legally convicted criminals may be sent to prisons. Prisons are called "correctional centers" because the goal is to transform the convict into a law-abiding citizen. However, this transformation is difficult. Before convicts can be rehabilitated, they need to take responsibility for their crimes and have a desire to change. Seasoned corrections officers easily identify unrepentant prisoners, predicting who will be reincarcerated after their release.

In the same way, we all sin. First John 1:8 says, "If we claim to be without sin, we deceive ourselves and the truth is not in us." We must take responsibility for our sin and have a sincere desire to change.

For all of us, transformation is difficult. But the Bible tells us how to be transformed with God's supernatural assistance. And that process starts with accepting God's call.

Grieving the Holy Spirit

We have previously discussed the Sinner's Prayer, also known as the Salvation Prayer. A sinner who accepts salvation through Christ must say the Sinner's Prayer in some form or fashion. By doing so, they give up their sins and ask Jesus to guide their life.

A believer who deliberately refuses to repent is grieving the Spirit. Therefore, we are commanded, "Grieve not the holy

Spirit of God, whereby ye are sealed unto the day of redemption" (Ephesians 4:30 KJV).

There are those among us who think they won't be held accountable for their sins if they never acknowledge them. Deep down, they desire to continue sinning, so they pretend that they do not know what sin is. There is something important that we need to understand here: there is no such thing as ignorance of sin.

> The wrath of God is being revealed from heaven against all the godlessness and wickedness of people, who suppress the truth by their wickedness, since what may be known about God is plain to them, because God has made it plain to them. For since the creation of the world God's invisible qualities—his eternal power and divine nature—have been clearly seen, being understood from what has been made, so that people are without excuse…
>
> …(Indeed, when Gentiles, who do not have the law, do by nature things required by the law, they are a law for themselves, even though they do not have the law. They show that the requirements of the law are written on their hearts, their consciences also bearing witness, and their thoughts sometimes accusing them and at other times even defending them.) (Romans 1:18–20; 2:15)

Even the most demented psychopath knows their predations are wrong. They will try to hide their crimes and will lie to police to avoid punishment. If they admit their guilt, it is in an arrogant and demeaning manner designed to inflict more pain.

Galatians 6:7 warns us, "Do not be deceived: God is not mocked, for whatever one sows, that will he also reap" (ESV). The biblical doctrine of the Trinity reveals to us that there is a mutual indwelling between the Father, the Son, and the Holy Spirit. Dr. R. C. Sproul explains:

> To put on Christ, then, is to put on the Father and the Spirit as well, and living out the new life in Christ according to the pattern He gives us pleases our triune Creator. On the other hand, violating the standards given to the disciples of Jesus not only grieves the Son of God but also the Father and the Spirit.

John Calvin (1509–1564), one of the great theologians of the same era as Luther and Erasmus, wrote:

> No language can adequately express this solemn truth, that the Holy Spirit rejoices and is glad on our account, when we are obedient to him in all things, and neither think nor speak anything, but what is pure and holy; and, on the other hand, is grieved, when we admit anything into our minds that is unworthy of our calling.

To grieve the Holy Spirit means that you are causing pain to Jesus Christ who loves you and does not want to see you or anyone else fall into the clutches of the devil. The Gospels also refer to the Holy Spirit dwelling within us as the Spirit of Truth (John 14:17), so anything false, deceitful, or hypocritical grieves him.

God loves us, and as we learn to love him, the fact that we have caused grief to him should have a profound effect on us. Charles Spurgeon (1834–1892) has been called the "Prince of Preachers," and he brings this commandment into a wonderful perspective when he writes:

> There is something very touching in this admonition, "Grieve not the Holy Spirit of God." It does not say, "Do not make him angry." A more delicate and tender term is used—"Grieve him not." There are…many of us who are scarcely to be moved by the information that another is angry with us; but where is the heart so hard, that it is not moved when we know that we have caused others grief?—for grief is a sweet combination of anger and of love. It is anger, but all the gall is taken from it. Love sweetens the anger, and turns the edge of it, not against the person, but against the offense.

There is no hiding from God's truth. The sinner cannot plead ignorance of sin, for the Bible says about the new covenant that Christ initiated, "This is the covenant I will make with them…says the LORD. I will put my laws in their hearts, and I will write them on their minds" (Hebrews 10:16). The Bible makes it clear that there is no excuse for any person to say, "I was never taught how to treat another human being," or "I don't know what God's laws are." The general laws of God are written on everyone's heart, and our conscience works with this law. Even a psychopath knows what is evil and tries to hide his crimes, but he will fail to keep his crimes in the dark; "For God shall bring every work into judgment, with every secret thing, whether it be good, or whether it be evil" (Ecclesiastes 12:14 KJV).

When the Bible says that God has written his law in our hearts, it is different from the Holy Spirit working in our hearts. The law is written in our hearts to make us aware of sin so our conscience can accuse us when we do wrong. By our heart, we know good and evil (Romans 2:15), and we often disobey the law. Fortunately for us, Hebrews 10:17 says we can be forgiven if we repent: "Their sins and lawless acts I will remember no more."

The Holy Spirit first works to call us to Christ. Then once we have repented and believed, God begins the slow, painful discipleship (read "discipline") work of conforming us into worthy servants of our Warrior-King, Jesus Christ and his greater purpose of saving souls.

WARNING #4: Next Level Battle Prep

➢   How have you grieved the Holy Spirit?

➤ How do you feel when God convicts you of sin?

➤ How do you feel about your sin when you pray to God?

➤ What sin are you holding back from God?

➤ Can you feel this unconfessed sin weakening your ability to fight evil?

➤ How frequently do you pray? Daily? Weekly?

➤ How can you pray with more urgency, asking for forgiveness?

FOURTH ORDER

MAKE CHRIST THE ONLY GUIDE
AND GOAL OF YOUR LIFE
Dedicate all your enthusiasm, all your effort, your leisure as well as your business.

(Erasmus)

"Love the Lord your God with all your heart and with all your soul and with all your mind." This is the first and greatest commandment. And the second is like it: "Love your neighbor *as* yourself." *All the Law and the Prophets hang on these two commandments.*
—Matthew 22:37–40

If we desire to make Christ our "only guide," if we truly wish to fully dedicate our enthusiasm, effort, leisure, and business toward that worthy goal, then we must constantly strive to get sin out of our lives. To win the battle against sin in our lives and take the next step in spiritual warfare and Christian growth, we must embrace repentance. The apostle Paul describes this process as the "renewing of your mind" (Romans 12:2).

Repentance Permits Sanctification

Know that God commands all people to repent (Acts 17:30). Repentance is by God's grace, offered as a gift to the believer, paid for by Jesus Christ on the cross. Why does God make repentance a command? Because our accepting God's invitation (through confession of sin and our plea that God take control of our lives) is necessary so that Jesus may send us the Holy Spirit.

Repentance is a prerequisite for sanctification and doing good works, and there is a penalty for refusal. You have a choice whether to obey or disobey the command (accept or reject God's invitation), but you must take responsibility for your answer.

The Bible says, "There is no one righteous, not even one" (Romans 3:10). Christian repentance starts with confession of your complete sinfulness. But repentance is more than confession. It must also be followed by sanctification—turning toward a God-honoring way of life, not only in your beliefs but in your actions as well.

> What good is it, my brothers and sisters, if
> someone claims to have faith but has no deeds?
> Can such faith save them? Suppose a brother or

a sister is without clothes and daily food. If one
of you says to them, "Go in peace; keep warm
and well fed," but does nothing about their
physical needs, what good is it? In the same way,
faith by itself, if it is not accompanied by action,
is dead. (James 2:14–17)

This is a major component in advanced spiritual warfare. Repentance and sanctification together build strong spiritual armor.

The Reverend Thomas Watson (1620–1686), an English Puritan pastor, wrote a helpful book called *The Doctrine of Repentance* (1668) in which he describes the "ingredients" for repentance. Watson describes "repentance" this way: "Repentance is a grace of God's Spirit whereby a sinner is inwardly humbled and visibly reformed." According to Watson, the six ingredients of true repentance are seeing your sin, feeling godly sorrow for your sin, confessing your sin, experiencing shame for your sin, hating of your sin, and turning from your sin.

Ingredient 1 – SEE Your Sin

Watson says you must first see your sin before you can repent of it. While faith is a gift from God and we cannot repent without the Holy Spirit, we are nonetheless responsible for what we do with God's gifts. The Bible tells us, "Do not grieve the Holy Spirit of God" (Ephesians 4:30), and it is therefore our responsibility to cooperate with the Holy Spirit and his work in our lives. When God makes us aware of our sin, when we *see* our sin, then as believers we must *confess* our sin.

Sinning is more than acting on temptation. We can sin even if we just submit to the temptation in our thoughts. As Jesus said, "You have heard that it was said, 'You shall not commit adultery.' But I tell you that anyone who looks at a woman lustfully has already committed adultery with her in his heart" (Matthew 5:27–28). Dwelling on and acting out the evil in our mind are enough to convict a person. It is indeed a blessing that the Holy Spirit makes us aware of sinful thoughts and desires: "Out of the heart of man, come evil thoughts, sexual immorality, theft, murder, adultery, coveting, wickedness, deceit, sensuality, envy, slander, pride, foolishness. All these evil things come from within, and they defile a person" (Mark 7:21–23 ESV).

Watson says, "A man must first recognize and consider what his sin is, and know the plague of his heart before he can be duly humbled for it…the eye is made both for seeing and weeping. Sin must first be seen before it can be wept for."

Ingredient 2 – SORROW for Sin

Next Watson tells us that true repentance must involve sorrow after you are made aware of your sinfulness (Psalm 38:18), as if your soul were crucified. This sorry should not be merely for the consequences of our sin against people but also for sinning against God and the free grace he has given us in Jesus. Watson tells us, "Godly sorrow is sincere. Hypocrites grieve only for the bitter consequence of sin [getting caught]… Godly sorrow, however, is chiefly for the trespass against God, so that even if there were no conscience to smite, no devil to accuse, no hell to punish, yet the soul would still be grieved because of the prejudice done to God." The psalmist expresses this well: "For I acknowledge my transgressions: and my sin is ever before me. Against thee, thee [God] only, have I sinned, and done this evil in thy sight" (51:3–4 KJV).

Ingredient 3 – CONFESSION of Sin

Third, Watson says true repentance must come with a sincere confession. As the psalmist confesses: "I acknowledged my sin to you and did not cover up my iniquity. I said, 'I will confess my transgressions to the LORD.' And you forgave the guilt of my sin" (32:5).

Watson says we must pray our confession with passion: "Those prayers God likes best which come seething hot from the heart." This is different from the Sinner's Prayer or the Salvation Prayer that we have already discussed. This involves believers acknowledging that they have fallen short of God's moral standard, that they have sinned against him.

Our confession can be simple, but it must be self-accusing: "I have sinned" (2 Samuel 24:17 KJV). Watson tells us: "When we come before God...we must accuse ourselves... And the truth is that by this self-accusing we prevent Satan's accusing."

Again, this is different from the Sinner's Prayer, the salvation prayer that acknowledged you are under God's authority and that salvation comes through the blood of Jesus. That was a one-time event, and that salvation can never be taken away from you. Accepting Jesus as your Savior, however, was just the beginning of your journey, pilgrim. The lifelong strife of spiritual battle begins in your heart and continues in your life.

We should confess our sins daily, in prayer, immediately upon recognizing that we have sinned. Additionally, we have sins of bitterness or lust or envy that we may have suppressed. But if we confess our *known* sins, then we are cleansed of "all unrighteousness":

> If we confess our sins, he is faithful and just to forgive us our sins and to cleanse us from all unrighteousness. (1 John 1:9 ESV)

> Who can discern his errors? Declare me innocent from hidden faults. (Psalm 19:12 ESV)

Ingredient 4 – SHAME for Sin

Shame for sin is similar to sorrow but even more intense (Ezekiel 43:10). Shame is total embarrassment before God: "I am ashamed and blush to lift my face to you, my God" (Ezra 9:6 ESV). For example, the repenting prodigal son was so ashamed of his sins that he thought himself "no longer worthy to be called your son" (Luke 15:21). Shame is an overriding sense of guilt.

Watson says, "Many sins which we commit are by the special instigation of the devil, and should not this cause shame?" These sins turn men into beasts: sly like foxes (Luke

13:32), ravenous like wolves (Matthew 7:15), stubborn like donkeys (Job 11:12), and greedy like swine (2 Peter 2:22).

After confessing your sin, it is normal and right to feel shame. Believers feel shame while the wicked do not (Zephaniah 3:5).

Ingredient 5 – HATRED of Sin

Watson goes on to say that the fifth ingredient of true repentance is hatred of sin: "It is more to loathe sin than to leave it. One may leave sin for fear…but…Christ is never loved till sin be loathed." Truly, God hates "every false way" (Psalm 119:104 KJV). And the wicked "flatter themselves too much to detect or hate their sin" (36:2).

Hypocrites only hate that which makes them look bad in front of others. But a penitent person hates what makes his soul sick. Watson says: "He who truly hates one sin, hates all sin. He who hates a serpent, hates all serpents."

Ingredient 6 – TURNING from Sin

Finally, Watson tells us, "This turning from sin is called a 'forsaking of sin'" (Isaiah 55:7). He says, "Dying to sin is the life of repentance…There is a change wrought in the life. Turning from sin is so visible that others may discern it. Therefore, it is called a change from darkness to light" (Ephesians 5:8). This is where the power of the Holy Spirit replaces sinful thoughts and actions with righteous thoughts and actions.

The turning *from* sin must be a turning *to* God. "Then Jesus said to his disciples, 'Whoever wants to be my disciple

must deny themselves and take up their cross and follow me'"
(Matthew 16:24).

The six ingredients of repentance are a guide. Sometimes
you need to add more of one ingredient than another or start
over and repeat the entire recipe. Watson warns, "If any one
ingredient is left out, it loses its virtue."

As we have said, repentance and sanctification are a
continuous part of our salvation. They grow through the power
of the Holy Spirit.

> I am happy, not because you were made sorry,
> but because your sorrow led you to repentance.
> For you became sorrowful as God intended and
> so were not harmed in any way by us. Godly
> sorrow brings repentance that leads to salvation.
> (2 Corinthians 7:9–10)

You may say to yourself, *I have sinned terribly against
God, and I try not to sin, but sometimes I still sin. How, then, can
I possibly be saved?* But that is what repentance is all about. God
offers unconditional forgiveness for the repentant sinner, with
sin's payment fully paid by Jesus Christ on the cross. When
Jesus was asked, "'Who then can be saved?' Jesus replied, 'What
is impossible with man is possible with God'" (Luke 18:26–27).

Sanctification: Set Apart for a Glorious Purpose

> We all, who with unveiled faces contemplate the
> LORD's glory, are being transformed into his image

with ever-increasing glory, which comes from the LORD, who is the Spirit. (2 Corinthians 3:18)

Completing repentance is a time to rejoice! Turning from sin toward service is called *sanctification*. *To sanctify* literally means "to be set apart for special use or purpose." At this stage of the pilgrimage, repentance has prepared you as a believer, and you are ready for the magnificent and glorious purpose of following Jesus. You have become a member of God's forever family: "Because you are sons, God has sent forth his Spirit of his Son into our hearts, crying, 'Abba! Father!' So you are no longer a slave, but a son, and if a son, then an heir through God" (Galatians 4:6–7 ESV).

Repentance and Sanctification: Two Parts of a Whole

We are saved by God's grace when we repent, and we are then called upon to serve by God's grace. It is God who graciously saves and sanctifies. By this the apostle Paul wrote: "Work out your salvation with fear and trembling, for it is God who works in you to will and to act in order to fulfill his good purpose" (Philippians 2:12–13). This is the deeper level of knowledge beyond salvation and confession of sin. As we stated earlier, repentance and sanctification are two sides of the same coin.

The apostle Paul prayed for the believers to be wholly sanctified: "May God himself, the God of peace, sanctify you through and through. May your whole spirit, soul and body be kept blameless at the coming of our LORD Jesus Christ" (1 Thessalonians 5:23). Paul understood that like repentance, the process of sanctification requires daily work. Paul bids us to be "fervent in spirit" (Romans 12:11 ESV). Watson says, "Prayer without fervency is like a sacrifice without a fire."

Continual Repentance Rejuvenates Sanctification

It is through Christ that we are daily transformed (Philippians 3:12) to fight in the battle against our own sinfulness and against evil in the world. Our Commander-in-Chief gives each of us sacred missions to carry out, some of which last throughout our entire lives: "I cry out to God Most High, to God who fulfills his purpose for me" (Psalm 57:2 ESV).

We are never truly done with the process of repentance. It is through daily repentance that a believer grows stronger in faith, recharges sanctification, and builds armor for battle against those demonic forces in the spiritual and worldly realms. This daily endeavor may seem difficult, but have faith! The Bible promises us that ultimately the devil and his followers will be defeated. At the final judgment, the apostle John reveals:

> The devil…was thrown into the lake of fire and sulfur where the beast and the false prophet were, and they will be tormented day and night forever and ever.
>
> …Then Death and Hades were thrown into the lake of fire. This is the second death, the lake of fire. And if anyone's name was not found

written in the book of life, he was thrown into the lake of fire.

...As for the cowardly, the faithless, the detestable, as for murderers, the sexually immoral, sorcerers, idolaters, and all liars, their portion will be in the lake that burns with fire and sulfur, which is the second death. (Revelation 20:10, 14–15; 21:8 ESV)

And those persons who are saved by grace and serve by faith will be with God:

I heard a voice from heaven saying, "Write this: Blessed are the dead who die in the LORD from now on." "Blessed indeed," says the Spirit, "that they may rest from their labors, for their deeds follow them!" (14:13 ESV)

Pray Wisely and Urgently

Erasmus said, "Prayer and knowledge [of God's Word] be the chief armor of a Christian man." At every level of repentance and sanctification, prayer and the wisdom of God's Word through Bible study are essential. The Bible tells us, "What am I to do? I will pray with my spirit, but I will pray with my mind also" (1 Corinthians 14:15 ESV).

Martin Luther advised people to "pray urgently!" There should be a sense of urgency in our prayers. A burning need to pray. Luther went on to say, "It is of great importance that the heart be made ready and eager for prayer."

Sometimes we are weak and do not know how to pray, so if we begin praying, the Holy Spirit can step in and articulate prayers for us. "The Spirit helps us in our weakness. We do not know what we ought to pray for, but the Spirit himself intercedes for us through wordless groans" (Romans 8:26). Whether we have the words or not, we always have the need. Luther says it well:

> Don't be foolish here; do you want to ask for faith, hope, love, humility, obedience, chastity, gentleness, peace, and righteousness? Do you want to be free of all your unbelief, doubt, pride, disobedience, unchastity, anger, covetousness, and unrighteousness? The more you find yourself in need, the more and more diligently you ought to pray or cry.

Pray Simply

Luther compares praying well to barbering well:

> So, a good and attentive barber keeps his thoughts, attention, and eyes on the razor and hair and does not forget how far he has gotten with his shaving or cutting. If he wants to engage in too much conversation or let his mind wander or look somewhere else he is likely to

cut his customer's mouth, nose, or even his throat.

Thus if anything is to be done well, it requires the full attention of all one's senses and members, as the proverb says…"He who thinks of many things, thinks of nothing and does nothing right." How much more does prayer call for concentration and singleness of heart if it is to be a good prayer!

Too much conversation and the mind wanders or looks somewhere else. He who prays of many things, prays of nothing. It's best to follow Jesus's counsel: "When you pray, do not keep on babbling like pagans, for they think they will be heard because of their many words" (Matthew 6:7). It's better to pray simply with singleness of heart.

Luther suggests a good place for our praying to begin: "A confession of sins is a good prayer to start; confess your own sin and then pray for everyone with earnestness and faith. Pray also for them that persecute you and insult you." To this he adds: "Study the Bible. Make daily use of those prayers which David prays: 'Lord, lead me in Thy path, and let me not walk in my own ways,' and many like prayers, which are all summed up in the prayer, 'Thy kingdom come.'"

Pray Immediately

Luther calls on every believer to "Guard yourself carefully against those false, deluding ideas which tell you, 'Wait a little while. I will pray in an hour; first I must attend to this or that.' Such thoughts get you away from prayer into other affairs which so hold your attention and involve you that nothing comes of prayer for that day."

Prayer is an essential activity for every Christian engaged in spiritual warfare. As Luther says: "Above all this, the strongest defense is prayer and the Word of God; namely, that when evil desire starts to stir, a man should flee to prayer, call upon God's mercy and help, read and meditate on the Gospel, and in it consider Christ's sufferings."

Pray "Amen"

Finally, mark this, that you must always speak the "Amen" firmly. Never doubt that God in his mercy has surely heard you. Never think that you are kneeling or standing alone, rather think that all devout Christians are standing there beside you. That is what Amen means.

Luther then concludes: "Confidently expect from God one of two things: either that your prayer will be granted, or that, if it will not be granted, the granting of it would not be good for you." Indeed, 1 John 5:14 tells us, "This is the confidence we have in approaching God: that if we ask anything according to his will, he hears us."

You Will Face Attacks

After you have been saved, anticipate temptations by the devil. He will attack you more fervently because you have now become a threat. Satan will attempt to undo your repentance by making you feel unworthy, unredeemed, and unjustified. Satan will whisper wicked thoughts of doubt and depression into your mind, and you must cast them aside!

In July 1530, Martin Luther shared this advice in a letter to a friend:

> Avoid entering upon a disputation with the devil and do not allow yourself to dwell on those deadly thoughts, for to do so is nothing short of yielding to the devil and letting him have his way. Instead, speak thus, "For I know One who suffered and made a satisfaction in my behalf. His name is Jesus Christ, the Son of God."

Beware a False Repentance

Beware lest repentance be a mere formula, resulting in nothing more than an empty statement made without heart. It is not good enough to just follow along in prayer without truly seeking God and embracing his truth.

We speak of God's grace for forgiveness of sins and receiving God-given faith, but the test of true repentance is being Christ-centered, and that entails embracing his command to love:

If I speak in the tongues of men or of angels, but
do not have love, I am only a resounding gong or
a clanging cymbal. If I have the gift of prophecy
and can fathom all mysteries and all knowledge,
and if I have a faith that can move mountains,
but do not have love, I am nothing. If I give all
I possess to the poor and give over my body to
hardship that I may boast, but do not have love, I
gain nothing. (1 Corinthians 13:1–3)

Your repentance is false if you do not love. What is
Christian love?

Love is patient, love is kind. It does not envy,
it does not boast, it is not proud. It does not
dishonor others, it is not self-seeking, it is not
easily angered, it keeps no record of wrongs.
Love does not delight in evil but rejoices with
the truth. It always protects, always trusts, always hopes, always perseveres. (vv. 4–7)

The Bible describes what happens in a false repentance:

When an impure spirit comes out of a person, it
goes through arid places seeking rest and does
not find it. Then it says, "I will return to the
house I left." When it arrives, it finds the house
unoccupied, swept clean and put in order. Then
it goes and takes with it seven other spirits more

wicked than itself, and they go in and live there. And the final condition of that person is worse than the first. (Matthew 12:43–45)

Love God, Love People

At the core of repentance is the call to love. Consider again Matthew 22:37–40 (this time with the power and majesty of the King James Version):

> Jesus said unto him, Thou shalt love the Lord thy God with all thy heart, and with all thy soul, and with all thy mind. This is the first and great commandment. And the second is like unto it, Thou shalt love thy neighbour as thyself. On these two commandments hang all the law and the prophets.

This commandment, "the first and greatest commandment," was addressed in detail in *On Spiritual Combat*. It can be summarized and effectively communicated into four words: "Love God, love people." This is our core mission here on earth. It is why we are here. Everything else flows from it. If we truly love people, then we will understand that the greatest gift we can share with others is eternal salvation through Jesus Christ. Which leads us to the Great Commission that Jesus delegated to us: "Go ye therefore, and teach all nations, baptizing them in the name of the Father, and of the Son, and of the Holy Ghost" (28:19 KJV).

WARNORD Recap

Advanced spiritual warfare requires understanding how repentance and sanctification interact so that we can be saved by the grace of God and serve by the faith that is imbued by the Holy Spirit.

God's goal for our lives is much greater than simply replacing bad thoughts. God's desire for our lives—the blessing that he wants us to embrace so we can have rich and abundant lives—is to make us more like Christ by loving God and by loving others.

God desires for us to be reconciled to him through Christ and then for us to do his good works as part of sanctification. Scripture reveals clearly:

A new command I give you: Love one another. As I have loved you, so you must love one another. (John 13:34)

For we are his workmanship, created in Christ Jesus for good works, which God prepared beforehand, that we should walk in them. (Ephesians 2:10 ESV)

Thus, Luther's warning reveals: the wicked—who are twisted and perverted and led by the devil—are in active battle against God. We can see that warning clearly stated in Martin Luther's own words in the magnificent hymn quoted at the beginning of this WARNORD:

For still our ancient foe
does seek to work us woe;
   his craft and power are great,
   and armed with cruel hate,
on earth is not his equal.

Therefore our order, the answer to this threat, is clearly stated in this same hymn. We defeat the enemy, and we are triumphant in this battle, by making Christ our guide and our goal:

Did we in our own strength confide,
   our striving would be losing,
were not the right Man on our side,
   the Man of God's own choosing.
You ask who that may be?
Christ Jesus, it is he.

Washington's Prayer of Confession

American President George Washington kept his religious beliefs private, but this prayer demonstrates his Puritan theology. He recognized "weak prayer" as one of his own sins. This passage, entitled "Sunday Evening Prayer," was found in his library and written in his own hand:

Most Glorious God, in Jesus Christ my merciful and loving father, I acknowledge and confess my guilt, in the weak and imperfect performance of the duties of this day.

I have called on thee for pardon and forgiveness of sins, but so coldly and carelessly that my prayers are become my sin and stand in need of pardon.

I have heard thy holy word, but with such deadness of spirit that I have been an unprofitable and forgetful hearer...

These weak petitions I humbly implore thee to hear, accept and answer for the sake of thy Dear Son Jesus Christ our Lord, Amen.

ORDER #4: Next Level Battle Prep

➤ Explain the six ingredients of true repentance.

- ○ Which ingredient resonates with you the most?
- ○ Which ingredient do you find the most challenging?

➤ Provide an example of a specific instance when prayer has helped you through a challenging time.

FIFTH WARNING

THE WICKED ARE BLINDED BY AMBITION

Whatever man loves, that is his god. For he carries it in his heart; he goes about with it night and day; he sleeps and wakes with it, be it what it may—wealth or self, pleasure or renown.

(Luther)

WARNORD #5

FIFTH ORDER

TURN AWAY FROM WORLDLY THINGS

If you are greatly concerned with success, you will be weak of spirit.

(Erasmus)

FIFTH WARNING

THE WICKED ARE BLINDED BY AMBITION

Whatever man loves, that is his god. For he carries it in his heart; he goes about with it night and day; he sleeps and wakes with it, be it what it may—wealth or self, pleasure or renown.

(Luther)

For where jealousy and selfish ambition exist,
there will be disorder and every vile practice.
—James 3:16 ESV

[Spoken Introduction]
While the storm clouds gather far across the sea,
Let us swear allegiance to a land that's free,

Let us all be grateful for a land so fair,
    As we raise our voices in a solemn prayer.

[Hymn]
God bless America, land that I love.
    Stand beside her,
    and guide her,
        Through the night,
        with the Light,
from above.

From the mountains, to the prairies,
    To the oceans, white with foam,
    God bless America, my home sweet home.

—"God Bless America," by Irving Berlin (1888–1989),
    written in 1918 while serving in the US Army

The Bible repeatedly warns us not to become obsessed with our earthly ambitions, for they can quite easily replace God in our thinking (Exodus 20:4–6; Matthew 19:17). Everything that is worldly is vanity: "For all that is in the world—the desires of the flesh and the desires of the eyes and pride of life—is not from the Father but is from the world" (1 John 2:16 ESV). These worldly loves become false gods, as Martin Luther observed: "Whatever man loves, that is his god. For he carries it in his heart; he goes about with it night and day; he sleeps and wakes with it, be it what it may—wealth or self, pleasure or renown."

Whoever Exalts Himself Will Be Humbled

Becoming obsessed with "wealth or self, pleasure or renown" is the same as creating a false idol. When the devil tried to tempt Jesus with *status*, Christ said, "Do not put the Lord your God to the test" (Luke 4:12). Jesus is God in human "flesh," "For God was pleased to have all his fullness dwell in him" (Colossians 1:19). But the devil assumed he could tempt Jesus because Jesus had taken on human form. Satan knew that even thinking about doing a sin is a corruption of the spirit (Mark 7:20–23). But James 1:13 tells us, "God cannot be tempted by evil, nor does he tempt anyone."

Jesus was "tested" in the wilderness (Matthew 4:1). Satan tried to tempt Jesus but totally failed. Jesus passed the test and remained sinless, making himself the only sacrifice worthy to take away the sins of mankind on the cross.

But like all sinners, Satan cannot see past his own temptations. The devil assumes that everyone is a sinner at heart just like himself. So Satan proceeded to test Jesus by trying to provoke pride. Jesus described the wickedness of *status* and *vanity*, two displays of the sin of pride that the Jewish religious leaders of his day shared:

> Everything they do is for show. On their arms they wear extra wide prayer boxes with Scripture verses inside, and they wear robes with extra long tassels. And they love to sit at the head table at banquets and in the seats of honor in

the synagogues. They love to receive respectful greetings as they walk in the marketplaces, and to be called "Rabbi." (23:5–7 NLT)

We all want to be successful in our careers and achieve recognition, honor, and status. We all want to feel joy and pleasure. We all want to store up wealth. These desires are natural, and psychologists refer to them as "inner drives." But, as we explained in *On Spiritual Combat*, we are to give the honor and glory to God, to publicly give God the glory. We should not let these natural wants become obsessions because they can become snares to us if left uncontrolled. In Matthew's Gospel, Jesus goes on to tell us, "Those who exalt themselves will be humbled, and those who humble themselves will be exalted" (v. 12 NLT). God corrects those who sin, so those who are arrogant and boastful will be shamed (Proverbs 11:2), and the proud will find only destruction (16:18).

Satan's False Doctrine of Success

Earlier we quoted pastor Dietrich Bonhoeffer, a German minister who studied theology in New York during the early 1930s. He also worked as a lay leader at an African American church in Harlem. Bonhoeffer was greatly impressed by the Puritan influence on the United States Constitution, with its checks and balances on human power.

Upon returning to Germany, Bonhoeffer was confronted with the totalitarian and racist ideology of the Nazi movement. In his book *Ethics*, he issued a dire warning about the ethics of success: "In a world where success is the measure and justification of all things...the world will allow itself to be subdued by success. The proposition that success is identical with good is followed by another...the proposition that only good is successful." The success that Bonhoeffer warns us of is "worldly success, that is, Satan's success—success without God, without Christ, without forgiveness of sins. To people who follow this path, God is dead and there is no accountability (Psalm 10:4–5)."

The Nazis used their early political and military successes to justify their evil ideology. They rationalized that their early success justified their actions, no matter how ruthless. Winston Churchill said that the Nazi logic was, "The victors write the history books," and therefore as long as we win, we will be the "good guys." Right? Wrong. The Bible warns against such perverse logic:

> For what is a man profited, if he shall gain the whole world, and lose his own soul? or what shall a man give in exchange for his soul? For the Son of man shall come in the glory of his Father with his angels; and then he shall reward every man according to his works. (Matthew 16:26–27 KJV)

Christians understand that the earthly success of individuals or nations is not an indicator of God's approval. This "winners will write the history books" mentality is the devil's own false doctrine.

One of the proofs of the divine influence in the Bible is that it does not glorify or exalt any person except Jesus Christ. Would all those kings and judges in the Old Testament write about and permit to have written all their failures and sustained those humiliations across the generations? Over and over again? Yes, the Bible recognizes the good kings. But even the record of one of the greatest, King David, reveals an array of great personal failures and disasters. But David (unlike the Nazis) repented of his sins and wrote psalms as a confession for all of us to admire and share. In human hands only, the Bible would have been focused on glorifying those kings and leaders. The authors would have been kissing up to their kings, and the kings would have been mercilessly destroying any authors and any text that told of their failures.

If you study the Bible, you will see that it exalts and glorifies no human being—except for a coming Messiah as foretold many times in the Old Testament. And this Messiah who was to come was Jesus of Nazareth, the Christ, and he fulfilled every one of those prophecies as the New Testament records. He will do the same during his second coming, fulfilling those prophecies that have to do with his future reign and judgment and the completion of all things (including of a new heavens and new earth) in him.

The Nazis, in their false doctrine that success justified their evils, went so far as to proclaim, "My conscience is Adolph Hitler," literally replacing Father, Son, and Holy Spirit with the mind of an evil and quite possibly demon-possessed man. Father Gabriele Amorth, who was the Vatican's chief exorcist, said in 2006:

> The devil exists, and he can not only possess a
> single person but also groups and entire popu-
> lations…I am convinced that the Nazis were all
> possessed…You can tell by their behavior and
> their actions, from the horrors they committed
> and the atrocities that were committed on their
> orders. That is why we need to defend society
> from demons.

Little wonder that the Nazis murdered so many inno-cent people; estimates of those murdered show six million Jews, seven million Soviet civilians, three million Soviet pris-oners, 1.8 million Polish civilians, up to two million civilians from various other countries, and untold number of political and religious opponents. There were an additional fifteen mil-lion Allied military casualties fighting the Nazis.

In 2006, the Vatican released secret documents show-ing that during World War II, Pope Pius XII attempted a long-distance exorcism of Hitler, which unfortunately failed. It was worth a try, but Father Amorth said that one of the key requirements for an exorcism to work is that the possessed person be present, consenting, and willing, and Hitler most definitely was not willing. But prayer is still a powerful tool in combating demons.

You might find it surprising that a possessed person must be "willing" to expel the demon. You might think, why would you not want the demon expelled? But think about it: people enjoy their demons (pride, greed, lust) like an addict enjoys a drug. As explained earlier, we are not God's puppets. To be saved, we need to implore and beseech God. We cannot expel the evil that is latched onto our soul unless we allow the Holy Spirit to enter us and replace the demon. James 4:7 says, (first) "Submit yourselves therefore to God," (then) "Resist the devil, and he will flee from you" (ESV). Submission to God precedes expelling evil.

The desire for worldly success stands in direct contrast to the standards established for followers of Jesus Christ. Those who worship success and personal achievement at all costs have been the cause of much evil across the centuries. We must worship God instead and ask for strength to resist the desire for worldly success.

Scripturally, there are two kinds of people. Worldly people and godly people:

- The world tells us, "Look out for number one."
- God tells us to "Store up your treasures in heaven" (Matthew 6:20 CEV).

Which kind of person would you want to have around you?

Which kind of person is most likely to contribute in a positive manner to the godly success of your community, your nation, and your civilization?

Which kind of person do you want to be?

WARNING #5: Next Level Battle Prep

➤ When have you let ambition blind you—choosing Satan's temptation over God's calling?

➤ How has Satan rewarded you under false pretense to corrupt your soul?

➤ When have you remained silent in the face of evil to protect your status?

➤ What is the most important requirement to "exorcise" an evil spirit that is corrupting your soul and influencing your behavior?

FIFTH ORDER

TURN AWAY FROM WORLDLY THINGS
If you are greatly concerned with success,
you will be weak of spirit.
(Erasmus)

Do not lay up for yourselves treasures on earth…but lay up
for yourselves treasures in heaven, where neither moth nor
rust destroys and where thieves do not break in and steal. For
where your treasure is, there your heart will be also…No one
can serve two masters…You cannot serve God and mammon.
—Matthew 6:19–21, 24 NKJV

In World War II Nazi Germany, we can clearly recognize one
end of the spectrum of evil. Horrific evil, on a vast scale, fed
by unchecked, ungodly, "wicked ambition" as warned of by
Luther. Against the vast evil of the Nazis, we set the humble

example of one man. A solitary Christian demonstrating the ultimate defiance of evil and the definitive example of Erasmus' call to "turn away from worldly things."

Here, then, is a role model and a set of Christian principles and ethics in the face of evil that has potential to do more good across the centuries than all the harm the Nazis could have ever imagined.

One Man, Standing Up to Evil

During the rise and reign of Nazi Germany, Lutheran pastor Dietrich Bonhoeffer developed an ethical system for Christian militancy to oppose Hitler. As a Lutheran, Bonhoeffer believed in salvation by grace. But he also believed that failing to oppose evil was "cheap grace" or cowardly, so he became an advocate for Christian action.

Bonhoeffer called it "cheap grace" when someone repented (accepted God's forgiveness) without completing sanctification (obedience to God). Bonhoeffer learned of the "saved by God's grace, serving by God's faith" attitude in the United States when he came to study at Union Theological Seminary in New York City during 1930–31. While in the United States, Bonhoeffer became a lay leader at the African American Abyssinian Baptist Church in Harlem. He observed, "Here one can truly speak and hear about sin and grace and the love of God." Bonhoeffer also admired the US Constitution:

> The American democracy is not founded upon emancipated man but, quite on the contrary,

upon the kingdom of God and the limitations of all earthly powers by the sovereignty of God... American historians can say that the federal constitution was written by men who were conscious of original sin and of the wickedness of the human heart.

Bonhoeffer's life and writings serve as just one example of what it means to spiritually engage the forces of evil. He said: "The theological question does not arise about the origin of evil but about the real overcoming of evil on the Cross." Christians who are biblically based can see through evil's machinations:

The great masquerade of evil has played havoc with all our ethical concepts. For evil to appear disguised as light, charity, historical necessity or social justice is quite bewildering to anyone brought up on our traditional ethical concepts, while for the Christian who bases his life on the Bible, it merely confirms the fundamental wickedness of evil.

Before WWII even started, Dietrich Bonhoeffer took a moral stand against Nazi doctrine. He felt that it was his Christian duty to warn people. In the middle of one of Bonhoeffer's radio broadcasts, the Nazis cut the power, inter-rupting his sermon. His reply: "Silence in the face of evil is itself evil." Think about that. It is *evil* to remain silent when you witness evil. This doctrine, if fully embraced by Christians everywhere, will do great good and could thwart horrific evil across the times yet to come.

Proverbs 25:26 tells us, "Like a muddied spring or a polluted fountain is a righteous man who gives way before the wicked" (ESV). This is a rebuke to those who see injustice and do nothing about it. A righteous peacekeeper is obliged to enforce the law. If he or she does nothing against the wicked and yields to their duplicity and their misdeeds, it is the same as condoning their wickedness.

Furthermore, recognize that this applies to the solemn responsibility of a believer in Christ who lives within a democracy or a republic such as America. Remember, in America, by casting our votes and selecting our leaders, we are ultimately the rulers. And if we do not use every bit of influence and authority that we have to move our nation toward righteousness, then we are like the wicked kings and evil nations of old. They did not escape God's judgment: "Therefore this is what the LORD Almighty says: 'I will punish them. Their young men will die by the sword, their sons and daughters by famine'" (Jeremiah 11:22).

Sadly, Bonhoeffer's warnings about Nazi success being no justification for their acts fell on deaf ears. Bonhoeffer also tried to warn the German people that the "Fuehrer" (Hitler) was *not* the "Father." At great risk to himself, Bonhoeffer wrote several books and sermons on Christ-centered ethics. He is most noted for his books *The Cost of Discipleship* and *Ethics*.

Many Germans of weak spiritual beliefs were obsessed and even possessed by Hitler's demonic speeches and diatribes.

Others were seduced by ambition and ignored God's great commandment: "Do to others what you would have them do to you" (Matthew 7:12). The Bible gives a dire warning to those who disobey what God commands us: "For wide is the gate and broad is the road that leads to destruction" (v. 13).

This warning was prophetic, describing the eventual destruction of Nazi Germany. Upon their final defeat in 1945, Germany was in ruins, with approximately 5.3 million military casualties and 1 million civilian casualties. But the overall cost of this spiritual failure was much greater. The millions of citizens murdered by the Nazis and the millions of soldiers killed by them in battle, coupled with the vast numbers who were mentally and physically maimed, are almost too great to comprehend. Everyone lost. Only Satan gained.

And yet, God can take the most tragic of all human events and sunder the darkest of evil with a mighty sunrise of good. The lessons that Dietrich Bonhoeffer gives us in Christian ethics, made clear at such a tragic price, are worthy of examination.

Bonhoeffer's Christian Ethics

Pastor Bonhoeffer designed three Christ-centered principles based on what he admired in Puritan America and the United States Constitution. Bonhoeffer wanted the German people to understand how true public servants should conduct themselves as protectors of God's people. Unfortunately, in Germany, the Nazis propaganda received more attention.

Bonhoeffer's three Christian ethical principles for public servants are these:

1. **Concept of the Mandate** – Peace officers and the military are sworn servants and should be constrained by "a higher law"—this is the "concept of the mandate." Pastor Bonhoeffer said, "Speak first of rights and only later of duties. One can have a natural right of one's own only if one respects the natural rights of others." The obedience of Germans to Adolf Hitler was "blind duty," devoid of Christ-centered obedience. Bonhoeffer warned that blind obedience to the rule of men would always result in serving the devil.

2. **The View from Below** – Understanding real human rights takes empathy; it means looking at life from the perspective of the victim, the helpless, sometimes even the criminal—this is the "view from below." Bonhoeffer said historians must also record history as it appears to those who are "below." Not, that is, from the viewpoint of the powerful and the wealthy, but "from the perspective of the outcasts, the suspects, the maltreated, the powerless, the oppressed, and the reviled—in short from the perspective of those who suffer." Bonhoeffer added, "Personal suffering is a more effective key" for understanding the world than "personal good fortune."

3. **Costly Grace** – The willingness to sacrifice your own safety or comfort to do what's right and combat evil is "Costly Grace." Bonhoeffer describes "Cheap Grace" as accepting Christ without picking up the cross. It's like accepting God's forgiveness without repenting. It's preserving your own safety and comfort at the expense of others. "Costly Grace" is discipleship. It asks that we be willing to take risks to do what is right. "Costly grace is the gospel which must be sought again and again…it is grace because it calls us to follow Jesus Christ."

Pastor Bonhoeffer lived up to these principles by working in the German resistance. He knew that faith without action was empty, but by his works, his faith was made perfect. "Do you see that faith was working together with his works, and by works faith was made perfect?" (James 2:22 NKJV).

Dietrich Bonhoeffer was eventually arrested for smuggling Jews out of Germany, and he was executed in Flossenbürg concentration camp on April 9, 1945. The SS doctor who witnessed Bonhoeffer's execution later confessed, "I have hardly ever seen a man die so entirely submissive to the will of God." Pastor Bonhoeffer was executed just two weeks before the US 90th and 97th Infantry Divisions liberated the camp and only a month before the surrender of Nazi Germany. Hitler tried to destroy as much innocence and righteousness as possible before he finally went down to defeat. Possessed by the devil, Hitler never repented or tried to make amends for his many evils. Instead, he committed suicide rather than face the justice coming to him from the Allies.

Before his death, Bonhoeffer had smuggled out one last letter to a friend in England. In it he said, "This is the end—for me the beginning of life." The Bible says, "Whoever loses his life for my sake will find it" (Matthew 16:25 ESV).

God is faithful and will never give you more than you can endure (1 Corinthians 10:13), so Pastor Bonhoeffer's God-given faith was most assuredly very strong. First Corinthians also tells us: "On the judgment day, fire will reveal what kind of work each builder has done. The fire will show if a person's work has any value. If the work survives, that builder will receive a reward" (3:13–14 NLT).

Pastor Bonhoeffer's final letters and papers survive today because some of his Christian guards smuggled them out of the concentration camp. They have been published as *Letters and Papers from Prison.*

Perhaps it is appropriate to take just a minute to thank God that the United States of America is a free country, where we swear to uphold justice and not obey the orders of a dictator. Our military and our police swear an oath to the Constitution, not to a king or a dictator. We are free to seek God, pray to God, know God, serve God, and learn about great disciples like Pastor Dietrich Bonhoeffer.

Alpha reader Leah Anaya observed that police and military must have discernment to assure that they are honoring the Constitution, and discernment comes from God. He gave us our Constitution, which closely mirrors New

Testament principles, and (as proclaimed in the Declaration of Independence) the rights of the people come from God.

The deep wisdom in Bonhoeffer's Christian ethics, combined with the powerful example of him literally living and dying by Christ's guidance, make Bonhoeffer a great and mighty martyr for the faith. And it bears repeating: it is truly possible that this example, embraced and applied across the centuries, can do more good than all the harm the Nazis inflicted in that horrific war.

Author and alpha reader Jeff Wolf says that "Dietrich Bonhoeffer continues the underlying theme of the responsibility of the righteous to stand up and act in the face of evil. We must ask God to help us discern what political plots are motivated by evil and stand up against them. Bonhoeffer did this by teaching and acting out God's word—even to death."

Always have faith in God. Never doubt his wisdom, his strength, and his love. Like the crucifixion of Jesus, that which the devil means for evil—what may even appear to us to be the triumph of evil—God *will* turn to good (Genesis 50:20). God will ultimately triumph over evil. Jesus' last words on the cross, "It is finished" (John 19:30), sealed Satan's doom and preserved the glorious life to come for all humans who follow Jesus.

Rules of Rescue: A Moral Progression

Bonhoeffer is an example of how a single Christian's goodness can transcend across centuries in the battle against unchecked ambition and evil. If the idea of such progress over time seems naïve to you, if you think the world doesn't work that way, then consider the steady progress of the "rules of rescue" across the centuries, as we will discuss below.

Christ sacrificed himself for our salvation, and he said, "Anyone who has seen me has seen the Father" (John 14:9), so we know that God is full of empathy and is unselfish in his service (Matthew 16:24). Jesus explained the concept of service: "Whoever wants to become great among you must be your servant, and whoever wants to be first must be slave of all. For even the Son of Man did not come to be served, but to serve, and to give his life as a ransom for many" (Mark 10:43–45).

It has taken many centuries for us to fully understand and embrace the example of Christ (John 10:30). Mankind has gradually moved from a time when selfish tyranny and predatory despotism were the only forms of authority, to a time in which the good of the people and the will of the governed are central to the rule of nations. Certainly, you don't have to look far for examples that tell us we have a *very* long way to go yet in fully embracing Christ's model. But a gradual movement, a steady progress in the right direction, can be seen in the rules of rescue during a disaster. When we look back only a few hundred years ago, the accepted rule of survival was "every man for himself," and unfortunately, many people still operate on this concept. Eventually, this was improved to "women and children first," which sometimes needed to be enforced at the barrel of a gun. Today, we teach that "the strong should protect the weak," and only the righteous can be counted on to uphold this principle when things get really bad.

In what follows, we will show a steady historical progression of individuals, in their finest hour, in the "last extremity," risking and giving their lives for others.

"Every Man for Himself"

1611 – "It's every man for himself, and Devil take the hindmost." This is a phrase, probably of a British military origin, that can be traced back to at least 1611, the same year the King James Bible was first published. When the situation has become hopeless, when it is the last extremity, the rule becomes survival of the fittest and "to hell with the unfortunate."

That is certainly the model that has been ascendant throughout most of human history. The authors of the book *No Mercy: True Stories of Disaster, Survival and Brutality* refer to this survival-of-the-fittest anarchy as the "Lord of the Flies Principle," after the famous novel by William Golding in which a group of schoolboys are marooned on an uninhabited island and quickly regress to a state of savagery and bloodlust.

"Women and Children First"

1852 – British Lt. Col. Alexander Seton, during the sinking of the HMS *Birkenhead*, established a new standard for rescue when a ship is going down. He commanded his soldiers that the priority was to be "women and children first." Of the 631 aboard, 438 died, almost all of them soldiers and sailors. One hundred and ninety-three were saved. Not a single woman or child was lost.

In his book *History of the Scottish Highlands*, Sir John Scott Keltie recorded this eyewitness account of Col. Seton and his men: "Side by side they stood at the helm, providing for the safety of all that could be saved. They never tried to save themselves." They died to a man so that others may live.

Keltie also immortalized Col. Seton as a person with "a clear head, perfect self-possession, a noble and chivalrous spirit, and a power of command over others which few men have the fortune to possess." The self-sacrifice of himself and his men, and their other personal qualities, are all manifestations of a Christlike character. They set a standard that lives on today.

"Recognize a Fellow Man"

1891 – The Royal Life Saving Society established a fully Christian-based ethos that the strong should protect the weak whenever there is danger. As said in the 1957 film *Abandon Ship!*, "The last extremity is when civilized man lives his finest hour."

This model takes the process a step further, from a simple rule, "women and children first," to an even higher principle of moral performance to be applied in a far wider set of circumstances. What you see here is also referred to as the progression of "Beneficence Ethics" or the ethics of doing good deeds. Ethicists use a "Beneficence Continuum," and you may find that it complements the police use-of-force continuum and the standards for other sheepdog professions.

There are four precepts that make up beneficence:

- Seek firstly to do no harm (if possible).

- Seek secondly to prevent evil or harm.
- Seek thirdly to remove evil or harm.
- Seek always to practice good.

As police Lt. David Kemp points out, "We are calling our Christian Spiritual Warriors to step into this ethical embodiment against the evils of today by representing Christ in this fallen world and engaging the Devil with works of Justice and Righteousness!"

For public servants, "Beneficence is the professional's moral imperative," says Dr. Frank Kinsinger, a pioneer in applied ethics for health care providers. Sadly, the devil has found a way to undermine beneficence and the ethos of sacrifice. The desire for worldly success stands in direct contrast to beneficence, and those who worship success will convince themselves that success justifies all manner of evil.

WARNORD Recap

In a nation where the will of the people and the consent of the governed are the foundation of authority, perhaps we can see the steady progress of turning toward Christ and away from unchecked ambition. Remember Alexis de Tocqueville's *Democracy in America* and his conclusion that "Despotism may govern without faith, but Liberty cannot." De Tocqueville went on to say, "In America, religion is the road to knowledge, and the observance of the divine laws leads man to civil freedom." This brings us back to the recognition of the fact that in our nation, we are the rulers, and we are called to be "the salt of the earth…the light of the world" (Matthew 5:13–14).

Our human politics may be splattered with imperfections and sinfulness, but Jesus Christ sent us the Holy Spirit to guide us and help us build better lives, families, and governments. Our forefathers proved that Christians can build a better government with God as our architect. And we must not destroy what they have accomplished thus far.

Like Bonhoeffer, we have a solemn obligation as believers and citizens in a democracy to move our nation toward paths of righteousness and godliness.

We began this WARNORD with "God Bless America," a song that is also a prayer. Irving Berlin, a Jewish immigrant, wrote these words while serving as a soldier in World War I, and then he used it to inspire America in the darkest hours of World War II. Study these words.

Is it wrong to make such a prayer? No. We would say it is not just good but also *essential* to make such a request to our loving Father. God's Word tells us: "All the nations are as nothing before him, they are accounted by him as less than nothing and emptiness" (Isaiah 40:17 ESV). Yet God also says: "Blessed is the nation whose God is the LORD" (Psalm 33:12 KJV). So maybe it is appropriate to join together in this solemn prayer:

God bless America, land that I love.
  Stand beside her, and guide her,
    Through the night, with the Light,
from above.

Bonhoeffer's Prayer

This prayer was written by Pastor Bonhoeffer while in a Nazi prison.

In me there is darkness,
But with You there is light;
I am lonely, but You do not leave me;
I am feeble in heart, but with You there is help;
I am restless, but with You there is peace.

In me there is bitterness,
But with You there is patience;
I do not understand Your ways,
But You know the way for me.

Lord Jesus Christ,
You were poor,
And in distress, a captive and forsaken as I am.

You know all man's troubles;
You abide with me
When all men fail me;

It is Your will that I should know You,
And turn to You.

Lord, I hear Your call and follow;
Help me. Amen.

ORDER #5: *Next Level Battle Prep*

- ➤ What is Bonhoeffer's "Concept of the Mandate"? Give an example.

- ➤ What is Bonhoeffer's "View from Below"? Give an example.

- ➤ What is Bonhoeffer's "Costly Grace"? Give an example.

- ➤ Consider Bonhoeffer's three Christian ethical principles. How have you prevented yourself from being pulled into something wrong?

- ➤ How have the rules of rescue improved with better understanding of Christianity? Do you still see people abiding by the "old" rules of rescue?

- ➤ Have you ever forfeited personal ambition or self interest in order to save, protect, or otherwise do the right thing? If so, provide an example.

SIXTH WARNING

THE WICKED SPREAD FALSE BELIEFS

The wicked are deluded by ideas hatched in
their own brains. They blasphemy the truth
with all kinds of falsehoods, calling evil good,
and good evil; they put darkness for light,
and light for darkness!

(Luther)

WARNORD #6

SIXTH ORDER

TRAIN YOUR MIND TO DISTINGUISH
THE TRUE NATURE OF GOOD AND EVIL

Let your rule of government be determined
by obedience to God, and the common good,
by the example of Jesus Christ our Savior.

(Erasmus)

SIXTH WARNING

THE WICKED SPREAD FALSE BELIEFS

The wicked are deluded by ideas hatched in their own brains. They blaspheme the truth with all kinds of falsehoods, calling evil good, and good evil; they put darkness for light, and light for darkness!

(Luther)

Woe to those who call evil good and good evil,
who put darkness for light and light for darkness,
who put bitter for sweet and sweet for bitter.
—Isaiah 5:20

Standing, like a lighthouse, on the shores of time,
Looking o'er the waves of darkness, sin and crime,

Open up your windows, there's a work sublime:
    Let the gospel light shine out.

There are human shipwrecks lying all around;
O what moral darkness ev'rywhere is found!
Warn some other vessels off from dang'rous ground:
    Let the gospel light shine out…

Try to live for Jesus till this life is o'er,
For along this pathway you will pass no more;
Till he bids you welcome on the other shore,
    Let the gospel light shine out.

—"Standing Like a Lighthouse," by Johnson Oatman
(1856–1922)

Christ is often described as a lighthouse in a storm. Jesus said, "I am the Light of the world. If you follow Me, you won't have to walk in darkness, because you will have the Light that leads to life" (John 8:12 NLT). And the Bible tells us to "Trust in the LORD with all your heart and lean not on your own understanding; in all your ways submit to him, and he will make your paths straight" (Proverbs 3:5–6).

During the storms in our lives, our faith determines just how closely we follow the Light that guides. Dr. John Leach, a military survival expert from the University of Portsmouth, conducted a study of decision-making skills during life-and-death disasters. He found that about 75 percent of the people in a disaster are unable to think and either try to run or simply freeze up, about 10 percent of the people freak out and become seriously dangerous to others, and only 15 percent of people in life and death disasters remain rational enough to make good decisions. This is reminiscent of the parable of the sower, which describes how most people forget God's word in times of hardship while only a few truly understand the Word and remain true (Matthew 13).

According to Dr. Leach, all you have to do is ask yourself one simple question: "If something bad happens, what is my first response?" If you answer that correctly, everything else will fall into place. Otherwise, one bad decision builds on another, eventually creating a disaster.

Faith*ful*ness and Faith*less*ness

In *No Mercy: True Stories of Disaster, Survival and Brutality*, Eleanor Learmonth and Jenny Tabakoff examine tragedies throughout history. Many of their findings reveal that, with each unique story, an instinctive leader emerges. Typically, they are unassuming people, such as an elderly woman or a young boy. Someone who may otherwise go unnoticed or not be listened to. Nevertheless, when called to action, they are seemingly guided by the Holy Spirit telling them the right thing to do. The question is, will anyone listen to them? As alpha reader Gene Blanton explains, "Not everyone who has worn a uniform is a warrior, and not every warrior has worn a uniform." Nothing better illustrates this than the old woman or young boy who is anointed by God in the midst of a disaster. God selects the sheepdog, "those who are called according to his purpose" (Romans 8:28 ESV).

Learmonth and Tabakoff's study of tragedies revealed a lot about *faithfulness* and *faithlessness* and how faithfulness leads to deliverance, while faithlessness leads to disaster. Those who follow the Lord in all circumstances will be rewarded: "Let us not grow weary of doing good, for in due season we will reap, if we do not give up" (Galatians 6:9 ESV). But those who abandon God's teachings will be chastised: "Just open your eyes, and see how the wicked are punished" (Psalm 91:8 NLT).

This research affirms Dr. Leach's findings, that approximately 15 percent of people remain faithful to God in challenging times.

1. **It's always the same.** Learmonth and Tabakoff said what was really eye-opening in their research is that nothing changes. In over two thousand years, the same two patterns emerge and play out. Some people leave civilization as normal respected people, and within hours of a tragedy, they have transformed: some become saints and life savers while others become part of the problem, and some even go on to become mass-murderers! The competition between good and evil leaders sets the stage for what happens. Satan will attempt to justify the wicked and condemn the righteous: "He who justifies the wicked and he who condemns the righteous are both alike an abomination to the LORD" (Proverbs 17:15 ESV).

2. **Early decisions set the pattern.** The decisions made in the first hours of a crisis have huge ramifications. It all

boils down to how the group prioritizes things. Those who showed compassion and empathy brought out the best in others and led the group to salvation. Those who hatched selfish ideas, spreading all kinds of falsehoods, calling evil good, led the group into hell. "For they proceed from evil to evil, and they know not me, saith the LORD" (Jeremiah 9:3 KJV).

3. **Carnage is the norm**. Unfortunately, in nearly every scenario outlined, it's the same tragic story: fear, panic, and hysteria. In a 2013 interview with *The Daily Telegraph*, Tabakoff said, "I think the ultimate horror is the thrill kills. The pandemonium killing; where people just kill for no reason." Once panic sets in, the survival rate drops quickly. When desperation drives decision-making, the result is carnage. They "are like wolves tearing their prey; they shed blood and kill people to make unjust gain" (Ezekiel 22:27).

4. **Selfishness is punished**. It's interesting how often compassion is rewarded and selfishness is punished. We think this is because God is always watching: "For your ways are in full view of the LORD, and he examines all your paths" (Proverbs 5:21). There is destiny in how things turn out. Those who had faith kept their compassion and God's protection. But those who cared only about their own survival were like demons unleashed upon the innocent, and for their punishment, they spent the rest of their lives

in misery. "For the eyes of the LORD range throughout the earth to strengthen those whose hearts are fully committed to him. You have done a foolish thing, and from now on you will be at war" (2 Chronicles 16:9).

5.   **Having compassionate leaders makes the difference**. The most important tool to ensure wellbeing is a sense of compassion from those in charge. In the case of the *Grafton*, shipwrecked for two years on a subarctic island, the survivors decided not to abandon a sick member of their crew. His knowledge and leadership turned out to be vital to their survival. When they were eventually rescued, their morality was intact. When choosing a leader, the Bible instructs: "Select capable men from all the people—men who fear God, trustworthy men who hate dishonest gain" (Exodus 18:21).

6.   **There is empathy in the good groups**. Godly survivors keep talking, share labor, and move people around so that they don't become resentful. These are the groups that make it. Survivors who looked out for each other and sacrificed for each other created an ethos of teamwork that enabled everyone to survive. "Let us consider how we may spur one another on toward love and good deeds" (Hebrews 10:24).

Jeff Wolf, author of *Blue Lies*, points out that Dr. Leach's research and the support of Learmonth and Tabakoff's stories are part of a growing body of empirical evidence that confirms the existence and intervention of God and his power in human lives. When a group of people are faced with a crisis of survival, someone will always emerge as a leader. If they are fortunate, it will be a righteous person who serves the Lord. And what a blessing it is to have a righteous leader. Proverbs 29:2 says, "When the righteous are in authority, the people rejoice" (KJV). The person with authority is not always the person with the title but with the commission of God to act.

Let us pray that *the people* will listen to God's chosen leader and not to the lies and threats of the devil's henchman.

No Guarantee of Safety on Earth

Let us be clear: God will not always rescue us *physically*. Being a Christian, even leading with Christian values, is not a promise of success and survival here on earth. God warns us that there will be times of great persecution for Christians. "Indeed, all who desire to live a godly life in Christ Jesus will be persecuted" (2 Timothy 3:12 ESV). Sometimes the persecution is mild, and sometimes it is intense and violent, but there is a price we must pay for being a Christian. Jesus said, "If the world hates you, keep in mind that it hated me first" (John 15:18).

Never forget that God's greatest miracle is to save our souls through the blood of Jesus Christ and to give us eternity in heaven. In the meantime, bad things will happen to Christians. "For it has been granted to you that for the sake of Christ you should not only believe in him but also suffer for his sake" (Philippians 1:29 ESV). We sometimes catch ourselves saying in the midst of tragedy that we are "going through hell." Of course, this is absurd. There is no cross that we must bear that resembles the suffering that sin and hell bring.

Still, there can be great blessing in virtuous, godly behavior here on earth. And when righteous men and women are in positions of authority, especially in times of crisis, good results are significantly more likely to occur. In contrast, when the ungodly and the wicked are in control, especially during disasters, it is almost a guarantee of tragic results.

The Sinking of the William Brown

One of the most infamous disasters that remains a topic of analysis was the sinking of the *William Brown*, which struck an iceberg off Newfoundland and sank on April 19, 1841. After striking the iceberg and realizing that they had to abandon the vessel, nine crewmen and thirty-two passengers piled into one longboat and moved away from the sinking ship. Fearing they would be capsized in rough water, the first mate, Francis Rhodes, ordered his seamen to throw fourteen men overboard to their deaths. When the crew refused to obey Rhodes, he told them: "Men, you must go to work, or we shall all perish." Rhodes chose to save the women, the children, and all of the crew to man the small ship, but all the male passengers were forced overboard.

In protest to Rhodes' decision, two women went in the water voluntarily to their own deaths rather than watch the murders that were taking place. Perhaps these two righteous women thought that their example might make Rhodes reconsider the error of his decision, to embrace a higher Christian morality. But unfortunately, Rhodes let these two women die and thus revealed his true motive: his own personal survival. Saving the women and children was only a pretext.

As things turned out, the lifeboat was found in less than two days, and the remaining survivors were rescued by the American ship *Crescent*. Had Rhodes chosen to keep the male passengers onboard, all of those on the longboat would likely have survived.

After returning to the United States, some of the surviving passengers filed a complaint against the crew with the US District Attorney. The first mate Francis Rhodes and the crew had gone into hiding. Officials could only find one low-ranking seaman, Alexander Holmes. Holmes was charged with manslaughter. While Holmes admitted to casting passenger Francis Askin overboard, he testified that he protested Rhodes' orders: "No, no more shall be thrown over. If any more are lost, we will all be lost together." Still, Holmes obeyed the orders he received.

Prosecutors argued that the danger to those in the boat wasn't eminent and that sailors should have prioritized the passengers' safety over their own: "The seaman, we hold, is bound, beyond the passenger, to encounter the perils of the sea. To the last extremity, to death itself, must he protect the passenger" (as recorded in the court proceedings US v. Holmes 1842). Here we see again the principle that the strong should protect the weak as a godly standard.

Many believe Alexander Holmes was a scapegoat, and the first mate Francis Rhodes should have been held responsible. The alibi that Holmes was "only following orders" has become a common defense for those accused and convicted of war crimes. Holmes, too, was convicted and served six months in jail.

What responsibility did he have as a low-ranking sailor to disobey an immoral order?

Today we see a new higher expectation on police officers to intervene when another officer is doing something wrong. It has taken one hundred eighty years to incorporate the lessons of the *William Brown*.

It Is Evil to Remain Silent in the Face of Evil

The sinking of the *William Brown* was a tragic situation. There is a very good chance that the first mate and the crew-members who sent those passengers to their deaths spent the rest of their lives in a living hell of guilt and fear of prosecution. "The wicked flee when no man pursueth" (Proverbs 28:1 KJV). People will bear many different afflictions and burdens for ungodly and wicked decisions, but never forget that God will forgive us and cleanse us of all sin if we confess our sin and turn to him (1 John 1:9).

There is a very good chance that some of the male passengers who were killed were Christians. They could go to their deaths knowing that they would be reunited with their loved ones in the Lord. But in this world, whether on the small scale of a single lifeboat or the vast global scale of a world war, great evil is unleashed when the wicked and ungodly are in control.

Like Pastor Bonhoeffer in the previous WARNORD, all Christians are called upon to confront evil and the false belief systems of the wicked, and we must always remember that solemn responsibility: "You are the salt of the earth…You are the light of the world…let your light shine before others, that they may see your good deeds and glorify your Father in heaven" (Matthew 5:13–16). Never forget the model set by Bonhoeffer and remember his words: "It is evil to remain silent in the face of evil." Indeed, we have a *duty* to intervene!

(Consider watching the movie *Abandon Ship!*, starring Tyrone Power, which is loosely based on the sinking of the *William Brown*. Here's the plot: It's shortly after World War II, and your cruise ship strikes a mine and quickly sinks, and there was no time to send a distress signal. You are the first mate in command of an overloaded lifeboat with limited food and water. What should you do?)

WARNING #6: Next Level Battle Prep

➤   What responsibility did Alexander Holmes have as a low-ranking sailor to disobey an immoral order?

➤   If you were on the jury, would you have convicted Alexander Holmes?

➤   What responsibility do low-ranking police and soldiers have to intervene when one of their comrades loses control?

➢ Describe a disaster in which a lack of Christian ethics resulted in bad decisions and made problems worse. What could have prevented these bad decisions?

SIXTH ORDER

TRAIN YOUR MIND TO DISTINGUISH THE TRUE NATURE OF GOOD AND EVIL

Let your rule of government be determined by obedience to God, and the common good, by the example of Jesus Christ our Savior.

(Erasmus)

Give your servant therefore an understanding mind to govern
your people, that I may discern between good and evil,
for who is able to govern this your great people?
—1 Kings 3:9 ESV

Let's examine another disaster, which was portrayed in the movie *Everest* (2015) and based on Jon Krakauer's book *Into Thin Air: A Personal Account of the Mt. Everest Disaster* (1996). On May 10, 1996, four separate groups of climbers set out to conquer Mount Everest. The subsequent deaths of eight climbers were a result of what is referred to as "Summit Fever."

The members of the Mount Everest expedition were keen on getting to the summit because of the time and money they had individually invested in it. This shared goal led to a fair degree of unity within each group and possibly caused some members to ignore warning signs, such as the forecast of a dangerous storm developing. Moreover, there was an unwritten code among the climbers: achieving the summit took priority over helping others; if another climber had trouble, he or she was on their own. They rationalized that it would be too dangerous to help someone else in the "death zone"—that altitude where oxygen was very thin, usually requiring the climber to use portable oxygen.

Climbers describe Summit Fever as the desire to make the summit at any costs, even at the risk of your own life or others. This mindset is sometimes called blind ambition, tunnel vision, or groupthink. Rational decisions and ethical choices become obscured in the pursuit of personal success. This drive becomes obsessive, contagious, and dangerous. And it proved so during this particular climb in 1996. After the Everest disaster, many of the survivors felt severe remorse for what happened, and they challenged their own priorities.

While the cost of aiding a distressed climber may mean risking your life and forsaking your summit ambition, we should think of it as the creation of a new summit quest—that of saving a human life. Isn't that worth more than climbing all the mountains in the world?

Make Jesus Your Lighthouse

You can ask yourself some questions, based on the lessons of the Everest disaster, to prepare yourself for future challenges. Answer each question with Jesus Christ as your guide:

1. What is so important that you are trying to achieve?
2. Are you using other people to further your own selfish ends?
3. What collateral damage could result from your ambition?
4. Establish a turnaround point: When is success too costly?
5. Do you have a survival plan in case things go terribly wrong?

This is a good place to recall what we addressed in *On Spiritual Combat*. As you answer questions 1 through 5 above, let the concepts that follow guide your answers. They make it clear why we are here:

1. To love the Lord God with all your heart, with all your soul, with all your mind, and with all your strength (Luke 10:27).
2. To love others as yourself (v. 27).
3. To fulfill the Great Commission because if we truly love people and if we love and obey God, then we will strive with all our heart to bring

others to the knowledge of salvation
(Matthew 28:19).

4. To be a powerful, living witness, bringing others to Christ by doing good deeds and never growing weary of doing good (Galatians 6:9).

5. To give the honor and glory to God (1 Corinthians 10:31).

6. To reap love, joy, and peace for ourselves (Galatians 5:22).

7. To dwell in heaven forever with our loving Father (Psalm 23:6).

The *Westminster Shorter Catechism* says that the "purpose of man" is to "Glorify God and enjoy him forever." Thus, our purpose can be defined in these thirteen words: We glorify God by obeying him and proclaiming him (as found in numbers 1 through 5 above) and enjoying him forever (numbers 6 and 7).

WARNORD Recap

This is how we make Jesus our lighthouse. Our Christian faith tells us what to do when things don't work out. Christianity is always optimistic because the nobility of our response to tragedy is completely in our hands through our Lord Jesus Christ.

Recall the hymn at the beginning of this WARNORD, and embrace these noble words:

Standing, like a lighthouse, on the shores of time,
Looking o'er the waves of darkness, sin and crime,
Open up your windows, there's a work sublime:
    Let the gospel light shine out.

There are human shipwrecks lying all around;
O what moral darkness ev'rywhere is found!
Warn some other vessels off from dang'rous ground:
    Let the gospel light shine out.

Try to live for Jesus till this life is o'er,
For along this pathway you will pass no more;
Till he bids you welcome on the other shore,
    Let the gospel light shine out.

It is our response to an evil world that makes us a winner or a loser. And never forget, we may not win in this world, but we can play the game knowing that we will always win in light of eternity. Our victory is already assured, and we yearn to hear those words, "Well done, thou good and faithful servant" (Matthew 25:21 KJV).

Sheepdogs! Make all your decisions knowing that the Great Shepherd is watching. "The eyes of the LORD are everywhere, keeping watch on the wicked and the good" (Proverbs 15:3).

Direct us, O Lord, in all our doings,
    With thy most gracious favor,
Further us with thy continual help;
    That in all our works begun,

Continued, and ended in Thee,
We may glorify thy holy Name,
And finally by thy mercy,
Obtain everlasting life,
Through Jesus Christ our Lord.
Amen.

—"Prayer for Direction," unknown author,
Soldier's Prayer Book (ca. 1863)

ORDER #6: *Next Level Battle Prep*

➤ Describe a crisis you have witnessed or experienced in which someone unexpectedly emerged as a leader to bring hope and righteousness to the situation.

   ○ What qualities did they demonstrate that alleviated the tragedy?

➤ Are there people in authority over you who don't fear God?

   ○ What compass do they follow?
   ○ How can you prevent the ship from crashing on the rocks?

SEVENTH WARNING

THE WICKED ARE EASILY DISTRACTED

Some people hear the Word, but when the world
brings them trouble, they quickly fall away.

(Luther)

WARNORD #7

SEVENTH ORDER

NEVER LET ANY FAILURE OR SETBACK
TURN YOU AWAY FROM GOD

We are not perfect;
this only means we should try harder.

(Erasmus)

SEVENTH WARNING

THE WICKED ARE EASILY DISTRACTED
Some people hear the Word, but when the world brings them trouble, they quickly fall away.
(Luther)

Jesus said…"Listen then to what the parable of the sower means: When anyone hears the message about the kingdom and does not understand it, the evil one comes and snatches away what was sown in their heart. This is the seed sown along the path. The seed falling on rocky ground refers to someone who hears the word and at once receives it with joy. But since they have no root, they last only a short time. When trouble or persecution comes because of the word, they quickly fall away. The seed falling among the thorns refers to someone who hears the word, but the worries of this life and the deceitfulness of wealth choke the word, making it unfruitful. But the seed falling on good soil refers to someone who hears the word and understands it. This is the one who produces a crop, yielding a hundred, sixty or thirty times what was sown."

—Matthew 13:18–23

O thou Rock of our salvation,
    Jesus, Savior of the world,
In our poor and lowly station
    We thy banner have unfurled.

Gather round the standard bearer;
    Gather round in strength of youth.
Ev'ry day the prospect's fairer
    While we're battling for the truth…

Gather round the standard bearer;
    Gather round in strength of youth.
Ev'ry day the prospect's fairer
    While we're battling for the truth.

—"O Thou Rock of Our Salvation,"
by Joseph L. Townsend (1849–1942)

The parable of the sower can be intimidating, even frightening, because it tells us how easy it is to become distracted and abandon the Lord. (But always remember, Jesus never abandons us.) No other parable shows us so clearly how the devil, the allure of the world, and the cares of life conspire to undermine the call of the Holy Spirit.

This parable explains how important it is to have the right state of our heart to receive the gospel. How do we stay focused on God, especially in the midst of the battle? This is a question that warriors have asked many times across the ages with one consistent answer.

The battlefield is a chaotic place, full of smoke, smells, loud noises, death, and other distractions. Like a soldier, a Christian knight can easily get confused and give up ground. As in the parable of the sower, the warrior can quickly lose sight of Jesus, our mighty Captain.

Gather Round the Standard Bearer

Centuries ago, before modern technology, military leaders needed a way to communicate with soldiers on the battlefield. The battlefield solution was the standard bearer—a soldier who would use a flag or banner to direct the troops. The banner was also an inspirational sign. In the national anthem of the United States, one of the key lyrics of that song is that "our flag was still there."

"The Star-Spangled Banner," our national anthem, was written during the War of 1812 by Francis Scott Key. On September 14, 1814, British ships bombarded Fort McHenry in the Baltimore Harbor. Over the fort flew a large flag with fifteen stars and fifteen stripes. It continued flying through-out the bombardment and provided inspiration for American patriots to fight on. The mere presence of the standard during the battle meant there was hope, which led to ultimate victory!

Christ is commonly depicted as waving the standard to signal his victory over sin and death and to inspire and regroup his soldiers in spiritual warfare. Jesus is our standard bearer, and we must keep our eyes on him and our ears tuned to him. Jesus said to those who followed him, "Blessed are your eyes, for they see: and your ears, for they hear" (Matthew 13:16 KJV).

"I'll Take a Bullet for You"

On December 2, 2015, two terrorists opened fire on a Christmas party held by the California Department of Public Health in San Bernardino County. The shooters murdered fourteen people and wounded twenty-two. In the midst of gunshots, chaos, blood, and death, Detective Jorge Lozano guided a large group of survivors—many of them bleeding and wounded—to safety. Some of the people Det. Lozano led out of this living hell were concerned that the killers might shoot them. Lozano's calm, laconic answer was, "I'll take a bullet before you do—that's for damn sure."

United States Poet Laureate Juan Felipe Herrera immortalized this courageous act of Lozano and his "follow me" leadership of these terrified and injured citizens in a poem titled "I'll Take a Bullet for You." What the enemy meant for evil, amidst the tragic murder of fourteen citizens, Det. Lozano embraced for good with this one incident of sacrificial, lead-from-the-front heroism.

"Follow me!" is the motto of my alma mater, the US Army Infantry School in Ft. Benning, Georgia, home of OCS and Ranger School. The words "Follow me!" are the condensed essence of combat leadership. And the understanding of everyone on the battlefield is that the person saying these heroic words will take the first bullet.

Along with leadership comes followership. And our mission is to follow through. Dr. Kevin Gilmartin, author of *Emotional Survival*, is a renowned law enforcement trainer and a Marine. (Marines will tell you there is no such thing as a "former" Marine.) He loves to tease USMC leaders, telling them that they have "adequate" leadership. But their great strength is that they have magnificent followership. Yes! *That* is the standard of followership that we must strive for.

Our Savior, the Lord Jesus Christ, is a true lead-from-the-front, "I'll take the first bullet" commander. He did take the first bullet. He is pierced by many wounds for us. He took that bullet, paid that price, laid down his life so that we do not need to. And all he asks of us can be said in two words: "Follow me!" (Matthew 8:22; 9:9; 10:38; 16:24; 19:21; Mark 2:14; 8:34; 10:21; Luke 5:27; 9:23, 59; 18:22; John 1:43; 10:27; 12:26; 13:36; 21:22). Christ calls to us, waves to us, implores us, "Follow me!" Jesus said "follow me" *over a dozen times* in the Gospels. Jesus could not be clearer in his commander's intent, in his mission statement to us. But so many cannot hear, cannot see.

Our mission is to follow Jesus and then to follow through. Follow through on our commitment to God. Follow through on those prayer drills. Follow through on our mission.

Follow through on loving God and loving others. Follow through on sharing the gospel. Follow through on doing good works and giving the honor and glory to God. Follow through with a life of selfless service and self-sacrifice. *Follow through to the end!*

Alpha reader Dr. Eric Murray said we must remember the words of the nineteenth century French writer Guy De Maupassant who wrote: "You have never lived until you have almost died, and for those who fight for it, life has a flavor the protected shall never know." And that is even truer for those who "fight the good fight" in spiritual warfare.

Luther warned us that the wicked will quickly fall away when the world gives them trouble. Why? Because the wicked have no godly faith to sustain them in a fallen world. They do not see Christ or hear him. In fact, as John says, "The world cannot accept him, because it neither sees him nor knows him" (John 14:17). The wicked fall away, but we who follow Jesus will not. We will follow through. As Theodore Roosevelt once said that we should spend ourselves for a worthy cause so that our "place shall never be with those cold and timid souls who neither know victory nor defeat."

WARNING #7: Next Level Battle Prep

➤ When have you struggled to achieve a goal and failed, only to realize later that it was not what God wanted you to do?

➤ What are some of the noises and distractions that prevent effective communication in your personal life? Professional life?

➤ Are you mentally, physically, psychologically, and spiritually prepared to take the first bullet for others just as Jesus did?

➤ What do you need to do mentally, physically, psychologically, and spiritually to be more effective at communicating with others during challenging times?

SEVENTH ORDER

NEVER LET ANY FAILURE OR SETBACK TURN YOU AWAY FROM GOD

We are not perfect; this only means we should try harder.

(Erasmus)

I can do everything through Christ,
who gives me strength.
—Philippians 4:13 NLT

Reverend Thomas Watson, the English Puritan pastor and reformer who embraced *grace* and *action*, was a diligent theologian and productive writer, and we have already discussed his ingredients for repentance in WARNORD #4.

Watson is probably most remembered for his book *The Christian Soldier: or Heaven Taken by Storm* (1669). Watson advises us to offer violence to ourselves, Satan, the world, and even to heaven. What is the violence advocated here? It is not violence in a physical sense. It is what we wage in the spiritual battle. Watson said: "Our life is military. Christ is our Captain, the gospel is the banner, the graces are our spiritual artillery, and heaven is only taken in a forcible way." When Watson talks about taking heaven in a forcible way, he is referring to doing good works: "Though heaven is given us freely—yet we must take pains for it." He reaffirmed the Puritan ethos that good works are not separate from faith; they are in conjunction with sanctification. Watson often accused people of spiritual laziness, accepting God's grace in repentance but failing to do God's work in sanctification.

While Martin Luther is remembered for emphasizing salvation by grace alone, he also wrote a sermon entitled "An Exhortation to Good Works," and he warned us in his treatise *On the Freedom of a Christian* that "Good works do not make a good man, but a good man does good works; evil works do not make a wicked man, but a wicked man does evil works."

In the same way, Watson wants us to be active Christian soldiers, recognizing that we are in God's service by grace, serving through the power of the Holy Spirit to do good works: "Jesus Christ went more willingly to the cross than we do to the throne of grace. Had not we need then provoke ourselves to duty?" And further on in *The Christian Soldier* he wrote, "If Christ thought the soul was worth the shedding of His blood, well may we think it worth spending our sweat."

How do we perform these godly works? By treating each act of service as if we were working for the Lord. Which we are!

> Whatever you do, work at it with all your heart, as working for the Lord, not for human masters, since you know that you will receive an inheritance from the Lord as a reward. It is the Lord Christ you are serving. Anyone who does wrong will be repaid for their wrongs, and there is no favoritism. (Colossians 3:23–25)

Dr. Martin Luther King Jr., another pastor and mighty man of God, a man named after the reformer Martin Luther, echoed these words. "Whatever your life's work is, do it well…A man should do his job so well that the living, the dead, and the unborn could do it no better." He went on to say:

> If it falls your lot to be a street sweeper, sweep streets like Michelangelo painted picture, like Shakespeare wrote poetry, like Beethoven composed music; sweep streets so well that all the hosts of Heaven and earth will have to pause and say, "Here lived a great street sweeper, who swept his job well."

Jeff Wolf says it is common to feel like you are not making a difference. Even members of the military, law enforcement, and ministry can feel small in the big picture. But the truth is quite the opposite. Nothing is futile! Nothing goes unnoticed!

You and what you do are significant in God's sight. "Indeed, the very hairs of your head are all numbered" (Luke 12:7).

"If a tree falls in a forest and no one is around to hear it, does it make a sound?" The answer, according to Bishop George Berkeley (the man attributed with first asking this question), is that it makes a huge sound because God hears it. In fact, God hears every leaf that falls. And if God can hear a leaf fall, he can surely hear your prayers.

Bishop Berkeley (1685–1753) was a Christian moralist. He addressed the concurrence that while the Bible says "Let everyone be subject to the governing authorities" (Romans 13:1), we need not obey usurpers or madmen. Satan is a usurper and perverter of God's design, and there are many worldly leaders who are usurpers and perverters of God's design—and they are all mad! To obey a usurper king would be to disobey God. If a leader like Hitler tells you to murder innocent children, you must disobey. When the king of Egypt told the Hebrew midwives to kill all newborn Hebrew boys, "the midwives feared God, and did not do as the king of Egypt had commanded them, but let the boys live" (Exodus 1:17 NASB). When the apostles were arrested and accused of blasphemy, Peter said, "We must obey God rather than men" (Acts 5:29 NASB).

While you may not think you are faced with life-and-death decisions, the Talmud (a collection of Jewish theology and commentary) explains that even the smallest acts have the power to destroy or save. There is a famous Talmud quotation that says, "Whoever destroys a single life is considered by Scripture to have destroyed the whole world, and whoever saves a single life is considered by Scripture to have saved the whole world." It should be made clear here that the word "destroy" is defined with several connotations:

- to put an end to one's existence (murder)
- to ruin someone emotionally or spiritually
- to ruin as if by tearing to shreds one's reputation
- to defeat someone utterly

Thus, the Talmud is referring to something far worse than taking a life. It also refers to "destroying" the human spirit.

Satan doesn't just want to murder you. He wants to ruin your salvation! Murder might not accomplish that. Better for the devil if he allows you to live long enough to turn away from God.

Nothing that we mortals do is meaningless. While Satan prefers that we sin and destroy, the sacrifice of Jesus Christ has enabled us to be servants of salvation with every small act of kindness that we perform.

The Hebrew word *hesed* (pronounced kheh-sed) is found 249 times in the Old Testament. Translated as "loving kindness" by God toward humanity and among people, *hesed* is a divine word that describes how even small acts of kindness can unleash godly power for good.

What about Killing?

Every sheepdog has asked themselves, what if I need to kill someone? Is that an unforgivable sin? Here is what the Bible says on *killing* versus *murder*.[4]

War

King David defeated the Philistines by following God's strategy concerning the battle (2 Samuel 5:23–25). God never tells people to sin, so when David and his soldiers waged war, they were not sinning. Killing in war cannot be equated with murder.

Self-Defense

Killing another person in an act of self-defense is permitted (Exodus 22:2). In fact, police are taught that they may use potentially fatal force only when an immediate threat to life exists. This response covers an officer's defense of his or her own life and the life of another person.

What about Murder?

You are probably wondering if God will ever forgive murderers.

Let's start with what the Bible teaches about murder. The Bible clearly says, "You shall not murder" (Deuteronomy 5:17). Jesus also said, "You have heard that it was said to those of old,

---

4   For more information on this topic, see *On Combat: The Psychology and Physiology of Deadly Conflict in War and Peace*, by Lt. Col. Dave Grossman with Loren W. Christensen, 4th ed. (KRG, 2008), chapter entitled "Thou Shalt Not Kill?," 350–54.

'You shall not murder; and whoever murders will be liable to judgment.' But I say to you that everyone who is angry with his brother will be liable to judgment; whoever insults his brother will be liable to the council; and whoever says, 'You fool!' will be liable to the hell of fire" (Matthew 5:21–22 ESV). This would seemingly condemn all of us.

Returning to the Old Testament, Israel's King David, most beloved by God, essentially murdered Uriah to steal his wife. David suffered every day for the rest of his life for this horrendous sin. But David openly confessed his grave sin to God (Psalm 51). He repented for his transgression, and he was severely punished. His sin cursed his family. When the prophet Nathan confronted David with his crime, David confessed, "'I have sinned against the LORD.' Nathan replied, 'The LORD has taken away your sin. You are not going to die'" (2 Samuel 12:13). God forgave David, even of murder.

I do not tell you this to lessen the severity of murder. I tell you this so that you know that even the sin of murder can be forgiven for those who repent, but there is a cost for such an egregious sin.

Our True North

We must aspire, strive, *yearn* to be a worldly saint—with earth as our sphere of activity and with heaven as our ultimate destination.

The world tells us that we are not perfect.

Erasmus says, "We are not perfect."

The Bible tells us we are not perfect.

But that only means we should try harder. And for maximum effectiveness, we must work in accordance with godly principles. We must follow God's mighty standard.

No, we are not perfect. But God is. "This God—his way is perfect; the word of the LORD proves true; he is a shield for all those who take refuge in him" (22:31 ESV). God the Father, God the Son, and God the Holy Spirit—they are perfect. And their standard is Christ's standard—the gospel. The gospel is the moral compass, and it will take our flawed, imperfect endeavors and guide our actions to great victory over the forces of evil.

So Christ is our true north, and his gospel is the standard that shines forth for us to order our lives toward. The Rend Collective song "True North" says God is our compass, and we can follow him into the dark.

I like to use the example of being "compass man" in Army Ranger School. On endless patrols in forests, mountains, and jungles, my Ranger buddy, Jim Boyle, and I were usually chosen to fill the position of compass man because of our proven past competence in that crucial job. When not assigned to a leadership position, you could usually find one of us up front, compass in hand. After days without sleep and food, at night in the pouring rain, soaking wet, with our rucksack and every other piece of equipment waterlogged and pulling down upon us even more than usual, chilled to the bone, we had to follow the pre-set azimuth on our compass, guided by that north-seeking arrow. The lesson learned, the magic ingredient of Ranger school that would stick with you throughout life, was a never-quit mindset. Just follow the compass!

Carved into your neurons was the same lesson the old knight, Erasmus, gives us: when things get bad, it just means you have to try harder. Just follow the Bible. As Navy SEAL and bestselling author Jocko Willink teaches, "Just say 'good!'" Or as the army teaches us, "Embrace the suck!" Tough it out and stay true. President Calvin Coolidge captured that never-quit spirit when he said:

> Nothing in this world can take the place of persistence. Talent will not; nothing is more common than unsuccessful men with talent. Genius will not; unrewarded genius is almost a proverb. Education will not; the world is full of educated derelicts. Persistence and determination alone are omnipotent. The slogan, "Press On!" has solved and always will solve the problems of the human race.

Most of all, consider that God sent Jesus Christ to this fallen world to sacrifice himself for a bunch of sinners, and the devil and the world opposed him at every step. Then his own disciple, Peter, out of selfish love, asked Jesus to take the easy way and forgo the crucifixion. Jesus responded, "Get behind me, Satan! You are a stumbling block to me; you do not have in mind the concerns of God" (Matthew 16:23).

Thus we have Jesus Christ. The universe condensed down to nothing but that glowing compass arrow to follow

God. That compass is the only constant, trustworthy thing that exists in a universe of darkness, pain, hunger, cold, and fatigue.

Like Christ and the persistence he showed, you can never quit because others are depending on you. That is what God's moral compass must be to us.

Erasmus reminds us to never let failures and setbacks turn us away from that godly compass. Ten thousand times the Ranger slips and falls in the mud and rain and absolute darkness. And ten thousand times he picks himself back up and drives on! *Though I be the lone survivor.*

WARNORD #7 Recap

We are not perfect, yet Jesus tells us we must be perfect. "You therefore must be perfect, as your heavenly Father is perfect" (5:48 ESV). Now, God does not give us any impossible tasks, so how do we, being imperfect, arrive at perfection? Jesus tells us how. We begin with the knowledge that "With man this is impossible, but with God all things are possible" (19:26 ESV). And to this, Paul adds his own testimony: "I can do all things through him who strengthens me" (Philippians 4:13 ESV). In other words, while we are not perfect, God is. And if we follow his standard, the gospel, the good news in his Holy Bible, then we cannot go wrong. God's Word, his guidance, is our "true north." It is the only trustworthy thing in a world of distractions, pain, fatigue, troubles, trials, and tribulations.

And when we fail, as Erasmus tells us, it only means we have to try harder. But always remember, without God on our side, our striving would be failing. So we follow his compass azimuth, and we gather around his standard.

"O Thou Rock of Our Salvation," from the beginning of this WARNORD, was written centuries after Luther and Erasmus' death, but we think they would have found pleasure in those words:

> We a war 'gainst sin are waging;
>> We're contending for the right.
> Ev'ry day the battle's raging;
>> Help us, Lord, to win the fight.
>
> Gather round the standard bearer;
>> Gather round in strength of youth.
> Ev'ry day the prospect's fairer
>> While we're battling for the truth.

ALMIGHTY GOD, our heavenly Father, Who, of his great mercy, hath promised forgiveness of sins, to all those who with hearty repentance and true faith turn unto him. Have mercy upon me; pardon and deliver me from all my sins; confirm and strengthen me in all goodness; and bring me to everlasting life, through Jesus Christ our Lord. Amen.

—Unknown author,
Soldier's Prayer Book (ca. 1863)

ORDER #7: Next Level Battle Prep

- ➤ What did Reverend Thomas Watson mean when he said we must "offer violence" to ourselves and to Satan?

- ➤ What did Bishop George Berkeley suggest we do if we find ourselves living under evil leaders who are "usurpers" of God's authority?

- ➤ What is the divine power behind the Hebrew word *hesed*?

- ➤ When have you endured—overcome resistance, distraction, and fatigue—to reach a godly ordained goal?

- ➤ How can you be a compass man or a compass woman?

EIGHTH WARNING

THE WICKED ARE EASILY TEMPTED BY SATAN

Satan reigns in us with full power, by temptation alone.

(Luther)

WARNORD #8

EIGHTH ORDER

FACE TEMPTATION WITH PRAYER, NOT WITH WORRY OR EXCUSES

Begin to worry when you do not feel temptation, because that is a sure sign that you cannot distinguish good from evil.

(Erasmus)

EIGHTH WARNING

THE WICKED ARE EASILY TEMPTED BY SATAN

Satan reigns in us with full power, by temptation alone.

(Luther)

Let no one say when he is tempted, "I am being tempted by God," for God cannot be tempted with evil, and he himself tempts no one. But each person is tempted when he is lured and enticed by his own desire. Then desire when it has conceived gives birth to sin, and sin when it is fully grown brings forth death.

—James 1:13–15 ESV

Let us work and pray together,
With a firm and strong endeavor;
Hearts and hands united ever
   In the service of the Lord:

In His constant love abiding,
And to Him our all confiding,
With His gentle hand still guiding,
   We shall conquer thro' His word...

Come and join the ranks before us;
Hark, their songs are floating o'er us;
Hear the glad the tuneful chorus,
   How it vibrates on the air:

Home is near, and toil is ending,
Soon the mount of joy ascending,
Where the blest their harps are blending
   We shall meet our loved ones there.

— "Let Us Work and Pray Together,"
by Fanny J. Crosby (1820–1915)

Martin Luther was fond of quoting St. Bernard: "The greatest temptation is to have no temptation."

Deception. Lies. Camouflage. They are all the same. This camouflage, or invisibility, is Satan's greatest instrument, says Luther. If men were aware of the devil's evil mischief, then he "would not be able to retain a single one of them."

Satan: Master of Deception and Lies

Father Gabriele Amorth, in his book *An Exorcist Explains the Demonic*, says, "Angels and men who follow Satan base their existence on three principles and practical rules of life," all of which are (of course) lies.

- "You can do what you want, that is, without subjugation to God's laws."
- "You obey no one."
- "You are the god of yourself."

And yet tragically and in the end, the wretched individuals who buy into these lies are not doing what they want; they have no free will at all. They obey only the evil one. And they may think that they are their own pitiful, pathetic god, but in reality, Satan is their god, and he owns their souls.

God will never use you (or anyone) as his puppet. He has given you (and all other people) free will. But Satan will ruthlessly and joyfully use you as his puppet if you let him into your life.

God gives all of us true freedom in this life, and he grants eternity in heaven to those who put their abiding faith in him. The evil one, however, steals your freedom in this life, and infinitely worse (literally, *infinitely* worse), he steals your eternal salvation. He is a liar and a thief, and his lies are how he steals the only eternal and truly precious thing on earth: our souls.

What sane, rational person would accept such slavery to Satan and sin? Who would willingly choose to be the mindless meat puppet of evil?

Defeat the Devil's Deception

Again, it is deception, the evil one's invisibility, that makes the devil's attacks possible. But God's Holy Word in the Bible and his Holy Spirit indwelling in you will allow you to see through the devil's deception. And if you accept Jesus as your Savior, God's power defeats *all* claims that Satan has ever had upon your soul.

Satan and his minions "come to you in sheep's clothing, but inwardly they are ferocious wolves" (Matthew 7:15), and they are experts in advertising and marketing. They will advertise evil as something normal and even patriotic. The devil is also a multi-level marketer. He wants to trick you into spreading his temptations and lies. He wants you to seduce others into sin by candy-coating evil and recruiting more marketers. The devil wants to build a pyramid scheme, with himself at the top of the pyramid and the only real winner. But the Bible warns us in Isaiah 5:20, "Woe unto them that call evil good, and good evil; that put darkness for light, and light for darkness; that put bitter for sweet, and sweet for bitter!" (KJV).

Broken Windows and Slippery Slopes

After we break one of God's laws, it gets easier and easier to sin. Martin Luther describes it this way: "We see here what an awful thing it is when the Devil begins to tempt a man. One lapse involves another lapse, and an apparently slight wrong brings about a prodigious lapse." We find ourselves on a slippery slope. In his book *Police Corruption: Exploring Police Deviance and Crime*, police sociologist Maurice Punch describes the "slippery slope" as starting with small deviant acts that become progressively more acceptable, and this gradually leads to participation in larger, more serious acts.

Police have another term for the slippery slope as applied to criminality; it's called the "broken windows theory." Developed by criminologists James Q. Wilson and George Kelling and published in a 1982 article for *The Atlantic Monthly*, the broken windows theory states that when minor crimes and anti-social behavior go unchecked in communities, it encourages further crime and disorder. Police have found that a broken-windows type of breakdown in a community is more likely to occur if there is a subculture within the community that encourages deviant behavior.

When a police officer goes bad, critics are quick to point out that it could have been prevented if disciplinary action had been quicker and more severe when the officer committed less serious infractions. But when a community is having a crime problem, police often get criticized if they step-up enforcement action to deter crime.

The Bible says: "When a crime is not punished quickly, people feel it is safe to do wrong" (Ecclesiastes 8:11 NLT). Read that line from Ecclesiastes again. This is a fundamental principle of criminology and of law and order. It is an undeniable aspect of human nature. It could have come straight out of a criminology textbook, but instead it was written about three thousand years ago and has supernatural divine power. Because "The word of God is alive and powerful," says Hebrews 4:12 (NLT). It applies to all people: police and criminal alike.

"I Saw Satan Laughing with Delight"

While there should sometimes be *punishment*, at other times, there should be *discipline*. Punishment as retribution can be just, especially for severe crimes, but punishment can also produce some negative side-effects. While punishment can create guilt, shame, and regret, which are important aspects of repentance, punishment can also create fear, self-pity, bitterness, and resentment. Jeremiah prayed to the Lord: "Correct me, LORD, but with justice; not with Your anger, or You will bring me to nothing" (Jeremiah 10:24 NASB).

God disciplines us like loving parents would correct their children: "The Lord disciplines the one he loves, and he chastens everyone he accepts as his son" (Hebrews 12:6). Likewise, loving parents also dispense discipline: "Whoever spares the rod hates their children, but the one who loves their children is careful to discipline them" (Proverbs 13:24). And all loving discipline is meant to influence change in the one disciplined and provide avenues to remedy wrongs. For example, God's discipline often provides the wrongdoer with an opportunity to right their wrongs through prayer and good works. This, too, should be our standard for justice for citizens and for police.

We must also remember that violent crime (interpersonal human aggression) is the most psychologically corrosive and traumatic event that can occur in anyone's life. And thus, an explosion of violence is the most toxic and destructive event (short of open warfare on our own soil) that can happen to any nation. Of course, this is exactly what Satan wants.

While Satan and his followers laugh at the calamity of others, the Bible says, "The Lord laughs at the wicked, for he knows their day is coming" (Psalm 37:13). God has the last laugh.

Proverbs also says, "When justice is done, it brings joy to the righteous but terror to evildoers" (21:15). It does not say, ignore the victim and justify the wicked. In fact, "Acquitting the guilty and condemning the innocent—the LORD detests them both" (17:15).

The Wicked Do Not Understand Justice

Author Jeff Wolf says that when a righteous person recognizes the evil plots and schemes of the wicked, he or she cannot understand why everyone else cannot see it. In other words, "Why doesn't everyone else see how insane this is?" But we shouldn't be surprised because "Evil men do not understand justice, but those who seek the LORD comprehend fully" (28:5 BSB).

Many people do not seek the Lord, so they do not understand justice. As a result, they do not care about the victims of crime or political injustice. They do not seek to protect the sheep from the predator. Quite the opposite, some people actually sympathize with those who rape, murder, and commit corruption.

Julia Swerdin, editor of *Horizon Newspaper*, in a 2019 article titled "Sympathy for Serial Killers Has Become a Hollywood Epidemic," says, "Not only are the murderers humanized, but they are even glorified." Swerdin explains, "We seem to overlook the cause of their infamy: They viciously murdered innocent people." Hollywood doesn't seem to care that media coverage elevates these murderers to a kind of celebrity status as long as there is money to be made.

Why do people bring images of such wretched, unrepentant evil into their lives? In some cases, they are trying to understand why someone would commit such horrendous crimes as rape and murder. However, there are some people who are actually attracted to the perpetrator. The desire to do evil and the attraction to evil is much the same. In Proverbs 4:13–17, a father gives this advice to his son:

> Hold on to instruction, do not let it go;
>   guard it well, for it is your life.
> Do not set foot on the path of the wicked
>   or walk in the way of evildoers.
> Avoid it, do not travel on it;
>   turn from it and go on your way.
> For they cannot rest until they do evil;
>   they are robbed of sleep till they
>   make someone stumble.
> They eat the bread of wickedness
>   and drink the wine of violence.

Scripture urges us to avoid those people who actually like to do evil things. At its most fundamental level, evil is disobedience to God's way. It is sin. When manifested on earth, evil is violent (Psalm 11:5), selfish (James 3:16), and tyrannical (Proverbs 28:16).

Who Protects the Helpless?

We as Christians must not allow evil to be glorified. We must warn our children about the false glamour of the wicked. Of equal importance, we as Christians must protect the vulnerable from being victimized by the wicked.

Who stands up for the victims of crime? The Lord and his sheepdog police officers and those prosecuting attorneys who seek justice in the courts. There are so many unsung heroes who go out every day to fairly enforce the laws and fairly prosecute crimes in the court. May the Lord strengthen them, protect them, and bless them.

Ultimately, the question is, how do we defeat evil? How do we defeat the devil? How can we stand against supernaturally empowered attacks and the devil's cunning, evil, persistent temptations? How can we find a road to justice, meting out punishment and discipline with a wise and loving hand? We defeat this supernatural evil by calling upon a vastly superior supernatural force of divine good. That is the *only* way to win in this battle. Otherwise, we are doomed.

One of the greatest spiritual weapons in our arsenal is prayer. We should follow the counsel of Erasmus: "Face temptation guided by God." Thus, we beseech the Lord: "Let us work and pray together," with police, first responders, and the whole community:

> Let us work and pray together,
> With a firm and strong endeavor;
> Hearts and hands united ever
>> In the service of the Lord.

Luther gave us the warning. Erasmus gives us the order. And (as you will see) God's Holy Word, combined with the sacrificial love of Jesus and the Holy Spirit working within us, will show us the way home from this dark and tragic realm.

WARNING #8: Next Level Battle Prep

> ➤ How does one sin grow into many sins in your home, at work, and in your country?

> ➤ What lie is Satan telling you (others)? What unholy promises has Satan tricked you (others) into believing in your home life, work life, or citizen life?

> ➤ Have you (others) tried using prayer to fend off evil and temptation?

EIGHTH ORDER

FACE TEMPTATION WITH PRAYER, NOT WITH WORRY OR EXCUSES

Begin to worry when you do not feel temptation, because that is a sure sign that you cannot distinguish good from evil.

(Erasmus)

Watch and pray so that you will not fall into temptation.
The spirit is willing, but the flesh is weak.
—Matthew 26:41

Deviant subcultures are a lot like the devil. They don't force you to do bad things. Instead, they seduce and coerce you into doing bad things. But the Bible says, if you "Resist the devil," then "he will flee from you" (James 4:7). Deviant subcultures are the same way; they don't want to be around an honest person. Honesty and lawful behavior remind them that they are doing something wrong, and they don't want to be reminded of that. If you could just share in their sin, even a little bit, then you wouldn't be a threat.

I like to use the example of my experience as a young soldier living in the barracks in Ft. Bragg, North Carolina, in 1975. When Ronald Reagan became president in 1981, the urinalysis program combined with anti-drug policies culled the drug users out of the US Armed Forces almost overnight. But prior to that time, the "druggies" ran the barracks. Like any deviant culture, the drug users and the dope dealers in the barracks could not stand someone who did not share in their crime. Refusing to do drugs made you a threat to them. If you didn't want to do drugs, you had to be prepared to fight.

The guiding political philosophy was that these drug-using "problem" soldiers were "socially deprived," and it was the military's job to provide them with "social mobility." This demand for the military to engage in such social engineering did great harm to our military readiness. You literally could not kick a bad soldier out of the armed forces. The military had to tolerate endless acts of disobedience and malfeasance. When they did mete out punishments, they were mild and ineffective. Our politicians did not see the military as an institution to win wars. To them, the US Armed Forces was an instrument to solve society's problems and a forum for endorsing and advocating whatever social experiment was in vogue at the time.

It was a bitter, dangerous, and tragic time in our nation, and a dark memory for many of our troops. During this time our armed forces were often (and quite rightfully) described as "broken" and "hollow." All because we failed to enforce the law and allowed a deviant criminal subculture to hijack our military at the grassroots level.

It is hard to understand how bad it was. It is a perfect case study of what happens when the wicked and unfaithful are in control. And it is an amazing testimony to the power of righteous actions to see how President Reagan, guided by virtuous principles, was able to defeat this evil within the first year of his term of office.

Work and Pray Together

Police officers, first responders, and all citizens who live in high crime areas need to defend themselves against the devil's subculture by praying and submitting themselves to God. Even if they do not fully share our faith, they can still be guided by—and blessed by—virtuous godly principles. Unfortunately, those individuals who refuse Christ will not gain the greatest of all blessings: eternity in heaven, which is why we need to pray that they find God. We don't want to leave anyone behind!

As for believers, we have a supernatural blessing and power available to us and to our community if we invite God into our lives and our cities through prayer and supplication. God's Word tells us, "Draw near to God, and he will draw near to you" (James 4:8 ESV).

There are honest kids in even the most crime-ridden neighborhoods. Police often find ways to reach out to these kids through after-school programs and sports. These are proven to be effective responses. But as believers in Christ, as sheepdogs under the authority of the Great Shepherd, we know that the ultimate solution is through God and his blessing upon our communities.

Many police officers and first responders have found it beneficial to attend religious services in their assigned communities. The Lord says, "For where two or three gather in my name, there am I with them" (Matthew 18:20). There is nothing more powerful for building trust between police and the community than praying together. This taps into a supernatural, divine source of blessing.

One of the most powerful and effective things any community can do is to integrate chaplains into their first responders and most especially into their police force. Local clergy should be invited and encouraged to work as chaplains. They can do ride alongs with police and respond to emergency calls with EMS.

In most cases, chaplains cost nothing. But a little bit of money invested in training and certification programs for chaplains can repay the investment many-fold. If a community's police department and other first responders are not actively seeking local clergy to volunteer as chaplains, then that should be a subject for concern for all godly citizens.

An article by Braswell et al. in the November 9, 2016, issue of the FBI's *Law Enforcement Bulletin* tells us that "Chaplains improve the overall functioning of law enforcement through involvement in correctional facilities, community-police relations, line-of-duty death notification and burial service facilitation, crisis intervention, and officer and department well-being." A February 9, 2018, article on Police1.com says:

> In addition to supporting officers struggling with issues such as burnout, stress or trauma, some chaplains also assist officers with some of their duties. These can include tasks like death notifications, crime victim support and homeless outreach…In some agencies, chaplains are also taking an active role in community policing, as law enforcement officers look to bridge the…divide and ease tensions. Chaplains accompany officers on the beat and serve as a calming presence in everything from traffic stops to domestic disputes.

Again, there should be concern about any agency and any community leadership that does not actively seek chaplains. All the items listed above are true and important. But even more important is the fact that the chaplain has a positive effect on the behavior of the police officer and on the actions of community members by reminding everyone of a shared set of positive and virtuous values and their accountability to the community and to a higher authority.

Most of all, what none of these secular articles can say but we will gladly proclaim here is that the chaplain can be a tool that will help to bring God's mighty blessing upon the community. Greg Amundson, in his excellent book *Gun in*

Hand, Gospel in Heart: A Theology of Combat Ministry, communicates this so very well:

> Chaplains present a valuable effort that can not only help counteract the toxicity of a long-term policing career but also serve as the one supernatural component in such a comprehensive effort…
>
> Officers need the spiritual care, love, and ministerial support that only chaplains can provide…Although the outer accoutrements issued to officers protect their physical body from attack, what matters most is the space between their ears.
>
> In this sense, oftentimes the first step to victory (both on and off duty) is for officers to embrace a warrior mindset. Officers who relate to themselves as a mighty warrior in a cosmic battle of good versus evil are predisposed to navigating the terrain features of a career in law enforcement with greater agility, courage, resilience and faith in a positive outcome.

Keith Overby, a retired deputy and an active chaplain in Oakland County, Michigan (and one of our alpha readers), describes the chaplain's mission very concisely as "responding first as a spiritual paramedic, with a short-term presence with the intent to listen with humility, attentively and thoughtfully, attempting to stabilize the safety and wellbeing of any person in need of help with missionary principles." Chaplains are one well-established and widely accepted resource that we can weave into the fabric of our community.

Another excellent opportunity to work and pray together is the National Day of Prayer, first proclaimed by President Harry S. Truman in 1952 to occur every year on the "first Thursday in May." It has been recognized by every US president every year since. This could and should be a time of celebration on par with Thanksgiving or Independence Day for those who love God across every community in our nation.

Look again at the hymn from the beginning of this WARNORD. A hymn written by Fanny Crosby, a mighty child of God who wrote more than eight thousand hymns and gospel songs! As of 2020, she is credited with having over a hundred million copies of her songs printed. She was blind from birth. A person who would have been abandoned, discarded, and rejected in most other nations throughout history. (Just one more reason why our nation is something worth fighting for.) Say these words aloud, and imagine that sweet godly soul looking over your shoulder (for there is no blindness in heaven) and passing her blessings on to us and to our communities and nation today:

> Let us work and pray together,
> With a firm and strong endeavor;
> Hearts and hands united ever
>   In the service of the Lord:

In His constant love abiding,
And to Him our all confiding,
With His gentle hand still guiding,
  We shall conquer thro' His word.

We can prevent many broken windows and much sliding down slippery slopes if we call upon God and work together with him to reject Satan's evil temptations and bind our social wounds. God has mighty blessings to bestow upon a community and a nation if those who love him will but work and pray together. "Seek the peace and prosperity of the city to which I have carried you into exile. Pray to the Lord for it, because if it prospers, you too will prosper" (Jeremiah 29:7).

Our national motto is "In God We Trust." And God promises that he will bless us with mighty blessings if we can become a nation that makes that motto more than just a trite phrase. Consider again 2 Chronicles 7:14, this time from the King James Version: "If my people, which are called by my name, shall humble themselves, and pray, and seek my face, and turn from their wicked ways; then will I hear from heaven, and will forgive their sin, and will heal their land."

Prayer for Protection

Almighty God,
    Defend our liberties; preserve our unity.
    Save us from lawlessness and violence;
    From discord and confusion;
    From pride and arrogance,

And from every evil way.
Endue with the spirit of wisdom
  those whom we entrust,
In thy Name with the authority of governance.
All which we ask for Jesus Christ's sake.
Amen.

—Unknown author,
The Campaign Prayer Book (1892)

ORDER #8: *Next Level Battle Prep*

➤ How can you (we) prevent one sin from becoming many sins? (Home? Work? Our country?)

➤ How has Satan and his followers pushed back against godly faith? How can you (we) prevent them from succeeding?

➤ What opportunities do you have at work to bring in a chaplain to lead a prayer of thanksgiving and for strength to defeat evil?

➤ What options do first responders have to pray with the community? List them.

NINTH WARNING

THE WICKED PRACTICE TRICKERY AND DECEPTION

The wicked seek their own gain through the other's loss and forget the rule which says: "Do unto others that which you wish they would do to you."

(Luther)

WARNORD #9

NINTH ORDER

ALWAYS BE PREPARED FOR AN ATTACK

Careful generals set guards even in times of peace.

(Erasmus)

NINTH WARNING

THE WICKED PRACTICE TRICKERY AND DECEPTION

The wicked seek their own gain through the other's loss and forget the rule which says: "Do unto others that which you wish they would do to you."

(Luther)

You belong to your father, the devil, and you want to carry out your father's desires. He was a murderer from the beginning, not holding to the truth, for there is no truth in him. When he lies, he speaks his native language, for he is a liar and the father of lies.

—John 8:44

Never lose the golden rule,
   Keep it still in view;
Do to others as you would
   They should do to you…

Love the Lord, the first command,
   With thy soul and mind;
Love thy neighbor as thyself,
   Both in one combined.
     —"Never Lose the Golden Rule,"
     by Fanny Crosby (1820–1915)

Consider for a moment the nature of the devil. He is often referred to as a snake or a serpent, and with good cause. In Genesis 3:1 it says, "Now the serpent was more crafty than any of the wild animals the Lord God had made. He said to the woman, 'Did God really say, "You must not eat from any tree in the garden"?'" The association of the devil with snakes is for good reason. "It is with the same serpent-like attack that he creeps upon, and deceives, simple souls," says Luther.

How Snakes Behave

Let us consider how snakes behave:

- Snakes are impulsive, seeking only to satisfy their yearnings.
- All snakes are carnivorous and predatory.
- Snakes are usually solitary creatures, hunting alone.

- Snakes prey on smaller or more vulnerable creatures.
- Snakes will flee from larger or more dangerous creatures.
- Avoiding detection is the snake's most important tactic.
- When stalking prey, snakes will generally find a place to hide.
- Snakes will wait patiently to ambush a victim then strike rapidly.

All these characteristics describe the evil one. But even more so.

At a fundamental level, this comparison is really an insult to snakes. Snakes were born that way, they have no other choice, and they are an important part of God's natural kingdom. Satan, on the other hand, had a choice. He made the decision to become the vilest of all creatures, literally lower than the lowest life-form on the face of the earth.

Talk to a cop who works sex crimes, and you will find that this pretty much describes a pimp or rapist: they use Satan-like, snake-like methods to commit their crimes. They move in slowly, then strike! All God's peacekeepers and all his faithful sheepdogs must educate themselves on the tactics of the enemy so they can detect evil and stop it before it does more harm. Stop it before it claims more souls and feeds on ever more innocence.

Modus Operandi: Satan's Method of Sin

A pimp is the classic psychopath, narcissist, and Machiavellian all rolled into one—Satan's perfect demonic tool. When pimps are arrested, they will minimize their crimes by telling police they are actually protecting the prostitutes. In truth, the prostitute is little more than property to a pimp. The pimps often force prostitutes to wear a tattoo branding them as belonging to the pimp. The pimp is callous, coercive, and predatory, often beating and raping the prostitutes as a means of control.

Pimps, like their father the devil, are experts at finding victims. Pimps seem to instinctively know when someone is vulnerable so they can be manipulated into "the life." Most prostitutes were previously abused and are runaways or social throwaways. Low self-esteem and desperation are exactly what pimps—and the devil—are looking for.

Sadly, for many years, society and law enforcement treated prostitutes as criminals when there is good cause to treat them as victims. Satan spreads the misinformation that adult women enter prostitution by choice. The truth is that most prostitutes are forced into human trafficking when they are minors.

For a minor, being kidnapped and raped by a pimp subconsciously creates a sense of utter hopelessness. This compels them to appease their abuser in order to survive. The victim focuses on survival rather than escape. Psychologists call this victim brainwashing process the Survival Identification

Syndrome or the Fawn Response. It was previously called Stockholm Syndrome.

Now you know why minors are the preferred victim of pimps. In 2013, the National Center for Missing and Exploited Children documented over ten thousand reports of child sex trafficking, admitting that reported cases probably represent a "tiny percentage" of actual child sex trafficking.

If you want to know Satan up close and personal, study pimps. They are the living embodiment of the devil—psychopath predators without a conscience.

Federal and state governments are now toughening enforcement on pimps and Johns, passing laws that say it shall be "presumed" a person under eighteen years of age was coerced into child sexually abusive activity.

Some would say that the prostitutes are criminals also and do not deserve to be protected by the law. Let us praise God that our heavenly Father doesn't think like this. This idea that the victim must earn our protection is one of the devil's lies.

Christians can have great empathy for others because we know that we are sinners, too, saved only by God's great grace. And as you will see, that empathy is the foundation upon which we will crush the snake.

God has commanded us to love, and with that divine commandment comes his supernatural ability that empowers us to love. Again, it comes back to Matthew 22:37–40: "Jesus replied: 'Love the Lord your God with all your heart and with all your soul and with all your mind.' This is the first and greatest commandment. And the second is like it: 'Love your neighbor as yourself.' All the Law and the Prophets hang on these two commandments."

Pimps, Human Snakes, and Vampires

There are many different types of pimps in the world today, committing vicious acts of deceit and betrayal every day. We can say that anyone who feeds off the soul of another human being is a pimp, a snake, or a vampire. All crimes are repugnant, but betraying someone's trust or innocence as a means to harm them is arguably the most despicable. Betrayal is not always about making money. People betray others for a lot of reasons, including ambition, for enjoyment, and even out of jealousy or spite. Betrayal, whatever the motive, always causes great emotional harm to the victim.

A dog will look down when he has done wrong, but a snake will look you straight in the eye. When someone looks you straight in the eye and betrays you, now you are talking about a premeditated evil. Someone who preys on others without remorse is a pimp, a human snake, a vampire—a psychopath.

Faithless criminals will manipulate you so they can take what they want. Or they will physically attack you and kill you, if need be, to get what they want. The Bible tells us that this is Satan's personality. He's a liar (manipulator) and a murderer (destroyer) and has been from the beginning (John 8:44).

What kind of sick "consumers" would inflict themselves upon such children? And what type of evil human being would be a "pimp" for these children, leading them into a living hell and ultimately to their early death? What kind of evil human being would do such things? Well, God's Word tells us, "Do to others what you would have them do to you" (Matthew 7:12). Or as Abraham Lincoln said: "Whenever I hear any one arguing for slavery [or, we would add, prostitution] I feel a strong impulse to see it tried on him personally."

These brutal "human snakes" have turned God's law on its head, and like a snake in nature, they are driven to take whatever they want with no concern for anyone but themselves. Father Flanagan, the founder of Boys Town, asks, "What sadder fate is there for any human being than to be left alone, forsaken, without a friend, to sink down into the cesspool of vice and sin?"

Love Triumphs over Evil

As to those who prey on these child prostitutes and all sexual predators who feed on the innocence of children, our nation has made a major, revolutionary step forward in the battle against such evil with the National Sex Offender Registry. This is law enforcement's way to always be prepared for an attack, to "set a careful guard" even in times of peace. The US Supreme Court has upheld the Sex Offender Registry as constitutional because sexual predators are not only dangerous but are extremely difficult to rehabilitate. What is the guiding principle behind such tactics for fighting sex crimes and other heinous acts? How can we consistently triumph in our battle against vicious, selfish, brutal evil?

First, we must accept that our purpose here on earth, the reason for our existence, is to *love* our fellow human beings, and that means we must *fight* such evil. "For our struggle is not against flesh and blood, but against…*spiritual forces of evil* in the heavenly realms" (Ephesians 6:12).

Second, we must understand that the evil one fears God! "*God is love*. Whoever lives in love lives in God, and God in them" (1 John 4:16). And evil is defeated by love, just as darkness is defeated by the light. *All* evil fears the power of God's love within you: "Like snakes crawling from their holes, they will come out to meet the LORD our God. They will fear him greatly, trembling in terror at his presence" (Micah 7:17 NLT).

Erasmus orders us to "set guards," but Luther tells us how. Luther gives us the "Golden Rule" as our "standing orders" for guard duty. This is the critical weapon built into Luther's warning, the weapon to wield against such evil: "Do unto others that which you wish they would do to you."

It is worth repeating that the opposite of evil is not good. The opposite of evil is love. And evil is the absence of love just as darkness is the absence of light. As light defeats darkness, love triumphs over evil. In the face of vicious, selfish evil, our guideline, our "standing order" for guard duty as we strive for justice, is love. We triumph over evil by asking the ultimate question, "How would you feel if someone did that to *you*? Or to *your* child?" We win by applying the Golden Rule.

Are you having trouble seeing how that works? Don't worry, we will make it clear next as we address Erasmus' ninth order.

Never lose the golden rule,
  Keep it still in view;
Do to others as you would
  They should do to you.

WARNING #9: Next Level Battle Prep

➤   How are sinners like snakes?

➤   What is Satan's modus operandi?

➤   Am I selective with those whom I think "deserve" to be treated with the Golden Rule?

➤   What do Satan and sinners fear most?

NINTH ORDER

ALWAYS BE PREPARED FOR AN ATTACK
Careful generals set guards even in times of peace.
(Erasmus)

Be sober-minded; be watchful.
Your adversary the devil prowls around like a roaring lion,
seeking someone to devour.
—1 Peter 5:8 ESV

"*Si vis pacem, para bellum*." Originally written by a Roman general, this Latin phrase means "If you seek peace, prepare for war." In Washington, DC, at the entrance to the National Archives of the United States, there is a statue that bears the inscription, "Eternal vigilance is the price of liberty." The original author of those words is uncertain although both Thomas

Jefferson and George Washington each said something similar, possibly paraphrasing that original Latin expression. Erasmus would certainly have been familiar with that Latin phrase, and—centuries before Washington and Jefferson—he gives it back to us here. The price of spiritual peace is to "set guards" at all times, under all circumstances. In other words, act with "eternal vigilance."

These "guards" are constantly on duty, prepared to give warning and take action against selfish, brutal evil. As Christians, we need to guard against Satan and his "meat puppets," the "human snakes" who do not follow the rule as cited by Luther, to "Do unto others that which you wish they would do to you."

Our Standing Order from God

All guards have "standing orders" and our guidance in this endeavor is *not* to respond to hate with hate. And we are *not* to respond to injury with injury.

Now in *On Spiritual Combat*, we talked about the evil one and how he will use human tools and that physical violence may be a part of what we must do to protect others. The Bible says that the leaders and authorities here on earth "beareth not the sword in vain" (Romans 13:4 KJV). A modern translation might be, "the police officer carries a gun for a very good reason." That verse also says, "If thou do that which is evil, be afraid…for he is the minister of God, a revenger to execute wrath upon him that doeth evil." Thus, when our sheepdogs must use force to protect innocent lives or to bring violent men to justice, they deserve our support.

But in the end, the tactic we must take to be truly triumphant against evil is to treat others as we would have them treat us. Starting in the early 1600s, people began to refer to this as the "Golden Rule," but that was just a new term for the commandment, or rule, that Jesus gave us. Jesus said, "In everything, do to others what you would have them do to you, for this sums up the Law and the Prophets" (Matthew 7:12). Jesus repeats the same concept in greater detail in 22:36–40 (love God, love others as yourself), which we addressed earlier in this section.

Matthew 22:36–40 can be encapsulated into four words: *Love God. Love people.* That is what that amazing hymnist Fanny Crosby was referring to in her powerful midrash, when she wrote:

> Love the Lord, the first command,
>   With thy soul and mind;
> Love thy neighbor as thyself,
>   Both in one combined…
> Never lose the golden rule.

What Makes a Great Investigator?

In the process of writing this book, Chris Pascoe sent me an email saying:

Say a prayer for me. Monday, I testify at one
of the biggest child abuse cases I've ever been
involved in. It sounds like the prosecutor is
putting me on the stand first and is going to start
off by asking me "why" I assigned the case to the
investigators who worked on the case. Of course,
I gave it to the two best investigators I could.

This led to his thoughts on the Golden Rule and "what makes
a great investigator."

Why were these investigators better than others? One
reason has to do with innate skill and intelligence. Furthermore,
most investigators are great communicators, observant, and
detail oriented. But there was something more than these characteristics that made them great. Great detectives are relentless
and never give up—they are "eternally" motivated.

But why were these select few individuals so motivated?
Chris provided insight. "Then," Chris said, "it finally came to
me, something I've heard countless great cops say: 'How would
you like it if someone did that to *you*? Or to *your* child?'" Yes,
you probably had your mother tell you this when you were a
child: "How would you feel if someone did that to you?" But
the great cops say this about investigations that they absolutely
refuse to give up on.

The morality of seeing someone victimized is so repugnant to men and women of conscience that it motivates them
to right the wrong. All faithful people feel this way, but there
are a select few who are willing to go above and beyond to

ensure that justice is done. These are the great detectives, and they are motivated by a profound sense of empathy, which is an outgrowth of love.

The Golden Rule

"How would you like it if someone did that to you?" is the essence of empathy in one sentence, and it is a variation of the Golden Rule: "Do to others whatever you would like them to do to you" (7:12 NLT). Many religions and cultures have a similar moral foundation. We call this the Golden Rule because it applies to everyone. Ethicists call this the natural moral law, which is universal. No one lives without it. It is one of those truths that we cannot *not* know. Paul in Romans 2:14–15 describes the universal moral law this way:

> Indeed, when Gentiles, who do not have the law, do by nature things required by the law, they are a law for themselves, even though they do not have the law. They show that the requirements of the law are written on their hearts, their consciences also bearing witness, and their thoughts sometimes accusing them and at other times even defending them.

Yes, there are universal ethics that apply to everyone. And we know where they originate: "In the beginning was the Word, and the Word was with God, and the Word was God. He was with God in the beginning. Through him all things were made;

without him nothing was made that has been made. In him was life, and that life was the Light of all mankind" (John 1:1–4).

God is the Source. God is the Word, and the Word is his Son, Jesus Christ our Lord. And the Word says, "Treat others as you would want them to treat you." The Word asks, "How would you like it if someone did that to you?"

The Golden Rule was brought to life, personified, and engraved in the spiritual DNA of all Christians when Jesus said on the cross, "Father, forgive them, for they know not what they do" (Luke 23:34 ESV).

It is the Word who gives power and energy to those who follow the Lord. God is the Word, and God is love. The Word is their "eternal motivation." Love and empathy are their superpowers!

The devil and those who obey him follow a different path: I do what I want, take what I want, no matter who I hurt in the process. But "The Light shines in the darkness, and the darkness has not overcome it" (John 1:5). As light defeats darkness, so love defeats evil.

Due Diligence

Diligence is an excellent word. Someone who is diligent in his work is serious and steady and is devoted to taking great pains to accomplish what he has set out to do. But diligence is also a legal standard for the attention and care a person is expected to give to a situation.

God commands us to be diligent, and every single aspect of that word applies here. "Ye shall diligently keep the commandments of the LORD your God, and his testimonies, and his statutes, which he hath commanded thee" (Deuteronomy 6:17 KJV). And the Bible promises us, "A sluggard's appetite is never filled, but the desires of the diligent are fully satisfied" (Proverbs 13:4).

Police officers and our military have learned that "diligence" is a key requirement in their professions. They must always be prepared for an attack. The enemy or criminals can show when you least expect them and where you least expect them.

And the virtue of diligence is essential to spiritual warfare. God tells us: "Be on your guard; stand firm in the faith; be courageous; be strong" (1 Corinthians 16:13). We are fighting a battle on enemy-occupied territory. Until Jesus comes again, the evil one and his countless minions—spiritual *and* physical—can be anywhere, and they can strike at any time.

Those who work in the legal or financial fields use a term called "due diligence." Due diligence describes the process of conducting a careful investigation to identify or exclude wrongdoing. While we are innocent until proven guilty in our court system, due diligence requires that the investigator take all allegations seriously.

In law enforcement, police conduct what is called a "terry pat down." This means that if they are legally detaining someone, the police can pat down the outside of their clothes to make sure they are not concealing any weapons. The US Supreme Court upheld "Terry" for the protection of the officers and other law-abiding citizens when there is reasonable suspicion or probable cause. It's just good sense to verify trust-worthiness in a fallen world.

And the police officer, or any sheepdog, must also always be prepared to use lawful force to protect innocent lives. There are blind optimists who assume the best in everyone. But Christians know that dark forces lurk within and without, and these dark forces are very powerful and always active. These dark forces must be defeated physically, but most importantly, they must be defeated spiritually. In God we trust. All others we search and check for warrants.

Our sheepdogs deserve our support when they must use force to protect innocent lives or to bring violent men to justice, but our most triumphal tactic against evil is to treat others as we would have them treat us while we cautiously prepare for the worst.

Never Assume the Devil Is "All Clear"

"All clear" is police code for "the danger is over." Now, any good police training officer will tell a rookie to never assume that a call they are responding to is frivolous and that they are "all clear." Unfortunately, advocates of defunding the police have advised police agencies that they can get by with fewer police officers if they quit wasting their time on frivolous nuisance calls.

Police know that the devil and crime (which are, in many ways, the same thing) are masters of camouflage. Experienced police officers understand that you never ignore a 911 call or walk in unprepared. The wicked are devious. They can quickly cover-up a crime or set an ambush for responding officers. Some of the worst crimes start out as only suspicious situations or "non-criminal" investigations. The faithless criminal will tell police:

- "Don't worry officer; everything is okay."
- "My wife is just overreacting."
- "The kids are telling lies."
- "There's nothing in the other room."
- "That's not blood."
- "I'm not carrying a weapon."
- "There's nothing to be found on my computer."
- "It's just a small accounting mistake."
- "You can totally trust me."

However, experienced police know: there are no routine calls. And experienced Christians know: there are no routine sins.

You must never assume that the devil is "all clear." Never assume that a sin is frivolous or trivial. The devil's favorite trick is to downplay the sin: "Everybody does it," or "You're under-appreciated, so go ahead and take it," or "If you want to fit in, this is what you need to do." Satan lies and deceives. He cannot be trusted—not ever!

WARNORD Recap

Our standard for behavior, for warfare, and for justice is the Golden Rule. "How would you like it if someone did that to *you*? Or to *your* child?"

Our first response upon hearing about a child prostitute dying—where children are alone and forsaken, without friends, having sunk to the bottom of the cesspool of vice and sin—should be, "What if it were my child?" Thus, we fight evil with love. We always remember that the opposite of evil is not good. The opposite of evil is love. And God is love. All love emanates from God. And love conquers evil, as water quenches fire, as light extinguishes darkness.

Love. Empathy. These truly are our superpowers. Given to us by a loving God.

God's foremost commandment to us is to *love*—"love God, love people." Love is our standing order to defeat selfish, vicious evil. It is how we defeat human snakes. It is how we must administer justice. It is how we build God's kingdom and do his will here on earth. "So now faith, hope, and love abide, these three; but the greatest of these is love" (1 Corinthians 13:13 ESV).

> Love the Lord, the first command,
>   With thy soul and mind;
> Love thy neighbor as thyself,
>   Both in one combined...

Never lose the golden rule,
   Keep it still in view;
Do to others as you would
   They should do to you.

Prayer for Love

O God of Love
   Giver of Concord
   through your only Son:
That we should Love one another
even as you have Loved us,
   the unworthy and the wandering;
and gave your Beloved Son
   for our life and salvation.
Lord, in our time of life on earth:
   give us a mind forgetful of past ill-will,
   a pure conscience and sincere thoughts,
and hearts to Love one another;
   for the sake of your Son,
Jesus Christ our Lord.
Amen.

                —Coptic Liturgy of St. Cyril
                (ca. fourth century AD)

ORDER #9: Next Level Battle Prep

- ➤ What is Luther's version of the Golden Rule?
- ➤ What is God's "standing order"?
- ➤ What makes a great investigator?
- ➤ What does "diligence" mean for a Christian?
- ➤ How can you identify the devil's stealthy schemes?

TENTH WARNING

THE WICKED FLEE FROM THE DEVIL

Submit yourselves, then, to God.
Resist the devil and he will flee from you.

(Luther)

WARNORD #10

TENTH ORDER

SPIT, AS IT WERE, IN THE FACE OF DANGER

Keep a stirring Bible quotation with you for
encouragement, so you may have courage
through the Lord thy God.

(Erasmus)

TENTH WARNING

THE WICKED FLEE FROM THE DEVIL

**Submit yourselves, then, to God.
Resist the devil and he will flee from you.**

(Luther)

God has not given us a spirit of fear,
but of power and of love and of a sound mind.
—2 Timothy 1:7 NKJV

Word of God, O sacred treasure!
  Sage and shepherd, king and priest,
Moved by God's own Holy Spirit,
  Brought to men thy wondrous feast.

Word of God, Word of God,
  Heaven's light abides in thee;

Through sin's darkness all abroad,
   Word of God, shine gloriously...

Word of God, thy theme is Jesus,
   Jesus and His dying love,
How from sin He fully frees us,
   How He points to realms above.

Word of God, thy open pages
   Call to service, banish fear;
None can idle be, or listless,
   If thy great commands they hear.

—"Word of God, O Sacred Treasure,"
  by William M. Runyan (1870–1957)

Perfect Love Casts Out Fear

Fear is a given. All men fear. General George Patton said: "If we take the generally accepted definition of bravery as a quality which knows no fear, I have never seen a brave man. All men are frightened. The more intelligent they are, the more they are frightened."

In the movie *The Last Full Measure*, which is about Medal of Honor recipient Airman First Class William "Pits" Pitsenbarger, there is this piece of wisdom: "Fear is good. It's a survival instinct. You're supposed to be afraid." Fear is a normal part of battle, but it can and must be overcome.

Pitsenbarger flew on almost three hundred rescue missions during the Vietnam War, serving as a US Air Force

Pararescueman (PJ). On his last mission, he "waved off" a damaged helicopter (so that it could make an emergency landing away from enemy forces) and stayed with a US Army unit that was surrounded, cut off, and taking heavy casualties. Pitsenbarger tended the wounded soldiers and fought in brutal close combat to protect the injured under his care even though he was wounded three times. The next day they found his body, one hand grasping a rifle and the other clutching his medical aid bag.

I wrote in my book *On Killing* about how medical personnel in combat draw their strength and courage in a unique manner, motivated from a powerful drive to protect.

> But they take not their courage from anger
>   That blinds the hot being;
> They take not their pity from weakness;
>   Tender, yet seeing.
>
> They endure to have eyes of the watcher
>   In hell and not swerve
> For an hour from the faith that they follow,
>   The light that they serve.
>
> This light, in the tiger mad welter,
>   They serve and they save.
> What song shall be worthy to sing them
>   Braver than the brave?

—"The Healers," by Laurence Binyon, World War I veteran

Airman First Class William "Pits" Pitsenbarger truly embodies 1 John 4:18 (NKJV), "Perfect love casts out fear."

While fear is a warning mechanism telling you there is danger around, it is also something you need to control, lest it control you. Patton said, "The courageous man is the man who forces himself, in spite of his fear, to carry on."

You may not see it, but there is an epic spiritual battle going on all around us. On one side, Satan and his army are working tirelessly to deter you from following Jesus Christ. Satan knows that to neutralize you, all he needs to do is over-whelm you with fear. The devil knows that fear can drain you of hope and keep you from fulfilling God's purpose for your life. Fear can keep you from acting on your faith and opposing evil.

Fear comes in all shapes and sizes. It can look a lot like worry, despair, depression, or anxiety—all of which seem to be occurring in epidemic proportions today. Fear can look like a lot of things, but its greatest damage is its ability to alter our decision-making abilities.

Every decision you make based solely on fear will not be in accordance with God's will. Following Jesus requires that we arm ourselves with his Word, and with his Word comes his love and his courage and every other promise that is in the Bible. God's divine power, as revealed in his Holy Word, can empower us. The Bible promises us: "God has not given us a spirit of fear, but of power and of love and of a sound mind" (2 Timothy 1:7 NKJV).

The wicked, the faithless, and those who are weak in their faith all fear the devil and flee from him when he attacks. But "Perfect love casts out fear" (1 John 4:18 NKJV), and God's perfect love empowers us. One of our spiritual superpowers is to receive the authority to use God's Word. If we face the devil with this God-given weapon, he will flee.

The Word of God

In *On Spiritual Combat*, we learned about the "Full Armor of God" from Ephesians chapter six. And one major part of that powerful panoply of spiritual warfare, the "basic issue" that we received upon enlistment into God's army, can be found in Ephesians 6:17, "the sword of the Spirit, *which is the word of God.*" The Word of God is a sword in our hand. It is "alive and powerful. It is sharper than the sharpest two-edged sword" (Hebrews 4:12 NLT). It is our Father's sword. It is that fateful, terrible, swift, lightning casting, +5 vorpal Sword of the Spirit!

Satan is no match for the Lord your God who loves you, and his Son Jesus Christ who died for you, and the Holy Spirit who indwells within you as a believer. We wield God's Word. It is our Father's sword. And we call upon his promise, in his Holy Word, to give us love and empathy and courage, through our Lord Jesus Christ, who manifested the ultimate in love and courage when he died for our sins.

Look again at the powerful words of the beautiful old hymn at the beginning of this section:

Word of God, thy open pages
    Call to service, banish fear;
None can idle be, or listless,
    If thy great commands they hear.

Amen, dear Lord!

We hold up God's Word, and we call upon God's divine power to banish all fear.

Luther tells us that "the wicked flee from the Devil." Like rabbits scrambling away from the devouring lion, so does the world flee the evil one. We who are in Christ belong to God, and he who is in us is far greater than he who is in the world (1 John 4:4). So *resist* the devil in God's power, and *he* will flee from *you*!

Now, let us look at some specific applications of using God's Holy Word at the moment of truth.

> Word of God, O sacred treasure!
>   Sage and shepherd, king and priest,
> Moved by God's own Holy Spirit,
>   Brought to men thy wondrous feast.

WARNING #10: Next Level Battle Prep

- ➤ What does human spiritual defeat look like in our earthly lives?

- ➤ What is Satan's weakness or greatest fear?

- ➤ How can we mortals defend ourselves against dark forces?

- ➤ How can we mortals defeat Satan in the realm of spiritual warfare?

TENTH ORDER

SPIT, AS IT WERE, IN THE FACE OF DANGER

Keep a stirring Bible quotation with you for encouragement, so you may have courage through the Lord thy God.

(Erasmus)

The word of God is alive and powerful. It is sharper than the sharpest two-edged sword, cutting between soul and spirit, between joint and marrow. It exposes our innermost thoughts and desires.

—Hebrews 4:12 NLT

The Bible gives us instructions for building our faithful courage. In the movie *Saving Private Ryan*, the Army Ranger and sniper Daniel Jackson would say a prayer, Psalm 25:2 (KJV), prior to and during an engagement. I've outlined here, providing some interpretation and application:

> *O my God, I trust in Thee.*
> *(O Father, I am your humble servant.)*
> *Let me not be ashamed;*
> *(O Jesus, guide my actions.)*
> *Let not mine enemies triumph over me.*
> *(May the Holy Spirit protect me and my comrades*
> *from danger.)*

This is a great example of a stirring Bible quotation being used for *encouragement* and *courage* through the Lord our God. In fact, Psalm 25 appears to have inspired the Code of the Knights Templar:

- Be without fear in the face of your enemies.
- Stand brave and upright, that the LORD may love thee.
- Speak the truth always, even if it means your death.
- Protect the helpless and do no wrong.

This is what Erasmus means when he tells us to "spit" in the face of danger. And what is the danger? It is always the same three foes: the devil (and his demons), the world, and the flesh, and the only force that can stand up to these enemies is the "holy water" that we spit in the face of evil—the Word of God.

"Divine Words" and Words of Power

In popular books, like the *Harry Potter* series, we often read about "magic" words. We all know that *Harry Potter* is fiction. But that fiction is a faint reflection of the reality of the power in God's Word. C. S. Lewis referred to this as the "Deeper Magic" that exists in God, in the Holy Spirit working within us, and in God's Holy Word. Magic is considered to be an illusion or a power from dark sources. But Lewis says that there is *divinity* in God's Word, and this divinity is much deeper than mere magic.

Divinity refers to the very nature of God's being. In Christianity, divinity belongs to God alone. But God's divine gifts have "given unto us exceeding great and precious promises: that by these ye might be *partakers of the divine nature*" (2 Peter 1:4 KJV).

Wrap your mind around the fact that God's Word, the Bible, is literally *alive*! And truly *powerful*. As we just read at the opening of this order, the Bible tells us that "the word of God is *alive* and *powerful*." These are "divine words," real words of power. Here are a few examples of my favorites.

"Amen"

This is a powerful term of affirmation. One useful definition of this word is simply "truth" or "so be it." But it is also a one-word prayer that means, "May it be so, Lord," and "We call for God's blessing upon this," and "I second the motion!" and "I love it!" and "Well said!" It is the "Swiss Army Knife" of

God's divine words. (And, yes, it is the holy equivalent of the Army's "Hooah!" and the USMC's "Semper Fi!") There is just so much power in this one word.

Use it to weave God's holy power into your language and your life.

> Amen, every saint is voicing;
>> Amen, is our heavenly song;
> Amen, there for aye rejoicing;
>> Amen, in God's joyous throng;
> Amen! Life comes from above;
> Amen! God alone is love!

—"Amen, Be His Word and Spirit," by C. K. Solberg
(1872–1954)

As Pastor Jeff Wolf explains it, whenever Jesus says, "Truly I say to you," in Scripture, the original Greek actually uses the Hebrew word *amen*. Thus, Jesus is saying, "Amen I tell you," or "What I'm about to say is truth." Whereas Scripture uses the word *amen* at the end of a sentence, Jesus uses it at the beginning. Why? Because what he says is always truth and doesn't have to be proven as true.

One last note on "amen." My right-hand assistant in my office is Sgt. Kathy Cusack, a retired police sergeant and a sister sheepdog under the authority of the Great Shepherd. She tells the story of how one night as a young police officer, exhausted by long hours of shiftwork and overtime, she briefly nodded off in her parked police car. She awoke to notice another police car that had pulled up beside her, quietly keeping watch over her as she napped. She says she just said "Amen!" and lifted her head up.

Truly, the "Swiss Army Knife" of God's divine words. As one unidentified person wrote, "Satan saw me with my head down and thought he'd won. Until I said 'Amen.'"

"Wherever two or three are gathered..."

I use this a lot when people are concerned that the audience is too small or the turnout is not enough or *whenever* someone thinks there are not enough people. These words come immediately to my mind. "For where two or three have gathered together in My name, I am there in their midst" (Matthew 18:20 NASB). One person with God is always a majority.

"Praise God!"

The Bible tells us that God inhabits praise (Psalm 22:3 KJV). Think about that. God actually *dwells* within our praise for him. This phrase should be something that comes out of your mouth all the time. Praise God!

"The Lord rebuke you"

When the archangel Michael was in spiritual battle with the devil, disputing over the body of Moses, "he did not presume to pronounce a blasphemous judgment" but simply said, "The Lord rebuke you" (Jude 1:9 ESV).

Like the archangel Michael, tell the devil, "The Lord rebuke you." Say this when you feel tormented and taunted with thoughts of anger, desire, or envy. Say it when you feel that icy cold presence of Satan, when you must overcome fear as you walk through the valley of the shadow of death. *Spit* in the devil's face with these words that summon the Lord to your defense. Tell the devil that God's going to cut him down. "The Lord rebuke you!"

"Iron sharpens iron"

Ah! A personal favorite. Allow me to expand and expound on this one.

In May 2015, in Garland, Texas, Officer Greg Stevens killed two would-be mass-murderers. It was "the first ISIS directed attack on American soil," according to the FBI. These two domestic terrorists had rifles, body armor, the element of surprise, and the intent to inflict a devastating attack upon helpless, unarmed American citizens.

They rolled out of their vehicle, and Greg Stevens, a fifty-nine-year-old traffic cop armed only with a pistol, killed them both. It was one of the greatest acts of courage and marksmanship in American history. The enemies shot over thirty rounds of rifle fire at Greg, but none of the rounds hit their mark. Greg, however, consistently hit his opponents with accurate and devastating pistol fire. Greg tells his audiences, "I am a man of faith. I feel like God put his hand on my shoulder and said, 'I'll take care of you. But you need to take care of them.'"

I tell my own audiences that I have had the honor to speak together with Greg Stevens in front of many different groups of people. Working with that man is one of the greatest and most humbling experiences of my life. Greg often tells his audiences, "I tried to tell Colonel Grossman what an honor it is to work with him. He looked at me, and you know what he said? 'Iron sharpens iron.'"

Boom. No more need be said. *That* is the living spirit and power within God's words.

"As iron sharpens iron, so one person sharpens another" (Proverbs 27:17). In other words, "This is a two-ways street, and you are a blessing to me as well." It says, "May God strengthen our friendship and our relationship, as he promises to do in these powerful words." And it calls for God to bless our relationship with his almighty and amazing power, grace, and love.

These, of course, are just a few examples.

One last thing. In *Harry Potter* and other such fantasy, "magical power" only works for those who have the "gift." With God's Holy Word, the "power" only works for those who have accepted the "gift" of God's grace. In John 15:7 (KJV), Jesus said, "If ye abide in me, and my words abide in you, ye shall ask what ye will, and it shall be done unto you." Think about that. If we abide in Jesus, then his words can actually *abide, indwell,* and *live* in us. But, if we do not abide in Jesus, the situation is completely different.

The Bible tells us about some would-be exorcists who tried to use the name of Jesus but were not Christians. They said to some demons:

"In the name of the Jesus whom Paul preaches,
I command you to come out." …The evil spirit
answered them, "Jesus I know, and Paul I know
about, but who are you?" Then the man who
had the evil spirit jumped on them and over-
powered them all. He gave them such a beating
that they ran out of the house naked and bleeding. (Acts 19:13–16)

WARNORD Recap

Do you truly want to put the power of what C. S. Lewis
called "Deep Magic" in your life? Do you want to be triumphant in your spiritual warfare against the forces of evil? Then
transcend the silliness of *Harry Potter* by first accepting Jesus
as your Savior and then embracing the true power of God's
Holy Word.

Wield the Sword of the Spirit. Erasmus tells us to "Spit,
as it were, in the face of danger." Thus, we are prepared to
instinctively, reflexively "spit" God's Word into the very face of
fear and death and evil.

Word of God, Word of God,
    Heaven's light abides in thee;
Through sin's darkness all abroad,
    Word of God, shine gloriously.

Prayer of Thanks for God's Holy Word

> *Lord God, heavenly Father,*
> *we thank you for giving us*
> *your holy Gospel and*
> *revealing your love to us.*
> *In your boundless mercy,*
> *help us hold on to*
> *this blessed light of*
> *your Word, and*
> *through your Holy Spirit*
> *govern and guide our hearts,*
> *so that we may never stray from it,*
> *but hold fast to it and*
> *finally be saved;*
> *through your Son, Jesus Christ our Lord.*

—From *Pomeranian Agenda*, possibly by Johannes
Bugenhagen
(sixteenth century AD)

ORDER #10: Next Level Battle Prep

➤   Describe an instance when a "divine" word or
     prayer activated spiritual strength in your life.

➤   Have you memorized a "divine" word, Scripture,
     or verse that brings you comfort in moments of
     fear or danger? Please share it with the group or

make it a goal to find a divine verse that comforts your soul.

➢ Have you memorized a "divine" word, Scripture, or verse that prepares your soul for battle against dark forces? Please share it with the group or make it a goal to find a divine verse that empowers your soul.

ELEVENTH WARNING

THE WICKED CRAVE STATUS

If you become concerned with popularity and neglect your duty, it is easy enough to fall into sin.

(Luther)

WARNORD #11

ELEVENTH ORDER

GUARD AGAINST TWO DANGERS: MORAL COWARDICE AND PERSONAL PRIDE

Dedicate all your effort and all your tribute to Jesus Christ our Savior.

(Erasmus)

ELEVENTH WARNING

THE WICKED CRAVE STATUS

If you become concerned with popularity and neglect your duty, it is easy enough to fall into sin.

(Luther)

Pride goeth before destruction,
and an haughty spirit before a fall.
—Proverbs 16:18 KJV

When we walk with the Lord
in the light of His word,
what a glory he sheds on our way!
While we do His good will,

He abides with us still,
   and with all who will trust and obey…

Not a burden we bear,
not a sorrow we share,
   but our toil He doth richly repay;
not a grief or a loss,
not a frown or a cross,
   but is blest if we trust and obey…

Then in fellowship sweet
we will sit at His feet,
   or we'll walk by His side in the way;
what He says we will do,
where He sends we will go;
   never fear, only trust and obey.

Trust and obey,
   for there's no other way,
to be happy in Jesus,
   but to trust and obey.

—"Trust and Obey," by John H. Sammis (1846–1919)

Pride and the desire for popularity and prestige are powerful cravings that form the root of so many sins, even cowardice. The proud will often avoid moral issues because it could jeopardize their positions. Calling out sinfulness could lose a person's support. If you become concerned with appearance and neglect your duty, it is easy enough to fall into sin. Thus, pride does make man a coward.

Ironically, avoiding a moral issue will lose you the very thing you are trying to protect. Just think how many leaders have lost their good reputation because they covered up a problem. If only they had attacked the problem head on the first time they learned of it.

> Pride goeth before destruction, and an haughty
> spirit before a fall. Better it is to be of an humble
> spirit with the lowly, than to divide the spoil
> with the proud. He that handleth a matter wisely
> shall find good: and whoso trusteth in the LORD,
> happy is he. (Proverbs 16:18–20 KJV)

Reverend Franklin Graham said, "Heaven is not for cowards!" Pastor Graham was referring to Revelation 21:7–8 that put cowards in the same category as murderers and rapists. He said those who are afraid to address moral issues are no better than those who commit transgressions.

When you accept a position of authority, you have accepted an obligation to work toward the benefit of mankind in the name of God. None of us is perfect; indeed, that is why you must pray for God's help when you find yourself in a dilemma. Pray for courage and direction, and the Lord God will send the Holy Spirit to help you. This is the testing of your faith—your trust in God.

The Baptist Pastor Adrian Rogers once said, "A faith that hasn't been tested can't be trusted." Even Simon, who would become the apostle Peter, was tested. Jesus said, "Simon, Simon, behold, Satan demanded to have you, that he might sift you like wheat" (Luke 22:31 ESV).

To strengthen courage, you must exercise it, like a muscle. God allows trials so that we may exercise the faith he has given us. Knowing that trials are intended to make us stronger does not promise they will be painless. Trials require the believer to rely on God more than ever before. The Bible says:

> Consider it pure joy, my brothers and sisters,
> whenever you face trials of many kinds, because
> you know that the testing of your faith produces
> perseverance. Let perseverance finish its work
> so that you may be mature and complete, not
> lacking anything. (James 1:2–4)

> The LORD disciplines those he loves, as a father
> the son he delights in. (Proverbs 3:12)

Fame: A Bottomless Pit of Despair

We said in *On Spiritual Combat* that we must do good deeds as a living witness. Someone who needs Jesus is watching you, and it is far better to live the sermon than to preach it. We also do good by sharing the gospel (which means "good news") and through our personal testimony. And we do good deeds through spiritual warfare: our endeavors to fight evil, guided by our love for others.

But we emphasized that you must give the honor and glory to God for all these good deeds. God doesn't need the honor and glory. God wants us to give that to him because he loves us with a love and wisdom that is "to infinity and beyond" any such that we can comprehend here on earth, and God knows that if we seek fame and honor and glory for ourselves, it will ultimately lead to a tragic, unhappy, and empty life for us. Seeking status and feeding personal pride is an attempt to fill a bottomless pit, and ultimately that pit leads to hell and gives the devil mastery over your life.

No matter what level of fame you ever accomplish in life, there will always be something you did not do, somewhere that you failed, somehow that you fell short. The mightiest athletes and the most beautiful stars will inevitably despair as they grow old and their bodies fail them. The greatest mind will become feeble, and astounding achievements of art and writing will be eclipsed by others and attacked by critics.

Thus, we must focus on doing good deeds and giving the glory to God, for truly, all the good that we do is because God has equipped and empowered us. By giving God the glory, we are being honest and just, and by accepting his blessing we are beneficiaries of boundless love, abundant joy, perfect peace, and many other great blessings. "The fruit of the Spirit is love, joy, peace, longsuffering, gentleness, goodness, faith, meekness, temperance: against such there is no law" (Galatians 5:22–23 KJV).

Doing good works is part of our spiritual duty. Erasmus tells us, "God knoweth not the fool…empty of good works." Erasmus understood that good works are a necessary part of our spiritual warfare mission. Always remember that mission, the reason why we are here: to love God and love people. That means bringing people to the knowledge of salvation. And *that* means doing good deeds to bring honor and glory to God and to let our lives be a living witness. It is better to live the sermon than to preach it. Thus, we are commanded: "Bear ye one another's burdens, and so fulfil the law of Christ" (6:2 KJV).

This is "the law of Christ." The Bible commands us to share in the hardships of others. We must be like Jesus and sacrifice ourselves as worthy sheepdogs, living up to the standard of love and sacrifice established by our beloved Master. This is the meaning of "good works." Erasmus recognized that cowardice and pride are obstacles to good works, and the devil seizes on this.

Fear—He Is a Liar!

First, the devil attacks "like a roaring lion" (1 Peter 5:8). In nature, when the lion attacks, its first weapon is its roar, which can defeat its prey before the fangs and claws even come into play. The lion's roar is an amazing feat of nature, functioning at multiple frequencies and harmonics, designed to stun and paralyze its victims.

Like the roaring lion, the devil wants to intimidate and paralyze you with fear and self-doubt. He wants to stop you from moving forward in serving the Lord. And the devil has many "frequencies and harmonics of fear" at his disposal to intimidate the believer:

- Fear of being unworthy
- Fear of making mistakes
- Fear of being opposed
- Fear of taking leadership
- Fear of intimacy and trust
- Fear of being alone
- Fear of hard work
- Fear of death

A popular Christian song by Zach Williams says that "Fear, he is a liar!" Amen!

All fear is designed to deceive and defeat us, says Reverend A. B. Simpson: "Fear is born of Satan, and if we would only take time to think a moment, we would see that everything Satan says is founded upon a falsehood."

If fear does not work, the devil can always fall back on pride. Everything we have or achieved was given by God, but the devil will trick you into believing that you have accomplished everything on your own. Even if we do "great works," they are not "good works" if we do them for our own merit. In other words, anything that raises our own ego works to displace Jesus Christ in our heart, and this is deadly.

You may have also noticed that as pride increases, charity decreases. The proud heart thinks that everyone gets what they deserve. If the proud person has a lot of material possessions, it must be because they are superior to everyone else. If you have nothing, it must be because you are lowly and deserve to be without.

All pride is designed to deceive and defeat us, which is why we should follow Simpson's counsel: "God give us humility! I think it is the prayer we covet most, that God will keep our spirit lowly and broken."

The devil is relentless and ruthless. He will test you repeatedly, trying to wear out your moral resolve. What are your weaknesses and temptations? The devil knows! But God is not trying to break you. To the contrary, call to the Lord for strength and he will refine your faith. Isaiah 48:10 says, "See, I have refined you, though not as silver; I have tested you in the furnace of affliction."

The devil will subject you to what is most likely to make you fall. But how we prepare and react to wickedness is all part of building our godly armor. This was Jesus' hope for Simon: "I have prayed for you, Simon, that your faith may not fail. And when you have turned back, strengthen your brothers" (Luke 22:32). And this Simon did, becoming the leader of the early church (Acts 2).

Jesus has prayed for all of us that we may overcome when the devil tests our faith, and that we may be a helper to our fellow believers by standing up for the truth. Jesus is ready to help you—if you ask him to.

Trust and obey,
for there's no other way,
to be happy in Jesus,
but to trust and obey.

WARNING #11: Next Level Battle Prep

➤ How does Satan utilize *pride* or *fear* in his spiritual attacks on humans?

○ When have you overcome pride or fear?
○ When have you failed to overcome pride or fear?

➤ What is (or was) the *fear* or *pride* that prevented or delayed you from repenting your sins and serving God?

➤ How has your faith been tested since you repented?

ELEVENTH ORDER

GUARD AGAINST TWO DANGERS: MORAL COWARDICE AND PERSONAL PRIDE

Dedicate all your effort and all your tribute to Jesus Christ our Savior.

(Erasmus)

Whatever you do, whether in word or deed, do it all in the name of the Lord Jesus, giving thanks to God the Father through him.

—Colossians 3:17

Luther tells us that "the wicked crave status," and Erasmus orders us to "guard against moral cowardice and personal pride." This topic has been "double-tapped" and clearly emphasized for us by Erasmus and Luther—two great, godly men.

In Step with the Spirit

Reverend Albert Benjamin "A. B." Simpson (1843–1919) was a Scottish Presbyterian raised in the Puritan tradition. His special emphasis in ministry was Christ-centeredness and missionary evangelism. His books include *The Christ Life* and *In Step with the Spirit: Discovering the Dynamics of the Deeper Life.*

Like Erasmus, Benjamin recognized that moral cowardice and pride are threats to our salvation, but these sins could be overcome if we learned to dedicate all our efforts to Christ. "Whatever you do, whether in word or deed, do it all in the name of the Lord Jesus, giving thanks to God the Father through him" (Colossians 3:17).

While holding to the Holy Trinity, it was Jesus' sacrifice that saved humanity from eternal damnation: "He himself bore our sins in his body on the tree, that we might die to sin and live to righteousness" (1 Peter 2:24 ESV).

When Jesus was resurrected, the bond between the Holy Spirit and the Son of God was so strong, so exclusive that, as Jesus told his disciples, unless he ascended to heaven, the Spirit could not be released to fall upon the disciples: "Very truly I tell you, it is for your good that I am going away. Unless I go away, the Advocate will not come to you; but if I go, I will send him to you" (John 16:7).

Becoming Christ-Centered

On January 19, 1861, A. B. Simpson published "A Solemn Covenant: The Dedication of Myself to God." It starts with a Sinner's Prayer of confession, followed by a promise to be Christ-centered. Here are excerpts:

> Simpson's Sinner's Prayer: "O Thou everlasting and almighty God...my 'heart is deceitful above all things and desperately wicked,' and I would not pretend to trust to it; but Thou knowest that I have a desire to dedicate myself to Thee for time and eternity."

> Simpson's Vow of Obedience: "I am now a soldier of the cross and a follower of the Lamb, and my motto from henceforth is 'I have one King, even Jesus.' Support and strengthen me, O my Captain, and be mine forever."

But Simpson knew that becoming Christ-centered is not as simple as saying a Sinner's Prayer (which is the first step) or taking a vow of obedience (which is part of being consecrated). While the Bible says we are all priests (1 Peter 2:9), there is a pilgrimage that we must complete (a spiritual journey). Likewise, even after police officers are "sworn" or "commissioned," there are years of obstacles they must overcome before they lose their rookie status.

The Hero's Pilgrimage

If you examine popular action-adventure movies, you see that many follow the same process as spiritual transformation—a pilgrimage in which the hero must overcome fear and pride in his effort to defeat an evil enemy. Likewise, A. B. Simpson developed a fourfold Christ-centered gospel that maps the pilgrim's progress to consecration.

1. **The Calling:** Christ the Savior (Acts 4:12); we must be saved, and salvation is found in no one else but Jesus Christ.

2. **The Separation Process:** Christ the Sanctifier (1 Corinthians 1:30); we must be separated from sin and connected to God by studying and following Jesus Christ.

3. **The Transformation:** Christ the Healer (John 14:12); anyone who has developed faith in Jesus will also do great things.

4. **The Victory:** Christ the coming King (Revelation 20); while the battle wears on, keep faith, for the Lord is returning in full victory over death and the devil.

The pilgrimage is available to everyone, especially to those who have been humbled by the hardships that the world inflicts on the faithful. Many action-adventure movies echo this holy process because it is real and compelling and because God has placed a deep-seated yearning within each of us to follow this path.

You will find in the movies a pale reflection of godly reality, that the hero is not the powerful, successful character (that is usually the bad guy). The hero turns out to be the person who has experienced loss and failure but overcomes himself and then overcomes evil. A. B. Simpson said it clearly: "God is not looking for extraordinary characters as His instruments, but He is looking for humble instruments through whom He can be honored throughout the ages."

The Bible tells us it is much more difficult to save a person who is full of pride and self-confidence. God seeks the humble to be his servants.

> Thus says the LORD: "Let not the wise man glory in his wisdom, let not the mighty man glory in his might, nor let the rich man glory in his riches; but let him who glories glory in this, that he understands and knows Me, that I am the LORD, exercising lovingkindness, judgment, and righteousness in the earth. For in these I delight," says the LORD. (Jeremiah 9:23–24 NKJV)

Step I: The Calling – Invitation to the Thirsty

The first step in the pilgrimage is to accept Jesus Christ as your Savior. God's invitation to the sinner is also called an "invitation to the thirsty" (Isaiah 55). Jesus referred to this passage from Isaiah when he cried out, "If anyone thirsts, let him come to Me and drink" (John 7:37 NKJV).

A. B. Simpson said: "God summons you to your knees. The very trial that has come upon you is His loving discipline, and He is bidding you seek His face and turn to His mercy before some greater calamity shall make it too late to pray."

As a young man, Simpson was profoundly influenced by the Puritan pastor Walter Marshall, who wrote *The Gospel Mystery of Sanctification* (1692), which said, "The first good work you will ever perform is to believe in the Lord Jesus Christ."

God calls upon you, but you must answer. "What meanest thou, O sleeper? arise, call upon thy God" (Jonah 1:6 KJV). The calling of the Holy Spirit will go away if left unanswered. Marshall says, "Believing on Christ, is a work that will require diligent endeavor and labor," but if you pray consistently, "praying at all times in the Spirit" (Ephesians 6:18 ESV), you will be empowered "so that Christ may dwell in your hearts through faith" (3:17).

So let the learning begin, and let the separation from sin start. Allow yourself to become one with the Lord:

> Thus saith the LORD…Call unto me, and I will answer thee, and show thee great and mighty things, which thou knowest not. (Jeremiah 33:2–3 KJV)

> Give ear and come to me; listen, that you may live. (Isaiah 55:3)

Step 2: The Separation – Practicing Christ's Presence

Simpson said that "separation" was God's strategy where the sinner would accept the Spirit and become an active servant of Christ. But separating oneself from sin and becoming connected to God isn't easy, and the pilgrim should expect to work hard at this process.

Learning to trust God is a vigorous process of growth, of insight into learning who he is, through his Son, Jesus Christ. It is not a reliance on a particular outcome in the human sense, for God's ways are not our ways: "'For my thoughts are not your thoughts, neither are your ways my ways,' declares the LORD. 'As the heavens are higher than the earth, so are my ways higher than your ways and my thoughts than your thoughts'" (Isaiah 55:8–9).

Becoming Christ-centered is often referred to as "practicing the Lord's presence." It means to develop awareness that God is always with you, always watching you.

You must undertake every action in full awareness that the Lord is watching and is available to guide you if you just ask. The Bible uses language such as "abiding" or "remaining" in Christ (John 15:4), "walking" with God (Deuteronomy 5:33), or keeping "in step with the Spirit" (Galatians 5:25). Simpson tells us this process can be difficult:

> Abiding [in Christ] must be established by a succession of definite acts of will, and of real, fixed, steadfast trust in Christ. It does not come as a spontaneous and irresistible impulse that carries you whether you will or not, but you have to begin by an act of trust, and you must repeat it until it becomes a habit. It is very important to realize this.

God often uses the cauldron of adversity to forge Christ-centered character in us. For when we face adversity, we are more likely to call on the Lord for assistance, and the more we call on God, the more likely it is to become a holy habit. Elsewhere Simpson writes: "Cultivate the habit of constant dependence. In everything let it be, 'Not I, but Christ,' until at last it becomes so natural that you do it without thinking, that almost mechanically you will find yourself saying, 'Jesus for this, What shall I do, Lord?'"

Satan knows that believers have the potential to oppose him, but he also knows that many people are too lazy to train for the faith. Satan is constantly searching for a weakness in you. If the devil sees that *fear* or *pride* controls an area of your life, he will continue to press into that area until it becomes a stronghold for demons.

In Psalm 29:1–2, David tells his demons: "Ascribe to the Lord, you heavenly beings, ascribe to the Lord glory and strength. Ascribe to the Lord the glory due his name; worship the Lord in the splendor of his holiness." David was an obvious target of evil supernatural forces—demonic forces at work in the world. He came to understand that he had no power against these forces aside from God. So David ordered his tormentors to "Ascribe to the Lord!" Then David warned his demons, "The voice of the Lord strikes with flashes of lightning" (v. 7). So demons beware!

With God's help, the trials or tests that the pilgrim undergoes in the separation process root out their own weaknesses and builds a connection to the Holy Spirit that proves to be much more powerful than the darkness. "The light shines in the darkness, and the darkness has not overcome it" (John 1:5).

Step 3: The Transformation – Setting the Example

The *transformation* requires the pilgrim to prove himself worthy and receive a final consecration or blessing. The pilgrim must show he is unselfish and brave.

Atonement refers to the necessary reconciliation between sinful mankind and the holy God, which was accomplished by Jesus Christ when he died for our sins (Romans 5:9–11). Only Jesus, the Son of God, could pay the hefty price for our sins, and he paid the price in full:

> Christ paid the price to free us from the curse
> that the laws in Moses' Teachings bring by
> becoming cursed instead of us. Scripture says,
> "Everyone who is hung on a tree is cursed."
> Christ paid the price so that the blessing promised to Abraham would come to all the people
> of the world through Jesus Christ and we would
> receive the promised Spirit through faith. (Galatians 3:13–14 GW)

How do we respond to this great gift? How do we accept it? As followers of Christ, we must set the example of being one with God: "Whoever is united with the Lord is one with him in spirit" (1 Corinthians 6:17). "On that day you will realize that I am in my Father, and you are in me, and I am in you" (John 14:20).

There is much to be ashamed of if we trample on God's gifts and set a poor example. After David had committed adultery with Bathsheba and arranged for her husband to be killed, the prophet Nathan rebuked David. Consider Nathan's indictment: "You have shown utter contempt for the LORD" (2 Samuel 12:14). David's sinfulness reflected poorly on the God he claimed to serve. This brought severe punishment to David, and he needed to restore his commitment to God. This required repentance and renewed obedience.

David's sins were great, but he was sincere in his repentance. Eventually, God forgave him, and Scripture frequently refers back to David as an example to other kings. For example, God said to King Jeroboam, "You have not been like my servant David, who kept my commands and followed me with all his heart, doing only what was right in my eyes" (1 Kings 14:8).

If David can be restored, so can we. Simpson said, "If our healing is provided for by Jesus Christ (1 Peter 2:24), then it is a redemption right which we may humbly yet boldly claim while walking obediently with the Lord." It is a gift of grace, it is a "right," and it "must be received wholly in His name, and in such a manner that He shall have all the glory." This is Christ-centeredness.

While pilgrims will make mistakes and need correction during the transformation process, they must never give up, always returning to God. Knights may get knocked down, but they return to their feet, brush themselves off, and carry on. God blesses the diligent! "Therefore, my dear brothers and sisters, stand firm. Let nothing move you. Always give yourselves fully to the work of the Lord, because you know that your labor in the Lord is not in vain" (1 Corinthians 15:58).

Step 4: The Victory – Trust and Obey the Lord

David began as a shepherd who believed in the almighty God and that, through him, he was an heir of the covenant God had made with Abraham and with Moses and Israel. God chose David to be king because David had a good heart. There was an innocence about him and a desire to do good works.

Even after much training and being consecrated, David faced temptations and numerous challenges in life. Throughout this experience, the prophet Samuel advised him. Still, David experienced doubts, despair, failure, and heartbreak. But he got back on his feet and succeeded when he finally surrendered himself completely to God. Trusting God means transferring your confidence and hope from yourself to him. Only when we fully put our trust in Jesus Christ are we one with the personal power who created the universe and sustains it by his word. Paul urges us, "Since, then, you have been raised with Christ, set your hearts on things above, where Christ is, seated at the right hand of God. Set your minds on things above, not on earthly things" (Colossians 3:1–2).

Serving the Lord may prove difficult at times. Sometimes we "think" we've lost contact with the Spirit; we second guess our mission or feel we have completely failed. When King David felt that God had abandoned him, he refocused: "I will remember the deeds of the LORD; yes, I will remember your miracles of long ago. I will consider all your works and meditate on all your mighty deeds" (Psalm 77:11–12).

David finally realized that he had created the expectations, and it was not God who failed to respond. By this time in his life, David had made many mistakes, and his feelings of guilt haunted him. His prayer says, "I will remember the deeds of the LORD." David reminded himself of all the miracles God had already performed, of all the times that God had used David as his instrument. God does not abandon his servants, and David reminded himself of that.

This prayer is a confession, a renewal of David's repentance:

> I cry aloud to God, aloud to God, that he may
> hear me. In the day of my trouble I seek the
> Lord; in the night my hand is stretched out
> without wearying; my soul refuses to be comforted. I think of God, and I moan; I meditate,
> and my spirit faints. Thou dost hold my eyelids
> from closing; I am so troubled that I cannot
> speak. (vv. 1–4 RSV)

A Christian knows, because of God's promise, that the Spirit never leaves or fails us. The spiritual struggle is part of growth, and the end result will be a strengthened faith and victory through Christ.

So when you are fighting for the Lord and the devil seems to be winning, just say, *This is really testing me, but with your help, Lord, I will make it.* Victory will come when you pray: *God, take control of my life.* God calls on us to let him be our Supreme Commander in spiritual warfare, to follow his lead, to do his work. That requires effort from us. We are not mere watchers but doers: "Get going with God."

WARNORD Recap

In all the hero accounts in Scripture, there are times when the devil triumphs in one of the battles, and the faithful person fails to do their duty. The devil, that great "accuser" who accuses us day and night (Revelation 12:10), wants us to burn for our transgressions—because that will be the devil's own punishment.

But unlike the devil who rejected God, the Lord sees redemption in humans. We have an advocate in Jesus Christ. An "advocate" denotes one who speaks for us, one who is at our side, and our helper (1 John 2:1). When we fail, the Lord finds a way to correct the mistake, like a father who corrects a child. We should accept this correction with gratitude as members of God's family.

> Endure your discipline. God corrects you as a
> father corrects his children. All children are dis-
> ciplined by their fathers. If you aren't disciplined
> like the other children, you aren't part of the
> family. On earth we have fathers who disci-
> plined us, and we respect them. Shouldn't we
> place ourselves under the authority of God, the

father of spirits, so that we will live? For a short
time our fathers disciplined us as they thought
best. Yet, God disciplines us for our own good
so that we can become holy like him. We don't
enjoy being disciplined. It always seems to cause
more pain than joy. But later on, those who
learn from that discipline have peace that comes
from doing what is right. (Hebrews 12:7–11 GW)

So, we will walk our hero's path. We will take the pilgrimage set before us, knowing the end of the story is sweet
victory in Jesus and blessed eternity in heaven.

Then in fellowship sweet
we will sit at His feet,
    or we'll walk by His side in the way;
what He says we will do,
where He sends we will go;
    never fear, only trust and obey.

Trust and obey,
    for there's no other way,
to be happy in Jesus,
    but to trust and obey.

A Soldiers' Prayer

O GOD our Father!
Wash us from all our sins in the Savior's blood,
   and we shall be whiter than snow.
Create in us a clean heart,
     and fill us with the Holy Ghost,
  that we may never be ashamed
  to confess the faith of Christ Crucified,
  and manfully to fight under His banner,
  against sin, the world, and the devil.
Looking to Jesus the great Captain of our
salvation,
  we ask it all, because He lived, died, rose again,
  and ever liveth to make intercession for us.
Amen.

—Unknown author, *Soldier's Prayer Book* (ca. 1863)

Order #11: Next Level Battle Prep

➤ When have you been "called" by the Spirit?

- ○ Share this experience.
- ○ Share "your" Sinner's Prayer.

➤ When were you "separated" from sin?

- ○ Write down your Sinner's Prayer in your notes or journal.
- ○ In the same place, describe how you became Christ-centered.

➤ When have you experienced the "transformation"?

- ○ How were you consecrated?
- ○ How did you make atonement?
- ○ What obstacles did you face?

➤ When did you truly trust and obey the Lord?

- ○ How do you demonstrate this trust and obedience in your life?
- ○ How do you fail to do so? What causes you to fail?

TWELFTH WARNING

THE WICKED ARE WEAK-MINDED

The conscience of the wicked is shattered and confused and retains neither faith nor works.

(Luther)

WARNORD #12

TWELFTH ORDER

TURN YOUR WEAKNESS INTO STRENGTH

Delight in weaknesses, in insults,
in hardships,
in persecutions, and difficulties.
Pray to Christ and say: "Lord, increase
my faith."

(Erasmus)

TWELFTH WARNING

THE WICKED ARE WEAK-MINDED

The conscience of the wicked is shattered and confused and retains neither faith nor works.

(Luther)

Of them the proverbs are true: "A dog returns to its vomit," and, "A sow that is washed returns to her wallowing in the mud."
—2 Peter 2:22

Faith is a living pow'r from heav'n
   That grasps the promise God hath giv'n,
A trust that cannot be o'erthrown,
   Fixed heartily on Christ alone.

Faith finds in Christ whate'er we need
   To save or strengthen us indeed,

Receives the grace He sends us down,
    And makes us share His cross and crown…

We thank Thee, then, O God of heav'n,
    That Thou to us this faith hast giv'n
In Jesus Christ, Thy Son, who is
    Our only fount and source of bliss.

And from His fullness grant each soul
    The rightful faith's true end and goal:
The blessedness no foes destroy,
    Eternal love, and light, and joy.

—"Faith Is a Living Power," by Petrus Herbertus (1530–1571),
    translated by Catherine Winkworth (1827–1878)

The New York City Police Department is the largest police department in the United States. The problems and the progress that NYPD have experienced is a history of the professionalization of all law enforcement over the last hundred years.

Unfortunately, the 1960s was a time when the flow of money through drugs, gambling, and prostitution had corrupted many police agencies. Crooked cops became the norm rather than the exception. As such, they came under the indictment that Moses brought against God's covenant people: "They have acted corruptly against Him, They are not His children, because of their defect; but are a perverse and crooked generation" (Deuteronomy 32:5 NASB).

"Crooked" is used in the Bible to describe all manner of betrayal, corruption, and hypocrisy, even apostasy. The

German theologian Max Scheler describes an *apostate* as someone who was once a Christian but now rejects Christ. In a similar way, crooked cops are *apostates* in that they once followed "the way" but now they violate the laws they once enforced. They willfully undermine and destroy the very thing they were entrusted to protect.

In 1970, the mayor of New York appointed the Knapp Commission to study the problem of police corruption. The result of the study described five types of police officer (three crooked, two faithful):

1. **Rogues:** extremely crooked cops who are willing to use violence to perpetrate all manner of crimes. Some say rogues are psychopaths who have somehow infiltrated law enforcement. Spiritually speaking, this is the person who does not understand the Word of God and follows Satan (Matthew 13:19).

2. **Meat Eaters:** corrupt cops who seek out situations where they can steal and shake-down bookies, drug dealers, and pimps. This is analogous to the person who hears the Word of God but quickly forgets it (vv. 20–21).

3. **Grass Eaters:** corrupt cops who take payoffs and bribes to look the other way. This is similar to the person who hears the Word, but the deceitfulness of wealth makes the Word unfruitful (v. 22).

4. **Straight Shooters:** honest officers who are dedicated to serving the public and refuse to work with corrupt police officers. This is like the person who hears the Word and understands it and produces a good crop (v. 23).

5. **White Knights:** officers who are straight shooters who eventually decide to make a stand against police corruption. They pull out the weeds planted by the devil by exposing "the people of the evil one" (vv. 37–43).

Serpico, the Straight Shooter

In 1959, Frank Serpico joined the New York City Police Department. As an officer, Serpico was a good, hardworking "straight shooter." In 1967, he was promoted to detective in a plainclothes vice unit. After he observed cops taking payoffs, it became obvious to Serpico that the entire plainclothes unit was involved in taking payoffs from drug dealers, gambling rackets, and pimps. The conscience of the detective bureau had become wicked, shattered, and confused, retaining neither faith nor works.

Being a straight shooter, Serpico sought a transfer out of the vice unit but was denied. Serpico then brought the corruption to the attention of superior officers. One top commander told Serpico to look the other way. He even went so far as to warn Serpico that he risked being found "floating dead in the East River" if he persisted. The problem was that many of the high-ranking officers were also benefiting from the corruption, which obviously deterred straight shooters from coming forward. Serpico just kept doing his job, even arresting people who were expecting "protection" from the police.

Frustrated, Serpico confided his situation to another honest detective, who contacted the City's Commissioner of Investigations. Sadly, someone leaked Serpico's name, which placed his life in peril.

On April 25, 1970, the *New York Times* printed a story on police corruption. Public outcry forced Mayor Lindsey to appoint a panel known as the Knapp Commission, and Serpico was pressured to be the primary informant.

Serpico, the White Knight—Why Me?

Serpico now faced a tough moral dilemma. He was a straight shooter, but the Knapp Commission wanted him to become a white knight. The problem with this was that Serpico didn't trust the NYPD command officers to cover his back. After all, the command officers were part of the corruption.

Then on February 3, 1971, while working undercover on a narcotics investigation, Serpico was shot in the face with a .22 pistol. The bullet struck just below the eye, lodging in his jaw. Serpico's police colleagues suddenly disappeared and never made a 10-13 request for assistance over the radio, indicating that an officer had been shot. The circumstances surrounding Serpico's shooting quickly came into question.

Fortunately, there was someone in an adjacent apartment who reported that an officer had been shot. One squad car arrived after hearing it was a narcotics officer (but Serpico's name was not attached to the incident). The officers transported him in the patrol car to Greenpoint Hospital. While in the hospital, the department called Serpico every two hours, conducting "welfare checks," both day and night, harassing him. The shooting and harassment made Serpico feel cornered. He must have thought to himself, *Why me?* When we ask that question, God's answer can be found in his Holy Word: "You have been set apart as holy to the LORD your God, and he has chosen you" (Deuteronomy 14:2 NLT).

By no intention or design of his own, circumstances had put Serpico front and center of the Knapp Commission hearing. God had apparently chosen Serpico to take down the entire criminal network within the New York Police Department. How daunting! Serpico must have felt betrayed and alone.

Alpha reader Gregory Guevara points out that it is at such times when we can always turn to the example of Job in the Bible. When Job had lost everything and was abandoned by his friends, he prayed: "Though [God] slay me, yet will I trust Him" (Job 13:15 NKJV). In the midst of our most difficult trials, we may feel abandoned, but this is when God is most powerful—if we will just trust him. Remember when David defeated the massive Philistine Goliath? David always had faith that God was with him.

As for the wicked, the book of Proverbs tells us, "As a dog returns to its vomit, so fools repeat their folly" (26:11), and Luther says that they return to their ways because "the wicked are weak-minded." But Erasmus tells us that the righteous "delight...in hardships and difficulties" and have faith that God has put them here "for such a time as this" (Esther 4:14).

Serpico had to make a choice: quit the NYPD and go into hiding or testify before the Knapp Commission. Serpico said his father always told him, "Never run when you are right." We'll tell the rest of Serpico's story in the Twelfth Order, which is coming up next.

WARNING #12: Next Level Battle Prep

➢ Describe the types of police officers that Detective Frank Serpico was forced to work with:

- ○ Rogues
- ○ Meat Eaters
- ○ Grass Eaters
- ○ Straight Shooters
- ○ White Knights

➢ What was Serpico's first reaction to being surrounded by corruption?

➢ What does God expect of us when we are faced with difficulties?

TWELFTH ORDER

TURN YOUR WEAKNESS INTO STRENGTH

**Delight in weaknesses, in insults,
in hardships,
in persecutions, and difficulties.
Pray to Christ and say: "Lord, increase
my faith."**

(Erasmus)

The apostles said to the Lord,
"Increase our faith!"
—Luke 17:5

On December 14, 1971, Serpico testified before the Knapp Commission. He was the first NYPD officer to testify openly about widespread corruption. Serpico refused to "rat" on low-ranking police officers at the hearing, describing them as "a few flunky cops dumped to the wolves." He feared that the low-ranking officers would become sacrificial lambs to protect high-ranking commanders. Serpico believed corrupt management should be held responsible for the "rotten barrel." The source of the corruption and cover-up was the police "bosses."

Deaf in one ear from the shooting, Serpico took a disability retirement on June 15, 1972, one month after receiving the NYPD's highest honor, the Medal of Honor, for being shot in the line of duty (not for standing up to corruption). Serpico said: "They handed the Medal of Honor to me over the counter like a pack of cigarettes. They never even had a ceremony for me."

We must understand that the world will seldom honor our works when we take a stand against evil, sin, and human folly. We will never truly find on earth our blessed assurance, our reward, and our peace because we store up our treasures in heaven (Matthew 6:20).

Serpico as Martyr

St. Augustine (354–430) said, "It is not the pain but the *purpose* that makes a martyr." And indeed, Serpico's purpose was always to do his job honestly, and he did not give in to the corruption that others were trying to force on him. But Serpico did endure the pain of being ostracized by his fellow officers and then being shot by an attempted assassin.

St. John Fisher's (1469–1535) description of a martyr may best describe Serpico's situation: "A good man is not a perfect man; a good man is an honest man, faithful and unhesitatingly responsive to the voice of God in his life." While Serpico may not consider himself a martyr, we think he would agree that in all his actions, he was just trying to be a good man. In this sense, we think Serpico deserves to be called a martyr in the cause of police professionalism.

No command officers were ever charged in the corruption that plagued NYPD during the seventies. However, in 1973, Al Pacino documented this saga in the movie *Serpico*. The impact of the movie was widespread across the country, and governments took a harder look at police operations and internal affairs. The reorganization of police departments to make corruption more difficult became known as the "Serpico Effect."

Thanks to Frank Serpico and the many white knights whom he inspired, police corruption is now a much smaller problem, and departments can quickly address it when it surfaces.

And what about crooked cops? Having been taught in "the way" and sworn to serve as a sheepdog, becoming "crooked" means a cop betrays the badge, the oath, and God himself when he or she becomes a servant of Satan. Can crooked cops ever redeem themselves? The Bible says, "What is crooked cannot be made straight, and what is lacking cannot be counted" (Ecclesiastes 1:15 ESV). The law states that "decertification" is permanent, and a crooked cop can never be trusted to serve as a police officer again. Rather than give in to what's wrong, we should heed the ancient wisdom expressed in Proverbs: "Guard your heart above all else, for it determines the course of your life" (4:23 NLT).

Pray for More Faith

When Christ defeated the devil on Calvary, he gave us the "divine power to demolish strongholds" (2 Corinthians 10:4). The Serpico Effect is the power of one honest cop destroying corruption. We could also call it the Rosa Parks Effect, which began when one righteous woman said no more discrimination. Through her single act of defiance, she helped changed the world.

How is such change possible? It occurs when we follow Jesus by challenging whatever and whoever goes against him. Paul did this in his day, and he pointed out that other faithful followers did the same. He wrote, "We destroy arguments and every proud obstacle to the knowledge of God, and take every thought captive to obey Christ" (v. 5 RSV). The ability to do this comes through the power of Pentecost, the Christian holiday that celebrates the fiftieth day after Easter Sunday. It celebrates the Holy Spirit descending upon the followers of Jesus Christ. "In the last days, God says, I will pour out my Spirit" (Acts 2:17). We tear down obstacles and challenges to Christ and live to him by the same power—the Holy Spirit of God.

When we see the Serpico Effect or the Rosa Parks Effect, we see the power of the Holy Spirit at work. Through him we face down evil. But even with him empowering us, the fight is never easy. When we engage in spiritual warfare against evil, sin, and human folly, we will inevitably find ourselves in situations where we may ask ourselves, *Why me?* At those times, we need to remind ourselves of the answer: because God has chosen you (Deuteronomy 4:12) for just such a time as this (Esther 4:14). You are God's man or woman for the job, and he is with you to help you toward victory.

Author Jeff Wolf explains that all through Scripture, God calls on men and women to stand up to wickedness (even among his own chosen people). For example, compare Detective Serpico to the prophet Jeremiah. God commanded Jeremiah, "Tell them all this, but do not expect them to listen. Shout out your warnings, but do not expect them to respond" (Jeremiah 7:27 NLT). Jeremiah was hated by the people he was calling out. Later, he was even arrested and beaten for prophesying judgment on those who would not turn from their wickedness (20:2).

God uses the sheepdog to pass judgment on the wicked. And where does the sheepdog get the strength? What can the sheepdog do when he or she stands alone against a multitude of sinners? The solution is to pray for more faith. But how do we do that?

First, understand that "faith is the assurance of things hoped for, the conviction of things not seen" (Hebrews 11:1 ESV). Thus, we begin our quest for more faith by understanding that faith is unseen. It is *spiritual*, and as such, it comes not by our power but from God. We have said it before, but we can never really say it enough: you can and *should* pray for more faith. The disciples begged Jesus to "increase our faith" (Luke 17:5).

A man came to Jesus beseeching him to heal his son, and Jesus said, "All things are possible to him that believeth." The man replied in anguish, "Lord, I believe; help thou mine unbelief" (Mark 9:23–24 KJV), and Jesus immediately healed his son. All God requires of us is to ask him for more faith. God wants us to ask. He implores us to ask!

It is like that great old World War II song based on the actual event of Chaplain Howell M. Forgy, passing ammo on the *USS New Orleans* during the Japanese attack on Pearl Harbor, "Praise the Lord and Pass the Ammunition!"

Faith is our ammunition. Belief is a choice. Choose to believe, then plant your little seed of faith and ask for more faith. Jesus even describes faith as a seed: "If you have faith as small as a mustard seed, you can say to this mountain, 'Move from here to there,' and it will move. Nothing will be impossible for you" (Matthew 17:20).

The Bible tells us that we must all face hardships as part of our spiritual growth and as a part of spiritual warfare. But be assured, "God is faithful; he will not let you be tempted beyond what you can bear. But when you are tempted, he will also provide a way out so that you can endure it" (1 Corinthians 10:13). Again: We. Cannot. Do. It. Ourselves. Our feeble human faith has no power. But when we ask God, he gives us faith strong enough to meet any test.

Unfortunately, as Police Lt. David Kemp points out, "Cops almost never ask for help because it makes them look weak or incapable. Most of us don't have partners, and we have to become self-sufficient. This can sometimes take officers down a long dark road of becoming control freaks, pessimistic, and not trusting anyone. For Christian cops, asking for help, even from Jesus, can sometimes be a struggle." This can get worse with PTSD. Worst of all, it can play into the devil's strategy of placing a barrier between police and God.

Prepare Yourself

Jeff Wolf tells us that you must prepare yourself ahead of time. Many believers have failed to accomplish what God has put in their heart because they couldn't overcome the devil's roar: criticism, discouragement, and recrimination—to name but a few of his tactics. The way to prepare ahead of time is to *immerse yourself* in God's Word in the Bible. His holy Word is more powerful than anything the evil one can say. Focus your attention on God's Word, and it will neutralize the devil's roar as water quenches fire.

Wherever you are, you can find God's Word. His Bible is in most hotel rooms, it can be found on numerous apps and websites, and it's available to every prisoner or patient in every prison and hospital.

Often, the person who becomes famous for some heroic act or gains status (like Serpico) doesn't seek it or really want it. But it was an unavoidable product of what they have accomplished. That exposure makes you a priority target for the evil one. However, anything great that God wants to do through you will require you to step out of the shadows and trust him to be your shield (Psalm 28:7). If you can't overcome the roar of the wicked, you will get stuck on your journey to fulfill God's plan for your life. So focus on God's Word and ask for more faith.

This roar gets louder and more ferocious when you step out to do mighty deeds for God. If you want to accomplish God's great plan for your life, you must neutralize the roar ahead of time by studying the Bible. And then you won't be paralyzed by tactics the devil uses against you. The roar will become just another noise. You'll find that you can defeat the roar if you let God's Word and the faith that he provides protect you.

> Faith finds in Christ whate'er we need
> To save or strengthen us indeed,
> Receives the grace He sends us down,
> And makes us share His cross and crown.

WARNORD Recap

Remember, God's plan for you to ace the test is not always *your* plan. He may give you grace and faith to die "a noble death." We will all die, sooner or later, and (as C. S. Lewis puts it) "a noble death is a treasure which no one is too poor to buy." (More about that in the next WARNORD.) But we will still be victorious, even in death. Because "to live is Christ, and to die is gain" (Philippians 1:21 KJV).

Erasmus and the Bible both exhort us to "Consider it pure joy...whenever you face trials of many kinds" (James 1:2). Trials can benefit us, and we can work through them and even overcome them with our faith in the almighty God. So keep asking him to give you more faith. This may be one of the most important lessons in advanced spiritual warfare. In the face of any temptation or trial, our first response should be to ask for more faith, and we should rejoice and exult in the opportunity to gain more faith. "Praise the Lord and pass the ammunition!" And Jesus assures us, he *promises* us, that "My grace is sufficient for you, for my power is made perfect in weakness" (2 Corinthians 12:9).

In February 2022, fifty years after the Knapp Commission, eighty-five-year-old Frank Serpico was finally awarded the authenticated Medal of Honor certificate and properly inscribed medal. Mayor Eric Adams, also a retired police officer, presented it to him. Adams said, "Serpico's bravery inspired my law enforcement career." Frank Serpico was finally officially recognized by the NYPD.

Serpico, an Army veteran, would tell us to keep in mind that many a hero has died without recognition, forgotten to history. The Tomb of the Unknown Soldier at Arlington National Cemetery is dedicated to such heroes. Fortunately, it is God who knows all, remembers all, and stores your treasure in heaven "where thieves do not break in and steal. For…there your heart will be also" (Matthew 6:19–21). Life can be hard, but God is always good.

> Faith is a living pow'r from heav'n
>   That grasps the promise God hath giv'n,
> A trust that cannot be o'erthrown,
>   Fixed heartily on Christ alone.

Prayer for Steadfast Faith

Lord God, heavenly Father, we are poor,
*   miserable sinners.*
We know your will, but we are too weak to fulfill it.
*   Our flesh and blood hold us back,*
*   and our enemy the devil will not leave us*
*   in peace.*
*   Pour your Holy Spirit in our hearts,*
*   that with steadfast faith*
*   we may cling to your Son, Jesus Christ,*
*   find comfort in his passion and death,*
*   believe the forgiveness of sin through him, and*
*   in willing obedience to your will, lead holy lives*
*   on earth*
until, by your grace, we depart from this world of
*   sorrow*
*   and obtain eternal life;*
*   through your Son,*
Jesus Christ our Lord,
*   who lives and reigns with you and the*
*   Holy Spirit,*
one true God, now and forever.

—Veit Dietrich (1506–1549)

ORDER #12: *Next Level Battle Prep*

➤ Describe an incident in which you stood up for what was right (to do a work for God) and faced persecution for doing so (were spiritually attacked by dark forces).

- ○ What was at stake?
- ○ What motivated the enemy?
- ○ What were the techniques of the enemy?
- ○ Describe others who were aware of the situation. Were they afraid to help? Did anyone step forward in faith?
- ○ Did you turn to God for more faith?
- ○ What actions did you take? (Right? Wrong?)
- ○ Would you do anything differently? Why or why not?
- ○ How should you look at such challenges in the future?

THIRTEENTH WARNING

THE WICKED RETREAT FROM THE HEART OF BATTLE

The wicked flee and yet cannot escape.

(Luther)

WARNORD #13

THIRTEENTH ORDER

TREAT EACH BATTLE AS THOUGH IT WERE YOUR LAST

And you will finish, in the end, victorious!

(Erasmus)

THIRTEENTH WARNING

THE WICKED RETREAT FROM THE HEART OF BATTLE

The wicked flee and yet cannot escape.

(Luther)

The wicked flee when no man pursueth:
but the righteous are bold as a lion.
—Proverbs 28:1 KJV

The final trump we soon shall hear,
  The great white throne shall then appear,
Ten thousand angels round:
  Jehovah turns the moon to blood,
  Blows out the sun, consumes the flood,
And burns the solid ground.

Arise, ye nations, and come forth,
    From east and west, and south and north;
Behold, the Judge is come:
    What horror strikes the guilty breast,
    Compell'd to stand the solemn test,
And hear their final doom.

"Depart, ye cursed, down to hell
    With howling fiends for ever dwell,
No more to see my face:
    My gospel calls you have withstood,
    And trampled on my precious blood,
And laughed at offered grace."

—"The Final Trump We Soon Shall Hear,"
author unknown (ca. 1850)

The story of *Beowulf* is a Christian allegory, written in Old English sometime between AD 700 and 800. Its author is unknown, but scholars surmise that it was written by a monk, perhaps as a resource to help other monks convert Vikings to Christianity since the writer uses both Christian and pagan references.

As a Christian allegory, *Beowulf* hides a biblical lesson. Perhaps the poem is most like the Old Testament story of Samson. Samson was also blessed by God with great strength, "dedicated to God" from birth (Judges 13:5). Samson defeated armies and lions singlehandedly, all by the power of God.

Likewise, consider the battle between the warrior Beowulf and Grendel. The story portrays the monster Grendel as a descendant of Cain, the son of Adam and Eve. Cain murdered his brother, Abel, and was condemned by God to wander the earth, whereupon Cain fathered many corrupt descendants who spread evil on earth. Grendel, like Cain, was a cold-blooded murderer. The first recorded use of the expression "cold-blooded" was in 1608 by an English soldier in his military commentaries. It means to be cold-blooded like a reptile, committing acts of violence without remorse. Yet, the cold-blooded know full well what evil they do, for they flee when there is risk of being held accountable for their horrible acts.

Furthermore, Grendel was caught "red handed." The Scottish started using this expression in legal matters around 1432, referring to a criminal caught with blood on their hands from murder or poaching. The Scottish eluded to the fact that when the evidence is clear and guilt is undeniable, the "red handed" culprit always runs.

The Wicked Flee

The monster wrenched and wrestled with him
   but Beowulf was mindful of his mighty strength,
the wondrous gifts God had showered on him:
   He relied for help on the Lord of All,
on His care and favour. So he overcame the foe,
   brought down the hell-brute…
Grendel escaped,

> *But wounded as he was could flee to his den,*
> His miserable hole at the bottom of the marsh,
>> Only to die, to wait for the end
> Of all his days…
> Beowulf…
> had killed Grendel,
> Ended the grief, The sorrow, the suffering.

Here we see the wicked Grendel flee when no one pursues. But (and this is the key) Beowulf does not boast, and he does not take the credit. When Beowulf relates his battle with Grendel's mother, he states: "The fight would have ended straightaway if God had not guarded me."

Lt. David Kemp points out that criminals (the wicked) flee from the heart of a battle because it is evil's nature not to want to confront the forces of good, which come from God. Even the toughest criminals will run from the police after a crime or when caught red-handed. They ambush police when they know there will not be a fight. And they cry for mercy when captured, vowing never to break the law again.

But Beowulf gives the honor and glory to God. What an astounding response that must have been to the fierce, vainglorious Vikings listening to the story of Beowulf! Nothing could more powerfully communicate to them the power and authority of God as proven by the way this epic poem has survived across the centuries. Beowulf credits his strength and victories to God, and this is the standard that we see throughout the Old

Testament. "My flesh and my heart may fail, but God is the strength of my heart" (Psalm 73:26).

One proof of the divine nature of the Bible is that it does not give honor and glory to men. Unlike every other historical work, in the Bible, even the greatest of kings have their failures and embarrassments preserved for eternity. As we noted in WARNORD 5, this is an act which—under any other circumstance than God's divine protection—would have led to the deaths of the chroniclers, scribes, bards, and priests who dared to record and retell the failures of kings and rulers.

When the "wicked flee before us" (as they will ultimately, always, flee from God), we must never lose track of the fact that God gave us the victory. Jeremiah 9:23–24 says:

> Let not the wise boast of their wisdom or the
> strong boast of their strength or the rich boast
> of their riches, but let the one who boasts boast
> about this: that they have the understanding to
> know me, that I am the LORD, who exercises
> kindness, justice and righteousness on earth, for
> in these I delight.

We must never forget that *all* the good that we do, God has done through us (Isaiah 26:12). In other words, everything good that we do in life is because of God. Jesus said, "Very truly I tell you, the Son can do nothing by himself; he can do only what he sees his Father doing, because whatever the Father does the Son also does" (John 5:19). When the apostle Paul commented on his missionary work, he said, "It was not I but God who was working through me by his grace" (1 Corinthians 15:10 NLT). When you accept Jesus as your Savior, realize that God is in control of all your battles and all your victories.

On the other hand, everything evil we do in life is because of our own sin. This should be a humbling realization. At a funeral, it is right and proper to give all the credit for good works to God. We cannot even take credit for our own confession and repentance because it was all the influence of the Holy Spirit.

But, from a different perspective, while John Calvin strenuously defended salvation by grace alone, he directed believers to look at a person's good works as comfort and evidence that God has saved them.

In Isaiah 42:8 God proclaimed, "I am the Lord; that is My name! I will not yield my glory to another or my praise to idols." God went on to say, "For my own sake, for my own sake, I do this. How can I let myself be defamed? I will not yield my glory to another" (48:11).

God cannot and will not share his perfect righteousness and power with sinners and certainly not with the devil. And he will not share the glory with us either! God is not being arrogant. To the contrary, he is motivated by perfect love. He protects us from ourselves because in his great love and wisdom, God knows that it would be harmful for us to seek the glory and honor for ourselves. So "be careful not to forget the covenant of the LORD your God that he made with you" (Deuteronomy 4:23). God gives generously, but God cannot give credit to others. Praise God, and pray to him for instruction, correction, and power against dark forces.

Ultimately, the wicked will flee from the heart of the battle. Satan and his minions are cowards. Some evil men die while hiding from judgment in a cave or a bunker, like Saddam Hussein, Osama Bin Laden, or Adolf Hitler. Other evil men try to destroy innocence as they shoot into a crowd or commit suicide with a bomb strapped across their chest.

But the righteous will even jump on a grenade to save others. Every soldier and first responder risks not going home to their loved ones, all for the sake of saving someone they don't even know while the wicked use their anonymity to deceive and destroy the innocent. True courage and self-sacrifice will not be found in the ranks of evil. By their very selfish and sinful nature, Satan, his demons, and unrepentant sinners are all cowards destined to eternal defeat.

The wicked will flee from the power of God. As for the faithful, even if we are not physically triumphant, when we die, we know that we will win spiritually because our souls are safe in the hands of a loving Father.

Always remember to give the honor and glory to God. Like Beowulf, we do not boast. But we can take satisfaction in seeing the Lord defeat Satan and cast down the demons of the evil one!

Depart, ye cursed, down to hell
    With howling fiends for ever dwell,
No more to see my face:

My gospel calls you have withstood,
   And trampled on my precious blood,
And laughed at offered grace.

WARNING #13: Next Level Battle Prep

➤ What is the wicked nature of doing something "cold blooded"?

➤ How do the wicked react when caught "red handed"?

➤ Using Beowulf as an example, how should police dedicate their arrests and convictions of criminal perpetrators?

➤ What realization should humble even the most righteous police officer?

THIRTEENTH ORDER

TREAT EACH BATTLE AS THOUGH IT WERE YOUR LAST
And you will finish, in the end, victorious!
(Erasmus)

Then there will be great tribulation, such as has not been from the beginning of the world until now, no, and never will be.
—Matthew 24:21 ESV

The battle against evil is not without its peril. Ultimately, the wicked will flee, but it is entirely possible that we will die physically long before we see God's ultimate victory over evil. So while our souls and our eternal salvation are safe in God's hands, we must fight as if the souls of others—the souls of the unsaved—depend on it. Because they do!

The wicked flee from the heart of battle, but we must stand fast. Our courage, our self-sacrifice, our living witness in the heart of the battle, and the good deeds that we do in God's power, giving God the glory, will make us a beacon of light in the darkness, calling others to Christ. Erasmus reassures us, "Treat each battle as though it were your last and you will finish, in the end, victorious!"

Victory, in the spiritual sense, does not mean you will follow your own path to your own concept of success. But whether we live or die, we will be victorious if we dedicate our battles to the Lord. "If we live, we live for the Lord; and if we die, we die for the Lord. So, whether we live or die, we belong to the Lord" (Romans 14:8).

Fighting for the Lord means that we must make our tactics and goals for the Lord's honor and in service of his mission. We cannot allow ourselves to adopt the tactics of the devil just to ensure victory because that is exactly what the devil wants us to do.

Living in service to the Lord and dying in glory for the Lord means we will continue to belong to the Lord no matter what happens. Stand or fall, life and service or death and glory, we do it all for the honor of Jesus Christ and the glory of God.

A Soldier's Courage

When we serve the Lord, we must not hold back. We must be all in for our Supreme Commander. This way, we fight every battle as though it were our last.

Each of us serves God's purpose differently. It is entirely personal, just between you and God. Consider Private First-Class Desmond Doss, a United States Army Medic during World War II. Doss was working in a shipyard at the beginning of the war and was entitled to a military deferment. But he quit his job and joined the Army because he believed in what America was fighting for. However, Doss was also a Seventh-day Adventist and a pacifist, so he refused to take up arms under any circumstances. Consequently, the Army made him a medic, but his views on fighting did not endear him to his fellow soldiers.

Doss' fellow soldiers severely harassed him in basic training. They even threw shoes at him when he prayed. But Doss told his commanding officer, "Don't ever doubt my courage because I will be right by your side saving life while you take life."

Doss finally had a chance to prove himself when his unit landed on the island of Okinawa and fought in the battle at Hacksaw Ridge, a jagged cliff where Japanese soldiers had dug in and were waiting.

The battle was close combat, and one of the bloodiest fought in the Pacific during WWII. There were so many casualties and such intense fire that Doss had to crawl from one body to another. Doss says: "I was praying the whole time. I just kept praying, 'Lord, please help me get one more.'"

In all, Doss saved seventy-five soldiers while being wounded four times, including by a sniper's bullet that fractured his left arm and by shrapnel when he attempted to kick an enemy grenade away from his men.

Daniel 5:27 says, "Thou art weighed in the balances" (KJV), meaning that our service to God is not "weighed" as mortals judge service but measured by the individual's response to the Lord's grace. Some people give more to God than others, based on what they have to offer. Doss refused to fight with a gun, but his courage was remarkable.

A fellow soldier said, "It's as if God had his hand on [Doss'] shoulder. It's the only explanation I can give." Doss had indeed responded to the Lord's grace. He had gone all in for God!

While the Army, at first, did not appreciate Doss and his conscientious objector status, soon they came to recognize that he was a man who did not have "the spirit of fear; but of power, and of love" (2 Timothy 1:7 KJV). Doss is the only conscientious objector to ever be awarded the Congressional Medal of Honor. Likewise, in God's kingdom, those who seem unimportant or even a burden may become the most honored by the Lord.

> Jesus sat down opposite the place where the offerings were put and watched the crowd putting their money into the temple treasury. Many rich people threw in large amounts. But a poor widow came and put in two very small copper coins, worth only a few cents. Calling his disciples to him, Jesus said, "Truly I tell you, this poor widow has put more into the treasury than

all the others. They all gave out of their wealth; but she, out of her poverty, put in everything— all she had to live on." (Mark 12:41–44)

End Times?

When Erasmus talks about your "last battle," we can also view his words from the perspective of *the* last battle. That final battle, known as Armageddon, which will be won at the return of Jesus, falls under the theological category called eschatology. Eschatology is the field of theology that studies death, judgment, final events, and the ultimate destiny of mankind, individually and collectively. *Eschatology* literally means "the study of last things" and is often lumped under the phrase "end times."

One of the most important events in the end times will be Jesus' second coming. As God's sheepdogs, we should yearn for Christ to come again, like a faithful dog waiting at the door for his beloved master to come home from work. The very last lines in the Bible powerfully reflect this deep yearning. There we are told: "He which testifieth these things saith, Surely I come quickly. Amen. Even so, come, Lord Jesus. The grace of our Lord Jesus Christ be with you all. Amen" (Revelation 22:20–21 KJV). Thus, we see that—other than a final blessing— the last verse in the Bible is a promise that Jesus will come again "quickly." Those words of promise were uttered two thousand years ago, indicating that "quickly" is a relative term for our timeless God. With it, however, comes a heartfelt plea: "Even so, come, Lord Jesus." No matter when he finally returns, we should always look for it, expect it, and count on it—for it will happen one day.

Christians throughout the centuries have many times thought they were facing the last days and therefore looked for Jesus to come soon. But God's Word tells us that we cannot know when he is coming. "Therefore you also must be ready, for the Son of Man is coming at an hour you do not expect" (Matthew 24:44 ESV). And with his return will come his final judgment upon the living and the dead, for all will stand before him and be judged "according to their deeds" (Revelation 20:12–13 NASB). Someday we will all be held accountable. So if you haven't already, repent now! And sanctify your repentance with service pleasing to God.

There were people who thought the Roman Emperor Nero, the fall of Rome, and then the dark times that followed marked the end times. Then, in more recent history, Napoleon, World War I, World War II, and the Cold War were all thought by some to be the final battle leading to the end times and Jesus' triumphant return. The great, self-supporting tension of Christianity is that we must build our nation as though our grandchildren will have to live and die in it while we live our lives and walk our pilgrim's path as though we might all be called to the judgment seat of Christ at any moment. In archi-tectural terms, an arch is a self-supporting masonry or stone structure made possible by the mutual tension or dynamic force coming from each direction. The dynamic force of Christianity (the *tension* that sustains that great arc across thousands of years) is this need to build for the future while also anticipating Jesus' return at any time.

Jeff Wolf explains that we can think of this "great, self-supporting tension" as being *in* the world but not *of* the world. Before his crucifixion, Jesus asked the Father to protect his followers: "My prayer is not that you take them out of the world but that you protect them from the evil one. They are not of the world, even as I am not of it" (John 17:15–16). So be a sheepdog and fear not, for Jesus Christ himself has prayed for your heavenly protection. Your soul is safe.

The "keystone" is a wedge-shaped stone at the apex of the arch. This is the final piece put in place during construction, which locks all the stones into position and allows the arch to bear weight. Of course, Jesus is the keystone in our arch. And he tells us that we cannot know the time of his return. Indeed, you can make a very good argument that it would be *harmful* to the great, self-sustaining arch of Christianity across the centuries if we were to know the time of Christ's return.

Thus, the solution to the tension dilemma is simple. Fight every battle as though it were your last. This is true on a personal level and on a global level. And that means fighting every battle as though it were *the* final battle.

Eschatology and Distraction?

Paul reveals that "all Scripture is God-breathed and is useful for teaching, rebuking, correcting and training in righteousness, so that the servant of God may be thoroughly equipped for every good work" (2 Timothy 3:16–17). *All*

Scripture is "useful." And that applies to all the verses that people seek out in their studies of end times. So as a sheepdog, you could also spend your time memorizing the book of Numbers, and that might be useful, but perhaps you could better spend your time studying elsewhere in Sacred Scripture.

To me, sheepdogs spending time and energy on end times and eschatology can be a distraction from the desperate spiritual battle of saving souls and pointing people to Christ in our day. In fact, as Chaplain Steve Sipe points out, Jesus mentioned eschatology only to provoke us to urgency about our work with people (Mark 13:37, "What I say to you, I say to everyone: 'Watch!'") and to assure us that the Father has a providential plan for dealing with the nations (Acts 1:6–8, "Then they gathered around him and asked him, 'Lord, are you at this time going to restore the kingdom to Israel?' He said to them: 'It is not for you to know the times or dates the Father has set by his own authority. But you will receive power when the Holy Spirit comes on you; and you will be my witnesses in Jerusalem, and in all Judea and Samaria, and to the ends of the earth.'").

One of the conditions for Jesus to return appears to be that "the gospel must first be preached to all nations" (Mark 13:10). And, I respectfully submit, repeated declarations that "This is the End Times!" is counterproductive to our personal witness and to the objective of bringing the whole world to the knowledge of salvation. Our guidance, our "order" from Erasmus, is very clear. We don't know when the Great Shepherd will come for his sheepdogs. So you must treat every battle like it is *your* last battle and like it is *the* last battle.

The Last Battle

> Remember that all worlds draw to an end and
> that noble death is a treasure which no one is
> too poor to buy.
>
>   —Roonwit, in *The Last Battle*,
>   by C. S. Lewis

The Last Battle by C. S. Lewis is the seventh and final book of his epic Christian allegory, *The Chronicles of Narnia*. Lewis was one of the greatest Christian writers in recent centuries. His books *Mere Christianity* and *The Screwtape Letters* should be required reading for all Christian spiritual warriors, but it is in his Narnia books that Lewis may have left his greatest legacy. In *The Last Battle*, we see Lewis' perspective on what God tells us about eschatology. For me, a lowly sheepdog, this is all I need to know about the subject.

Facing their inevitable death against overwhelming evil forces, those who participated in spiritual warfare, those who had led epic adventures in Narnia, find themselves asking the question, "Was it all worthwhile?" Will you regret your spiritual endeavors against evil if they end in your physical death? Jill, a young girl facing death in battle, says, "I was going to say I wished we'd never come. But I don't, I don't, I don't. Even if we *are* killed. I'd rather be killed fighting for Narnia than grow old and stupid at home and perhaps go about in a bathchair and then die in the end just the same."

The Unicorn agreed, "I would choose no other life than the life I have had and no other death than the one we go to."

Yes! Let us choose no other life and no other death than to die in God's service. Our life comes from God, and we give it back to him, knowing that only he can truly keep us safe.

Jill sheds tears of fear and sorrow, bravely awaiting death in the ranks with her bow and quiver of arrows. And she is told, "If you must weep, sweetheart…turn your face aside and see you wet not your bowstring."

Yes! If a bowstring gets wet, it will not be effective. We may shed a tear as we face our death, and no one will hold it against us, but do not let it interfere with your final battle. Don't let your emotions weaken your witness in this crucial hour. Do not let your tears "wet your bowstring" and prevent you from gaining a noble death as you fight your final battle. Because a "noble death is a treasure which no one is too poor to buy."

We may fight our final battle in some swirling maelstrom of death and danger. But it is more likely to come, inevitably and inexorably, as we face old age. We *can* become better people as we grow older, teaching our dear ones how to live and laugh and love. And then, finally, we can teach them how to die.

No acrimony, no anger. Nothing but gentleness and graciousness to all, we pray Lord, as we face our final battle. Ask God for more faith. And then, as you face your death with courage and confidence that you will spend eternity with our loving Father, you can be a mighty spiritual beacon, giving the most powerful possible witness, and win the final battle in triumph.

And Then...?

Then—whether it be *the* final battle of all or just *our* final battle—we will be in heaven. Lewis gives us a faint understanding, as good a description as the most gifted wordsmith and wisest theologian could possibly craft for us, of what it will be like after we die in Christ:

> I have come home at last! This is my real country! I belong here. This is the land I have been looking for all my life, though I never knew it till now. The reason why we loved the old Narnia is that it sometimes looked a little like this.
>
> …All their life in this world and all their adventures in Narnia had only been the cover and the title page: now at last they were beginning Chapter One of the Great Story which no one on earth has read: which goes on for ever: in which every chapter is better than the one before.
>
> …The term is over: the holidays have begun. The dream is ended: this is the morning. (C. S. Lewis, *The Last Battle*)

WARNORD Recap

Heaven is going to be amazing! But here is one last quote from *The Last Battle*, to join these others, perfect for all God's lowly sheepdogs: "This is the marvel of marvels, that he called me Beloved, me who am but as a dog."

We are told that we can't know the hour of Christ's return. So one last time: treat every battle like it is your last. And like the faithful dog waiting for the joyous moment when his master returns at the end of the day, we will wait for Jesus to come. Because God promises that "they who *wait* for the LORD shall renew their strength; they shall mount up with wings like eagles; they shall run and not be weary; they shall walk and not faint" (Isaiah 40:31 ESV).

Then, in the fullness of time, the final battle will come, and it will be a glorious thing to behold!

> The final trump we soon shall hear,
>   The great white throne shall then appear,
> Ten thousand angels round:
>   Jehovah turns the moon to blood,
>   Blows out the sun, consumes the flood,
> And burns the solid ground.
>
> Arise, ye nations, and come forth,
>   From east and west, and south and north;
> Behold, the Judge is come.

Prayer for the Coming of Jesus

> *Lord God, heavenly Father,*
> *by your Son you have revealed to us*
>   *that heaven and earth will pass away,*
>   *that our bodies will rise again, and*
>   *that we all must appear*

before the judgment throne.
Keep us by your Holy Spirit in your Word,
  establish us in the true faith,
  graciously defend us from sin and
  preserve us in all temptations,
that our hearts may not be obsessed
  with carousing,
  drunkenness, and
  foolish cares,
  but that we may always
watch and pray and
  trust fully in your grace,
await with joy
the glorious coming
of your Son and
  at last, obtain eternal salvation,
  through your beloved Son,
Jesus Christ our Lord, who lives and reigns
  with you and the Holy Spirit,
one true God, now and forever.
  Amen.

—Veit Dietrich (1506–1549)

ORDER #13: *Next Level Battle Prep*

➤ Read the last chapter of the Bible (Revelation 22) and explain the "invitation" and the "warning."

➤ What opportunities does your job provide to serve God? By what acts and words?

➤ What is your interpretation of "being in the world but not of the world" as you read John 17:14–16?

➤ What is the "last battle"?

FOURTEENTH WARNING

THE WICKED DECEIVE THEMSELVES

No one has sunk so deep into wickedness as those men who do many good works of their own.

(Luther)

WARNORD #14

FOURTEENTH ORDER

DON'T ASSUME THAT DOING GOOD ALLOWS YOU TO KEEP A FEW VICES

The enemy you ignore is the one who conquers you.

(Erasmus)

FOURTEENTH WARNING

THE WICKED DECEIVE THEMSELVES

No one has sunk so deep into wickedness as those men who do many good works of their own.

(Luther)

Glory belongs to God, whose power is at work in us. By this power he can do infinitely more than we can ask or imagine.
—Ephesians 3:20 GW

Humility, thou secret vale,
    Unknown to proud in heart;
Where show'rs of blessing never fail,
    And glories ne'er depart.

Humility, how pure thy place!
   Thou seat of holiness!
Thou door of entrance into grace
   And everlasting bliss!

Humility, how calm the breast
   That knows thy peace sublime!
Within thy courts our perfect rest
   Grows sweeter all the time.

—"Humility, Thou Secret Vale," by William Gallio Schell
(1869–1940)

In the previous WARNORD, we discussed how Beowulf defeated both Grendel and Grendel's mother, all with God's help. After his victory, the Danish King Hrothgar thanked Beowulf but also warned him that with victory comes temptations.

Success can sometimes be a curse. Jeff Wolf reminds us that failure and humiliation can teach us to realize our innate sinfulness and vulnerability, forcing us to seek God, so that we can appreciate future success as a godly gift, not as a sign of our own superiority, which is a lie.

The greatest temptation in any success, the one that will sink you deep into wickedness, is pride. In *Mere Christianity,* C. S. Lewis tells us that "a proud man is always looking down on things and people; and, of course, as long as you are looking down, you cannot see something that is above you."

Referred to as "Hrothgar's Sermon," the Danish King advises Beowulf "do not give way to pride," for it is better to seek God's "eternal" reward. Here is part of what Hrothgar says to Beowulf:

> O flower of warriors, beware of the trap.
>   Choose, dear Beowulf, the better part,
> eternal rewards. Do not give way to pride.
>   For a brief while your strength is in bloom
> but it fades quickly; and soon there will follow
>   illness or the sword to lay you low,
> or a sudden fire or surge of water
>   or jabbing blade or javelin from the air
> or repellent age. Your piercing eyes
>   will dim and darken; and death will arrive,
> dear warrior, to sweep you away.

King Hrothgar appears to be using Ephesians 3:20–21 to warn Beowulf of pride, reminding him: "Glory belongs to God, whose power is at work in us. By this power he can do infinitely more than we can ask or imagine" (GW). Luther reminds us, "Our own will, especially our corrupt will, cannot of itself do good."

Beowulf's victory over Grendel was God-given, but King Hrothgar worries that Beowulf will forget this and take the credit. Taking credit for God's good work will bring emotional and spiritual harm upon the arrogant. Because of his deep, divine love, God cannot allow his power to be credited to men, and "God cannot be mocked" (Galatians 6:7).

Next, King Hrothgar tells Beowulf that life is fleeting and that he should orient himself toward serving God, which brings eternal rewards. This advice comes from the book of Matthew, where Jesus says:

> Do not store up for yourselves treasures on earth, where moths and vermin destroy, and where thieves break in and steal. But store up for yourselves treasures in heaven, where moths and vermin do not destroy, and where thieves do not break in and steal. (Matthew 6:19–20)

What an amazing lesson this must have been! What a complete transformation in the mindset of the prideful, arrogant Vikings! Yet it worked. No other lore, no other saga or ode or epic poem has endured from this culture and time like *Beowulf*.

Lt. David Kemp says there is a lesson here for police officers and for *all* sheepdogs who are good people doing God's work. The danger is that they may believe that they have earned the right to go to heaven because of the tough job and the dangerous life that they have led. What a dangerous thing to believe! Police cannot "badge" their way into heaven. Sheepdogs need to repent and be sanctified just like everyone else. But police are indeed blessed to be in positions of authority from which they can carry out God's work.

But be warned: "From everyone who has been given much, much will be demanded; and from the one who has been entrusted with much, much more will be asked" (Luke 12:48). Being a police officer means that you will be held to an even higher standard upon meeting Jesus for final judgement. Never doubt that your salvation is assured, but you will have to answer for what you have done with your life. "The Father judges no one, but has entrusted all judgment to the Son, that all may honor the Son just as they honor the Father. Whoever does not honor the Son does not honor the Father, who sent him" (John 5:22–23). Now is the time to ask yourself if you are honoring Jesus Christ.

Works without God Are Empty

Luther takes us a step further than just warning against pride. He focuses this warning on "men who do many good works of their own." Luther tells us, "No one has sunk so deep into wickedness." No one has *sunk so deep*? What is so bad about doing many good works? Ah, the key here is "good works *of their own*."

When we do good deeds for God and give him the glory and honor, then we are on a path of true happiness. When we do good deeds for any other reason, then we are on a path to despair.

People who assume they are good, begin to assume that all their deeds are for a good reason. This is when they begin to do very selfish, wicked, things. They justify their wickedness: "It is all for a good cause" (*their* good cause). The Bible warns those who say, "'Let's do evil, that good may come?' Those who say so are justly condemned" (Romans 3:8 WEB).

Lewis tells us in *Mere Christianity* that "a moderately bad man knows he is not very good: a thoroughly bad man thinks he is alright. This is common sense really. You understand sleep when you are awake, not when you are sleeping." The problem is that you will be trapped into thinking you are a good person, and of course, "good people" go to heaven because of their good deeds. The world today makes it so very easy for us to take pride in our achievements.

Online and in person, vast numbers of people may honor and respect you because of your accomplishments, your money, your skills, even your good looks. But all those are "wood, hay, and straw" (1 Corinthians 3:12 CEV) that will be diminished in this life as we age and finally burned away in the judgment of that day when Christ examines the quality of our lives. Without God, "all our righteousnesses are as filthy rags" (Isaiah 64:6 KJV). Lewis tells us:

> If you have sound nerves and intelligence and health and popularity and a good upbringing, you are likely to be quite satisfied with your character as it is. "Why drag God into it?" you may ask.
>
> A certain level of good conduct comes fairly easily to you. You are not one of those wretched creatures who are always being tripped up by sex, or dipsomania [alcoholism], or nervousness, or bad temper. Everyone says

you are a nice chap and (between ourselves) you agree with them.

You are quite likely to believe that all this niceness is your own doing, and you may easily not feel the need for any better kind of goodness. Often people who have all these natural kinds of goodness cannot be brought to recognize their need for Christ at all until, one day, the natural goodness lets them down and their self-satisfaction is shattered.

The problem here is pride, and what makes it even worse is that those individuals Lewis describes do not think they are being prideful, but everyone else knows it and sees it. And both God and the world loathe and despise pride.

There is one vice of which no man in the world is free; which everyone in the world loathes when he sees it in someone else; and of which hardly any people, except Christians, ever imagine that they are guilty themselves…

There is no fault which makes a man more unpopular, and no fault which we are more unconscious of in ourselves…

The vice I am talking of is Pride or Self-Conceit: and the virtue opposite to it, in Christian morals, is called *Humility*.

Ah! Here we see the answer to the problem of pride. The opposite of pride is humility. Humility quenches pride, as water quenches fire. Because "God opposes the proud but shows favor to the humble" (James 4:6). Thus, we will call upon Samson, Beowulf, and Lewis again to help us find the path to humility.

> Humility, how pure thy place!
>> Thou seat of holiness!
> Thou door of entrance into grace
>> And everlasting bliss!

WARNING #14: Next Level Battle Prep

➤ What is a very dangerous assumption that public servants make?

○ Do you live your life with the arrogant belief that you are going straight to heaven, no questions asked?

➤ What does "honor" have to do with salvation?

➤ When have you taken credit for God's glory?

➤ What secret sins are you hiding? (Not from God but just fooling yourself.)

➤ Have you used your position to obtain favors, take bribes, or conceal an extramarital affair?

FOURTEENTH ORDER

DON'T ASSUME THAT DOING GOOD ALLOWS YOU TO KEEP A FEW VICES

The enemy you ignore is the one who conquers you.

(Erasmus)

"God opposes the proud but shows favor to the humble."
—James 4:6

In the Bible, Samson is betrayed by his lover Delilah. Samson was a great warrior and protected his people, but he had an unconfessed sin: lust. Erasmus reminds us, "Don't assume that doing good deeds allows us to keep a few vices. The enemy you ignore is the one who conquers you."

While Samson slept, Delilah cut off his hair (which embodied his oath to God), and God allowed this to occur because of Samson's sins. The Philistines then blinded Samson and made him a slave to his enemies. "Then the lords of the Philistines gathered them together for to offer a great sacrifice unto Dagon their god, and to rejoice: for they said, Our god hath delivered Samson our enemy into our hand" (Judges 16:23 KJV). The Philistines were proud, and they were defiant of the Hebrew God. But eventually, humbled and broken, Samson conquered his pride and regained God's favor when he prayed: "O Lord God, remember me, I pray thee, and strengthen me, I pray thee, only this once, O God" (v. 28 KJV). When Samson was brought into the enemy's temple for their entertainment, he regained his strength, toppled the temple, and crushed those who denied the true God.

The message of Samson's story is that when he was humble and beseeched the Lord out of weakness, it was then that he became strong. "The Spirit of the LORD came mightily upon him" when Samson killed a lion with his bare hands (14:6 KJV). "The Spirit of the LORD came upon him" before Samson went and killed thirty Philistines (v. 19 KJV). "The Spirit of the LORD came mightily upon him" before Samson slaughtered a thousand Philistines with a donkey's jawbone (15:14–15 KJV). And finally, when Samson was chained in the temple of the false god, the Spirit of the Lord rushed upon him, "so the dead which he slew at his death were more than they which he slew in his life" (16:30 KJV).

> What shall I more say? For the time would
> fail me to tell of Gedeon, and of Barak, and of

> Samson, and of Jephthae; of David also, and
> Samuel, and of the prophets: Who through faith
> subdued kingdoms, wrought righteousness,
> obtained promises, stopped the mouths of lions.
> Quenched the violence of fire, escaped the edge
> of the sword, out of weakness were made strong,
> waxed valiant in fight, turned to flight the ar-
> mies of the aliens. (Hebrews 11:32–34 KJV)

The story of Samson is an epic tale designed to teach a powerful lesson. That lesson is summed up in James when the Bible says that God "gives grace to the humble," but also warns, "God opposes the proud" (James 4:6 NLT). God deserves our praise for an unlimited number of reasons, among which is the fact that our loving Father forgives those who openly confess their sins: "Whoever conceals their sins does not prosper, but the one who confesses and renounces them finds mercy" (Proverbs 28:13).

It is *essential* that we recognize our weakness and thank God for our blessings in order to stay humble and remember where our power truly comes from. Paul said, "For Christ's sake, I delight in weaknesses, in insults, in hardships, in persecutions, in difficulties. For when I am weak, then I am strong" (2 Corinthians 12:10).

A Secret Sin?

The devil and the world tell us that we are truly good people, and the one bad thing that we hide is balanced out by all the good that we do. Thus, many people sleep peacefully with their secret sin, not knowing that the Bible tells us quite the opposite, that the secret sin destroys *all* the good that we do. This is why Erasmus warns us, "The enemy you ignore is the one who conquers you." Likewise, it was in a letter to Erasmus that Luther reveals what may be the most dreadful and terrifying warning in the Bible: "For whosoever shall keep the whole law, and yet offend in one point, he is guilty of all" (James 2:10 KJV). That's correct. One sin committed makes us guilty of all sins! That is why we need the willing sacrifice of Jesus (who was without sin) to enter into heaven. Our salvation *is* assured when we sincerely pray the Sinner's Prayer, but only wholehearted and total repentance can lead us back to sanctification and the completion of our godly hero's journey.

Our world is filled with people who do great harm to others, and many of them do this from a clean and orderly office, and then they go home and lead perfectly ordinary lives. Like the executives in the tobacco industry, sitting in their offices for decades, fighting tooth-and-nail over one thing: to keep selling cigarettes to children. Or perhaps developers and marketers in the video game industry who fought all the way to the Supreme Court (and they fought dirty) to sell any game to any kid at any age. (More about that in my book, *Assassination Generation*.)

For those who do not believe in Jesus, this banality of evil is a path straight to hell. For those who have accepted Jesus as their Savior, it is a satanic trap to undermine your witness, destroy your good godly influence upon this earth, and ultimately defeat you in spiritual warfare.

In his book *The Screwtape Letters*, C. S. Lewis wrote about "the greatest evil" being done in the "office of a thoroughly nasty business concern."

> The greatest evil is not now done in those sordid "dens of crime" that Dickens loved to paint. It is not done even in concentration camps and labour camps. In those we see its final result.
> But [evil] is conceived and ordered (moved, seconded, carried, and minuted) in clean, carpeted, warmed and well-lighted offices, by quiet men with white collars and cut fingernails and smooth-shaven cheeks who do not need to raise their voices. Hence, naturally enough, my symbol for Hell is something like the bureaucracy of a police state or the office of a thoroughly nasty business concern.

Of course, our secret sin (or sins) could also be pornography or alcohol or anger or lust or slander or gossip. And we will be destroyed by that one thing. We must let go of our pride, confess our sin to God, and ask him for more faith so that we can defeat this evil.

We are playing games with our secret sin thinking that it is okay because we are such good people in all other respects. And we are fooling no one, certainly not ourselves and least of all God. This is the most arrogant, prideful, and pathetic sort of pseudo-intellectual mind game. In *Mere Christianity*, Lewis warns us that "God is no fonder of intellectual slackers than He is of any other slacker." And God's Word tells us, "Everyone who is arrogant in heart is an abomination to the LORD; be assured, he will not go unpunished" (Proverbs 16:5 ESV).

Or a Secret Vale of Humility?

Luther reminds us that we are "justified freely," but this is not a license to sin. God's Word tells us, "Shall we continue in sin, that grace may abound? God forbid" (Romans 6:1–2 KJV). God forbid, indeed! Instead of harboring a secret sin, let us have a secret vale of humility.

Humility, thou secret vale,
   Unknown to proud in heart;
Where show'rs of blessing never fail,
   And glories ne'er depart.

But what *is* humility, and how do we get some of this humility stuff? In a blog on the *Gentle Christian Parenting* website, we find this wonderful definition: "Biblical humility means believing what God says about you over anyone else's opinion, including your own. It requires embracing who you are in Christ over who you are in the flesh. To be biblically humble is to be so free of concern for your own ego that you unreservedly elevate those around you."

Humility is really the first step toward salvation, and St. Augustine said, "Humility is the foundation of all other virtues."

Philippians 2:3 urges us, "Do nothing out of selfish ambition or vain conceit. Rather, in humility value others above yourselves." Thus, we see that humility is about the Golden Rule, "Do unto others as you would have them do to you." But it takes it a step further by commanding us to value others *above* ourselves. What does this look like? In *Mere Christianity*, C. S. Lewis helps us with this:

> Do not imagine that if you meet a really humble man he will be what most people call "humble" nowadays: he will not be a sort of greasy, smarmy person, who is always telling you that, of course, he is nobody.
>
> Probably all you will think about him is that he seemed a cheerful, intelligent chap who took a real interest in what *you* said to *him*.
>
> If you do dislike him it will be because you feel a little envious of anyone who seems to enjoy life so easily. He will not be thinking about humility: he will not be thinking about himself at all.

That gives us a good feel for what humility is and what it looks like in action.

How do we get humility? As in all things spiritual, we must pray and ask for God to come into every aspect of our lives. In *Mere Christianity*, Lewis offers this advice: "Look for yourself, and you will find in the long run only hatred, loneliness, despair, rage, ruin, and decay. But look for Christ and you will find Him, and with Him everything else thrown in." And among all that Jesus gives us is the path to humility and faith. Lewis tells us:

> Give up yourself, and you will find your real self. Lose your life and you will save it.
>
> Submit to death, death of your ambitions and favorite wishes every day and death of your whole body in the end: submit with every fiber of your being, and you will find eternal life. Keep back nothing. Nothing that you have not given away will be really yours. Nothing in you that has not died will ever be raised from the dead.

That's hard. How can anyone possibly do that? By praying. Ask for it. And ask for more faith while you're at it. "Praise the Lord and pass the ammunition!"

WARNORD Recap

The answer to the problem of pride is to seek humility. Again, the opposite of pride is humility. Humility quenches pride as water quenches fire. And like faith, we can increase our humility by coming to God in humble prayer and asking for it.

Finally, for all us lowly sheepdogs—off the leash, rolling in stinky stuff, and running into the neighbor's yard—Lewis gives us this consolation:

> But if you are a poor creature—poisoned by a wretched up-bringing in some house full of vul-

gar jealousies and senseless quarrels—saddled, by no choice of your own, with some loathsome sexual perversion—nagged day in and day out by an inferiority complex that makes you snap at your best friends—do not despair. He knows all about it.

You are one of the poor whom He blessed. He knows what a wretched machine you are trying to drive. Keep on. Do what you can. One day...He will fling it on the scrapheap and give you a new one. And then you may astonish us all—not least yourself: for you have learned your driving in a hard school.

Furthermore, God's Word says, "Pride brings a person low, but the lowly in spirit gain honor" (Proverbs 29:23). So maybe when it comes to humility, the lowly sheepdogs who yearn only to rest at the Master's feet will have a little bit of an advantage.

Humility, how pure thy place!
　　Thou seat of holiness!
Thou door of entrance into grace
　　And everlasting bliss!

Prayer for Humility

> *O sweet Jesus!*
> *meek and humble of Heart,*
> *make my heart like unto Thine,*
> *and give me the grace of final perseverance.*
> *Amen.*

—Margaret Mary Alacoque (1867)

ORDER #14: Next Level Battle Prep

- ➤ Have you been honoring Jesus Christ with the authority that has been entrusted to you? If so, how?
- ➤ When have you praised God for allowing you to be a servant of his great power and authority?
- ➤ Have you confessed your secret sin to God? Have you asked God for strength to defeat this sin in your life? If not, why?
- ➤ Describe an adversity in your life that taught you humility and later produced fruit that would never have come had you not been through the experience.

FIFTEENTH WARNING

THE WICKED ARE EASILY PROVOKED

Man's heart and senses are inclined always to do evil, that is, to pride, disobedience, anger, and hatred.

(Luther)

WARNORD #15

FIFTEENTH ORDER

A GOOD KNIGHT WEIGHS HIS ALTERNATIVES CAREFULLY

The wrong way will often seem easier than the right way.

(Erasmus)

FIFTEENTH WARNING

THE WICKED ARE EASILY PROVOKED

Man's heart and senses are inclined always to do evil, that is, to pride, disobedience, anger, and hatred.

(Luther)

Hate evil, love good;
maintain justice.
—Amos 5:15

Straight is the gate and narrow the way
    That leads unto life eternal;
Christ is the way to the realms of day,
    Where all is bright and vernal.

Come, dear sinner, mercy is free,
    That gate stands open wide for thee;
For thee, for thee,
    Stands open wide for thee…

Straight is the gate and narrow the way,
    But let us press on united;
Come, you may enter the gates of day,
    For every soul's invited.

—"The Open Gate," by F. D. Barnes (1837–1916)

Psychologists describe *hostile aggression* as intense anger or rage that seeks to inflict pain for enjoyment or revenge. In contrast, the desire to achieve a positive goal (as should be the case whenever law enforcement officers use force) is a form of "righteous" or "just" aggression.

All of us intuitively understand that something is wrong if a police officer is seeking revenge. There is nothing wrong with taking satisfaction, even joy, in stopping criminals. But the court system is to determine punishment, and the police officer (or any other sheepdog lawfully using force to protect others) must not use any more force than is necessary to arrest and control a suspect.

The devil is a psychopath, and he is the ultimate case study in hostile aggression. He wants to inflict pain and cause destruction, without any positive or just objective or goal. The devil's only motive is sick pleasure and revenge upon God by inflicting suffering on his creations.

Perhaps most tellingly, many convicted serial killers are devil worshipers. Satan is the very manifestation and source of hostile aggression.

Satan Is a Terrorist

What is Satan's *motive* for his crimes? He covets what he cannot have and seeks to destroy others out of resentment and anger. Psychologists have long identified "frustration-aggression" and "narcissism-aggression" as underlying causes of terrorism. The devil is the ultimate frustrated terrorist, and the father of terrorism.

Dr. Robert Hare, a criminal psychologist who is an expert in psychopathy, has found that psychopaths have frequent temper tantrums and rage-induced aggression. Psychopaths are likely to experience anger in response to frustration, especially in the context of money or sexual gratification. (More on frustration-aggression in WARNORD #18).

Satan, and those inspired by him, are indeed, as Luther tells us, "easily provoked." The devil's behavior, and the behavior of most terrorists, can be seen as one vast temper tantrum.

The devil, or *diablo* in Spanish, comes from the Greek word *diabolos*, which means one who accuses, separates, or divides. Satan wants to divide people from the love of God. Satan wants to divide everyone: nations, religions, races. In short, the devil wants to put everyone at each other's throats.

Creating division is one of Satan's most diabolical tactics, his *modus operandi* or *method of operation*. Satan, the father of lies (John 8:44), wants you to believe that God is behind all destruction, crime, and sin. Satan wants to shift the blame from himself to God. This is part of what makes the devil the ultimate terrorist. Psychologists Jerrold M. Post, author of *The Mind of the Terrorist*, says a particularly striking personality trait of people who are drawn to terrorism is "externalization" and "splitting." These individuals—and Hitler can definitely be included in this group—need an outside enemy to blame for their own inadequacies and weaknesses.

While the devil has come to destroy, the Lord our God sent his Son, Jesus Christ, to save. Jesus said: "The thief [devil] comes only to steal and kill and destroy; I have come that they may have life, and have it to the full" (John 10:10).

The devil further seeks to divide by setting people of faith against each other. The Bible tells us:

> Brothers and sisters, do not slander one another. Anyone who speaks against a brother or sister or judges them speaks against the law and judges it. When you judge the law, you are not keeping it, but sitting in judgment on it. There is only one Lawgiver and Judge, the one who is able to save and destroy. But you—who are you to judge your neighbor? (James 4:11–12)

Christians unabashedly proclaim that Christ is the way, the truth, and the life (John 14:6), but we are not to judge the salvation of others. We know that, as Dietrich Bonhoeffer wrote, "The evil in the other person is exactly the same evil as in ourselves." The Bible tells us that Christ alone will judge the living and the dead (2 Timothy 4:1). But as Christians, we are responsible for carefully judging the behaviors and decisions of others, just as Paul judged that he needed to confront Peter's actions favoring the Judaizers in respect to circumcision and salvation (Galatians 2). In the same way, police officers have to make judgments in the field about a person's statements and actions; if they don't do this, they will find themselves conned and even wounded or dead.

The apostle Peter said: "I now realize how true it is that God does not show favoritism but accepts from every nation the one who fears him and does what is right" (Acts 10:34–35). The Bible says Jesus shed his blood for *all* people: "God in all his fullness was pleased to live in Christ, and through him God reconciled everything to himself. He made peace with everything in heaven and on earth by means of Christ's blood on the cross" (Colossians 1:19–20 NLT).

So we need to view all people as loved by God and potential spiritual children of God. The former is true no matter what, but the latter is subject to a condition for it to be realized. That is, we actually become children of God by coming into his family by faith. And this step of salvation is available to all human beings, no matter their ethnicity, economic or social status, political party, geographical location, or anything else that differentiates you from me and from others. No one is left out of what God offers in Christ, but we must freely accept it for it to become a reality in our lives. God doesn't force himself on anyone.

Satan Hates the Jewish People

When it comes to creating division and prejudice, the devil particularly hates the Jewish people. The devil finds a way to create anti-Semitism even in areas where there are very few Jewish residents or where the perpetrator has never even had contact with Jews.

One convicted killer, after being arrested for shooting a woman at a synagogue on April 27, 2019, said he was inspired by Adolf Hitler. He said he did it "because Jewish people are destroying the white race."

The man who murdered eleven people and wounded six others in an attack on a Pittsburgh synagogue on October 27, 2018, told police, "I just want to kill Jews." (Note that the authors of this book try to avoid giving criminals any recognition or reward for their actions and generally will not use their names.)

Anti-Semitism is so irrational as to appear insane. And its pervasive nature proves it has a very sinister source. Understanding the vile satanic foundation of anti-Semitism and confronting this evil, irrational behavior are vital aspects of advanced spiritual warfare.

The Lie: Exposing the Satanic Plot Behind Anti-Semitism, a book by Bruce Booker, explains that anti-Semitism is a lie created and spread by the king of liars, Satan. The devil has targeted the Jews because they were specifically chosen by God (Isaiah 44:1). Thus we can understand that anti-Semitism is a plot to discredit God, destroy his first chosen people, and thwart his plans.

Isaiah 11:11 explains that God has promised to regather the Jews from the four corners of the earth. Satan does not want this to happen, so he works against it. But every attempt Satan makes to destroy the Jews only works to drive them back to their promised land and fulfill God's prophecy.

The return of the Jews to their homeland—a return that began in earnest in the late 1940s—is so miraculous that it could only have occurred by the hand of God. In an article called "What Does the Bible Have to Say about the Return of the Jews to Their Homeland," published on the International Christian Embassy Jerusalem website, author Susan Michael points out: "No other people group has managed to survive two exiles—much less one that was 2,000 years long—and then return to reestablish national sovereignty."

Anti-Semitism and the Holocaust are satanic acts of vengeance against the Jewish people. Ultimately, these are acts of evil attacking the greatest good the world has ever seen: the Jewish Messiah, Jesus the Christ.

In an address during his visit to the Nazi extermination camp at Auschwitz on May 28, 2006, Pope Benedict XVI said, "They [the Nazis] wanted to kill God." He explained that the Holocaust was motivated by a hatred of God himself and Satan's attempt to destroy Christianity:

> The rulers of the Third Reich wanted to crush the entire Jewish people, to cancel it from the register of the peoples of the earth.

Thus, the words of Psalm 44, "We are being killed, accounted as sheep for the slaughter," were fulfilled in a terrifying way.

Deep down, those vicious criminals, by wiping out this people, wanted to kill the God who called Abraham, who spoke on Sinai and laid down principles to serve as a guide for mankind, principles that are eternally valid.

If this people, by its very existence, was a witness to the God who spoke to humanity and took us to himself, then that God finally had to die and power had to belong to man alone—to those men, who thought that by force they had made themselves masters of the world.

By destroying Israel, by the Shoah, they ultimately wanted to tear up the taproot of the Christian faith and to replace it with a faith of their own invention: faith in the rule of man, the rule of the powerful.

Satan covets God's prominence, and having failed to steal God's power, the devil seeks to destroy God's first chosen: the Jewish people who were witnesses to God and his Holy Law. And it was Jesus' Jewish disciples who witnessed and proclaimed the death and resurrection of the Jewish Messiah as foretold in the Jewish Holy books in what Christians call the Old Testament.

The devil continues to plant seeds of anti-Semitism in the ear of anyone who does not have the Holy Spirit. For example, the Nazi swastika, the SS "lightning bolts," and the SS "black sun" have become symbols for satanic cults, and thus anti-Semitism has become an undeniable and inseparable aspect of all satanism.

Like the twisted, sick mass murderers slaughtering innocent children in our schools, Satan seeks to destroy those he resents, without mercy, without exception, and without shame. The devil continues to seek nothing less than the total extermination of God's first Chosen People, and the Bible warns us that we can recognize Satan's wretched minions by their evil "fruit" (Matthew 7:15–20).

Fortunately, God can undo all the damage of the Holocaust. In his infinite power, wisdom, and love, God will bring back to life all who have died: "The Lord himself will come down from heaven, with a loud command, with the voice of the archangel and with the trumpet call of God, and the dead in Christ will rise first" (1 Thessalonians 4:16).

An omnipotent God can also take away the pain from the Holocaust: "See, I will create new heavens and a new earth. The former things will not be remembered, nor will they come to mind" (Isaiah 65:17).

And God *will* punish the devil and his followers: "The King will turn to those on the left and say, 'Away with you, you cursed ones, into the eternal fire prepared for the devil and his demons'" (Matthew 25:41 NLT).

Satan: The Ultimate Hypocrite

Would the Nazis have liked it if they were herded like cattle into gas chambers? No! They would cry racism. All incidents of terrorism, harassment, and oppression are acts of hypocrisy.

Would a corporate swindler like it if someone stole his pension? No! He would call the FBI. All incidents of fraud and trickery are also acts of hypocrisy.

Jesus pronounced a curse on hypocrites seven times in Matthew: "You clean the outside of the cup and dish, but inside they are full of greed and self-indulgence...On the outside you appear to people as righteous but on the inside you are full of hypocrisy and wickedness" (23:25, 28). In fact, from one powerful perspective, all sin is hypocrisy. Hypocrisy is the ultimate failure to follow the Golden Rule. Hypocrisy is the act of doing things unto others that you would not have done to yourself. Hypocrisy is the "Dark Rule," the exact opposite of the Golden Rule. The Dark Rule is sacrificing others for your own advantage, whatever it takes to get ahead. The Dark Rule is manipulating people or taking credit for their work. The Dark Rule is complete selfishness, not caring about what happens to others as long as it's not happening to you. As alpha reader Gregory Guevara points out, Satan is the ultimate hypocrite: while he rejects God (the unpardonable sin), he also wants to *be* God. And since he cannot be God, the devil will try to destroy everything that God created.

It is hypocrisy if we lie, cheat, steal, or assault others. It is hypocrisy if we praise God on Sunday mornings but do not follow his decrees all week long. It is hypocrisy if we say we are Christians but do nothing to oppose evil. Any time we see politicians establish "rules for thee but not for me," it is the clear manifestation of a hypocrite.

Satan Uses Sin to Create Hate

People will wrong us throughout our lives. They will lie to us, steal from us, cheat us, manipulate us, betray us, and humiliate us. And most of the time, we are not just imagining it. Responding with resentment and bitterness is understandable, but Jesus calls Christians to a higher standard.

If we have trouble praying for a person who has harmed us or if we find ourselves wishing for wicked things to occur, then these are symptoms that Satan has done his job and done it well. Not just to the offender but also to the victim.

Satan is indeed a terrorist; he seeks to use one sinner to knock out several righteous people at the same time, like a suicide bomber. If Satan can corrupt one person at the right time, that person can spread a blast pattern of bitterness and spiritual death. These contagious suicide-bomber sinners destroy their own souls and then the souls of their victims by creating anger and hate.

Satan can achieve nuclear scale results (wars, massacres, pogroms, or campaigns filled with hate, death, and destruction) if he can convince people to use stereotypes by bringing different races or groups against each other. Satan must love mass media because it allows him to take one terrible act that one person commits and use it to create bitterness and anger among thousands, even millions of people. Satan knows that our human response to a perceived injustice is to "do them one better."

The writer of the book of Hebrews knew full well about seeking revenge and warned us: "Look after each other so that none of you fails to receive the grace of God. Watch out that no poisonous root of bitterness grows up to trouble you, corrupting many" (Hebrews 12:15 NLT). One sinner's act of deceit or violence can spread a root of bitterness among many people, and this is a poisonous root: "corrupting many."

Jesus Christ knew the devil would use this poisonous weapon of mass destruction and made sure that his followers received the appropriate antitoxin: "I say unto you, Love your enemies, bless them that curse you, do good to them that hate you, and pray for them which despitefully use you, and persecute you" (Matthew 5:44 KJV).

How can we love our enemies and pray for those who have done us wrong? This sounds impossible!

Hate Evil, Love Good, Maintain Justice

First, we must understand that just because we forgive someone doesn't mean we trust them or release them from justice. Forgiveness means that we accept what happened and have let it go. We are trusting God and working with the established authorities to ensure justice.

My favorite verse for spiritual warfare is Amos 5:15. This verse was first called to my attention by Kristine Paulsen, my wonderful friend and coauthor of our book *Assassination Generation: Video Games, Aggression, and the Psychology of Killing,* and it was influential in naming her grandson, Amos. I try to have a verse that I include when I sign copies of my books, and the verse I use for *On Spiritual Combat* is Amos 5:15, "Hate evil, love good; maintain justice." Boom. Spiritual warfare in six words.

Thus, when faced with the devil's terrorist behavior, it is appropriate to "hate evil." We can *hate* the *evil* deed. In fact, we are commanded to hate the evil behavior, but we must be very cautious about hating the person. Scripture tells us, "The LORD tests the righteous, but his soul hates the wicked and the one who loves violence" (Psalm 11:5 ESV). But we don't know who can be saved as God does, we cannot judge accurately as God does, and we are not good as God is. So what or whom we hate must always be tempered and moved by love and prayers for the salvation of others.

To "love good" is to "love God and love others as yourself." We are all wretched sinners, and God died for that sinner just as he died for you. God loves *all people,* including violent criminals. We must strive to do the same. How does this look, or how do we practice this? Romans 12:17 says, "Repay no one evil for evil, but give thought to do what is honorable in the sight of all" (ESV). For police officers and soldiers, this means abiding by the law and the Geneva Convention. It means performing your duty by the Spirit of the Law and praying for justice.

And to "maintain justice" is to ensure that evil deeds are judged and punished by the courts and by God. We must never seek vengeance, because "Vengeance is mine, I will repay, says the Lord" (v. 19 ESV).

This is hard. "Hate evil, love good, maintain justice." We can say it in six words, but achieving it will take a lifetime of striving, and it takes God's almighty power working in us to do so (see Philippians 4:13). This is the "narrow gate" that we must take. The devil and those who follow him take the "easy road." They take the road that is "broad, and its gate is wide for the many who choose that way." But we know that road is, indeed, "the highway to hell" (Matthew 7:13 NLT). And. It. Is. *Not*. For us! Because we have chosen to follow Jesus.

> Straight is the gate and narrow the way,
>   That leads unto life eternal;
> Christ is the way to the realms of day,
>   Where all is bright and vernal…
>
> Come, dear sinner, mercy is free,
>   That gate stands open wide for thee.

WARNING #15: *Next Level Battle Prep*

➤ What is Satan's "hostile aggression"? Describe some examples.

➤ What are Satan's terrorist tactics? Describe some examples.

➤ Why does Satan hate the Jews, and how does he inflict his hate?

- ○ Have you ever seen anti-Semitism in people even though they have had little or no contact with people of the Jewish religion? Tell about an incident.
- ○ How can you recognize anti-Semitism for its satanic origin?

➤ How is hypocrisy the devil's "Dark Rule"? Describe some examples.

FIFTEENTH ORDER

A GOOD KNIGHT WEIGHS HIS ALTERNATIVES CAREFULLY

The wrong way will often seem easier than the right way.

(Erasmus)

You can enter God's Kingdom only through the narrow gate. The highway to hell is broad, and its gate is wide for the many who choose that way.

—Matthew 7:13 NLT

The Bible tells us that "The LORD is compassionate and gracious, slow to anger, abounding in love" (Psalm 103:8). But God is also "just" and "righteous," and this means that he *must* punish sin. The Bible tells us that when people sin, God can be provoked to righteous anger:

- **God gets angry at human violence:** "The LORD tests the righteous, but His soul hates the wicked and the one who loves violence" (Psalm 11:5 ESV).

- **God gets angry at dishonest people:** "Your rich people are violent; your inhabitants are liars and their tongues speak deceitfully. Therefore, I have begun to destroy you, to ruin you because of your sins" (Micah 6:12–13).

- **God gets angry at injustice and bad government:** "Your rulers are rebels, partners with thieves; they all love bribes and chase after gifts. They do not defend the cause of the fatherless; the widow's case does not come before them. Therefore, the LORD, the LORD Almighty, the Mighty One of Israel, declares: 'Ah! I will vent My wrath on my foes and avenge myself on my enemies'" (Isaiah 1:23–24).

- **God gets angry at arrogance and pride:** "The LORD, the God of their ancestors, sent word to them through his messengers again and again, because he had pity on his people and on his dwelling place. But they mocked God's messengers, despised his words and scoffed at his prophets until the wrath of the LORD was aroused against his people and there was no remedy" (2 Chronicles 36:15–16).

- **God gets angry at those who are ungrateful:** "The people complained about their hardships in the hearing of the LORD, and when he heard them his anger was aroused. Then fire from the LORD burned among them and consumed some of the outskirts of the camp. When the people cried out to Moses, he prayed to the LORD and the fire died down" (Numbers 11:1–2).

- ***God gets angry at those who refuse to repent:*** "Because of your stubbornness and your unrepentant heart, you are storing up wrath against yourself for the day of God's wrath, when his righteous judgment will be revealed" (Romans 2:5).

God Is a Righteous Judge

God gives warnings to people and governments to ensure justice, to defend the weak, and protect foreigners:

This is what the LORD says: Do what is just and right. Rescue from the hand of the oppressor the one who has been robbed. Do no wrong or violence to the foreigner, the fatherless or the widow, and do not shed innocent blood in this place. (Jeremiah 22:3)

God's Word wisely advises us: "My son, do not make light of the Lord's discipline, and do not lose heart when he rebukes you, because the Lord disciplines the one he loves, and he chastens everyone he accepts as his son" (Hebrews 12:5–6).

The Lord seeks to correct sinfulness and promote righteousness. Remember, once you have accepted Jesus as your Savior, you do not lose your salvation because of sin. But, like a loving father who will punish a child who has done something harmful to themselves or others, so, too, does God our Father respond to our sin.

And if we fail to obey God, if we fail to use all the authority he has given us to ensure justice, then God is stirred to "righteous anger."

Vengeance Is Mine, Says the Lord

In law enforcement, on rare occasions, a police officer might seek revenge on a criminal. This is called "extrajudicial punishment" or "vigilante enforcement" because it is not within the law. Only the judiciary may inflict punishment. How could a police officer become so influenced? Like anyone else, seeing evil can make a person want to seek vengeance. But the Bible says:

> Repay no one evil for evil, but give thought to do what is honorable in the sight of all. If possible, so far as it depends on you, live peaceably with all. Beloved, never avenge yourselves, but leave it to the wrath of God, for it is written, "Vengeance is Mine, I will repay, says the Lord." To the contrary, "if your enemy is hungry, feed him; if he is thirsty, give him something to drink; for by so doing you will heap burning coals on his head."

Do not be overcome by evil, but overcome evil with good. (Romans 12:17–21 ESV)

It is illegal and immoral for police to act as a judge and punish a criminal. Additionally, police know that treating criminals with respect has a purpose. Detectives know that "if your enemy is hungry, feed him; if he is thirsty, give him something to drink" (12:20) are exactly what you need to do before conducting an interrogation.

There is a well-known 2003 video of a police officer bringing Ricardo Alfonso Cerna into an interrogation room. During his apprehension, Cerna shot a police officer twice in the abdomen (ultimately, the officer survived). The desire for the police to seek vengeance upon this individual must have been very powerful, but it is clear that they treated him with dignity. Indeed, the video shows an officer setting down a bottle of water for Cerna. Then the cop leaves for a minute, and you watch in horror as the camera catches Cerna reaching into his pants, pulling out a pistol, and shooting himself dead. Trainers often use this video as a tool to emphasize how important it is to thoroughly frisk a suspect. (They took the gun used in his crime, and everyone just assumed that was the only gun he had.) But there is a second, much more important message here. That criminal was willing to die. He wanted to die, as proven by his actions.

Cerna had grievously injured and attempted to murder a police officer. So if he had a gun, why didn't he use that gun to kill a cop (or two or three) and *then* kill himself? I believe it was because the police treated him with dignity. And I think the simple, compassionate act of giving that suspect a bottle of water saved that cop's life. The Cerna incident is a powerful example of police showing an act of mercy in the midst of a terrible crime. Having someone die by suicide is not a desired outcome for police and most certainly not for God. Every human life is precious. But Cerna is a powerful example of the impact of mercy in the face of vicious behavior.

Consider the transcendent impact of the book and musical *Les Miserable* and Inspector Javert, who hounded and persecuted Jean Valjean for decades. When Valjean had Javert's life in his hands and permitted his tormentor to live, it was an act of mercy that rocked Javert's bitter, hate-filled belief system to its very core, resulting in Javert's suicide. Cerna was a real-life Javert!

To dig deeper into *Les Miserable,* Jean Valjean was offered God's mercy and grace when the bishop gave him a second candlestick instead of having him arrested for stealing the first one. Valjean accepted this gift and was transformed by this one deed into a person who dedicated his life to doing good and striving to manifest God's love on earth. Inspector Javert rejected God's mercy and grace when Valjean offered it to him and rejected the offer of life freely given to him.

Imagine being given the gift of forgiveness and life and yet rejecting the gift! That is what Javert did, and that is the foolish, tragic mistake that we make if we reject the grace, mercy, and eternal life that God offers to each of us.

Belief is a choice! Salvation is a choice! Javert had a choice, and in the same way, each and every one of us has the choice to accept life or death. And we must always strive to treat everyone with the same love, mercy, and grace that God has given to us. It can be one of the most powerful of all possible witnesses we can ever offer to anyone.

"If your enemy…is thirsty, give him something to drink" (12:20). Amen! Think about that verse, and Ricardo Alfonso Cerna, and just say, "Amen."

For justice to be done, a legal interrogation requires that police respect the rights of all people, even the cruelest criminal: "For by so doing you will heap burning coals on his head" (v. 20 ESV). This verse is an excellent example of why we must always take God's Word in context. Just prior to that verse, Paul commanded us not to respond to evil with evil. The context makes it clear that your act of love and kindness can make someone burn with shame! That is how we heap "burning coals" on their head.

It is easy to change *behavior* with cruelty—for a little while. But it always comes with a backlash of resentment and hate, and it will always be counterproductive in the long run. If you want to change *attitude*, if you want a lasting change, then respond to people with love and kindness, no matter how much you hate their actions—like handing a bottle of water to a man who just shot a fellow cop. That can cause someone to have shame and repentance for their actions, and that can be a powerful tool for true change.

What good has a police officer accomplished if he punches a ruthless criminal out of revenge and the criminal then has his charges dismissed? And then the criminal sues the police officer? It is better to protect the Constitution and the rights of that suspect and conduct a good interrogation.

Now look at that verse again and understand the power of God's guidance for us in conducting virtuous spiritual warfare: "Do not be overcome by evil, but overcome evil with good." Indeed!

Keep Your Anger Righteous

A "righteous anger" is like that of a loving parent correcting a child. God's anger is to make things "right," it is *instrumental*—meaning it has a purpose, to prevent further infractions and instruct proper actions. Likewise, a lot of police enforcement action is instrumental, designed to deter further violations and instruct in proper behavior.

When a serious crime occurs, both God and police are stirred to righteous action—not out of hostility but to set things right, to save the innocent from destruction.

Consider what happened on May 18, 2019, a mother's worse nightmare, straight out of hell. A child molester kidnapped an eight-year-old girl right out of her mother's arms. Neighborhood surveillance video shows the suspect knocking the mother to the ground and then speeding away in his automobile with the child.

The entire Fort Worth Police Department and city mobilized with the power of God, and they would not quit searching. Off duty officers rushed in to assist. Finally, a tip led them to a hotel where someone had seen a vehicle matching the suspect's. The police conducted a raid more than eight hours after the girl was abducted and found the child, stripped of clothing, and stuffed in a laundry basket. The child had been abused but was rescued. "We got her, we got her!" officers announced on their radios. "He's in custody; we have her."

During the interrogation, the suspect admitted he threatened the girl, telling her not to move when the police came in the hotel room: "I told her if she said anything, that I would do something to her parents, and if I was in jail, I would have my friends do it."

It took a jury less than ten minutes to convict the suspect, who received a life sentence, and US Attorney Nealy Cox said of the victim, "She knows that there is evil in this world." Cox went on to give thanks that the victim was rescued and that the suspect can never be a danger to anyone else in the community, saying, "A dangerous predator is spending the rest of his life behind bars because law enforcement and citizen volunteers worked tirelessly to safely bring the victim home."

God bless the police and citizens of Fort Worth, Texas! They demonstrated real service by faith. And may God especially bless the victim; may she heal and grow stronger.

When we serve the Lord, getting angry is a warranted response if you see an injustice happening, and serving God means we should try to confront the injustice with all our hearts and souls.

*May God bless all victims of evil; give us strength,
Lord, to battle evil and protect the weak, in Jesus'
name. Amen.*

How to Pray for Those Who Do Wrong

When David was being attacked by political rivals, he
made such a terrible prayer for revenge that God would never
respond: "May his children be fatherless and his wife a widow.
May his children be wandering beggars" (Psalm 109:9–10).
Here we see one of the most revered and virtuous of *Old
Testament* kings depicted in a very negative light. The Bible
tells us that God will not respond to unrighteous prayers with
wrong motives (John 5:14–15; James 4:3). Remember, God
calls on us to *love* our enemies and *pray* for those who persecute us (Matthew 5:43–48).

Pray for justice instead of revenge, for we must all stand
before Jesus Christ and be judged: "God will bring into judgment both the righteous and the wicked" (Ecclesiastes 3:17).
Perhaps we can pray for justice like this:

*Oh Lord, bring "darkness into the light" (Job
12:22); "convict the guilty" (Proverbs 24:25);
bring "joy to the righteous but terror to evildoers"
(Proverbs 21:15); "let justice roll on like a river"
(Amos 5:24); and may everyone learn to do right,
seek justice, defend the oppressed, take up the*

cause of the fatherless, and plead the case of the
widow (Isaiah 1:17).

By praying for those who do evil, you can free yourself from
hate, anger, and the devil.

Perhaps we can pray for sinners like this:

Oh Lord, may my oppressors realize their sins and
confess to you (Acts 2:38); may my enemies "Turn
from evil and do good" (Psalm 37:27).

Pray that your enemies will realize their sins and confess to God with a whole heart so that they will be transformed
and forgiven just as you pray to be transformed and forgiven.
"He has shown you, O mortal, what is good. And what does
the LORD require of you? To act justly and to love mercy and to
walk humbly with your God" (Micah 6:8).

Prayer Prevents Hostile Anger

A study on the "Effects of Prayer on Anger and
Aggression" was conducted by Bremner, Bushman, and Koole
at the University of Michigan, Ohio State, and VU University
Amsterdam. (It was perhaps a miracle that researchers from the
University of Michigan and Ohio State could play on the same
team!) The study showed that people who prayed silently going
into a bad situation were almost four times "less likely to be
provoked" than those who just used thinking to control their
behavior. Science confirms what theologians have known for
centuries: prayer is a powerful force. It changes how we think,

analyze, and perform. But those of us with faith know that prayer's effect and its benefits are not just biological. It influences all we are and do, especially in our relationship with God.

A Good Knight Carefully Weighs His Alternatives

Thus, as Erasmus tells us, we must choose our responses very carefully. To make a wise and ethical decision, we must first remind ourselves that we are saved by God's grace to do his good works (Ephesians 2:10). So we are concerned with three questions: What would God have me do? How would he have me do it? What risks would God have me take?

This is hard! This is the "narrow way." It is an arduous, stony, uphill trek on a difficult route, but it is the path that God commands us to take.

Let us consider God's instructions.

1) Am I doing my duty?

In the Old Testament, God made a covenant that men should obey the commandments and do their duty unto the Lord (Deuteronomy 7:12–13). Police—and all sheepdogs who follow the virtuous path of spiritual warfare—have a duty to protect the innocent from those who lie, cheat, steal, or assault others. To "do your duty" means that you do your job admirably.

If you are a sheepdog under the authority of the Great Shepherd, and if you have chosen to protect others from physical aggression, then it is your duty to enforce the law while protecting the rights of both the victim and the accused. If the action you are considering violates God's law, the US Constitution, or—if you are a law enforcement officer—department policy, then you must stop immediately. In summary: *Don't do wrong!*

If there are no issues so far, then proceed to the next ethics question.

2) Am I enforcing the law fairly?

In the New Testament, Jesus summed up the law: "In everything, do to others what you would have them do to you, for this sums up the Law and the Prophets" (Matthew 7:12). This is the root of police discretion, and it is at the heart of all virtuous, godly, spiritual warfare. Discretion is one of the most precious powers entrusted to any sheepdog. Police, and any sheepdog dedicated to protecting others, must use their discretion to balance enforcement with fairness.

If sheepdogs abuse their discretion, then the courts or legislature will take it from them. God's sheepdogs should constantly challenge their decisions: Am I making the proper enforcement action to protect others? How would I feel if someone were doing the same thing to me? Am I showing favoritism? Am I being biased? Am I using the proper amount of force?

In summary, *Do what's right!*

If there are no issues here, then proceed to the next question.

3) Am I acting honorably? Am I willing to make a "peace offering"?

In the Bible, a "peace offering" was a voluntary sacrifice. Jesus Christ made the supreme peace offering and established a new covenant when he died for our sins:

> He is the mediator of a new covenant, so that those who are called may receive the promised eternal inheritance, since a death has occurred that redeems them from the transgressions committed under the first covenant. (Hebrews 9:15 ESV)

We are fortunate that Jesus Christ made a sacrifice that saves those who follow him. But as followers of Christ, sometimes our service also requires a sacrifice: time, resources, and exposure to danger. But Jesus promises, "If anyone serves Me, him My Father will honor" (John 12:26 NKJV).

In summary, *Do what's honorable and serve Jesus!*

WARNORD Recap

In summary, "It doesn't take a hero to order men into battle. It takes a hero to be one of those men who goes into battle."
—Gen. H. Norman Schwarzkopf

In the US Armed Forces, the Medal of Honor is the highest military decoration that the United States government can award. It is presented only to those who distinguish themselves through extraordinary gallantry and at the risk of life, going above and beyond the call of duty.

Honor can be found in heroism, accepting physical or social risk for the greater good. Pray for God's protection (Psalm 91:2–4), but also prepare yourself for worst-case scenarios (Ephesians 5:16). Ask yourself:

- "Am I willing to risk myself to save another?"
- "Am I willing to stop a friend or a colleague before they do something wrong?"

This is the narrow way. This is the hard right versus the easy wrong. *This* is the hero's pilgrimage. *This* is the road we must travel.

> Straight is the gate and narrow the way,
>   But let us press on united;
> Come, you may enter the gates of day,
>   For every soul's invited.

A Prayer for Protection

> *I will say of the Lord,*
>   *He is my refuge and my fortress:*
> *my God; in him will I trust.*
> *Surely he shall deliver thee*
>   *from the snare of the fowler,*
>   *and from the noisome pestilence.*

He shall cover thee with his feathers,
*   and under his wings shalt thou trust:*
his truth shall be thy shield and buckler.

—Psalm 91:2–4 KJV

ORDER #15: *Next Level Battle Prep*

➤ What does God get angry about?

➤ How do people express their anger:

  ○ Positively?

  ○ Negatively?

➤ Have you ever caught yourself thinking of seeking revenge? If so, when?

➤ What are some things that make you frustrated in your personal life? In your professional life?

➤ How can you release frustration so it doesn't take control of you?

➤ How can you keep your anger righteous instead of hostile?

➤ Why is it important to show respect even to criminal suspects?

  ○ What is the lesson we can learn from the case of Ricardo Alfonso Cerna?

➤ Have you ever asked yourself:

- ○ "Am I doing my duty?"

    - › "Am I following procedure and obeying the Ten Commandments?"

- ○ "Am I enforcing the law fairly?"

    - › "Am I applying the Golden Rule as part of my discretion?"

- ○ "Am I an honorable person?"

    - › "Am I willing to risk myself to save another?"
    - › "Am I willing to stop a friend or a colleague before they do something wrong?"

SIXTEENTH WARNING

THE WICKED SAY "THE DEVIL IS TOO STRONG"

The devil convinces those weak in faith that all their good efforts are worthless and condemned, and one might as well remain a sinner.

(Luther)

WARNORD #16

SIXTEENTH ORDER

NEVER ADMIT DEFEAT EVEN IF YOU HAVE BEEN WOUNDED

The good soldier's painful wounds spur him to gather his strength.

(Erasmus)

SIXTEENTH WARNING

THE WICKED SAY "THE DEVIL IS TOO STRONG"

The devil convinces those weak in faith that all their good efforts are worthless and condemned, and one might as well remain a sinner.

(Luther)

Woe to the inhabiters of the earth and of the sea! for the devil is come down unto you, having great wrath, because he knoweth that he hath but a short time.
—Revelation 12:12 KJV

When wounded sore, the stricken soul
Lies bleeding and unbound,

One only hand, a pierced hand,
    Can salve the sinner's wound,
    Can salve the sinner's wound.

When sorrow swells the laden breast,
    And tears of anguish flow,
One only heart, a broken heart,
    Can feel the sinner's woe,
    Can feel the sinner's woe…

'Tis Jesus' blood that washes white,
    This hand that brings relief;
This heart that's touched with all our joys,
    And feeleth for our grief,
    And feeleth for our grief.

Lift up thy bleeding hand, O Lord,
    Unseal that cleansing tide;
We have no shelter from our sin
    But in thy wounded side,
    But in thy wounded side.

—"When Wounded Sore," by Cecil
F. Alexander (1818–1895)

Hidden Wounds

There are many wounds that the world will inflict upon those engaged in spiritual warfare. In many ways, the physical wounds are the easiest to deal with. But there is a different kind of wound—often hidden, more intimate, always personal. These wounds attack at the spiritual level. We call it PTSD (post-traumatic stress disorder), or depression, or failure of faith. Usually there is no physical evidence of these wounds, and too often there is no support from other people in the face of these trials. These wounds can be the most devastating and debilitating, and—as always—they create a battle at the spiritual level. A battle that we can only win in Jesus. We. Cannot. Win. It. In our own strength!

> For though we live in the world, we do not wage war as the world does. The weapons we fight with are not the weapons of the world. On the contrary, they have divine power to demolish strongholds. We demolish arguments and every pretension that sets itself up against the knowledge of God, and we take captive every thought to make it obedient to Christ.
> (2 Corinthians 10:3–5)

The world says that evil is too strong, that the devil is too strong. But the world is wrong. Its way leads us down a path of despair and depression and ultimately even to self-murder. We will never find solution in this tragic, fallen world. The answer, the healing, the one who can salve the wounded sore and the stricken soul is Jesus.

Look again at these lines, and the answer within them:

When wounded sore, the stricken soul
   Lies bleeding and unbound,
One only hand, a pierced hand,
   Can salve the sinner's wound,
   Can salve the sinner's wound.

The "pierced hand" belongs to Jesus. Pierced on the cross for us. Our battle is spiritual, and only he who was wounded and pierced for us, only Jesus, can heal us of our hidden wounds.

A Sense of Futility

The madness you see in the world makes it all too easy to lose faith, and this is exactly what the devil wants. Without the Lord's assistance, this constant battle breaks down our defenses and defeats us.

Luther himself struggled with doubt and despair, which he called *Anfechtung*. The Protestant historian Roland Bainton defined *Anfechtung* as "a trial sent by God to test man, or an assault by the Devil to destroy man. It is all the doubt, turmoil, pang, tremor, panic, despair, desolation, and desperation which invade the spirit of a man."

Professor Edwin Delattre, author of *Character and Cops*, says, "Police loss of faith in mankind generally spawns individual and departmental corruption...It [leads to] diffuse feelings of hate and envy, impotent hostility, and the sour-grapes pattern."

In his essay "The Theme of 'Futility' in War Poetry," Professor Ahmad Abu Baker says that in war poetry (and especially in poetry written by individuals who are in combat), you can very often perceive a sense of futility, betrayal, and loss of faith. Soldiers find that doing the right thing is often followed by tragedy, when innocent civilians are killed and brave soldiers die.

Siegfried Sassoon, considered one of history's great war poets, was a captain in the British Army during World War I. He was deeply respected for his courage, which grew more reckless in the face of ever greater casualties, earning him the nickname "Mad Jack." On July 27, 1916, Sassoon was awarded the Military Cross for bravery, making him a hero back in England. Sassoon's popularity made it difficult for his commanders to deal with his growing disillusionment as a frontline participant in one of the most tragic, destructive, and horrendous of all wars. Consider Sassoon's poem, "Suicide in the Trenches," published in his collection, *Counter-Attack and Other Poems* (1918):

> I knew a simple soldier boy
>> Who grinned at life in empty joy,
> Slept soundly through the lonesome dark,
>> And whistled early with the lark.
>
> In winter trenches, cowed and glum,
>> With crumps and lice and lack of rum,
> He put a bullet through his brain.
>> No one spoke of him again.

You smug-faced crowds with kindling eye
    Who cheer when soldier lads march by,
Sneak home and pray you'll never know
    The hell where youth and laughter go.

Police officers, like soldiers, must see horrors that the public knows little about. And they, too, can bear hidden wounds. Compare Sassoon's poem to "I Am the Officer," composed by an anonymous police author (the first stanza is often used for fallen officer memorials):

I have been where you fear to be,
    I have seen what you fear to see,
I have done what you fear to do,
    All these things I have done for you.

I am the person you lean upon,
    The one you cast your scorn upon,
The one you bring your troubles to,
    All these people I've been for you.

The one you ask to stand apart,
    The one you feel should have no heart,
The one you call "The Officer in Blue,"
    But I'm just a person, just like you.

And through the years I've come to see,
    That I am not always what you ask of me;
So, take this badge…take this gun…
    Will you take it…will anyone?

And when you watch a person die
    And hear a battered baby cry,
Then do you think that you can be
    All these things you ask of me?

You can sense the futility in both poems; the soldier and police officer feel disconnected and unappreciated by the public, and they feel that the battle has no end. As you begin to question your religious foundations in a world that seems indifferent to human suffering, you can experience a futility of *faith*, like these men did. There can also occur a feeling of futility of *the system* in response to feelings of betrayal by an indifferent bureaucracy, inept leadership, or corrupt politicians. And ultimately you can experience a futility of *purpose* as you struggle to find meaning in the midst of madness.

When sorrow swells the laden breast,
    And tears of anguish flow,
One only heart, a broken heart,
    Can feel the sinner's woe,
    Can feel the sinner's woe.

Post-Traumatic Stress Disorder

Martin Luther recognized that the constant battle against evil wears us down and makes us feel like we failed God. Feelings of alienation from God are described perfectly in Psalms:

O God, You have cast us off;
You have broken us down;
You have been displeased;
Oh, restore us again! (Psalm 60:1 NKJV)

How do you develop post-traumatic stress disorder (PTSD)? According to the DSM (the "bible" of psychiatry and psychology), there is first an overwhelming event causing stress. This is usually a life-and-death situation that one experiences or witnesses others experiencing.

Next, the DSM explains that there is a response to this event that involves "intense fear, helplessness or horror." It is important to understand that what causes an intense response can vary greatly. Police, EMTs, and coroners see events every day (mutilated bodies, decayed bodies, crime scenes, or accident scenes) that are normal to them but might cause an intense response in the average person. Thus, stressful events affect everyone differently based on many factors, including timing, context, and previous experiences.

People often think that PTSD is confined to a life-and-death experience, but it can be far more complex than that. For example, Dr. Joel Brende and Fr. Elmer McDonald conducted the study "Post-Traumatic Spiritual Alienation and Recovery in Vietnam Combat Veterans." They uncovered that feelings of futility and guilt are primary factors causing PTSD.

Furthermore, what we consider to be "threatening" appears to be based on universal norms that all human beings share. Philosopher Immanuel Kant tells us that there are four fundamental norms or laws: (1) Don't lie to me; (2) Don't cheat me; (3) Don't steal from me; (4) Don't hurt me. These are, of course, from the Ten Commandments, and Kant referred to all universal norms or laws as "categorical imperatives." A categorical imperative creates a universal expectation and a universal duty. We expect not to be lied to, and we have a duty to prevent people from spreading lies. We expect not to be assaulted, and we have a duty to protect people from assault.

In the January 2012 issue of the journal *Psychological Trauma*, Crystal L. Park et al. published a study showing that anytime a categorical imperative is violated in our lives, we experience it as a form of betrayal, and this creates trauma. Whether you were physically attacked or swindled, you experienced it as a betrayal of God's universal law, and it could potentially cause post-traumatic stress disorder. The research found that "appraisals of the extent to which the trauma violated one's beliefs and goals related fairly strongly to PTSD… These findings support the cognitive worldview perspective."

For example, co-author Chris Pascoe dealt with an elderly lady who gave a large sum of money to a charity that turned out to be fraudulent. She was utterly despondent and in tears, not only because she had been betrayed but also because the money she gave never helped anyone. To help the lady make sense of the trauma, Chris reassured her that God would cherish her generosity and would somehow make good on her gift.

God has written his laws into the hearts of all people (Hebrews 8:10), and nobody wants another person to lie to, cheat, steal from, or assault them. God's laws are unchangeable, but we can find ways to build resilience and dampen the trauma of having our God-given rights violated.

What It's Like to Have PTSD

Remember, the vast majority of combat veterans, cops, EMTs, and coroners do *not* get PTSD. To understand what PTSD is and is not, let us consider the true example of a dog named Flash. He was an aptly named Border Collie who was quick as a flash. Unfortunately, Flash took up chasing cars due to a lack of sheep in the area. No amount of training or scolding could stop Flash from chasing cars. Then one day he was hit by a car, causing him considerable pain. But fortunately the car did not kill him. The experience of being hit by a car was a traumatic event, and Flash never again chased another car. That is *not* post-traumatic stress. That is *learning* from a traumatic experience. This is a survival mechanism for those who are lucky enough to survive a bad experience. Our brain says: "Avoid this in the future."

Now, if Flash whines and gets nervous whenever he gets close to a car or if Flash whimpers whenever he is in a car, then that would be a good example of post-traumatic stress. But if Flash refused to ever get near a car and ran away when anyone tried to put him in a car, then *that* would be post-traumatic stress disorder. PTSD is debilitating. If Flash really had PTSD, then he would be unable to do his job if he were a police dog, and he would no longer act as a normal dog or serve as a companion. Also, according to the DSM, such debilitating responses must last for at least a month to be classified as PTSD.

From this perspective you can begin to understand that the media and the public will far too often wrongfully declare someone to have PTSD. Always keep in mind that the various symptoms of PTSD can be quite normal and common. It is only a post-traumatic stress *disorder* if (1) the symptoms persist for at least a month *and* (2) they cause "clinically significant distress or impairment" in some important part of your life.

Our mind and body can have many ways of telling us to stay away from danger and to avoid interpersonal aggression. In my book *On Combat*, I demonstrated that interpersonal human aggression is the universal human phobia. But avoidance of danger and dangerous people can become dysfunctional when facing danger is part of your job. For example, what if you are a police officer? We all understand that police cannot avoid driving in their patrol car or dealing with aggressive people. And there are many others who will face human aggression daily in their lives.

In *On Spiritual Combat*, we discussed in detail how spiritual warfare can often take the form of facing human aggressors. The attacker is the devil, the battle is spiritual, but the evil one will often use human instruments in his vicious endeavors to destroy all that we love: our family, our community, and our nation. And *always remember*, we battle against the forces of evil in the most vital of all battles: the fight for our immortal souls and eternity in heaven through the saving grace of Jesus Christ.

Now, a quick reminder, keeping us grounded in triumphant, Christ-centered spiritual warfare. Everyone will die, physically. The critical question is: Will you live eternally? Never forget that this is what spiritual warfare is all about. There is no victory for Satan if he takes our feeble, mortal shells. There is great tragedy if he takes our eternity.

Perhaps you can begin to understand that in spiritual warfare—especially in facing the psychological trauma hateful human aggressors inflict—we can never truly prevail unless we have the supernatural force of God on our side in this battle. God's force of love will always be triumphant over evil and fear. God's universal gift of love, sacrifice, and salvation purchased by Christ's blood, suffering, and death upon the cross can defeat the universal human phobia.

Even empathy (a manifestation of God's love) can sometimes work against you. It is called "vicarious trauma." You can actually experience post-traumatic stress by the remorse you feel when another officer gets hurt or when helping victims cope with their trauma. We don't want to turn off our empathy (as some first responders try to do) in order to cope. With God, all things are possible, and we *can* keep our empathy (which is, again, a manifestation of God's all-conquering love) and be resilient.

An important aspect of empathy for those in law enforcement (and in many other fields) is to remember that the PTSD symptoms they experience are often the same symptoms victims of crime experienced. Keep this in mind when you are interviewing a victim of sexual assault and notice that their emotions range from laughter to crying to being emotionally flat.

Make Meaning of Stress

Human beings are able to give meaning to their stressful experiences. Whether we are resilient or we develop post-traumatic stress disorder all depends on how we interpret our experiences. In the research paper "Trauma, Faith, and Meaning-Making," psychologists from the VA Healthcare System have found that people who have experienced trauma can "reconcile their experiences" through faith and spiritual beliefs. As the paper states, "Writings as far back as the Book of Job document the common struggle to reconcile one's faith and expectations of a just world with the devastation of trauma and loss."

"Meaning-making" is a spiritual process, and it can be one of the great secrets to handling traumatic experiences. After Satan had killed most of Job's family and destroyed everything he had, the devil predicted that Job would curse God to his face (Job 1:11). Job suffered greatly and went through much soul searching trying to make sense of his trauma. But he was able to eventually find deliverance. Job said:

> I know that my redeemer lives,
>   and that in the end he will stand on the earth.
> And after my skin has been destroyed,
>   yet in my flesh I will see God. (19:25–26)

Grow in Faith and Resilience

It is important to note that PTSD is not like cancer. Either you have cancer or you don't; there's no middle ground, no other option. Post-traumatic stress, however, can come in varying degrees.

Remember Flash the dog. Not chasing cars anymore: good learning experience. (Good boy!) Whining in cars: post-traumatic stress. (What's wrong, buddy?) Running away when anyone tries to put him in a car: post-traumatic stress *disorder*. (Bad dog!) And we can all imagine variations among these three responses.

Early psychologists took the term "stress" from the engineering world, where it refers to the amount of pressure, weight, or load upon a certain structure or part of a structure. It is useful to go back to that definition and think of stress as being like weight on our body. Stress can come in one massive event, or it can be cumulative (or both), but for the purpose of our model, it is all additional weight, and we need to find a way to burn it off before it creates a serious health problem. Most of us carry around some extra pounds, and we can think of that as post-traumatic stress. This could be some aspects of our memories that mildly distress us when we experience similar situations or perhaps if we just think about it. But post-traumatic stress *disorder* is a debilitating amount of PTS. It is like being obese: persistent, inescapable, and debilitating to many aspects of a healthy life. (Again, think of Flash running from anyone who tries to put him in a car.)

As an aside, there has been a wide movement in recent decades to talk in terms of "post-traumatic stress *injury*," or PTSI, and in many ways that terminology provides a better understanding of what is happening. Most of us recognize that there are a wide variety of injuries, and if we lay out a "spectrum of injuries"—with bruises on one end and multiple compound fractures on the other end—at some point these injuries become debilitating.

The key objective here is to understand that with God's help, we can heal from PTSD, and it can become post-traumatic *growth*, a rich area of research highly recommended for further study and application to spiritual warfare.

In *On Spiritual Combat*, we referred to German philosopher Friedrich Nietzsche, who said, "That which does not kill us, makes us stronger."

> Ha! Nietzsche stole that from the Bible! Almost
> two thousand years before Nietzsche, God's Word
> told us: "We glory in tribulations…knowing
> that tribulation worketh patience; And patience,
> experience; and experience, hope: And hope
> maketh not ashamed; because the love of God
> is shed abroad in our hearts by the Holy Ghost
> which is given unto us" (Romans 5:3–5 [KJV]).

Now we will take this to the next level to help you understand PTSD as a dysfunctional reaction to tribulation and how (with God's help) it can become post-traumatic growth—something we can truly glory in.

God uses an analogy of "burning off" unwanted "weight." In Isaiah 48:10, God's Word tells us, "I have refined you, though not as silver; I have tested you in the furnace of affliction." The analogy here is to refining the dross from silver or gold in order to have a more pure and valuable substance. When we take in too much, our burden grows, so we need to "burn" it off. Thus, the affliction, the wounds we suffer, can be a key factor in our resilience and our growth in godly spiritual warriorhood. It may seem counterintuitive, but the stress we experience can actually make us more resilient and better prepared for future missions if we process it correctly. And thus we "glory" in tribulation.

First, faith acts like a denominator, dividing and reducing the effects of trauma. Next, faith acts as a multiplier, increasing our resilience by giving meaning to our lives. Remember in *On Spiritual Combat* we said, "Joy shared is joy multiplied. Pain shared is pain divided." Now we can take that to the next level in spiritual warfare, with God "supercharging" this joyful, healing growth process. So let us pray with fervor, just as the apostles pleaded with the Lord, "Increase our faith!" (Luke 17:5).

Stop Your Stinking Thinking

The devil wants us to obsess over our bad experiences so we become too afraid to serve Jesus Christ. The devil can most definitely use PTSD against you. Evil gets involved and convinces you to think in self-destructive ways:

1. **Victim Thinking:** seeing oneself as permanently damaged, unworthy, unlovable, with no redemption; "I'm no good" thinking.

2. **Erroneous Beliefs:** viewing the whole world as lost to evil, without God's salvation, unsafe, unpredictable, and feeling that everyone is untrustworthy; "Everyone is out to get me" thinking.

3. **Ruminate Repeatedly:** the "loss cycle," worrying, brooding, dwelling on the past, pining over failures and missed experiences; "Woe is me" thinking.

4. **Sweating the Small Stuff:** being ungrateful, engaging in comparison with those whom you think have more, being preoccupied with what others think; "If only" and "Why me" thinking.

5. **Avoiding Life:** suppressing thoughts, abusing alcohol or drugs; "I just won't deal with it" thinking.

This list is an integration of the negative aspects of PTSD, depression, and anxiety, and it is all "stinking thinking." It is exactly what the devil wants you to believe. The combination of stress and stinking thinking eventually overwhelms the coping mechanisms in your brain. The result can be *reexperiencing the event*, with physiological arousal (heart rate goes up, fight-or-flight mechanisms kick in), along with flashbacks, anger, and more stinking thinking.

Lone Survivor: A Case Study in Post-Traumatic Growth

Many of us know the story of Navy SEAL Marcus Luttrell, from the book and movie entitled *Lone Survivor*. The short version of the story is this: Luttrell was on a mission in Afghanistan in 2005. Taliban fighters attacked his SEAL team and wiped them out, and he was the "lone survivor." He managed to escape with the help of some nearby villagers. Ultimately, Army Rangers rescued him, and he returned to duty in the US Navy. He was awarded the Navy Cross (our nation's second-highest award for valor) and the Purple Heart, for his actions against Taliban fighters.

Marcus Luttrell has a podcast called "Team Never Quit." I had the honor to be on the podcast, and I asked his permission to share my involvement with him and his team. He is a gracious and good man, a brother Christian, and he gave me permission.

At one time or another, spanning three decades of war, I have had the honor to teach every branch of the US Armed Forces and most of our Special Operations Units. And I had the privilege to present to Marcus Luttrell's unit, before and after that event.

After listening to my presentation, Marcus' military mental health provider used the "overweight/obese" analogy to describe Marcus' condition. The doctor said that when Marcus was rescued, he was "five hundred pounds PTSD"—totally debilitated. A year later, the doctor said he was "fifty pounds PTSD." I was able to tell Marcus at the time: "Look how far you have come. Your doc tells me that a year ago you were 'five hundred pounds PTSD.' Do you remember those days? Now he says you are 'fifty pounds PTSD.' Look how far you have come and be confident you can come farther."

Today Marcus Luttrell tells us that he is 100 percent PTSD free and stronger for the experience. He is a great example of post-traumatic growth and of God's power in our lives.

In his autobiographical book *Lone Survivor: The Eyewitness Account of Operation Redwing and the Lost Heroes of SEAL Team 10,* Marcus gives this powerful testimony:

> With absolutely no one to turn to, no Mikey, no Axe, no Danny, I had to face the final battle by myself, maybe lonely, maybe desolate, maybe against formidable odds. But I was not giving up.
>
> I had only one Teammate. And He moved, as ever, in mysterious ways. But I was a Christian, and He had somehow saved me from a thousand AK-47 bullets on that day. No one had shot me, which was well-nigh beyond all comprehension.

Marcus Luttrell includes these lines as a bit of personal testimony. A diligent search has failed to identify the original author, but it is a new verse to that magnificent, centuries-old and still strong midrash, "Eternal Father" (which is often called the "Navy Hymn") written by William Whiting in 1860:

> Eternal Father, faithful friend,
> Be quick to answer those we send
> In brotherhood and urgent trust,
> On hidden missions dangerous,

O hear us when we cry to Thee,
   For SEALs in air, on land, and sea.

Let us conclude by reaffirming two critical facts about PTSD and spiritual warfare. First, there are many tools that modern mental health professionals have available to treat and fully recover from PTSD. And every year the body of scientific knowledge makes ever greater strides in this arena. The wise warrior will draw from a full armory of weapons (mental health tools and resources) and allies (mental health providers) in the battle against PTSD or *any* mental illness. If one weapon isn't effective, don't surrender! Never give up! Roll right into another and another and keep fighting until you are victorious.

Secondly, your faith and the power of God in your life form a foundation upon which you can base all other endeavors. Faith can interact with and amplify every other possible mental health resource. There is nothing dishonorable or shameful about a Christian warrior having felt the injuries and sorrows of trauma. It means you have put yourself in harm's way and that you care. Have faith, for our wounds enable us to heal—ultimately to be stronger—as we will see in the Sixteenth Order.

Lift up thy bleeding hand, O Lord,
   Unseal that cleansing tide;
We have no shelter from our sin
   But in thy wounded side,
   But in thy wounded side.

WARNING #16: Next Level Battle Prep

- ➢ Have you recognized yourself or others losing faith as spiritual warriors?
- ➢ What are the negative results of losing faith?
- ➢ What are some factors that have caused this loss of faith?
- ➢ Give some examples of stinking thinking that reinforces the loss of faith.

SIXTEENTH ORDER

NEVER ADMIT DEFEAT EVEN IF YOU HAVE BEEN WOUNDED

The good soldier's painful wounds spur him to gather his strength.

(Erasmus)

*We glory in tribulations…*knowing that tribulation worketh patience; and patience, experience; and experience, hope: and hope maketh not ashamed.
—Romans 5:3–5 KJV

The Stockdale Paradox

Admiral James Stockdale was a prisoner of war in Vietnam for seven and a half years. When asked about the POWs who didn't make it, Stockdale described them as the "optimists." They were the ones who said, "We're going to be out by Christmas." When that didn't happen, they said, "We're going to be out by Easter." The date kept changing while it remained unrealistic. Stockdale went so far as to say, "I think there was a lot of damage done by optimists," and other writers from other wars have come to similar conclusions. Blind optimism is not faith in a biblical sense. Refusing to deal with reality can become a case of the blind leading the blind over a cliff. Here is how Admiral Stockdale defines hope and faith, now known as the Stockdale Paradox:

> Stockdale Paradox: You must maintain unwavering faith that you can and will prevail in the end, regardless of the difficulties; and at the same time, have the discipline to confront the most brutal facts of your current reality, whatever they might be.

Stockdale said that faith was essential, but realism was also important in maintaining that faith. In his bestselling book *Good to Great*, author Jim Collins coined the phrase "Stockdale Paradox" to describe this *realistic faith*. Stockdale told Collins:

> I never lost faith in the end of the story…I never doubted not only that I would get out, but also that I would prevail in the end and turn the experience into the defining event of my life… [but] You must never confuse faith…with the discipline to confront the most brutal facts of your current reality, whatever they might be.

Stockdale's attitude was to have faith while confronting reality. Scripture supports this approach. In the Gospel of Matthew, Jesus counsels: "Do not worry about tomorrow, for tomorrow will worry about itself. Each day has enough trouble of its own" (Matthew 6:34). This is similar to the Alcoholics Anonymous Serenity Prayer: "God, grant me the serenity to accept the things I cannot change, courage to change the things I can, and wisdom to know the difference."

Deal with It!

This "realism and faith" approach doesn't require that we give up and become defeatist. Rather, we must accept the reality of the situation and pray for the strength to be a good Christian in the midst of suffering. Author Jim Collins said he carries a mental image of Stockdale admonishing the optimists in the prison camp: "We're not getting out by Christmas; deal with it!"

A similar theme can be seen in the early church as people wanted to believe that Jesus was coming back soon. The apostle Paul was faced with individuals who would not get a job and who would not do good works. They were content to sit and wait for Jesus to come. Thus Paul wrote:

We command you, brothers and sisters, to
keep away from every believer who is idle…
we worked night and day, laboring and toiling
so that we would not be a burden to any of you.
We did this…as a model for you to imitate…we

gave you this rule: "The one who is unwilling to work shall not eat."

We hear that some among you are idle and disruptive. They are not busy; they are busybodies. Such people we command and urge in the Lord Jesus Christ to settle down and earn the food they eat. And as for you, brothers and sisters, never tire of doing what is good. (2 Thessalonians 3:6–13)

I feel like I can hear Paul saying, "Jesus is probably not coming back this year; deal with it!" His primary message is

- Go get a job! And
- Go do good works in the name of Jesus.

I feel like a similar message is appropriate for some Christians today: "Jesus is probably not coming back in your lifetime; deal with it!"

Pray for Something Bigger than Yourself

For people suffering like our POWs, telling them to "count your blessings" is shallow advice. How can you console someone who has been horribly victimized, suffered debilitating injury or illness, or unexpectedly lost a loved one? We live in a fallen world, and it has been tragically unfair to countless people throughout history, just as it was unfair to the Vietnam POWs.

Sometimes suffering is so severe that faith is at its breaking point. Luther says, at these times, we must eventually sacrifice the emotion of grief because it can become too destructive. This is when we as believers can only point to the infinite and unconditional love of God. This is when the victim must sacrifice their grief and focus on something bigger outside of themselves.

Stockdale said that success in a long-term survival situation means getting up and fighting each day. In his book *A Vietnam Experience: Ten Years of Reflection*, Stockdale describes survivors as being like Senator John McCain, who was a Navy pilot shot down over Hanoi then held prisoner for six years. "It was the persistent practitioner of endurance who carried the day for courage. The game of physical intimidation was not won or lost in one grand showdown. The hero of us all was the plucky little guy who made them start all over every day."

John McCain said his own religious awakening began in that communist prison camp, as he became the "room chaplain" to his fellow prisoners of war. His spiritual philosophy was simple: commitment to a cause greater than oneself. In fact, McCain urged his fellow prisoners not to pray for their release or their own personal success. McCain wrote that when he was in solitary confinement, "I also prayed more often and more fervently than I ever had as a free man." In an article for CNN in 2018, Maeve Reston reported that McCain told a friend: "I prayed to do the right thing, so I won't look back in regret or embarrassment or even shame that I betrayed my principles and my faith."

Psychologist John Leach wrote in his book, *Survival Psychology*, "Personal spirituality functions in a deceptively simple way...people who possess a personal ideal will take it with them, wherever they go, and wherever they happen to find themselves."

God's Formula for Overcoming Adversity

Let us combine what we learned from Stockdale and McCain to discern a godly formula for overcoming adversity.

Stockdale Paradox: Acknowledge the brutal facts of your reality while exercising faith.

\+ **McCain's Axiom:** Pray for the faith and strength to confront this reality.

= **Trust in God**

Stockdale said that the optimists prayed only to escape reality and died for lack of strength. But the faithful prayed for the strength to confront reality and survived on God's terms.

"In God We Trust" is the official motto of the United States. It is also found in the Old Testament: "I will say of the Lord, He is my refuge and my fortress: my God; in him will I trust" (Psalm 91:2 KJV). And in the New Testament: "Who delivered us from so great a death, and doth deliver: in whom we trust that he will yet deliver us" (2 Corinthians 1:10 KJV).

Trust is belief in God's truth, ability, and strength. Trusting is believing in the promises of God in all circumstances, even in those where the evidence seems to be to the contrary. Thus, the "paradox," always remembering that "with God all things are possible" (Matthew 19:26 KJV).

> The LORD is my rock and my fortress and my deliverer, my God, my rock, in whom I take refuge, my shield, and the horn of my salvation, my stronghold. (Psalm 18:2 ESV)

- **Trust Is Not Blind** – God has revealed himself through Scripture: "Faith cometh by hearing, and hearing by the word of God" (Romans 10:17 KJV).

- **Trust Is Not Gullible** – Even Christian scholars get fooled by bad philosophy. Knowing Scripture isn't enough. To *beware* of bad philosophy one must be *aware* of bad philosophy. "See to it that no one takes you captive through hollow and deceptive philosophy, which depends on human tradition and the elemental spiritual forces of this world rather than on Christ" (Colossians 2:8).

- **Trust Is Not Weak** – Weakness comes from relying just on yourself or others. True strength can come only from God and the example of Jesus Christ who endured all things for our sake. "Look to the LORD and his strength; seek his face always" (1 Chronicles 16:11).

- **Trust Is Not Avoiding Reality** – Jesus Christ has told us, "In the world you will have tribulation. But take heart; I have overcome the world" (John

16:33 ESV). The Bible promises us that we can claim the victory that Jesus won. "Everyone born of God overcomes the world. This is the victory that has overcome the world, even our faith" (1 John 5:4).

Suffering Makes You Bitter or Better

In a study by A. Feder et al. called "Post-traumatic Growth in Former Vietnam Prisoners of War" researchers found that "it is possible to achieve long-lasting personal growth even in the face of prolonged extreme adversity." The concept of post-traumatic growth is one of the most important lessons to learn about post-traumatic stress. You can come out the other end and be stronger as a result of the bad things that happened to you. As Paul wrote two thousand years ago: "*We glory in tribulations*…knowing that tribulation worketh patience; and patience, experience; and experience, hope: and hope maketh not ashamed" (Romans 5:3–5 KJV). Erasmus tells us, "The good soldier's painful wounds spur him to gather his strength," and he means it literally. In a spiritual sense, your wounds will teach you to "gather your strength" (just as you might gather your wits) and thereby become much stronger spiritually.

"Breaking bad" refers to post-traumatic stress disorder that has become destructive to both self and others. "Breaking good" refers to post-traumatic growth when someone with PTSD has been able to recover and become stronger from their negative experience.

Captain Charlie Plumb was twenty-four-years old, flying his seventy-fifth mission over North Vietnam—five days before the end of his tour—when he was shot down, captured, and tortured. Plumb said that when he was first captured, he started complaining to another prisoner; the prisoner told Plumb, "Get over it…We're warriors and we're going to persist until our last breath."

Plumb said that overcoming adversity is a choice: "Each of us had to make a choice, to succeed, or to become the victim of circumstances." Captain Plumb served as the de facto "POW Chaplain" for two years of his captivity and became one of the key Christian disciples of the prison camp.

When Captain Plumb was finally released and returned to the United States, he found out that his wife had left him for another man. Military psychologists told him: "If anyone has a right to be bitter, *you* have a right to be bitter!" His blunt response was, "That's like saying I have the right to have diarrhea." He tells us that bitterness gives away control of your life.

Plumb said that while he was in the prison camp, "One of the guards came in with his girlfriend to show her how tough he was. He beat me up with his rifle butt and I had so much bitterness."

Plumb's experience is like that of the WWII POW, Lt. Louie Zamperini, who was featured in the book, and movie by the same name, *Unbroken*. In an article entitled "After 'Unbroken'" by Kristy Etheridge on the Billy Graham Evangelistic Association website, we get a more complete understanding of Zamperini's spiritual journey. The truth is,

Zamperini was broken. He was so bitter about the Japanese guard who had abused him that he became filled with hate and obsessed with revenge after the war. Zamperini said that he had almost destroyed his own life and marriage, but then he attended a Billy Graham crusade and found Jesus Christ. Like Plumb, Zamperini's healing could never be found in bitterness and revenge. True healing can only be found in God.

Plumb says that suffering can make you bitter or it can make you better, and both options are a choice. "A lot of people will pity themselves or blame other people in difficult situations. But I encourage you to really take on and accept that adversity in your life."

Another Vietnam POW survivor, Congressman Sam Johnson, wrote in a Politico.com article: "I got through those hellish years by the grace and mercy of God who provided me with a strong POW support system." Research shows that one of the primary reasons why POWs had lower rates of PTSD, compared to other Vietnam vets, was having a strong spiritual support system to help them make sense of the futility. The POWs needed to create a spiritual support system in the prison in the face of persistent and brutal attempts by the guards to prevent any religious observances. You can make a powerful argument, and many researchers and POWs agree, that it was the necessity to worship God in the face of persecution, torture, and punishment that helped prevent PTSD. Chaplain Steve Sipe points out, "It takes a true warrior ethic to live out the Christ life."

Disciples like Stockdale, McCain, and Plumb carried the cross of Jesus for other prisoners. United, the prisoners refused to cooperate with their captors and confess to war crimes in exchange for early release, knowing it would dishonor their country.

In his 1886 poem *Ichabod!*, the American Quaker poet John Greenleaf Whittier wrote, "When faith is lost, when honor dies, the man is dead." And the opposite is also true: as long as we have faith, we thrive. And when we die, it's even better! Remember, the world says, "Life is hard, then you die." But God offers us an alternative: "To live is Christ and to die is gain" (Philippians 1:21).

Psychologists who work with the military, police, and victims have concluded that mental health outcomes are poorer for those who lose faith in the context of trauma, creating more severe PTSD. Anna Harper and her fellow authors, in the study "Trauma, Religion, and Spirituality: Pathways to Healing" concluded that "For better or worse, people often draw upon religion and spirituality in the wake of traumatic events." The "for worse" part refers to victims who have had their faith shaken and did not receive spiritual assistance after their trauma. The research gave one example of a woman who had been a victim of child abuse and incest, and she blamed God for abandoning her. However, she said that her greatest desire was to find God again. This indicates the absolute need for "spiritual first aid."

Harper and her co-authors also wrote about a study of families who had survived Hurricane Katrina. One twenty-five-year-old man who survived explained, "I believe He (referring to God) has his reason, and it is not for us to understand; it is for us to accept." His faith and beliefs helped him deal with the trauma of the event.

"To gain mastery and control in response to calamity," these researchers found that survivors also pursued "a collaborative problem-solving partnership with God." As one female breast cancer survivor stated, "God would help me, but I had to do my part too; that was expected of me by the Providence to which I trusted my life."

Our alpha reader chaplains, like Keith Overby, are fully trained in Critical Incident Stress Debriefing. We already discussed debriefing in *On Spiritual Combat*. Suffice it to say here that not only do our first responders need chaplains but so do the victims of crime and natural disasters. This is a demanding job, and our chaplain programs need to be greatly expanded.

Erasmus tells us that "The good soldier's painful wounds spur him to gather his strength." Belief is a choice. Faith is a choice. And we *choose* to "consider it pure joy, my brothers and sisters, whenever you face trials of many kinds" (James 1:2).

> 'Tis Jesus' blood that washes white,
>   This hand that brings relief;
> This heart that's touched with all our joys,
>   And feeleth for our grief,
>   And feeleth for our grief.

God, please give us the strength to live with our memories.

WARNORD Recap

There can be no doubt that the path to true recovery, the road to post-traumatic growth, is *spiritual*. Dr. Paul T. P. Wong, clinical psychologist and Christian minister, has been credited with this powerful quote: "When you are able to harness your anger and pain into motivation, when you are able to turn your need and frustration into faith and imagination…You will be unbeatable, unstoppable, and undefeatable, because you will have discovered the hidden paths to all the resources in Heaven and on Earth."

The world will, indeed, attack "our body, goods, and honor." The devil's evil goal is always "to bring upon us sickness, poverty, and shame." But God can use these painful wounds to spur us to even greater spiritual strength. What the devil meant for evil, God can turn to great good.

> When wounded sore, the stricken soul
>   Lies bleeding and unbound,
> One only hand, a pierced hand,
>   Can salve the sinner's wound,
>   Can salve the sinner's wound.

Prayer: "I Asked God"

I asked God for strength, that I might achieve.

I was made weak,
that I might learn humbly to obey.
I asked for health, that I might do greater things.
I was given infirmity,
that I might do better things.
I asked for riches, that I might be happy.
I was given poverty, that I might be wise.
I asked for power
that I might have the praise of men.
I was given weakness,
that I might feel the need of God.
I asked for all things, that I might enjoy life.
I was given life, that I might enjoy all things.
I got nothing that I asked for
but got everything I had hoped for.
Almost despite myself,
my unspoken prayers were answered.
I am, among all people, most richly blessed.

—Unknown author; found on the body
of a dead soldier after the Battle of
Richmond (1864)

ORDER #16: Next Level Battle Prep

➤   What is the Stockdale Paradox, and how can you
use it to reinforce your faith?

➢ What is the McCain Paradox, and how can prayer be used to prevent post-traumatic stress disorder?

➢ What does it mean to trust in God?

➢ How have psychologists duplicated the spiritual support system that POWs created in Vietnam?

SEVENTEENTH WARNING

THE WICKED CREATE CONFLICT AMONG THE FAITHFUL

Sin doth corrupt and decay that which was
well created, sowing the poison of dissension.

(Luther)

WARNORD #17

SEVENTEENTH ORDER

ALWAYS HAVE A PLAN OF ACTION

So when the time comes for battle,
you will know what to do.

(Erasmus)

SEVENTEENTH WARNING

THE WICKED CREATE CONFLICT AMONG THE FAITHFUL

Sin doth corrupt and decay that which was well created, sowing the poison of dissension.

(Luther)

I urge you, brothers and sisters, to watch out for those who cause divisions and put obstacles in your way that are contrary to the teaching you have learned. Keep away from them. For such people are not serving our Lord Christ, but their own appetites.

—Romans 16:17–18

We gather together to ask the Lord's blessing;
He chastens and hastens His will to make known.

The wicked oppressing now cease from distressing.
 Sing praises to His Name; He forgets not His own.

Beside us to guide us, our God with us joining,
 Ordaining, maintaining His kingdom divine;
So from the beginning the fight we were winning;
 Thou, Lord, were at our side, all glory be Thine!

We all do extol Thee, Thou Leader triumphant,
 And pray that Thou still our Defender will be.
Let Thy congregation escape tribulation;
 Thy Name be ever praised! O Lord, make us free!

—"We Gather Together," by Adrianus Valerius (1575–1625)

One of Satan's oldest tricks is sowing chaos, friction, and discord. Creating conflict among God's children is one of the devil's prime objectives. He is the "father of lies," and his deceptions have caused great harm.

A Tragic History

For centuries, the dispute between Catholic and Protestant traditions wreaked havoc among believers around the world. Erasmus spoke about this, referring to it as an absurdity: "What an absurd thing it is, that there should be almost continuous warfare between those who are of the household of one Church, who are members of the same body and glory in the same Head, that is Christ…[who are] fighting under the same commander…having a common enemy in the Devil."

In his book *Mere Christianity,* C. S. Lewis observed: "The devil always sends errors into the world in pairs—pairs of opposites. And he always encourages us to spend a lot of time thinking which is the worse. You see why, of course? He relies on your extra dislike of the one error to draw you gradually into the opposite one." How the evil one must have laughed in delight as followers of Christ felt they had to make a choice between Catholics and Protestants—with Protestants attacking Catholics and Catholics attacking Protestants.

Fortunately, the antagonism has lessened considerably on both sides, with numerous Protestants and Catholics realizing how much more they have in common than they differ on. In fact, in the first half of the 1990s, leaders and laypersons in both traditions drafted and signed a document titled "Evangelicals and Catholics Together: The Christian Mission in the Third Millennium," in which they affirmed their commonalities without denying their differences and affirmed their desire to work together for the good of humanity and the glory of God. Across traditions and denominations, more and more Christians now accept and embrace each other, understanding that division in Christ's body serves Satan's interests, not God's.

We have already discussed how anti-Semitism is a major indictor of evil at work, another of the devil's attempts to sow discord. In centuries past, there have been dark deeds between God's children (followers of Christ and Christianity) and his chosen (followers of Moses and Judaism). Many times those who claimed allegiance to Christ and his church committed evil against those of the Jewish faith. In more recent history, the pogroms in Czarist Russia were directed against Jews, and complicit in that were leaders of the Russian church. Here we see another of Satan's evil sending of errors in pairs, presenting a choice between Christians condemning Jews or Jews condemning Christians. Today we should hope to manifest God's love in that relationship, and we should take a degree of solace in the fact that many members of the Christian church in Germany stood against Hitler and the Nazis and even risked their lives to protect Jews and their families from government-sanctioned harm.

The December 23, 1940, issue of *Time* magazine (issued almost a year before America entered World War II) quotes German Pastor Martin Niemöller who said, "Not you, Herr Hitler, but God is my Führer." In response to which Hitler raged: "It is Niemöller or I." *Führer* means "leader," and Hitler portrayed himself as a father figure, but Niemöller would have no other God but our Father in heaven: "Not you, Herr Hitler"!

> So [wrote the editor of *Time*] this second Christmas of Hitler's war finds Niemöller and upwards of 200,000 other Christians (some estimates run as high as 800,000) behind the barbed wire of the frozen Nazi concentration camps. Here men bear mute witness that the Christ—whose birth the outside world celebrates unthinkingly at Christmas—can still inspire a living faith for which men and women even now endure imprisonment, torture and death as bravely as in centuries past…[T]he best tribute to the

spirit of Germany's Christians comes from a Jew and agnostic, the world's most famous scientist, Albert Einstein.

Now the article's author quotes Einstein from the September 23, 1940, issue of *Time* magazine:

> Being a lover of freedom, when the revolution came in Germany, I looked to the universities to defend it, knowing that they had always boasted of their devotion to the cause of truth; but, no, the universities immediately were silenced. Then I looked to the great editors of the newspapers whose flaming editorials in days gone by had proclaimed their love of freedom; but they, like the universities, were silenced in a few short weeks...
>
> Only the Church stood squarely across the path of Hitler's campaign for suppressing truth. I never had any special interest in the Church before, but now I feel a great affection and admiration because the Church alone has had the courage and persistence to stand for intellectual truth and moral freedom. I am forced thus to confess that what I once despised I now praise unreservedly.

The full articles are readily available online. They are quite lengthy, very informative, and worthy of extensive study to see how Satan can sow discord and evil. And to understand how the believers of Jesus Christ can be a powerful force for good in this world.

In the book of Leviticus, a sacred text for Jewish and Christian faiths alike, we are commanded, "Do not stand idly by when your neighbor's life is threatened" (Leviticus 19:16 NLT). In one of history's darkest hours, German Christians stood up for their Jewish neighbors. From one powerful perspective, Hitler had to break the Christian church before he could begin the process of destroying the Jews.

If such a challenge were to arise today, would we stand beside Bonhoeffer, Niemöller, and the hundreds of thousands of other Christians who went to concentration camps and died to protect our persecuted neighbors? Let us pray that, should our day come, we could do as well. Remember these words of Niemöller, now featured at the United States Holocaust Memorial:

> First they came for the Communists,
> and I did not speak out
> Because I was not a communist…
> Then they came for the trade unionists,
> and I did not speak out
> Because I was not a trade unionist.
> Then they came for the Jews,
> and I did not speak out
> Because I was not a Jew.
> Then they came for me,
> and there was no one left
> to speak for me.

It is entirely possible that—across the untold centuries to come—God will work greater good from this historical example and this extraordinary lesson than all the harm the Nazis ever imagined. Furthermore, an omnipotent God can raise the dead and redeem the loss and suffering from this great evil. Like the torture and murder of God's Son here on earth, what Satan would consider his greatest victories, God can turn into amazing blessings.

> God moves in a mysterious way,
>   His wonders to perform;
> He plants his footsteps in the sea,
>   And rides upon the storm.
>
> Ye fearful saints fresh courage take,
>   The clouds ye so much dread
> Are big with mercy, and shall break
>   In blessings on your head…
>
> His purposes will ripen fast,
>   Unfolding ev'ry hour;
> The bud may have a bitter taste,
>   But sweet will be the flow'r.
>
>   —"God Moves in a Mysterious Way,"
>   by William Cowper (1731–1800)

A Spiritual Warfare Perspective

There is a tremendous amount of excellent material available online (books, articles, blogs, and much more) concerning the issue of discord and strife within the church. As Luther tells us, the "wicked" do indeed "create conflict among the faithful." And "sin" does indeed "corrupt and decay that which was well created, sowing the poison of dissension."

The goal in this book is to take a unique approach, to make a singular contribution to the study of spiritual warfare by applying a systematic police and military methodology. Thus, we bring to this subject the insights of Sgt. Chris Pascoe and the work he has developed as a police officer, law enforcement trainer, and an adjunct professor.

Fewer Cops, More Crime

This model for understanding stress in police officers could apply equally to churches, congregations, businesses, and virtually any other group under spiritual assault. The difference is that in the police world, failure becomes immediately obvious, undeniable, and irrefutable—and often very public. When a business fails, people lose their jobs. When the police fail, people die.

We can see this in cities like Portland, Oregon, where the defund-the-police movement and embracing the bizarre theories of social anarchism have resulted in an explosion of violence. In 2020, Portland had a 68 percent increase in homicides over the previous year. In 2021, there was another huge increase in homicides, surpassing the all-time record high in 1987. But, as we discussed earlier in the Second Warning, we know the comparison between 2021 and 1987 completely breaks down because of huge increases in life-saving medical technology since 1987. In other words, medical advances have helped decrease the number of fatalities, so the number of people who would have died without those advances would be even higher than they are now. Put another way, murder is undercounted year by year because of medical technology. Moreover, for every murder prevented there is an ever larger ratio of citizens assaulted. Putting fewer police on the streets has not curbed crime; it has only exacerbated it, and that includes the murder rate.

The reduction of police department budgets and number of officers greatly accelerated in 2020 and 2021, with tragic effect. But the problem of defunding police has actually been going on for *many* years, in *many* states. For example, in Chris Pascoe's home state of Michigan, since the 9/11 attacks, overall police numbers have decreased from over twenty-two thousand officers in 2001 to just over eighteen thousand in 2021. Compare this statewide total for Michigan to New York City that has thirty-six thousand officers just for one city. The city of Detroit attempts to cover 139 square miles with just two thousand five hundred police officers as of 2023. When police departments are so short-staffed, the working police officers and the public are both casualties.

The devil desires to create conflict and prevent us from doing good works. He has many means at his disposal to accomplish this. For police officers, short staffing is one of the most demoralizing and antagonizing assaults the devil could devise.

With the fall into sin, the world entered into an unnatural state of chaos and suffering, which the devil propagates. It is the job of every pilgrim to fight against this chaos. But the devil knows it is hard to fight chaos on the outside when there is chaos on the inside of your own organization.

It is well established that the downsizing of police departments creates conditions that are chaotic and stressful for police officers. Police departments are routinely short staffed, and the defund-the-police movement has only made the problem more critical. Those who advocate the defunding of police fail to realize that reducing the number of police officers does not reduce the workload. Police continue to receive ever-increasing numbers of 911 calls and criminal investigations regardless of how many police officers are on duty.

Chronic stress in police work creates health problems and increases the chances of developing post-traumatic stress disorder. Chronic stress also affects officer performance by creating conditions known as "hyper-arousal" and "hypo-arousal."

Hypo-arousal is defined as emotional numbing, restricted functioning, social withdrawal, and a disconnect between body and feelings. For some people, a perceived threat, traumatic memories or reminders, or specific emotions can trigger temporary states of hypo-arousal. The public witnesses officers to be slow in responding to dispatched runs, remiss in returning phone calls, and disrespectful to victims.

Other people adapt to complex trauma by devising ways to keep themselves in constant states of alertness in preparation for combat. This is called hyper-arousal. It has been shown to increase the potential for accidental or excessive use of force. The public witnesses officers to be always on edge, short-tempered, and suspicious of everyone.

Matthew Yglesias wrote an article in *Vox* entitled "The Case for Hiring More Police Officers: A Crime-Fighting Idea That Actually Works, and New Exclusive Polling Shows It's Popular across All Racial Groups." He concluded that "tired officers, across a variety of studies, generate more complaints from the civilians they interact with."

Fewer cops means more crime. Bad things happen for everyone.

The crazy part, the *important* part, is that the opposite is true as well. From Cesare Beccaria over two hundred years ago to National Public Radio in 2021, the results are in: *more* cops means *less* crime. Beccaria is widely acknowledged as "the father of criminal justice." In 1764 he wrote, "Crimes are more effectively prevented by the certainty of getting caught than by the severity of punishment." As with so many things, profound words written by humans can be found first in the Bible, and that is the case here. In the Old Testament, Solomon wrote, "When a crime is not punished quickly, people feel it is safe to do wrong" (Ecclesiastes 8:11 NLT). Thus, it is a fundamental principle of criminal science, from Ecclesiastes to Beccaria, that the effectiveness of our justice system depends much more on the certainty and swiftness of punishment than on its severity.

Adding their voice to that conclusion is NPR in 2021, reporting on the study, "Police Force Size and Civilian Race," by Aaron Chalfin et al. The study concluded that employing one additional police officer to a city, prevents approximately 0.06 to 0.1 homicides per year. So if a city hires ten to seventeen new cops, they will save one life a year. That would cost taxpayers between $1.3 and $2.2 million a year. The US government places the value of a "statistical life" at approximately $10 million. So, concluded NPR, "from that perspective, investing in more police officers to save lives provides a very good bang for the buck." It is sad to think that we must put a price tag on a human life to justify police officers, but that is how the world measures things. In God's eyes, every life is precious, and this equation jumps exponentially in favor of doing what it takes to save lives.

Additionally, of course, more police officers also reduce robbery, rape, and aggravated assault. (Never forget that medical technology is holding down the murder rate year-by-year. For every murder prevented, there is an ever-greater ratio of people assaulted and horrifically injured, with the application of modern lifesaving technology being the only reason "murder" was prevented.) Interestingly, a larger police force also results in "Black lives saved at about twice the rate of white lives."

A 2018 study by Chalfin and McCray looked at a large body of police and crime data for mid-to-large cities from 1960 to 2010. They found that every $1 spent on increased policing generates $1.63 in social benefits through fewer murders. And they concluded that just the *presence* of more cops reduces crime by deterring criminals.

Studies of "high alert" periods in Washington, DC, found that when more officers surged onto the streets, crime came down by measurable amounts. In a study of federal grant programs to increase the number of police officers, cities that received grants had a 3.5 percent increase in police officers and a 3.5 percent decrease in crime.

The data is irrefutable: more cops means less crime, lives saved, and a better quality of life for just about everyone.

As always, God said it all first. He called on his people long ago to do what we could to prevent harm and not ignore the problem:

> Rescue those being led away to death; hold back
> those staggering toward slaughter. If you say,
> "But we knew nothing about this," does not he
> who weighs the heart perceive it? Does not he
> who guards your life know it? Will he not repay
> everyone according to what they have done?
> (Proverbs 24:11–12)

The Bible also tells us that the police officer (law enforcement) is "God's servant" to bring blessings upon those who obey the law:

> For rulers hold no terror for those who do right,
> but for those who do wrong. Do you want to be

free from fear of the one in authority? Then do
what is right and you will be commended.

> For the one in authority is God's servant
> for your good. But if you do wrong, be afraid,
> for rulers do not bear the sword for no reason.
> They are God's servants, agents of wrath to bring
> punishment on the wrongdoer. (Romans 13:3–4)

Once we have concluded that we need more cops, there
is just one additional little problem. Far fewer people today
want to become cops. Recruiting is down, and retention is
down. Who would want to be a cop in the face of the current
political situation? Who would want to do this job? We think
the job needs

- People who are courageous.
- People who care.
- People who want to use their lives and their gifts to
  make the world a better place.
- People who love enough to put their lives on the line
  for others. For strangers. For people they don't even
  know.
- Christians who are called by the Great Shepherd to
  be sheepdogs.

Those stepping forward today are like the greatest generations that have gone before them. They are volunteers in a time
of great peril. When all looks lost, that is when God's sheepdogs

emerge. When the wolf is at the door, who will defend us? The sheepdog! Under the authority of the Great Shepherd.

Sometimes the greatest love is not to sacrifice your life but to live a life of sacrifice. And being a cop in this dark hour is one of the most sacrificial, selfless, courageous actions a Christian could ever make. God has put them here "for such a time as this" (Esther 4:14 KJV).

Fifteen Signs of Pushing People Too Hard

The devil knows well that he can undermine God's peacekeepers by sowing dissension in the ranks. Short-staffing police agencies creates all sorts of problems. Here are some symptoms, fifteen warning signs that we are pushing officers too hard, based on Chris Pascoe's research as an adjunct professor.

With each of these fifteen warning signs is one or two Bible verses of encouragement and guidance for those of us who find ourselves in similar situations. Not just cops, but *all* of us face some of these spiritual attacks, and the answer is in God's Word combined with prayer.

God's answer is not necessarily easy. But always remember that his Word is "alive and powerful," and there is divine power in claiming these verses and using them to strengthen you. There is great solace and authority in God's Word, even when it seems like his advice is a loving—and God is *always* loving since he *is* love—reminder to "Suck it up and drive on, soldier! You got this!" Here are the warning signs, each of which we have followed up with God's counsel:

1. No specialized training for frontline officers—
   "just get out there and work!" "Train yourself to
   be godly. For physical training is of some value,
   but godliness has value for all things, holding
   promise for both the present life and the life to
   come" (1 Timothy 4:7–8).

2. Long work hours and unpaid overtime—but
   still falling behind. "Come to me, all you who
   are weary and burdened, and I will give you rest.
   Take my yoke upon you and learn from me, for I
   am gentle and humble in heart, and you will find
   rest for your souls. For my yoke is easy and my
   burden is light" (Matthew 11:28–30). "Rejoice
   and be glad, because great is your reward in
   heaven, for in the same way they persecuted the
   prophets who were before you" (5:12).

3. Lack of employee initiative—stepping back,
   passing the buck, no volunteers, nobody wants
   to take overtime anymore. "Arise, for it is your
   task, and we are with you; be strong and do it"
   (Ezra 10:4 ESV). "I can do all this through him
   who gives me strength" (Philippians 4:13).

4. Habitual lateness—people begin to dread going
   to work. "Do not fear or be in dread…for it is
   the LORD your God who goes with you. He will
   not leave you or forsake you" (Deuteronomy
   31:6 ESV). "Whatever you do, work at it with

all your heart, as working for the Lord, not for human masters" (Colossians 3:23).

5. More employees calling in sick—workers need mental health days to survive. "Seek the LORD and his strength, seek his face continually" (1 Chronicles 16:11 KJV). "We gave you this rule: 'The one who is unwilling to work shall not eat.' We hear that some among you are idle and disruptive" (2 Thessalonians 3:10–11).

6. No time for team bonding—staggered shifts and short staffing mean no time for picnics or get togethers; employees don't even have time to meet for coffee while working. "Therefore encourage one another and build each other up" (1 Thessalonians 5:11). "Nevertheless I am continually with You; You have taken hold of my right hand" (Psalm 73:23 NASB).

7. Lack of teamwork, every man for himself—it's become selfish survival by dodging work and throwing other people under the bus. "Do nothing out of selfish ambition or vain conceit. Rather, in humility value others above yourselves, not looking to your own interests but each of you to the interests of the others" (Philippians 2:3–4). "Each one should test their own actions. Then they can take pride in themselves alone, without comparing

themselves to someone else, for each one should carry their own load" (Galatians 6:4–5).

8. Decreased citizen/customer satisfaction— clearance rates (the number of cases solved) are dropping or being faked by upper management. "For even the Son of Man did not come to be served, but to serve, and to give his life as a ransom for many" (Mark 10:45). "Whoever can be trusted with very little can also be trusted with much, and whoever is dishonest with very little will also be dishonest with much" (Luke 16:10).

9. Employee suggestions go nowhere. Why? Management has given up. "Let the wise listen and add to their learning, and let the discerning get guidance" (Proverbs 1:5).

10. Limited time for personal life or inability to enjoy personal life—too stressed out to enjoy family time. "May the God of hope fill you with all joy and peace as you trust in him, so that you may overflow with hope by the power of the Holy Spirit" (Romans 15:13).

11. Finger pointing and backstabbing—the creation of sacrificial lambs. "Rid yourselves of all malice and all deceit, hypocrisy, envy, and slander of every kind" (1 Peter 2:1). "Whoever is evil must go on doing evil, and whoever is filthy must go

on being filthy; whoever is good must go on doing good, and whoever is holy must go on being holy" (Revelation 22:11 GNT).

12. Heightened emotional displays. Angry outbursts—quickly reaching the breaking point. "Refrain from anger and turn from wrath; do not fret—it leads only to evil" (Psalm 37:8).

13. Making officers work without adequate resources or officer backup—increasing the level of force a single officer may need to use, a delayed response waiting for backup, or worse: aggression/fear response. "For God hath not given us the spirit of fear; but of power, and of love, and of a sound mind" (2 Timothy 1:7 KJV). "The eye cannot say to the hand, 'I don't need you!' And the head cannot say to the feet, 'I don't need you!'" (1 Corinthians 12:21).

14. Increased employee turnover or transfers out. *I can't take it anymore; get me the hell out of here!* "Let us not become weary in doing good, for at the proper time we will reap a harvest if we do not give up" (Galatians 6:9). "No temptation has overtaken you except what is common to mankind. And God is faithful; he will not let you be tempted beyond what you can bear" (1 Corinthians 10:13).

15. No celebration of employee excellence—no awards, no retirement parties, because everyone is too tired. "If one part suffers, every part suffers with it; if one part is honored, every part rejoices with it" (1 Corinthians 12:26). "Be thou faithful unto death, and I will give thee a crown of life" (Revelation 2:10 KJV).

If you find yourself in any of these situations or similar situations—and all of us have at one time or another—then claim these verses. Hold those promises up in prayer and ask God to give you the faith to be a mighty witness in the face of such attacks.

Law enforcement leaders must stand up and confront false doctrine, such as the movement to defund police departments. But regardless of funding, staffing will always be a problem, and even in the best of times, the best solution is to foster an atmosphere of teamwork. The same can be true in many other circumstances. From a spiritual warfare perspective, you should think of yourself and your organization as engaging in intense daily combat against forces of evil every bit as much as the beleaguered police officers of Detroit.

Thus, the goal is to strive to find ways to counter this kind of assault. And the police community—the magnificent men and women who go into harm's way every day so that others may live—have much to teach us.

We'll address the history behind this amazing hymn, this great piece of Christian midrash soon, but for now consider these five-hundred-year-old thoughts on defeating the wicked who seek conflict among God's people.

> We gather together to ask the Lord's blessing;
>   He chastens and hastens His will to make known.
> The wicked oppressing now cease from distressing.
>   Sing praises to His Name; He forgets not His own.

WARNING #17: Next Level Battle Prep

- ➤ How do the wicked create conflict among the faithful?
- ➤ What are the results of asking too much of police while providing them with too few resources and little support?
- ➤ How does chronic stress affect police performance?
- ➤ Describe "hyper-arousal."
- ➤ Describe "hypo-arousal."
- ➤ What can police (and others in similar situations) do to strengthen their spirits in times of hardship?

SEVENTEENTH ORDER

ALWAYS HAVE A PLAN OF ACTION
So when the time comes for battle, you will know what to do.
(Erasmus)

May the God who gives endurance and encouragement give you the same attitude of mind toward each other that Christ Jesus had, so that with one mind and one voice you may glorify the God and Father of our Lord Jesus Christ.
—Romans 15:5–6

Christians have always understood that teamwork can greatly help advance God's battle plan against the devil:

> Let us consider how we may spur one another on toward love and good deeds, not giving up meeting together, as some are in the habit

of doing, but encouraging one another—and
all the more as you see the Day [of his return]
approaching. (Hebrews 10:24–25).

In the Bible, teamwork is an act of faith, illustrating that
God's soldiers are united with the same purpose. This is what
all organizations should be striving for—to build a culture of
many people who are working as one. The Bible talks about
the church as one body: "Just as a body, though one, has many
parts, but all its many parts form one body, so it is with Christ"
(1 Corinthians 12:12). And it is useful and biblical to think of
any team or organization in the same way.

"Theory Z" Servant Leadership

Team Policing, called "Unit Beat Policing," was created
in the County of Coventry, England in 1966 to overcome a
shortage of manpower. While the officers patrolled separately,
a supervisor coordinated their responses and investigations to
foster cooperation and teamwork.

There is much talk about "reforming" police, but the
truth is that police are constantly evolving and reforming.
Other than the military in time of war, there is no institution
that is subject to a more severe daily acid test. Remember, failure in this business means people die, which is just one reason
why you'll not find another organization more dedicated to
constant improvement than policing.

Thus, the Team Policing concept was adopted in the
United States and became known as "Neighborhood Team

Policing." Team Policing reduces stress and increases the success rate of solving crimes because cases no longer fall between the cracks in a busy bureaucracy. Moreover, the strengths of one team member often compensate for the weakness of others on the team, which brings out the best in everyone.

The traditional authoritarian approach to leadership is called "Theory X," and it was described by Dr. Douglas McGregor, a management professor at MIT, and proposed in his 1960 book *The Human Side of Enterprise*. Authoritarian leadership is good at holding people accountable because we are all sinners. The problem with authoritarian leadership, however, is that it discourages growth since the individual worker tends to do only what is necessary to stay out of trouble.

A "delegate and trust" approach to leadership is called "Theory Y" and offers individual freedom, but this allows for corrupt behavior to grow and fester. Moreover, individual workers tend to focus only on their own assignments, and this creates competition and discourages teamwork.

The leadership that Jesus demonstrated was one of holding his disciples accountable for their actions, while encouraging questions and initiative. Jesus always led by example, as a *servant-leader*, and was out there with the disciples in the field. This approach is called "Theory Z" leadership, suggested by Dr. William Ouchi in 1981 after he studied the management systems of highly productive Japanese and American companies.

One example of Theory Z is in Luke 9, when Jesus sends out the twelve apostles with instructions for carrying out their mission. When they return to him, they debrief, telling him all they did. In Luke 10, Jesus sends out seventy disciples in pairs. After they return, Jesus assesses their work and continues teaching them. In John 14, Jesus says he will be with the disciples by the Holy Spirit. This Spirit-led work begins in Acts 2, when the Spirit comes upon Jesus' followers and empowers them to carry out ministry in Jesus' name. Thus, Christ is still leading us through the Spirit's inner work. The leadership of Christ is available to anyone who is willing to follow him as his disciple.

The Voice Bible translation does an excellent job of capturing the "Theory Z" servant-leader model that God wants for his church and, ideally, for any other godly organization. Jesus said:

> Do you want the Kingdom run like the Romans run their kingdom? Their rulers have great power over the people, but God the Father doesn't play by the Romans' rules. This is the Kingdom's logic: whoever wants to become great must first make himself a servant; whoever wants to be first must bind himself as a slave—just as the Son of Man did not come to be served, but to serve and to give His life as the ransom for many. (Matthew 20:25–28 VOICE).

Notice here that the ancient Romans were a great example of Theory X, and Jesus gave us a perfect example of Theory Z servant leadership.

You Never Stop Policing Brass

Some departments have been very successful with Team Policing and establishing Theory Z servant leadership. In other agencies, these models have failed due to weak execution from top management, poor information exchange between teams and shifts, and a lack of commitment by the officers themselves. Team Policing requires strong leadership to effectively coordinate different officers and shifts so they work as one investigative unit.

We must not allow the devil to destroy our unity. And Theory Z servant leadership requires setting examples and instilling values from other servant leaders throughout your career—an approach you take until you are the one in charge and you know what to do because you have seen it throughout your career.

We must gather together to develop protocols and resources to communicate effectively. And it is an ongoing, ever enduring process to nurture servant leaders from generation to generation. In the military, there is that endless endeavor to establish servant leaders. The core of this model almost always consists of Christians among the officers and senior sergeants.

In my own career, servant leadership and leading by example were instilled in us by such principles as "officers eat last." We would be soaked with rain all day, and then it would freeze at night. We would be a miserable huddle of shuddering, shivering corpse-cicles when morning broke and the big heat-tab in the sky began to bring blessed warmth into the world. It is hard to communicate what a mighty blessing it was on those frozen days when a steaming hot breakfast arrived in insulated mermite containers. But I had company commanders like Captain Ivan Middlemiss, who insisted that all the troops ate first. If there wasn't enough food, we didn't eat. It was one application of Jesus' servant-leadership approach: "Even the Son of Man did not come to be served, but to serve, and to give his life as a ransom for many" (Mark 10:45). There were a fair number of occasions when we went hungry, as my fellow lieutenants and I scraped out the last little bit of cold food to have something to eat. Lessons like that taught you sacrificial, servant leadership. It also taught you to make dang sure the mess hall provided enough food for all the troops!

Maybe the most enduring lesson I learned about servant leadership and leading by example was that you never stop policing brass. In basic training at Ft. Ord, California, in 1974, as a young Private Grossman, I found out that I liked to shoot, and I found out that I was really good at it. For me it was one of the most enjoyable things that I did in the army. But at the end of the day, we had to police up all the expended brass. The ejected shell-casings for our ammo were made of brass, but what picking up the brass had to do with "policing" is something that I never have completely understood. Anyway, policing brass was *not* fun, especially at the end of the day when it was usually cold and we were tired and hungry. It was a tedious, boring, backbreaking endeavor. As a young private, I looked at the drill sergeants and said to myself, *Someday I'm gonna be a sergeant, and I won't have to police brass.*

Then in 1976, Sergeant Grossman went to the XVIII Airborne Corps NCO Academy at Ft. Bragg, North Carolina. We had lots of time on the range, and at the end of every day, all us sergeants had to police the brass. I thought, *Someday I'll be an officer, and I won't have to police brass.*

In Officer Candidate School (OCS) in Ft. Benning, Georgia, in 1978, I understood that we were back to basic training, with a mountain of books on top, and policing brass was part of the drill. But it broke young Second Lieutenant Grossman's little pea-pickin' heart when we went to the Ft. Benning Infantry Officers Basic Course and we had to—yes, police the brass.

Well, as a young lieutenant and then a captain assigned to infantry units in the years to follow, when we were out on the range, there was just something in me that couldn't stand back and do nothing while the troops were doing something that I hated. And a lot of the time we were short-handed and working on tight schedules. So what else could I do but jump in and assist with policing brass.

Jump forward to 1994 when Lieutenant Colonel Grossman was commanding the ROTC Battalion at Arkansas State University. Bill Clinton was president, the Cold War was over, and I was happy as a clam to volunteer to wrap up my military career in Arkansas as far away from any commanding officer as humanly possible. My four years there were joyful ones. I started with twenty cadets and had over two hundred when I left, but we were always short-handed. And when we went to the range, of course I found myself leading by example, which involved helping to police the brass.

Twenty years later I pursued my love of the martial arts and my love for shooting and earned my black-belt in Hojutsu, the martial art of the gun. One time out on the Hojutsu range, at the end of a hard day of runnin'-and-gunnin', I was helping to police brass. Jeff Hall, the founder of Hojutsu (a man with legendary combat qualifications in both the military and law enforcement, with many different martial arts black-belts to his name, and a supernatural pistol shot) came by and said, "Sensei [black-belt], you don't need to do that."

I responded, "Soke [founder, 10th degree black belt], it's leadership by example, the only kind I know." He gave a nod of approval and moved on. The "nod" from that man was one of the highest rewards I'll ever get on this earth.

Of course, the lesson is, you never stop policing brass. If you think the day will come when you don't have to do it any-more, then you haven't figured it out yet. Servant leadership never ends. Remember: "If one of you wants to be great, you must be the servant of the rest" (Matthew 20:26 GNT).

I was far from perfect in my military career. I messed up a lot of things across the years. But I think one lesson I stumbled upon and figured out, one thing burned into my neurons by good leaders and God's mighty blessings was the concept of servant leadership. Consider again what God tells us in 1 Peter 5:2–3 (this time in the New Living Translation):

> Care for the flock that God has entrusted to you.
> Watch over it willingly, not grudgingly—not for
> what you will get out of it, but because you are
> eager to serve God. Don't lord it over the people
> assigned to your care, but lead them by your
> own good example.

You see a flash of servant leadership sometimes, if you look for it. A restaurant manager who will bus tables during the rush hour. A police chief who will help set up chairs for a presentation. A supervisor (Sergeant? Lieutenant? Captain? Chief?) who will buy hot food out of their own pocket and deliver it to their people working outside on a miserable night. "Whosoever shall exalt himself shall be abased; and he that shall humble himself shall be exalted" (Matthew 23:12 KJV).

But for a police department—or any other organization—that is trying to instill that kind of leadership from the ground up, it is *hard*. It takes decades, even generations, of building, nurturing, and sustaining that kind of leadership. Furthermore, it is almost impossible to do it without a core of faithful Christian leaders.

Unfortunately, it can be lost in a single generation. As Martin Luther warned us, "Sin doth corrupt and decay that which was well created." Like all good things, establishing servant leadership takes prayer, Scripture, hard work, and sacrifice to create and sustain it. But creating an environment of true servant leadership is absolutely worth the effort. It is a critical part of our mission statement: To do good deeds, never grow weary of doing good, and then giving the honor and glory to God.

Servant leadership, at its highest level or over extended periods of time, can become sacrificial leadership. Sacrificial leadership is not always about sacrificing your life, although that is the standard set by Jesus. Very often, sacrificial leadership can be found within a family. A loving mother, who sacrifices and labors devotedly for her family, for a lifetime. A loving father, who works decade after decade at a demanding, difficult daily job, sacrificing every day for his family to put food on the table. Most of the time sacrificial leadership is not about sacrificing your life. Rather, it is about *living* a life of sacrifice. Ultimately, servant leadership and sacrificial leadership are the glue that holds together our godly endeavors.

De-Escalation: The Three Most Important Sentences

"Blessed are the peacemakers, for they will be called children of God" (Matthew 5:9). Police officers are given the sacred duty as servant leaders to bring peace wherever they can. De-escalation is communication designed to reduce an emotional crisis and prevent violence, to bring about a needed level of peace in the situation. When it comes to de-escalation communication, you will find that there is congruence between what clergy and first responders say to help resolve an emotional crisis.

At the heart of all de-escalation communication are three sentences:

1. "Please tell me what's wrong."
2. "I'm sorry for what happened to you."
3. "I will do everything in my power to help you."

Let us examine each of these three sentences separately and understand why they are so important.

"Please tell me what's wrong"

This is called "catharsis." By patiently listening while someone expresses their feelings, you can reduce their stress level. Venting allows them to get some of their upset off their chest and thereby provide relief from strong or repressed emotions. Even if they are making threats or belligerent statements, it is better than if they are taking hostile actions. "My dear brothers and sisters, take note of this: Everyone should be quick to listen, slow to speak and slow to become angry" (James 1:19).

"I'm sorry for what happened to you"

This is called "emotional validation." By expressing empathy for a person's situation, you can start building a relationship. You are acknowledging that something must have occurred that triggered their crisis. By validating, you are reducing their cortisol levels. Cortisol is our body's primary stress hormone. It acts as nature's built-in alarm system; it triggers fight, flight, or freeze. "Blessed are those who mourn, for they will be comforted" (Matthew 5:4).

"I will do everything in my power to help you"

This is called "emotional support." By pledging yourself to help the other person, you can encourage their cooperation. By showing support, you are increasing their oxytocin levels. Oxytocin is a hormone that reduces stress. The release of oxytocin will help the person regain control of their behavior. Oxytocin also crystallizes emotional memories, allowing you to find out more information in cases where the person has been victimized. "We must help the weak, remembering the words the Lord Jesus himself said: 'It is more blessed to give than to receive'" (Acts 20:35).

Congruence between Clergy and First Responders

Whether you are a pastor or first responder, assisting someone during an emotional crisis is part of your godly assigned job. Now think about this: when we beseech God in prayer, this is exactly what God is doing for us. He is responding to our emotional crisis. Praise the Lord!

When you practice de-escalation communication, you are truly serving others, just as God serves humanity. "Blessed are the peacemakers: for they shall be called the children of God" (Matthew 5:9 KJV).

De-escalation communication can be used to help anyone experiencing an emotional crisis. While it may not work in some cases where the person is on drugs or is experiencing a psychotic episode, such as hallucinations, it will at least buy time so you can arrange for back-up or a safer use of force.

And don't forget to use de-escalation communication with victims of crime. Using the three sentences will substantially improve victim interviews. Police officers should be using the three de-escalation sentences weekly, if not daily. Write these sentences down, memorize them. Use them regularly. And mean them sincerely!

1. "Please tell me what's wrong."
2. "I'm sorry for what happened to you."
3. "I will do everything in my power to help you."

(For more information on de-escalation, see "A Trauma Informed Approach to Law Enforcement First Response"; the YouTube address is available in the bibliography.)

Plan of Action? Pray!

Erasmus tells us, "Always have a plan of action, so when the time comes for battle, you will know what to do." In this case, the plan of action we have outlined here is about godly inspired and empowered cooperation, teamwork, and servant, sacrificial leadership.

But, at one essential, vital, spiritual warfare perspective, our plan of action should *always* include prayer. When we teach our "Sheepdog House of Worship Safety Courses," we teach that there should be someone on every team whose job it is to immediately pray. They should have their back to the wall, and their eyes open. It really is okay to pray with your head up and eyes open—ready to move to safety if needed.

This is the part of the church body that my wife calls "the praying pinkie toe." Like the pinky toe, you thought that old church lady was of little use in a violent incident until the moment of truth when her timely prayer might be the most vital spiritual contribution. And maybe she isn't just the pinky toe. Maybe she and her faithful fervent prayers are the secret beating heart of the church body.

There is a section on prayer we are saving for the end of this book, but it could fit well in so many places, and this is one of them. Always remember that prayer should very often be your instinctive, automatic response. Prayer should be your "plan of action, so when the time comes for battle, you will know what to do." And when you pray, in the absence of anything more specific, always remember to pray for more faith. "Praise the Lord and pass the ammunition!"

One other critical point on prayer. God promises us a special blessing, an extra power that comes with joint prayer. "For where two or three are gathered together in my name, there am I in the midst of them" (Matthew 18:20 KJV). Always strive to remember the power of group prayer. In every partnership, in every endeavor, let this be a critical part of your plan of action.

WARNORD Recap

Consider now the hymn "We Gather Together," written by Adrianus Valerius in 1597, after the Protestant Dutch nation had won a mighty victory in a war of national liberation from the Catholic ruler, King Phillip II of Spain. It had special meaning and application to the Dutch, because prior to their liberation, they had been forbidden to gather together in Protestant worship.

In 1894, Theodore Baker translated this hymn into English, and, in my opinion, he deserves extra credit. Translating poetry is hard work. Not only did he translate it well, but he caught all those wonderful internal rhymes that make this hymn such a joy to sing.

Today, "We Gather Together" is often associated with Thanksgiving, and it is so very powerful for that purpose. It is God's mighty blessing to give us this hymn for such an occasion. We have so many traditional hymns for Christmas, and those Christmas carols are an important part of the blessings of that season. We should strive to have hymns to be traditionally used for other occasions, seeking to find and establish the Christian midrash that can illuminate our faith and magnify the blessings of those holidays as well.

Look again at the words of this hymn, and answer the question, "What, then, is our 'plan of action' in response to this threat?"

Our plan of action? To pray!

We gather together to ask the Lord's blessing;
 He chastens and hastens His will to make known.
The wicked oppressing now cease from distressing.
 Sing praises to His Name; He forgets not His own…

We all do extol Thee, Thou Leader triumphant,
 And pray that Thou still our Defender will be.

Let Thy congregation escape tribulation;
*   Thy Name be ever praised! O Lord, make us free!*

Jesus Prays for Unity

I am praying not only for these disciples but also for all who will ever believe in me through their message. I pray that they will all be one, just as you and I are one—as you are in me, Father, and I am in you. And may they be in us so that the world will believe you sent me.

I have given them the glory you gave me, so they may be one as we are one. I am in them and you are in me. May they experience such perfect unity that the world will know that you sent me and that you love them as much as you love me. Father, I want these whom you have given me to be with me where I am. Then they can see all the glory you gave me because you loved me even before the world began!

O righteous Father, the world doesn't know you, but I do; and these disciples know you sent me. I have revealed you to them, and I will continue to do so. Then your love for me will be in them, and I will be in them. (John 17:20–26 NLT)

ORDER #17: Next Level Battle Prep

> Why is it important for a leader to help with the regular work?

> What can you do as a leader to encourage everyone to jump in and "police the brass"?

> The best way to share your Christian faith is by example. What can you do to demonstrate your devotion to God?

> Have you ever utilized or observed someone who understood how to de-escalate an agitated situation? What was the result?

EIGHTEENTH WARNING

THE WICKED ARE ENVIOUS OF OTHERS

The devil provokes jealousy, back-biting,
vengeance, and all manner of angry works
and words.

(Luther)

WARNORD #18

EIGHTEENTH ORDER

CALM YOUR PASSIONS BY SEEING HOW LITTLE THERE IS TO GAIN

We often worry and scheme about trifling
matters of no real importance.

(Erasmus)

EIGHTEENTH WARNING

THE WICKED ARE ENVIOUS OF OTHERS

The devil provokes jealousy, back-biting, vengeance, and all manner of angry works and words.

(Luther)

Where you have envy and selfish ambition,
there you find disorder and every evil practice.
—James 3:16

Have we laid up our treasures in heaven?
The land where no moth shall consume,
No beautiful links shall be riven,
No frost blight the lily's fair bloom…

Have we laid up our treasures by caring
    For those who are lonely and sad?
Each gift and each happiness sharing,
    To make others grateful and glad…

Have we laid up our treasures in heaven,
    Rich treasures of faith, hope and love?
If so, what bright stars shall be given,
    What blessings await us above!

—"Have We Laid Up Our Treasures in Heaven,"
    by Eliza E. Hewitt (1851–1920)

The evils prohibited by the first nine of the Ten Commandments are such that one could be tried and found guilty of committing a specific *physical* action. But the tenth commandment deals most specifically with the sins of the heart.

The "heart" is the center of both sinfulness and faithfulness; therefore, coveting will most assuredly block out faithfulness. The tenth commandment states, "You shall not covet your neighbor's house. You shall not covet your neighbor's wife, or his male or female servant, his ox or donkey, or anything that belongs to your neighbor" (Exodus 20:17).

The Core of Darkness

Coveting is such a despicable force for darkness that it was the one sin that resulted in the devil and one third of the angels being expelled from heaven (Revelation 12:4). For you see, Satan coveted God's power:

How you are fallen from heaven,
　　O Day Star, son of Dawn!
How you are cut down to the ground,
　　you who laid the nations low!
You said in your heart,
　　"I will ascend to heaven;
above the stars of God
　　I will set my throne on high;
I will sit on the mount of assembly
　　in the far reaches of the north;
I will ascend above the heights of the clouds;
　　I will make myself like the Most High."
(Isaiah 14:12–14 esv)

Like Satan, it was covetousness that expelled Adam and Eve from the garden of Eden. When Adam and Eve sinned, they coveted what was not theirs. God gave them every fruit, a garden, the whole world. But it was not enough. It is prophetic that covetousness was able to flourish in the minds of both Adam and Eve even though they wanted for nothing.

Adam and Eve succumbed to the temptation of that serpent, the devil. The fruit was desirable to their eyes, *to be like God*, knowing good and evil. As Adam swallowed the fruit, sin and death would swallow humanity.

Satan so coveted God's power that he convinced Adam and Eve to covet, to see if the knowledge of good and evil would force God into surrendering. Satan also coveted the Son of God because Jesus was one with God and shared in God's power. Jesus demonstrated his oneness with God by becoming flesh and sacrificing his life for many—including you! But Satan did not share in God's loving character, and the devil's covetousness turned to hate and murder.

This is the source of the dark energy that we analyzed in WARNORD #3. The "core of darkness" is covetousness. It is such a dangerous force that God reserved his tenth commandment to forbid this sin of sins. Covetousness can be seen as the one sin that gives birth to all the others.

Coveting is a combination of pride, envy, and irresistible desire. It is most often the motive for human criminality: a thief covets his neighbor's wealth; a warring nation covets its neighbor's property; corporate executives commit fraud because they covet their competitor's patents; a rapist or murderer covets his neighbor's life. Through coveting we come under God's indictment: "Your eyes and your heart are set only on dishonest gain, on shedding innocent blood and on oppression and extortion" (Jeremiah 22:17).

The Puritan Pastor William Gurnall (1616–1679) is best known for his book *Christian in Complete Armour*, which is considered a classic on spiritual warfare. He describes envy as an affront to God:

> Envy is an affront to the character and person of God. When you envy, you are questioning God's right to administer His gifts as He sees best. You are also maligning the goodness of God. You are angry that God wants to bless someone besides

you. Would you not have God be good? You might as well say you would not have Him be God, for He can no more cease to be good than He can cease to be God! When your envy prods you to belittle the gifts of other Christians, you are really belittling God who gave them.

Cain: A Covetous Killer

Cain and Abel were making offerings to God. In Hebrews 11:4, we read that Abel's sacrifice was by faith and was acceptable to God, but Cain was merely going through the motions of worship. Cain did not truly love God; he only sought to please God in order that he might receive God's favor. God could see inside Cain's heart and gave little regard for his offering. But God could see Abel had faith and smiled on him, and this made Cain furious (Genesis 4:5). Cain became jealous that Abel's sacrifice was accepted and his was not. It appears that Cain was unable to appreciate why his offering was rejected.

God speaks to Cain with truth and love, coming to him with a question and a warning, the same way God spoke to Jonah.

> The Lord said to Cain, "Why are you angry? Why is your face downcast? If you do what is right, will you not be accepted? But if you do not do what is right, sin is crouching at your door; it desires to have you, but you must rule over it." (vv. 6–7)

Later, Cain tells Abel, "Let us go out to the field." There Cain sneaks up and murders Abel, cold blooded and premeditated. "Then the LORD said to Cain, 'Where is your brother Abel?' 'I don't know,' he replied, 'Am I my brother's keeper?' The LORD said, 'What have you done?…Your brother's blood cries out to me from the ground'" (vv. 8–10).

God works justice against Cain by expelling him to be "a restless wanderer" (v. 12) the rest of his life. God forbids that anyone should kill Cain so as to lengthen Cain's suffering.

Cain's response to God shows that he had not changed. Instead of confessing and praying for forgiveness, Cain complains that he is being punished more than he deserves: "My punishment is more than I can bear" (v. 13). This probably sounds familiar to police when a criminal goes before the court for sentencing.

Cain is still being self-righteous even after murdering his own brother out of jealousy. He doesn't show remorse or regret for his crime; his only regret is that he was caught. (Note that in the allegory of *Beowulf*, the demon Grendel is said to be the descendant of Cain.)

Do not become like Jonah or Cain, angry at God because God doesn't give you everything you want. God shares his love and forgiveness with all his children. Here is James 1:13–15, one last time, from the King James Version:

Let no man say when he is tempted, I am tempted of God: for God cannot be tempted with evil, neither tempteth he any man: But every man is

tempted, when he is drawn away of his own lust,
and enticed. Then when lust hath conceived, it
bringeth forth sin: and sin, when it is finished,
bringeth forth death.

The devil knows that humans live in a competitive world
of material needs and human desires, and this gives the devil
ample ammo to create jealousy and selfish desire. "Thou shalt
not covet" is God's greatest warning.

Envious, Covetous School Killers

God created us with the ability to have desires, but when
we fixate on a desire, it becomes very destructive, and this is
what the Bible usually refers to as *coveting* or *lusts*.

To covet is usually thought of as longing after another
person's property, but some people have a desire to dominate,
to assert their will, and to have control. Coveting in this context correlates to power. In the Old Testament, Abimelech's lust
for power resulted in his murdering seventy of his own breth-
ren to obtain the throne (Judges 9:1–5).

Coveting can also refer to longing after another person's
popularity, beauty, performance, or prestige. Unfortunately,
many school massacres have been motivated by such jealousy.
Even the "revenge motive" (attributed to some of these killers)
can be seen as the evil fruit of envy and covetousness. Many
of the killers were bullied, but they were not satisfied with just
killing the bully. Their rampage becomes devoted to murdering as many people as possible, destroying the lives and the

gifts that they can't have. Their goal is to hurt the world and steal the happiness that they believe was denied them.

The terms "school shooters" and "school shootings" are often used to refer to these mass murders. It represents the depth of our depravity and denial that we cannot call these crimes what they are—sins of envy and covetousness.

Shooting is an Olympic sport, a deeply respected and admired activity. Shooting baskets is something that earns basketball players millions of dollars. Shooting a movie or a show is a creative artistic endeavor that can win an Oscar or an Emmy. Shooting is what soldiers and cowboys do in movies, and it is almost always depicted as a courageous and noble act. *The Shootist* is a John Wayne movie in which he plays the greatest gunfighter of all, referred to as, yes, "*the* shootist." In almost every other context, shooting is a positive, respected, praiseworthy, and admirable action.

We must demand: "Stop calling murderers shootists!" These are massacres and slaughters committed by killers and mass murderers. By calling these *shootings* instead of *vicious, depraved criminal acts*, we are actually giving the killers the respect and recognition they covet and inciting others to do the same.

On the National Center for Biotechnology Information website (a sub-set of the National Institutes of Health), you will find a scholarly article from 2017 entitled "Mass Shootings: The Role of the Media in Promoting Generalized Imitation." The authors, James N. Meindl and Jonathan W. Ivy, describe in scientific detail how the media can promote the imitation of these mass murders by giving the killers an elevated status and rewarding them for their behavior. And yet they repeatedly use the terms *shooting* and *shooter* to refer to these evil acts. Again, in virtually every other context, these terms are used for individuals and behaviors that have highly elevated status in our society and are richly rewarded for their outcomes. But not once do these authors use the words *murder*, *murderer*, *mass murder*, *massacre*, or *homicide*. This is an example of how Satan's evil is rooted deep in this fallen world. So often the banality of evil allows it to hide right before our eyes.

The phrase *banality of evil* comes from Hannah Arendt, who fled Nazi Germany in her youth and then, in 1963, reported on the trial of Adolf Eichmann, one of the key Nazi perpetrators in the Holocaust. Arendt expected to find a vicious, depraved monster in Eichmann, but instead she found a horrifically normal little bureaucrat.

Banal is an apt word. It means "boring," "vapid," or "commonplace." And it is the very normality of the evil all around us that makes it so difficult to even see it, let alone confront it. Evil is perpetuated by the scholarship of banal bureaucrats who will write a whole article about mass murders, consistently using positive, even laudatory terms to describe these killers and their crimes but never once using the words *murder* or *homicide*, not even recognizing the evil they are perpetuating in doing so.

God has made his thoughts on such matters very clear. Here is Isaiah 5:20, this time from the Good News Translation: "You are doomed! You call evil good and call good evil. You turn darkness into light and light into darkness. You make what is bitter sweet, and what is sweet you make bitter."

Unlike the media and academia—which is largely of the world and thus controlled by the devil—we must always call these massacres exactly what they are. They are *not* shootings. They are the vicious, cowardly mass execution of innocent, harmless, helpless victims, motivated by the core of darkness and the root of all evil: coveting.

While many school killers have claimed they were only reacting to bullying, the truth is that most had fixated on what they *didn't* have. They were coveting the attributes of others. Dr. Peter Langman, author of *School Shooters: Understanding High School, College, and Adult Perpetrators*, calls it "Murderous Envy." (Yes, once again we see in the book's title that thoughtless use of the word *shooter*.) For example, one of the perpetrators of the Columbine school massacre in Littleton, Colorado, wrote in his journal, "I see jocks having fun, friends, women…I hated the happiness that they have."

Before the killer went on his murderous rampage at Thurston High School in Springfield, Oregon, he had circled the face of a player on the football team photograph and wrote "kill" next to it. The circle happened to target the best player on the team, who was also dating a girl that the killer was attracted to.

Note that we haven't used any of these killers' names. Just like not calling them "shooters," not using their names confronts another aspect of their sinful, spiteful, covetous motivation. It is another indicator of the thoughtless depravity of our society, when we give these killers recognition and celebrity in return for committing these mass-murders.

God tells us: "Do not love the world or anything in the world. If anyone loves the world, love for the Father is not in them. For everything in the world—the lust of the flesh, the lust of the eyes, and the pride of life—comes not from the Father but from the world" (1 John 2:15–16).

But the "payoff" for these vicious school killers is when the world gives them fame and celebrity. They seek to covetously, sinfully, spitefully, steal for themselves the renown and recognition they envy in their murdered victims. And we give them renown and recognition every time anyone (including the media) says their names.

FBI director James Comey, in response to the 2016 mass-murder of forty-nine people in an Orlando night club, said: "Notice I am not using the killer's name…Part of what motivates sick people to do this kind of thing is some twisted notion of fame or glory, and I don't want to be part of that…so that other twisted minds don't think that this is a path to fame and recognition."

To refuse to say their name is one thing that we *can* control along with the terms we use to describe these mass murderers and their massacres. It is one influence that we *do* have. Thus, we must take the influence we have been blessed with and use it well so that we deny the killers what they so sinfully craved. We can see the spiritual emptiness in our world because "they loved the glory that comes from man more than the glory that comes from God" (John 12:43 ESV).

After the 2019 mosque massacres in New Zealand, Prime Minister Jacinda Ardern refused to say the killer's name. She said, "He may have sought notoriety, but we in New Zealand will give him nothing, not even his name." Yes! *Here* is someone who understands. Give the killers nothing. Make them nobody. Refuse to even say their name. *That* is punishment. We will not give them the respect, the fame, the recognition that they sinfully covet. And it is indeed the sin of coveting that largely motivates these vicious, depraved criminals.

Before the Virginia Tech college massacre, the killer criticized his targets, saying, "Your Mercedes wasn't enough, you brats. Your golden necklaces weren't enough, you snobs." Yet, he wished he could have been one of them: "Oh the happiness I could have had mingling among you." But God's Word tells us: "Keep your lives free from the love of money and be content with what you have, because God has said, 'Never will I leave you; never will I forsake you'" (Hebrews 13:5).

Dr. Langman has found that these mass murderers are more likely driven by envy than by revenge. Ingratitude is a precursor to envy, and those who covet have forgotten their own gifts and have focused all their energy on desiring the gifts given to others. This leads to dark fixations and predatory actions.

The evidence is clear: breaking the tenth commandment sets off a chain reaction that destroys others before it finally consumes the self. We must count our own blessings and pray to God to remove jealousy from our heart so that perverse desire never turns into an action.

The solution is, first, to focus on the gifts and opportunities that God has given to us. Then to use those gifts to do good as we give the honor and glory to God. Thus, we become mighty, godly witnesses to the world, and we reap love, joy, and peace for ourselves.

We must always ask ourselves, "Who am I trying to please?" As the apostle Paul said long ago, "Am I now trying to win the approval of human beings, or of God? Or am I trying to please people? If I were still trying to please people, I would not be a servant of Christ" (Galatians 1:10).

We also should recall that our great reward comes not in the brief, fleeting time on this earth, but in eternity in heaven.

> Have we laid up our treasures in heaven?
>   The land where no moth shall consume,
> No beautiful links shall be riven,
>   No frost blight the lily's fair bloom.

WARNING #18: Next Level Battle Prep

- ➤ Discuss the tenth commandment (Thou shalt not covet) and how it affects criminality.

    - ○ What worldly things do you covet?
    - ○ What blessings do you take for granted?
    - ○ How does coveting affect your behavior?
    - ○ Can you find an example of coveting in the news?

- How has coveting affected your community?
- How has coveting affected your country?

EIGHTEENTH ORDER

CALM YOUR PASSIONS BY SEEING HOW LITTLE THERE IS TO GAIN

We often worry and scheme about trifling matters of no real importance.

(Erasmus)

> Be thou faithful unto death,
> and I will give thee a crown of life.
> —Revelation 2:10 KJV

The Bible says that we are all blessed with intrinsic value as God's children. This is evidenced in all the ways he provides for us:

> [God] is not served by human hands, as if
> he needed anything. Rather, he himself gives
> everyone life and breath and everything else.

> From one man he made all the nations, that they should inhabit the whole earth; and he marked out their appointed times in history and the boundaries of their lands. God did this so that they would seek him and perhaps reach out for him and find him, though he is not far from any one of us. "For in him we live and move and have our being." As some of your own poets have said, "We are his offspring." (Acts 17:25–28)

This passage also reveals to us that God marks out our appointed times in history and the boundaries of our possessions. The Bible says we covet when we are unsatisfied with our lives, when we want the gifts that God has given to others.

Humility Comes before Honor

The Bible teaches us, "Before a downfall the heart is haughty, but humility comes before honor" (Proverbs 18:12). Humility destroys covetousness just as it destroys pride. Humility means being content with what God has given you. Humility means that the devil and envy are not your master. "Humility comes before honor" because humility allows faithfulness to flourish in your heart. Humility enables you to perform godly service in keeping with honor.

An anonymous Catholic priest has been credited for the wise saying, "I became a free man once I decided that I did not care if I ever became a bishop." Likewise, police and military should serve in humility, accepting promotion as a heavy responsibility if it comes, but accepting God's path for themselves if promotion is not offered or sought after.

Politics is an aspect of all earthly ranks, and it is easy for covetousness to turn into anger when someone appears to or actually does use influence to obtain a promotion. But to grow enraged is to doubt God's power and divine plan. When advancement, prestige, and money all mean *less* to us than our devotion to Jesus Christ, then and only then are we truly free to serve God.

> You must have the same attitude that Christ Jesus had. Though he was God, he did not think of equality with God as something to cling to. Instead, he gave up his divine privileges; he took the humble position of a slave and was born as a human being. When he appeared in human form, he humbled himself in obedience to God and died a criminal's death on a cross. (Philippians 2:5–8 NLT)

Jesus Christ (who was by nature God) humbled himself and became a man, a true servant leader. He was a perfect sacrifice for our sin because he did not sin. He was the Messiah foretold countless times in the Old Testament, the only human being ever born who did not sin. This same Jesus became a sacrificial leader and made himself a sacrifice so we might receive forgiveness of our sins. Satan (who coveted God's power and stature above all else) was defeated, once and for all time, when Jesus willingly died for our sin.

Count Your Blessings

The answer to covetousness is not the absence of all desire but rather the cultivation of contentment and gratitude (1 Timothy 6:6–10). "Give thanks unto the Lord, for he is good: for his mercy endureth for ever" (Psalm 107:1 KJV).

Dr. Norberto Eiji Nawa conducted a study of college students at Ritsumeikan University and published in ScienceDaily on May 13, 2021. Nawa asked the students to keep an online "gratitude journal" by recording up to five things they felt grateful for each day. The researchers found that keeping a gratitude journal increased the students' academic motivation not only during the study but even three months after it ended. The researchers discovered that keeping daily gratitude journals decreased the perception that one's actions are irrelevant, which can lead to feelings of helplessness. In other words, feelings of gratitude were directly correlated to feelings of control and optimism for one's own future.

When you feel blessed, coveting the blessings of others is no longer necessary because you have everything you need.

Five Blessings to Be Grateful For:

1. The Lord is good, and his love endures forever (Psalm 100:5).
2. Nothing can ever separate us from God's love. Not death, not demons, not even the powers of hell (Romans 8:38).

3. God so loved us that he sent his Son as an atoning sacrifice for our sins (1 John 4:10).

4. Whoever cries unto the Lord will be saved (Romans 10:13).

5. And you shall dwell in the house of the Lord forever (Psalm 23:6).

Scrooge and His "Sinner's Prayer"

Let us examine the classic novel *A Christmas Carol* (1843), by Charles Dickens. The lead character, Ebenezer Scrooge, is a particularly despicable and sinful man. His heart is full of greed, selfishness, and resentment.

But Scrooge is fortunate. In his mercy, God saw fit to send three spirits to warn him of his pending damnation: the Ghost of Christmas Past, the Ghost of Christmas Present, and the Ghost of Christmas Yet to Come. The last spirit was by far the worst. The spirit takes Scrooge to the cemetery to point out Ebenezer's lonely, unmourned death without salvation.

Ebenezer Scrooge was "broken bad" because his father blamed Ebenezer for his mother's death in childbirth. As a young man, Ebenezer chose to seek wealth rather than have a family. But the three spirits forced Scrooge to truly observe the empty, joyless abyss of his life and mercilessly judge it. As the spirits showed Scrooge his past, present, and future, he was brought to sincere sorrow for choosing a life of coveting instead of a life of love. Scrooge confessed his sins, and his heart softened so the Holy Spirit could enter.

This produced a remarkable transformation as Scrooge expressed his repentance in thankfulness and love of his fellow man. Scrooge had now "broken good," and he expressed his sanctification by becoming a charitable man and by truly honoring Christmas—which ultimately means to honor Christ.

Scrooge's prayer of repentance is worthy of examination. Here is a true Sinner's Prayer:

> "Spirit!" he cried, tight clutching at its robe, "hear me! I am not the man I was. I will not be the man I must have been but for this intercourse. Why show me this, if I am past all hope!"
>
> For the first time the hand appeared to shake.
>
> "Good Spirit," he pursued, as down upon the ground he fell before it: "Your nature intercedes for me, and pities me. Assure me that I yet may change these shadows you have shown me, by an altered life!"
>
> The kind hand trembled.
>
> "I will honor Christmas in my heart, and try to keep it all the year. I will live in the Past, the Present, and the Future. The Spirits of all Three shall strive within me. I will not shut out the lessons that they teach. Oh, tell me I may sponge away the writing on this stone!"

Gain the World, Lose Your Soul?

The verse that may best define Scrooge's repentance is Mark 8:36, where Jesus says, "For what does it profit a man to gain the whole world and forfeit his soul?" (ESV). Everything that the world can possibly give us is absolutely trivial and miniscule compared to eternity in heaven.

The spirits taught this lesson to Scrooge by showing him the past and allowing him to see those things that endured from the years gone by—virtues such as joy, fellowship, and love. By seeing the present, Scrooge understood that Bob Cratchit and his family (although profoundly impoverished) had great joy and love in their lives while Scrooge had only a joyless existence filled with covetous greed. But seeing the future had the greatest impact of all, for Scrooge learned that he would die with an empty, hollow life—a life unmourned and unloved.

On earth, *love* is the characteristic, the action, and the result of a life that is most pleasing in the sight of man and God. As Paul reveals to us:

> I may be able to speak the languages of human beings and even of angels, but if I have no love, my speech is no more than a noisy gong or a clanging bell. I may have the gift of inspired preaching; I may have all knowledge and under- stand all secrets; I may have all the faith needed to move mountains—but if I have no love, I am nothing. I may give away everything I have, and

even give up my body to be burned—but if I
have no love, this does me no good.

Love is patient and kind; it is not jealous
or conceited or proud; love is not ill-mannered
or selfish or irritable; love does not keep a record of wrongs; love is not happy with evil, but
is happy with the truth. Love never gives up; and
its faith, hope, and patience never fail.

Love is eternal. There are inspired messages,
but they are temporary; there are gifts of speaking in strange tongues, but they will cease; there
is knowledge, but it will pass…Meanwhile these
three remain: faith, hope, and love; and the greatest
of these is love. (1 Corinthians 13:1–8, 13 GNT)

Remember that the greatest commandment that God
gives us is to love:

Jesus answered, "'Love the Lord your God with all
your heart, with all your soul, and with all your
mind.' This is the greatest and the most important
commandment. The second most important commandment is like it: 'Love your neighbor as you
love yourself.' The whole Law of Moses and the
teachings of the prophets depend on these two
commandments." (Matthew 22:37–40 GNT)

Thus, we must always remember, if we truly love God and
love people, then the most important thing we could *ever* do is

to bring them to the knowledge of salvation. And everything—our every action, our purpose here on earth, everything!—flows from that beautiful, glorious foundation of love.

God *is* love, as the apostle John tells us (1 John 4:8). One implication of this is brought out by C. S. Lewis in his book *The Four Loves*: "In God there is no hunger that needs to be filled, only plenteousness that desires to give." Scrooge had no love in his life. The absence of love is evil, just as dark is the absence of light. Scrooge was evil, and he was on a path leading straight to hell.

> To love…is to be vulnerable. Love anything, and your heart will certainly be wrung and possibly be broken. If you want to make sure of keeping it intact, you must give your heart to no one, not even to an animal. Wrap it carefully round with hobbies and little luxuries; avoid all entanglements; lock it up safe in the casket or coffin of your selfishness. But in that casket—safe, dark, motionless, airless—it will change. It will not be broken; it will become unbreakable, impenetrable, irredeemable. The alternative to tragedy, or at least to the risk of tragedy, is damnation. The only place outside Heaven where you can be perfectly safe from all the dangers and perturbations of love is Hell. (Lewis, *The Four Loves*)

Again in *The Four Loves*, Lewis rightly tells us, "Affection [love] is responsible for nine-tenths of whatever solid and durable happiness there is in our natural lives." God knows that we need love and that we need to give love to others. So he loves us, and his foremost desire is for us to love. If we ask God, he will help us in that endeavor. God gives us clear instructions on how that love should manifest itself: "Do nothing out of selfish ambition or vain conceit. Rather, in humility value others above yourselves, not looking to your own interests but each of you to the interests of the others" (Philippians 2:3–4).

When we love others as we should, we find confirmed what Lewis observes in *The Four Loves*: "The worldly man treats certain people kindly because he 'likes' them: the Christian, trying to treat every one kindly, finds him liking more and more people as he goes on—including people he could not even have imagined himself liking at the beginning."

Scrooge learned, the hard way, that spirits exist. If they do, then there is life beyond natural, biological life. There *is* something beyond what we can see and touch. If you believe that, even a little bit, then you may realize that what comes after this life is infinitely more important than anything that can happen in this life. And this is what Scripture affirms.

Never lose track of the fact that eternity hangs in the balance. We must never lose that eternal perspective that guides God's interaction with us and with the world. Thus, this is perhaps Erasmus' most important order, his wisest advice: "Calm your passions by seeing how little there is to gain." Nothing, nothing, *nothing* on this planet is remotely as important as eternity in heaven with God. If you truly, mathematically, philosophically grasp the unthinkable enormity of eternity, then everything else—your life, the life of our planet, the lifespan of our sun—shrinks to an insignificant, miniscule *nothing* by comparison. No pain on this earth, no suffering in this fallen world, nor any reward that this existence can possibly give us, *none of it* is remotely important compared to your salvation and bringing others to that saving life in Christ.

WARNORD Recap

One of the deepest and most important verses in the Bible—so simple and basic that we too often treat it like a nursery rhyme and fail to grasp its majesty and grandeur—tells us that we must focus our attention on what comes *after* we die. Pastor Doug Winkler says that we should stay focused on the "profits" in the "spreadsheet" of our *heavenly account*.

> Do not store up for yourselves treasures on earth, where moths and vermin destroy, and where thieves break in and steal. But store up for yourselves treasures in heaven, where moths and vermin do not destroy, and where thieves do not break in and steal. For where your treasure is, there your heart will be also. (Matthew 6:19–21)

Do you find yourself consumed with worry and scheming about trivial, inconsequential matters? Then stop. Take a deep breath. And remember that our reward is in heaven.

Start living your earthly life as God commands—*not* as the world says—and store up treasures in heaven. Treasures full of faith, hope, and love. And the greatest of these is love. "With malice toward none, with charity for all, with firmness in the right as God gives us to see!" (Abraham Lincoln's Second Inaugural Address).

God promises us, "Be thou faithful unto death, and I will give thee a crown of life" (Revelation 2:10 KJV).

> Have we laid up our treasures in heaven,
>   Rich treasures of faith, hope and love?
> If so, what bright stars shall be given,
>   What blessings await us above!
>
> Wonderful treasures, heavenly pleasures,
>   Never to perish, nor fade away;
> Wonderful treasures, heavenly pleasures,
>   Are we laying up treasures today?

Prayer: Giving Thanks and Promising Service

ALMIGHTY God, Father of all mercies,
we, thine unworthy servants,
do give thee most humble and hearty thanks
for all thy goodness and loving kindness
to us, and to all men.
    We bless thee for our creation, preservation,
and all the blessings of this life;
but above all, for thine inestimable love in the

redemption of the world by our Lord Jesus Christ;
for the means of grace, and for the hope of glory.
  And, we beseech thee,
give us that due sense of all thy mercies
that our hearts may be unfeignedly thankful:
and that we may show forth thy praise,
not only with our lips, but in our lives;
by giving up ourselves to thy service,
and by walking before thee
in holiness and righteousness
all our days;
  through Jesus Christ our Lord,
to whom, with thee and the Holy Ghost,
be all honor and glory, world without end.
  Amen.

—Unknown author, *Soldier's Prayer Book*
(ca. 1863)

ORDER #18: Next Level Battle Prep

➤   How do you count your blessings?

  ○   How do you thank God?
  ○   How do you grieve God?

➤ Is there someone in your life you need to show appreciation to?

    ○ Is there someone you take for granted?

    ○ What can you do to make amends?

NINETEENTH WARNING

THE WICKED DO NOT FEEL SORROW FOR THE PAIN THEY CAUSE

The devil tempts us to bring shame and hurt on our mothers, fathers, wives, and children.

(Luther)

WARNORD #19

NINETEENTH ORDER

CONSIDER THE IMPACT ON YOUR FAMILY

"If I do what I am considering, would I want my family to know about it?"

(Erasmus)

NINETEENTH WARNING

THE WICKED DO NOT FEEL SORROW FOR THE PAIN THEY CAUSE

The devil tempts us to bring shame and hurt on our mothers, fathers, wives, and children.

(Luther)

Jesus said, "Let the little children come to me, and do not hinder them, for the kingdom of heaven belongs to such as these."
—Matthew 19:14

Happy the home when God is there,
    And love fills every breast;
When one their wish, and one their prayer,
    And one their heav'nly rest.

Happy the home where Jesus' name
    Is sweet to every ear;
Where children early speak His fame,
    And parents hold Him dear.

Happy the home where prayer is heard,
    And praise is wont to rise;
Where parents love the sacred Word
    And all its wisdom prize.

Lord, let us in our homes agree
    This blessed peace to gain;
Unite our hearts in love to Thee,
    And love to all will reign.

— "Happy the Home When God Is There," by Henry Ware
(1793–1843)

In this nineteenth WARNORD, Luther and Erasmus both focus on our families. Our responsibility toward these dear ones is so profound; it is a mighty motivator for sacrificial love. And envisioning the remorse we would feel for causing them shame can motivate us to do what is good and godly in the face of temptations.

A 2021 study, "A Psychological Intervention Reduces Doping Likelihood," from the University of Birmingham, UK, by Professor Maria Kavussanu and others, published in the journal *Psychology of Sport and Exercise,* found that, "Appealing to athletes' sense of 'future guilt' through psychological intervention, could prove a powerful weapon in the fight against doping."

> Researchers discovered that making elite athletes picture how guilty they might feel about using banned performance enhancing drugs, produced a more powerful initial reaction than initiatives educating sports people about the health risks of doping.

In the same way, envisioning the sorrow, pain, and shame we would inflict upon our loved ones can motivate us to stay on the straight and narrow path of God's will. We would contend that we should focus our greatest motivation, inspiration, and sacrifice upon our children. We must always ask if our actions are bringing them to the knowledge of God's plan of salvation.

Sgt. York: From Dishonor to Medal of Honor

Alvin Cullum York, also known as Sergeant York, was born December 13, 1887, in Pall Mall, Tennessee, in the Valley of the Three Forks of the Wolf River. He was one of the most celebrated heroes of World War I, receiving the Congressional Medal of Honor.

The monument to him on a small hill outside the French village of Chatel-Chehery reads, "Armed with his rifle and pistol, his courage and skill, he silenced a German battalion of 35 machine guns, killed 25 enemy soldiers and captured 132." It also quotes the French Marshal Foch, who said that what York did "was the greatest thing accomplished by any private soldier of all the armies of Europe."

In the book, *Sgt. York: His Life and Legacy*, John Perry describes how Alvin York went from being an unreliable drinker and brawler to a pacifist to a humble war hero and family man.

Alvin grew up in a small cabin with ten brothers and sisters. His father was a farmer and blacksmith, and his mother was a hardy but loving pioneer woman. Alvin received minimal schooling before joining his father on the farm. When Alvin was twenty-four, his father passed away, and then his two older brothers married and moved away. Alvin was forced to become head of the household at a young age, and he rebelled. He hung out with a rough group and became something of a carouser: smoking, gambling, swearing, and drinking. He became an insolent sort and didn't mind bringing dishonor upon his family. This is what Luther meant when he said, "The wicked do not feel sorrow for the pain they cause." Alvin York was a classic example of the devil tempting us to bring dishonor, shame, and hurt to our loved ones. On one occasion he got drunk and disrupted a community picnic. By the age of twenty-nine, Alvin had a bad reputation, and it looked like he would only get worse.

Then late one night, Alvin returned home after another night of drinking. To his surprise, Mother York was wide awake, waiting for him in her rocking chair by the fire. His mother was a hard-working woman, and she never stayed up late. As Alvin walked in the cabin, his mother looked at her son, and in a soft but firm voice asked: "Alvin, when are you going to be a man like your father and grandfather?" Alvin's father was always strong and reliable, a good Christian man. His grandfather was a pillar of the community. His mother's simple question pierced Alvin like a knife and left a scar that would not heal.

Mother York had tears in her eyes. Alvin later said it was the first time he had ever seen his mother cry. It was at this time, Alvin said, something inside him started to break. Suddenly he felt the shame and dishonor he had inflicted upon his family. Would he break bad or good?

Martin Luther likens such moments to being hit by a thunderbolt. In the 1941 movie *Sergeant York*, Alvin is literally struck by lightning while on his way to murder a man who cheated him out of a piece of property he was determined to buy. (Another example involving the tenth commandment.) Fortunately, God hits Alvin with a thunderbolt not too far from the church. Alvin is drawn to God (John 6:44) by the Holy Ghost. Alvin gets up from the ground and walks into church while they are singing a hymn "Old Time Religion," and he ends up praying with his family. Alvin accepts Jesus Christ as his Savior (in spirit, not just in words or acts), and he is born again (3:3–8). At that moment, Alvin makes a promise to his mother that he would become like his dad.

Abrupt change in a wayward person is unforeseen, even when yearned and prayed for. In Alvin York's case, it occurred when his mother invoked the lineage of his father and grandfather. That connection made Alvin break for the good.

A few weeks later, Alvin confessed his sins and was saved at a church revival meeting. He had seen the light and became the Sergeant York of legend: a conscientious objector who opposed all violence but eventually decided he had to fight against evil. Alvin's company commander, Captain Edward Courtney Bullock Danforth, quoted Scripture that convinced Alvin that it was sometimes necessary to fight for a cause. In particular, the verses Danforth used to enlighten Alvin were John 18:36 (KJV), "If my kingdom were of this world, then would my servants fight," and Luke 22:36 (KJV), "He that hath no sword, let him sell his garment, and buy one." Captain Danforth convinced Alvin that *faith* also requires *works*, and this sometimes involves very difficult decisions.

That is how one man went from being Alvin York to the legendary Sgt. York. That is how he went from dishonor to the Medal of Honor. In doing so, his mighty deeds brought honor and glory to God, and across the years, the story of this virtuous Christian warrior has inspired millions.

In many ways, you can say that York's mother, and maybe Captain Danforth, were the real heroes in this story. Remember, your greatest contribution to God's kingdom might not be something you do but someone you raise or perhaps someone you teach about God's Word.

Every mother and father should also pray, work, and strive (like Mother York) for their child to be "born again."

Lord, let us in our homes agree
This blessed peace to gain;
Unite our hearts in love to Thee,
And love to all will reign.

What Does It Mean to Be "Born Again"?

To be "born again" is a phrase that comes from Scripture: "Jesus replied, 'Very truly I tell you, no one can see the kingdom of God unless they are born again…Very truly I tell you, no one can enter the kingdom of God unless they are born of water and the Spirit'" (John 3:3, 5). To be born again refers to a spiritual rebirth brought about by the Holy Spirit when a person puts their faith in Christ. We cannot be born again apart from the Spirit's work of conversion. To be born again requires you to accept Jesus as your Savior and confess your complete sinfulness. Everyone who is born again has come to Christ and disclosed their shame: "Whoever lives by the truth comes into the light, so that it may be seen plainly that what they have done has been done in the sight of God" (v. 21). However, those who have refused the Holy Spirit have not been born again. They are holding on to their sins and are afraid to repent of their sins before Jesus Christ: "Everyone who does evil hates the light, and will not come into the light for fear that their deeds will be exposed" (v. 20).

Each person has the choice to receive or reject God's salvation gift through faith (Ephesians 2:8–9). In the next

WARNORD, we will discuss how we disciples of Christ can help others respond to God's call.

> Children are a heritage from the LORD,
>   offspring a reward from him.
> Like arrows in the hands of a warrior
>   are children born in one's youth.
> Blessed is the man
>   whose quiver is full of them.
>
> —Psalm 127:3–5

From the Movie *Sergeant York*, directed by Howard Hawks (1941)

"Satan's got you by the shirttail, Alvin."

"Sure has."

"He's going to yank you straight down to Hell."

"You are plumb right, pastor."

"You got to make him let loose of you before it's too late."

"I sure wish I knowed how."

"Wrestle him, Alvin, wrestle him like you would a bear."

"I done wrestled him, pastor, but old Satan, he hangs on tight."

"You and the Lord could throw him, Alvin. Why, 'twixt the two of you you'd have old Satan down in a jiffy."

"I sure wish the Lord would throw in."

"He will if you ask him."

"Oh, I done prayed, pastor, till I was blue in the face. But it weren't no use."

"It ain't only praying, Alvin. It's believing."

WARNING #19: Next Level Battle Prep

➢ How can an intervention that creates anticipated guilt of future misbehavior change a person's perspective?

➢ How could this be used in police training?

➢ What did Mother York say that changed Alvin York's sense of guilt?

➢ What is the difference between a *receptive* person and a *resistant* person during an intervention?

NINETEENTH ORDER

CONSIDER THE IMPACT ON YOUR FAMILY

"If I do what I am considering, would I want my family to know about it?"

(Erasmus)

Anyone who does not provide for their relatives, and especially for their own household, has denied the faith and is worse than an unbeliever.
—1 Timothy 5:8

When considering the enticement of sin, think of the impact it will have on your family. Your integrity. Your career. But most of all and above all, eternity. Remember, science tells us that anticipating future shame can be a powerful tool to guide us on the straight and narrow road that leads to eternity with God.

In our book *Bulletproof Marriage: A 90-Day Devotional* (coauthored with Adam Davis), we share stories—many from Adam's own experiences—of how our sinful desires have an impact on others. Some may call this fallout collateral damage, but it is better understood as the fruit of sin.

The lure of the devil and the allure of sin affects every area of our lives, especially our families. The fruit of sin may not blossom immediately, but it will in time. It affects our communication in marriage, our parenting styles, our children's destinies, and the future of our families. Yes, the enemy, known as the devil, will entice us to sin, and the results of our sin will bear a cost. For evil actions, there are always consequences.

But, my dear friends, fellow pilgrims, beloved sheepdogs under the authority of the Great Shepherd, rejoice in the hope of Christ. Redemption is nearer and dearer to us than the enticement of sin. Yes, the devil may tempt us, and he will indeed attack us. But closer to our lives than the taste for sin's pleasure are our families and the redemption of the Lord.

When we rebel against God in sin, death and tragedy are our reward. Even if we are saved, our actions could cause others to reject salvation. Oh, but when we rebel against hell's grip of sin, what joy awaits! What hope abounds! What grace may await!

Your marriage, your family, your career, your community, and your nation, all deserve the best rebellious effort against hell and its temptations. Your marriage vows, your oath, and your responsibility to your family are all manifestations of your integrity. Some of you say, "No, I didn't swear an oath as a law enforcement officer." Or "No, I didn't swear an oath of enlistment in the military." That is not the oath I'm talking about. At least if you are an American, much of your integrity is reflected and affirmed in the solemn oath we swore from our youngest days: "I pledge allegiance to the Flag of the United States of America, and to the Republic for which it stands, one Nation under God, indivisible, with liberty and justice for all."

The relation of sin and integrity is powerful. One calls us to evil and the other to honor, "with liberty and justice for all." In Adam Davis' book *Behind the Badge: 365 Daily Devotions for Law Enforcement,* he spends an entire month on the topic of integrity matters. Adam had a heart to write this book in short, easy-to-read bites. It is a way to focus your eyes on what is most important, and it will certainly help you get a deeper hunger for God's Word. As Adam Davis says in his powerful and inspirational presentations, "Resist the temptation presented by the enemy, and if you are equipped with the armor of God and His Word, you will be ready for battle!" Adam tells his audiences, "You need to fight with everything you have for your families. Because hell is fighting for them too!"

Moral Epiphanies: "I have seen the Light!"

When we are sinful, our families often suffer for our actions. A sinful person is usually blind to the pain and shame they inflict upon others. But sometimes, when a loved one seems "lost" to sin, a family intervention can make the sinner suddenly aware. As in the case of Alvin York, whose mother asked a simple question that sparked his conscience: "Alvin, when are you going to be a man like your father and grandfather?" Psychologists now refer to these unexpected feelings of guilt and empathy as "moral epiphanies."

Moral epiphanies are sudden realizations of right and wrong—and they are, sadly, as rare as "the appearance of a rainbow in the clouds on a rainy day" (Ezekiel 1:28).

Psychologists say that moral epiphanies are difficult to understand because morality involves several overlapping areas in the brain. It could be that such moral epiphanies are caused by a sudden new brain connection. It is certainly within the power of the Holy Spirit (1 Corinthians 6:11) to rewire our brains and show us the light. And there is a way that we can reach others who are trapped in bad lifestyles and addiction.

Tough Love

Sometimes an intervention is needed to help create a moral epiphany. Police know that tough love is a valuable alternative when everything else has failed.

Tough love occurs when a sheepdog (that can be police, family members, or anyone who wants to move someone to "safe meadows") does the tough thing out of the love of their heart to protect a soul from further damage by the devil. This is active spiritual warfare against the devil, who will do anything he can to keep a soul from healing. "No discipline is enjoyable while it is happening—it's painful! But afterward there will be a peaceful harvest of right living for those who are trained in this way" (Hebrews 12:11 NLT).

Addiction is one of the most dangerous tools of the devil. The Bureau of Justice Statistics reports that nearly 50 percent of violent offenders were using alcohol or drugs at the time of their arrest. When a person becomes addicted, their brain is rewired to seek the drug, now regarded as something necessary to survive, more important than food or water. Addiction is so powerful it replaces God and family, no matter the consequences. So quite obviously, Satan utilizes addiction whenever he can; it is perhaps his most powerful tool to separate people from God.

Anyone who has experienced the horror of a loved one possessed by addiction will tell you, as the addiction worsens, the addict will increasingly lie, steal, shift blame, manipulate, and become abusive. Brain scans of drug addicts reveal that their brains slowly transform and begin to resemble the brain scans of psychopaths.

The good news is that rewiring can work both ways. There are generally three stages in the recovery process for addiction: abstinence, repair, and growth. Unfortunately, according to "The Stages of Recovery" by Fort Behavioral Health, abstinence lasts from one to two years and repair lasts two to three years. The question is, what can we do to attain years of cooperation from the addict? Many families spend their entire life savings to fund treatment only to watch their loved one repeatedly quit treatment and return to addiction. Police and probation officers often hear from addicts, "Whatever you do, don't send me to rehab!" It's a myth that addicts want to get off drugs. Many addicts want to keep drinking or using the drug.

The National Institute on Drug Abuse reports that it is a myth that an addict must be ready and willing to enter treatment. It is also a myth that an addict must hit rock bottom before they can be helped. If you wait that long, the mental and physical damage could be devastating.

Studies by the National Institute on Drug Abuse show that legal pressure by the criminal justice system on the addict can produce higher attendance rates in drug treatment. Participants remaining in treatment for longer periods of time can have results as good or better than voluntary participation.

Police realize that not bringing criminal charges could be the worse decision for some drug addicts. Many states now have drug courts or problem-solving courts that are set up to supervise drug rehabilitation.

Police have learned that they should seize even small amounts of evidence or drug paraphernalia for lab analysis or even obtain blood samples so that the addict can be charged with possession or drug use.

Critics accuse the police of "zero-tolerance" enforcement, just to make an arrest. But families of the addict will say that enforcement of drug laws is tough love when everything else is failing. Many of these families have learned what Scripture affirms: "Those who spare the rod of discipline hate their children. Those who love their children care enough to discipline them" (Proverbs 13:24 NLT). And, when necessary, law enforcement can support the efforts of families by bringing their own brand of tough love into the picture.

Sometimes mandatory rehabilitation is the only door to a cure. Without rehabilitation and the help of professionals, only a very few people would ever overcome addiction.

WARNORD Recap

We are called to "rescue" the perishing (24:11), just as we are called to bring others to the knowledge of salvation. And that responsibility is first and foremost to our loved ones. Another amazing old Fanny Crosby hymn tells us:

> Rescue the perishing, Care for the dying,
>   Snatch them in pity from sin and the grave;
> Weep o'er the erring one, lift up the fallen,
>   Tell them of Jesus the mighty to save.
>
> Rescue the perishing, Duty demands it;
>   Strength for thy labor the Lord will provide;
> Back to the narrow way patiently win them;
>   Tell the poor wanderer a Savior has died.

Meanwhile, when it comes to taking that first step down the self-destructive path of sin, Erasmus powerfully establishes one effective tool to guide us on God's chosen path: Think of it this way, "If I do what I am considering, would I want my family to know about it?"

As always, the best guideline for our priorities can be found in God's Holy Word: "Anyone who does not provide for their relatives, and especially for their own household, has denied the faith and is worse than an unbeliever" (1 Timothy 5:8).

Happy the home where prayer is heard,
    And praise is wont to rise;
Where parents love the sacred Word
    And all its wisdom prize.

Prayer for Our Children

Blessed Lord Jesus,
    Who hast taught us
    that we must be as little children
    in order to come to Thy Kingdom, and
Who didst love and bless them most tenderly:
Grant that our children
    may be drawn unto Thee
    by Thy good Spirit and
    ever kept in Thy service,
    so that walking in Thy way,
    they may ever show forth Thy praise and
be one with us in the confession of Thy holy Name;
Who livest and reignest
with the Father and the Holy Ghost,
ever One God, world without end.
    Amen.

—Common Service Book of the Lutheran Church (1918)

ORDER #19: Next Level Battle Prep

- ➤ How has guilt changed your life?
- ➤ What does "born again" mean to you?
- ➤ Have you ever had a moral epiphany? What was it?
- ➤ Have you ever seen a Christian use tough love? What did that look like, and how effective was it?

TWENTIETH WARNING

THE WICKED HAVE NO DIVINE AUTHORITY

Evil is at its worse when the rule of man is preferred over the authority of God.

(Luther)

WARNORD #20

TWENTIETH ORDER

VIRTUE HAS ITS OWN AUTHORITY

Once a person has Christ in their heart, they would not exchange His authority for anything.

(Erasmus)

TWENTIETH WARNING

THE WICKED HAVE
NO DIVINE AUTHORITY

Evil is at its worse when the rule of man is preferred over the authority of God.

(Luther)

Where you have envy and selfish ambition,
there you find disorder and every evil practice.
—James 3:16

The sacred joy which virtue brings,
   The lasting joy of truth,
Depends not on the blooming scene,
   The scene of transient youth.

Through nature's great and constant change,
    Unconscious of decay,
It views unmoved the scythe of time
    Sweep all besides away.

While every short-lived flower of sense,
    Destructive years consume.
Through virtue's fair, delightful walk,
    Unfading blossoms bloom.

—"The Sacred Joy Which Virtue Brings," by Mrs. Carter
(ca. 1826)

Virtue, Authority, and Responsibility

The Scottish poet Sir Walter Scott once mused, "How rare is virtue on a throne!" In the US military, there is a blunter way of saying the same thing: "You can delegate *authority*, but you can't delegate *responsibility*." *Authority* refers to the power given to an individual to take certain actions. It may include the ability to spend time in a certain way, to have access to certain resources, or to delegate work to other people. *Responsibility* refers to taking ownership for a project, task, or course of action. Even though a leader may supervise people working on a project or a mission, he or she is still in charge of the entire process and should be held accountable for the end result.

You may have noticed that a lot of people want *authority* and all the perks that come with power and prestige, but they don't want the *responsibility* that comes with the promotion.

The devil is like this: he wants God's power but not God's virtue; he wants authority but not responsibility. The Bible warns us that a lot of leaders will be like this: "The people all said to Samuel, 'Pray to the LORD your God for your servants so that we will not die, for we have added to all our other sins the evil of asking for a king'" (1 Samuel 12:19).

After the people asked God to give them a king, they soon regretted it. It takes virtue to assume responsibility for other people's problems, and God cannot give authority to those who will not assume responsibility. If people had God's power but kept their own sinful character, imagine the evil they would commit. It would be like a nightmare out of some *Harry Potter* movie. That is what the devil wants.

The Bible warns us about selfish ambition: "If you harbor bitter envy and selfish ambition in your hearts, do not boast about it or deny the truth. Such 'wisdom' does not come down from heaven but is earthly, unspiritual, demonic. For where you have envy and selfish ambition, there you find disorder and every evil practice" (James 3:14–16). This explains why people in power commit so much evil.

The Puritans were correct in wanting to limit power—a view and desire worked out politically in the US Constitution's separation of governing powers. America's founders understood that sinful people with centralized power in their hands were prone to terrible abuses, so they sought to curtail that consequence by a series of checks on power and balances of power that decentralized it and made the power-holders accountable to the people they governed. Power coupled with built-in limits, responsibilities, and accountability—a critical combination for preserving and protecting human freedom and rights.

Jesus referred to those who want authority without responsibility as hypocrites because the language of their lips does not match the living of their lives (Matthew 15:7–9). Bad leaders have the Machiavellian and narcissistic qualities of their father Satan. But the awesome *virtue* and *authority* of the Holy Spirit awaits those leaders ready to take responsibility in the name of Jesus Christ our Lord.

Then we have examples of just the opposite, says alpha reader Gene Blanton, where a low-ranking person assumes the responsibility of those high commanders who are failing to do their job. Gene says, "I've seen it where people were given huge amounts of responsibility without being 'knighted' with the deserved authority." Just think of all the organizations being held together by those "at the bottom" of the chain-of-command. It's not right; it's not fair, but God bless those at the bottom, who live a life of quiet service and sacrifice.

The Virtue of Defiance in the Face of Evil

If you search online for August Landmesser, you will find an amazing photograph from 1936 taken in Nazi Germany. You'll see a virtual *sea* of men, giving the Nazi salute, but one man stands in defiance with his arms crossed. Many people believe that this is August Landmesser, who was engaged to a woman who was Jewish. The couple were arrested, and ultimately, they both died at the hands of the Nazis.

However, a man named Gustav Wegert is also considered by many to be that one individual who stood defiant in the face of evil. He worked at that location in those years, he looked very much like the man in the picture, he was a devout Christian, and he refused to render the Nazi salute. However, unlike Landmesser, Wegert ultimately survived the war.

Was it the love of a Jewish woman that inspired such defiance? Or was it the love of the Lord? Either way it was love, and "Whoever does not love does not know God, because God is love" (1 John 4:8). Landmesser and Wegert in this instance form a kind of divine quantum physics in which God can allow both possibilities to be true at the same time. And either way, the evil of the Nazis should have been obvious to all at that point in history both because of Hitler's attacks on the Jews and his attacks on the Christian church. What is astounding is not this one man of virtue standing in defiance of evil but rather the vast majority who did not see the evil or saw it and went along with it. It is the banality of evil again. It is evil so entrenched and commonplace that one person of virtue becomes the extraordinary exception.

The Nazis replaced the fear of God with a fear of man. "For they loved the praise of men more than the praise of God" (John 12:43 KJV). This is one of the devil's favorite traps or snares. "Fear of man will prove to be a snare, but whoever trusts in the LORD is kept safe" (Proverbs 29:25).

Luther warns us that "The wicked have no divine authority." And it is very clear that evil is indeed "at its worst when the rule of man is preferred over the authority of God."

We need look no further than the horrors and mass murders perpetrated by Nazi Germany, Soviet Russia, or Communist China to see ghastly examples of this fundamental truth. As the power of man goes up and the power of God goes down, evil ascends.

Those who obey God's Word have got their priorities right. "I tell you, my friends, do not be afraid of those who kill the body and after that can do no more" (Luke 12:4).

In our moment of truth, would we have the virtue to stand up in defiance of evil?

> The sacred joy which virtue brings,
>   The lasting joy of truth,
> Depends not on the blooming scene,
>   The scene of transient youth.

Thy word is a lamp unto my feet, and a light unto my path.
—Psalm 119:105 KJV

WARNING #20: Next Level Battle Prep

➤ Give an example of someone holding authority but not fulfilling their responsibility.

➤ Give an example of someone serving with responsibility but not being given the appropriate authority.

> ➤ "The fear of the LORD is the beginning of wisdom"
> (Proverbs 9:10). Do you fear something that
> supersedes your fear of the Lord? If so, what is
> it? What can you do to subject that fear to God
> and let him work through you to lessen it or even
> remove it from your life?

TWENTIETH ORDER

VIRTUE HAS ITS OWN AUTHORITY

Once a person has Christ in their heart, they would not exchange His authority for anything.

(Erasmus)

For this very reason, make every effort to supplement your faith with virtue, and virtue with knowledge.
—2 Peter 1:5 ESV

Adrian Rogers, a renowned preacher and bestselling author, wrote a book called *The Incredible Power of Kingdom Authority: Getting an Upper Hand on the Underworld*. Pastor Rogers uses the legal authority of a police officer as an analogy to a Christian acting with God's kingdom authority. Allow us to summarize. When a police officer knocks at the door and says,

"Open, in the name of the law," most citizens will wisely open the door. Why? Because the officer has authority. The police officer is under the authority of the United States Constitution and all the power assigned under local, state, and federal law. Incredible authority stands behind that one officer, but it is nothing compared to a Christian acting under God's spiritual authority.

Consider the authority delegated by Jesus and given to the apostles:

> One day Jesus called together his twelve disciples and gave them power and authority to cast out all demons and to heal all diseases. Then he sent them out to tell everyone about the Kingdom of God and to heal the sick. "Take nothing for your journey," he instructed them. "Don't take a walking stick, a traveler's bag, food, money, or even a change of clothes." (Luke 9:1–3 NLT)

The apostles understood that their material needs would be provided by God. However, this is one of those verses that must not be taken out of context.

Later, as the time was drawing near for Jesus to be arrested and executed on the cross, circumstances had changed completely, and he gave his disciples new guidance. Notice Jesus did not take away authority, but he gave them additional responsibility to protect themselves and others in the violent times to come. Thus, one of Jesus' last commandments to his disciples was to arm themselves! "He said to them, 'But now if you have a purse, take it, and also a bag; and if you don't have a sword, sell your cloak and buy one'" (22:36). It must be understood that carrying a sword was legal and appropriate in that place and time. (Now, if you "live by the sword"—in other words, if you use violence against lawful authority—then the situation is completely different.)

We must always remember that all legitimate authority comes from God. And as Christians waging spiritual warfare against forces of evil, we have the ultimate authority on our side.

Virtue Has Its Own Reward

We, too, can have God's power to perform good works. Pastor Rogers says, "In Christ we have incredible *authority*. Why? Because we are united with Jesus in His death, burial, resurrection, ascension, and enthronement (see Rom. 6:3–9). Our authority comes from Him." When we live our lives as faithful believers, we are under heavenly authority (1 Peter 3:22). However, if police officers violate the Constitution, they are no longer under constitutional authority, and they become liable for what they do. Likewise, if a Christian is disobedient to God, they are no longer under God's kingdom authority, and they become liable for what they do.

Pastor Rogers explains that all authority is linked to obedience. A police officer cannot have legal authority until he gets under the authority of the Constitution, and a Christian cannot have spiritual authority until he gets under the author-ity of Jesus Christ. This is the reason that Satan works so hard to have us disobey God. When we disobey the Lord, we forfeit the spiritual authority of Jesus Christ. Pastor Rogers says, "God does not give Kingdom authority to rebels. If you do not learn to be under, you will not be over."

Now ask yourself, says Rogers, "Are you under the Word of God? Is the Bible your mandate for life? Are you loving it, reading it, obeying it, and living it?" We can become virtuous, and God, through the work of his Spirit and our study of and application of his Word, will help us accomplish that.

Becoming virtuous will certainly benefit others, but it will also improve us in so many ways that it becomes its own reward. Being a servant of the Lord gives astounding *joy* because you know deep in your soul that something powerful and wonderful has been accomplished, and the Lord chose you to be part of his plan. When that happens, you can't help but think, *Wow! A sinner such as me, to be selected by God to serve his noble purpose. Thank you, Lord. Praise God!*

Our strength for spiritual combat against dark forces comes from the authority and virtue of Jesus Christ our Lord and Savior, who is seated at the right hand of the Father. With that authority and virtue comes joy.

"Serve the LORD with gladness!" (Psalm 100:2 KJV)

"These things have I spoken unto you, that my joy might remain in you, and that your joy might be full." (John 15:11 KJV)

Obedience. Virtue. Joy. None are optional. All are achievable with God's help. All benefit us. And God has ordered us to pursue them. What a joy to be divinely commanded to do what is good for us! Our God is incredibly good.

Now let's put all of this within the context of the mission that Jesus has passed along to us. When you accept Jesus Christ as your Savior and love God, then you can be a sheepdog under the authority of the Great Shepherd, empowered by God's virtue, protecting the flock, and accomplishing mighty deeds in a life filled with great joy. How wonderful is that!

His Virtue Gave Authority to the Badge

We can find an outstanding example of God's authority and virtue from one of the bravest US Marshals the wild, wild West ever knew. His name was Bass Reeves.

Bass Reeves was born a slave in the Arkansas household of state legislator William S. Reeves. William Reeves refused to let young Bass learn to read and write, considering it too dangerous for a slave. But his owner did teach Bass to shoot so he could hunt for food and later serve as a bodyguard.

William Reeves forced Bass to accompany him to Paris, Texas, in 1846. Later, William made Bass accompany his son, Capt. George Reeves, to fight for the Confederacy.

One night, Bass escaped to Indian Territory in an area now part of Texas, Oklahoma, and Arkansas. It was a region ruled by five Native American tribes (Cherokee, Seminole, Creek, Choctaw, and Chickasaw). These tribes had been forced to move there due to the Indian Removal Act of 1830. It was also a place where escaped slaves and criminals could hide.

Bass lived with the Native Americans, and over the years, he learned their language, the territory, and the skill of tracking. Bass is believed to have served with the Indian forces loyal to the Union during the Civil War.

After the Civil War, US Marshal James Fagan, a former officer in the Confederate Army, recruited Bass to assist in upholding the law and confronting the criminals that plagued the land. Fagan had heard about Bass, that he knew the Indian Territory and could speak Native languages. Bass Reeves became the first black Deputy US Marshal west of the Mississippi, and he went on to work thirty-two years as one of "Hanging" Judge Isaac Parker's most valued deputies.

Bass often worked with a Native American Tribal Officer, like the Choctaw lawman Charles LeFlore. Bass would occasionally pretend to be an outlaw (working undercover) to get the jump on wanted criminals. He stood six foot two and had a reputation for being able to "whoop" any two men in a fist fight.

Bass' great grandnephew, Federal Judge Paul Brady, said Bass was well versed in the Bible. When Bass was a child, his mother would sit him in her lap and teach him Bible passages. Whenever Bass took someone into custody, he made sure to witness to them from the multitude of Scripture verses he had memorized. While Bass could not read, he had a perfect memory, and as a Marshal he would have others read the warrants to him.

Bass Reeves would surely have known Romans 13:1, which establishes the lawman's authority: "Let every person be subject to the governing authorities. For there is no authority except from God, and those that exist have been instituted by God" (ESV). God's Word is clear. We are to submit to lawful authority. But there are exceptions. God blessed the endeavors of the rebels who stood up against the tyranny of King George III and founded the United States of America. Look at the Declaration of Independence to understand their call to divine authority in doing so. We also honor men like Bonhoeffer and Niemöller for standing up to the evil of Hitler and Nazi Germany.

The authority of the police comes from the Constitution, but ultimately even constitutional authority comes from God. And Bass Reeves understood and represented that at a gut, basic, fundamental level.

In the 2015 television series *Legends & Lies*, when outlaws would question the authority of Bass Reeves because of his race, Bass would quote John 8:24: "If ye believe not that I am he, ye shall die in your sins" (KJV). And then he would ask, "Do you want to die in your sins?" Few outlaws would question the authority of Bass Reeves.

By the time he retired in 1907, Bass had arrested over three thousand felons. He brought in some of the most dangerous outlaws of that time and was never wounded despite having been ambushed and even having his hat shot off. He killed fourteen outlaws to defend his own life.

According to TrueWestMagazine.com, contemporary newspapers said about Bass Reeves, "He is…a holy *terror* to the lawless characters in the west." This was a direct reference to Romans 13:3–4:

> For rulers are not a *terror* to good works, but to the evil. Wilt thou then not be afraid of the power? do that which is good, and thou shalt have praise of the same: For he is the minister of God to thee for good. But if thou do that which is evil, be afraid; for he beareth not the sword in vain: *for he is the minister of God, a revenger to execute wrath upon him that doeth evil.* (KJV)

Or we could pull from Proverbs 21:15: "When justice is done, it brings joy to the righteous but terror to evildoers." Thus, we have Bass Reeves, a true terror to the lawless, God's minister to bring "joy to the righteous" and to "execute wrath" upon those who do evil. And it was his godly virtue that made it possible.

While Bass was widely known for his courage, it was his virtuous character that gave authority to the badge. Even outlaws regarded Bass for his integrity, as he was incorruptible and considered impossible to pay off. As Scripture says, "An overseer must be above reproach" (1 Timothy 3:2 ESV). Bass even arrested his own son, Bennie. Bennie had killed his wife during a domestic dispute. When Bass overheard that another marshal had the warrant, Bass stepped in, quietly saying, "Give me the writ." Bass took the responsibility to arrest his own son, who was later sentenced to prison.

The story of Bass Reeve's life may sound familiar: honesty, bravery, working covertly with a Native American as his comrade. In fact, it sounds a lot like the Lone Ranger! And, according to historian Thaddeus Morgan on History.com, the real Lone Ranger was a black man, an escaped slave, and possibly the greatest US Marshal who ever lived.

Virtue Has Its Own Authority

One last thing about the US Marshals. The word *marshal* goes back across many centuries, with hundreds of military leaders using the title Marshal to denote their authority. The rank of Field Marshal has been used for at least eight hundred years, going back to the Middle Ages.

Most authorities trace the word *marshal* back to a French or German word meaning "keeper of the horses." But words retain their power and prestige across the centuries for multiple reasons. *Marshal* breaks down into "Mars" (the Roman god of war) and "hall." Thus, a "Marshal" could be thought of as someone in charge of the warrior's hall. The word also breaks down into "Mars" and "shall" as in the *will* of Mars. Both of these have powerful connotations of authority and prestige going back to the legendary days of the Roman Empire. In addition, the word marshal is a homonym for "martial" derived from the Roman "Mars" meaning "of war," as in the "martial arts." Even to this day a king or queen has a lineage to establish their prestige, based on a concept of divine right going back to the ancient Egyptians and into the mists of time. So, too, a marshal can call upon the heritage of the mighty empire of Rome to establish their authority and stature.

Today, instead of "Mars" we might speak in terms of "Saint Michael the Archangel," the patron saint of police and military. But (and here is the point) it all comes back to *authority*. A marshal's authority might derive from the Romans or from Saint Michael or from the US Constitution.

Our authority as believers in Christ comes directly from the Lord God, our loving Father, Creator of the universe. There is no higher authority than that. "Jesus came to them and said, 'All authority in heaven and on earth has been given to me'" (Matthew 28:18).

WARNORD Recap

Truly, truly, as Erasmus tells us, "Once a person has Christ in their heart, they would not exchange His authority for anything."

Never give in to the temptations of this mortal realm. Everything that this fallen world has to offer us is unimportant compared to God's authority over life, death, and eternity. Never forget that we are the beloved children of God, adopted into the family of our loving Father. We are sheepdogs under the authority of the Great Shepherd. The minions of hell cannot compete with that.

If you ever get a chance, visit the US Marshals Museum in Fort Smith, Arkansas, and see the Bass Reeves Monument and exhibit. There you will see the living embodiment of

God's power and Erasmus' teaching, that "*virtue* has its own *authority*."

> While every short-lived flower of sense,
>   Destructive years consume.
> Through virtue's fair, delightful walk,
>   Unfading blossoms bloom.

Prayer for Virtue

> *O Lord, impart to us Thy grace,*
> *that we may add to our faith virtue,*
>   *and to virtue knowledge,*
>   *and to knowledge temperance,*
>   *and to temperance patience,*
>   *and to patience godliness,*
>   *and to godliness brotherly kindness,*
>   *and to brotherly kindness charity:*
> *that so, we may be fruitful in good works*
>   *through Jesus Christ our Lord. Amen.*

> —*Euchologion: A Collection of Prayers for the Use of Families* (1847)

ORDER #20: Next Level Battle Prep

➤ Under what authority are you operating?

- ○ Are you operating under the Constitution?
- ○ Are you operating under God?

➤ How did US Marshal Bass Reeves keep the Constitution and exert the spirit of the Lord?

➤ How do you fulfill your responsibility?

- ○ How do you keep the Constitution?
- ○ How do you exert the Spirit of the Lord?

➤ Have you ever violated your holy responsibility?

- ○ What does God do to those who transgress?
- ○ How can you amend the violation?

TWENTY-FIRST WARNING

THE WICKED DO NOT KNOW GOD IN CHRIST

And if you do not know God, you cannot worship Him, praise Him, give Him thanks, nor serve Him.

(Luther)

WARNORD #21

TWENTY-FIRST ORDER

LIFE CAN BE SAD, DIFFICULT, AND QUICK: MAKE IT COUNT FOR SOMETHING

Since we do not know when death will come, dedicate yourself to Christ every day.

(Erasmus)

TWENTY-FIRST WARNING

THE WICKED DO NOT KNOW GOD IN CHRIST

And if you do not know God, you cannot worship Him, praise Him, give Him thanks, nor serve Him.

(Luther)

The hope of the righteous shall be gladness:
but the expectation of the wicked shall perish.
Proverbs 10:28 KJV

Faith of the martyrs, living still
in spite of dungeon, fire, and sword;
oh, how our hearts beat high with joy
whene'er we hear of them, dear Lord!

The martyrs chained in prison cells
    were still in heart and conscience free,
and bless'd would be their children's fate
…if they, like them, should die for thee!

Faith of the martyrs, we will love
    both friend and foe in all our strife,
and preach thee, too, as love knows how,
    by saving word and faithful life!

—"Faith of Our Fathers," by Frederick William Faber
(1814–1863)

In *On Spiritual Combat*, the first book in this series, we taught you the old soldier trick of keeping one eye closed to protect your night vision. We applied that to the concept of keeping a spiritual eye protected from the things of this world so that your spiritual knight vision will not be blinded by the world.

While we can protect ourselves from the world's spiritual darkness, those outside of Christ cannot. In fact, those who do not know Christ are completely blinded by the world. So the unsaved may say, "Thank God!" But we need to gently and lovingly point out to them that they cannot thank God, or (as Luther points out) "worship Him, praise Him,…nor serve Him," if they do not *know him*.

Consider once again the example of August Landmesser. Use his name to do an online search for that photo again. Look at the huge mass of people mindlessly giving the Nazi salute while one man stands there with his head up and his arms crossed. Recognizing that it could be Landmesser or Wegert in that picture, the point is that only this one man can perceive the evil around him. That is what Luther is talking about! That is what it is like to be blinded by the world.

Proverbs 10:28 (KJV) rightly tells us that, as Christians, our "Hope…shall be gladness." But all the hopes and dreams and expectations of the unsaved tragically "shall perish." C. S. Lewis said, "When the whole world is running towards a cliff, he who is running in the opposite direction appears to have lost his mind."

Consider now this allegory of a Christian knight, the hope of gladness, and the bitter emptiness of the unsaved.

Yearn to Make a Difference

The 1957 movie *The Seventh Seal*, directed by Ingmar Bergman, is about a knight named Antonius Block. The story is suggestive of the wood carving, *Knight, Death, and the Devil*, by Albrecht Dürer, that can be found at the beginning of this book.

Antonius Block is returning home to Sweden after fighting in the Crusades. He has experienced intense combat and seen barbarity committed by armies on both sides of the conflict. He has lost faith in his soldiers, himself, and the cause he was fighting for. It appears he has post-traumatic stress disorder, but there was no name for it then, other than "loss of faith."

Upon returning to Sweden, Antonius Block finds the land infested with a deadly plague. Block seems to know his time is running short. The Angel of Death finally comes to Block and tells him, "I've already walked by your side for quite some time." But before Death can take him, Block challenges the angel to a game of chess. Block had heard stories that the Angel of Death enjoys the game. Death accepts the challenge, but the angel reminds Block that he has never lost: "No one escapes me." Block does not expect that he will defeat Death, but he is using the chess game as a distraction to buy time—time to do one good work or deed that will give his life meaning. In the end, Block finds a way to do a good deed and regain his faith.

The message of *The Seventh Seal* is that life can be sad, difficult, and quick. In the end, all people must stand before God for judgment. As faithful followers of Jesus, we should hunger, we should ache, we should yearn to make a difference, to contribute to God's kingdom during our brief time here on earth.

Remember, your greatest contribution to God's kingdom might not be something you do but someone you raise. The prayer warrior providing heavenly artillery support for other endeavors is also a worthy calling. There are many ways to contribute. Sometimes the greatest love is not to sacrifice your life but to live a life of sacrifice.

Jesus did not die for your salvation just so you could have a good time in this life—although, that is part of the blessing. God intended and empowered you to make a difference! And just as surely as God wants you to have a positive impact, Satan will surely try to stop you.

Antonius Block's sin was doubt and fear. He doubted God's willingness to forgive him after all the sins he had committed. And he feared for his very soul. He said, "I see myself…

and I am filled with fear and disgust." Block thought he had committed the unpardonable sin. (More about that critical subject shortly.) Even Martin Luther and John Bunyan, who wrote *Pilgrim's Progress*, were obsessed with this fear. But they defeated their doubts and depressions by accepting the sacrifice that saves, the love of our Savior Jesus Christ.

The good news is that God is always with us and ready to help us make a difference. We just don't realize it. Psalm 139:8 (CEV) says: "If I were to climb up to the highest heavens, you would be there. If I were to dig down to the world of the dead you would also be there." God is always with us whether we sense him or not. And his love will always be with us no matter what. As the apostle Paul said: "I am persuaded, that neither death, nor life, nor angels, nor principalities, nor powers, nor things present, nor things to come, Nor height, nor depth, nor any other creature, shall be able to separate us from the love of God, which is in Christ Jesus our Lord" (Romans 8:38–39 KJV).

Erasmus tells us, "Wherefore if thou dedicate thyself wholly to the study of scripture and exercise thy mind day and night in the law of God, no fear shall trouble thee, neither by day nor night: but thou shalt against all assaults of thine enemies be armed and exercised also." What a powerful concept. Since we do not know when death will come, we must dedicate ourselves to Christ every day. Then we will perform acts praiseworthy in God's eyes, and no fear will trouble us. And we shall be armed against the assaults of our enemy the devil. Because we are confident in God's loving kindness toward us. "'I know the plans I have for you,' declares the LORD, 'plans to prosper you and not to harm you, plans to give you hope and a future'" (Jeremiah 29:11).

The Golem Effect

Of course, Satan does not want you to know or feel God's presence. Satan knows that he can sometimes block God out of your life, with feelings of anger and pain. In fact, the devil would like nothing better than to banish believers from the rest of society and separate the sheepdogs—especially the police—from the love of the flock and the authority of the Shepherd. God's Word makes it very clear that our God stands for justice and against lawlessness: "I, the LORD, love justice; I hate robbery and wrongdoing" (Isaiah 61:8). And what better way to destroy a nation than to neutralize its protectors, destroy justice, and incite lawlessness?

Satan has found a way to manipulate some people—in many cases this is being used against the very citizens that police protect—into attacking and demoralizing God's sheepdogs. Psychologists call this the "Golem Effect." The Golem Effect describes a psychological phenomenon in which lower expectations placed upon people lead to poorer performance. It is a self-fulfilling prophecy. The Golem Effect is a form of bias resulting in prejudice against certain groups, like minorities or police officers. The danger is that these lower expectations can lead to poorer performance.

The "Golem" was a soulless creature in Hebrew mythology. In one story, the creature was created to protect the Jews of Prague, but it grew more and more violent, eventually attacking its own creators. The metaphor of the Golem has inspired such characters as Frankenstein and The Terminator.

The first study to demonstrate the Golem Effect was published in the *Journal of Educational Psychology* in a 1982 article called "Pygmalion, Galatea, and the Golem: Investigations of Biased and Unbiased Teachers" by Babad, Inbar, and Rosenthal. When arbitrarily informed that certain students were "bright" or "dull," the teacher's behavior seemed to favor the bright students and become biased against the students labeled as dull. The students themselves started to behave in line with their labels.

Remember, Satan is referred to as the "accuser of our brothers and sisters, who accuses them before our God, day and night" (Revelation 12:10 CSB). The devil is the ultimate Golem Maker, name caller, insulter, and demeanor. He will use all hypocrites to be his surrogate bullies.

Dr. Rick Trinkner, Arizona State University, published a paper entitled "The Force of Fear." He demonstrated that the "racist police officer" stereotype is in fact undermining the moral authority of police officers, thereby creating a Golem Effect. While most police perform admirably, the over-publicizing of a few tragic events has created a "bandwagon" of anti-police sentiment and thus magnified the Golem Effect.

The Golem Effect works like this: (1) Bias and hostility are expressed to police. (2) This diminishes police morale. (3) Police begin to treat the public worse. (4) This reinforces negative beliefs about police, and the pattern repeats.

This is Satan's perfect storm! A vortex of evil like Dante's Inferno, it can reinforce itself, pulling police and society down into a living hell on earth. And then, even worse, it pulls souls down into hell.

Jeff Wolf begins his book *Blue Lies: The War on Justice and the Conspiracy to Weaken America's Cops* by saying:

> Imagine an America without law and order,
> a mobocracy where the government submits
> to the demands of domestic terrorists, where
> criminals are glorified and police are vilified,
> where your child's killer walks free because an
> activist prosecutor failed to appear in court,
> where drug traffickers are given free rein of our
> highways, where you are charged with a crime
> for defending your home against riotous thugs,
> where cop killers sit in seats of government,
> where entire police forces quit, and others no
> longer come when you call. Imagine an America
> where good is evil and evil is good. Sadly, this is
> our America.

A godly nation must anticipate attacks on the concept of law and order, which is essential for our nation. And police must anticipate spiritual attacks because they serve the Lord. They work with other authorities on the side of law and order as "God's servants, agents of wrath to bring punishment on the wrongdoer" (Romans 13:4).

The propaganda campaign to attack, defund, and delegitimize our police is just another scheme of the devil's, even if those who are demanding these actions don't realize it. Ivy League Professor Glen Loury, on his *The Glenn Show* video blog, observes that the national media have "buckets of blood" on their hands for law enforcement "delegitimization." The Bible warned us that God's people will be attacked, and the persecutors will claim they are serving God. Jesus warned the disciples, "Indeed, the hour is coming when whoever kills you will think he is offering service to God. And they will do these things because they have not known the Father, nor me" (John 16:2–3 ESV).

The devil knows many tricks of distraction and deception. The devil knows how to cut straight to the heart of a godly nation and destroy it from within. The Golem Effect is just one of the many methods the devil uses to turn people against each other and away from their Creator and Savior.

Defeating the Golem Makers

The first step to overcoming the Golem Effect is being aware of it. Society as a whole, God's people, and most specifically our police must learn to be mindful of this evil phenomenon.

The second step to overcome the Golem Effect is for police to reinforce positive expectations for themselves and reward positive performance. Indeed, our goal, like God's, is to "let justice roll down like waters, and righteousness like an ever-flowing stream" (Amos 5:24 ESV).

In a 2019 *Psychology Today* article (intriguingly entitled: "Why the Weak Sometimes Win and the Strong Never

Learn"), Anthony Lopez outlines research demonstrating that when people view the low expectations of critics as unfair, high personal expectations can boost performance, creating the "Underdog Effect." Next, we'll learn about that and how it has been in play throughout the history of the Christian church, and most especially among the "ultimate underdogs," the martyrs of the church.

> Faith of the martyrs, living still
> in spite of dungeon, fire, and sword;
> oh, how our hearts beat high with joy
> whene'er we hear of them, dear Lord!

WARNING #21: Next Level Battle Prep

- ➤ When attacked in your life, how have you reacted?
  - ○ Like a Golem, becoming the monster you are accused of being?

- ➤ Describe the Golem Effect.
  - ○ Why does the devil use this form of attack?

- ➤ What is the message of the movie *The Seventh Seal*, about a knight named Antonius Block? (Suggestive of the wood carving, "Knight, Death and the Devil," by Albrecht Dührer, found in the front of the book.)

TWENTY-FIRST ORDER

LIFE CAN BE SAD, DIFFICULT, AND QUICK: MAKE IT COUNT FOR SOMETHING

Since we do not know when death will come, dedicate yourself to Christ every day.

(Erasmus)

I saw under the altar the souls of them that were slain for the word of God, and for the testimony which they held.
—Revelation 6:9 KJV

Malcolm Gladwell, in his book *David and Goliath: Underdogs, Misfits, and the Art of Battling Giants,* explains that a struggle to succeed against seemingly insurmountable odds (like David against Goliath, or the American Revolution against the vast British Empire) can be a vital component for growth and success.

David's faith is the quintessential American ideal. Our nation, God's people, and the police in these dark times must be like David in order to dismiss the doubters, stand tall against giants, and work hard to overcome all obstacles and prejudices.

The Underdog Effect

Let us examine how the "Underdog Effect" works, using police as an example. (1) Negative criticisms are expressed to police. (2) Police and society reject the criticisms as unfair. (3) This causes police to work harder, which (4) results in advances and innovations developed by police.

Police officers are classic underdogs defeating Satan, just as David defeated Goliath, because the battle is the Lord's, and he is their help. Underdog success stories create role models for police officers to emulate and high ideals to strive for.

When police reject negative criticisms and take action to refute them, they set an example for other police officers to do the same. This becomes its own positive, self-fulfilling prophecy: "Let your light shine before others, that they may see your good deeds and glorify your Father in heaven" (Matthew 5:16).

Underdogs are the innovators who improve the system and promote police professionalism. The last time police were "Golemmed" was after the tragic Rodney King beating in 1991. After this brutal assault by only a few officers, all police were categorized as monsters. But how did the police respond to these accusations? The police said, "The actions of a few do not define our profession." Police developed and implemented the "Use of Force Continuum" that is now the foundation of all police training.

Sadly, today police are again being subjected to the Golem Effect as they are repeatedly demeaned and challenged when they do their job. The devil knows that this contributes to hypervigilance. Hypervigilance is a state of elevated defensiveness that can provoke the Golem response, a self-fulfilling prophecy where police learn to disrespect themselves. Common triggers of hypervigilance include the following:

- feeling judged
- feeling abandoned
- feeling emotional distress
- feeling trapped or unwelcome
- being reminded of past traumas
- anticipating pain, fear, or judgment
- being around the random, chaotic behaviors of others
- hearing loud noises (especially if they're sudden or emotionally charged), which can include yelling at police

Police are sworn to stay out of politics, so they may feel defenseless against political attacks. But the Bible reminds us that God loves the righteous underdog. "God chose what is weak in the world to shame the strong" (1 Corinthians 1:27 ESV).

It is our prayer that this very book will serve a small part in God's plan to build resilience in our nation's protectors and in all of God's faithful sheepdogs. We believe that a Christian

"Sheepdog revival" has begun to empower our nation and our protectors. We can see it as a godly inspired *underdog response* to the repeated Golem attacks on police. Not only will this advance law enforcement as a profession, but more importantly, it will save souls.

Courtesy Is Our Superpower

Remember the bottle of water a detective gave to Alfonso Cerna, the man who had just shot a police officer? This is an example of Romans 12:20: "If thine enemy hunger, feed him; if he thirst, give him drink: for in so doing thou shalt heap coals of fire on his head" (KJV). The context of this verse makes it clear that your act of love and kindness can make someone burn with shame! *That* is one sure way to create a lasting change in people.

For police, one of their most powerful tactics is persistent courtesy. In the face of disrespect, the most powerful response is tenacious, persistent, constant courtesy. Yes, police always have a plan to use force, even deadly force if necessary, to defend the lives of self and others. But right up until the moment that force is used, courtesy is the watchword. Remember our standing order is always the Golden Rule. Such courtesy in the face of disrespect can be "coals of fire" to make people "burn with shame."

Courtesy in the face of anger.

Courtesy in the face of insults.

Courtesy in the face of false accusations.

Courtesy in the face of hatred for no reason.

This is what Jesus means when he said to turn the other cheek. In Matthew 5:38–39, Jesus says, "You have heard that it was said, 'Eye for eye, and tooth for tooth.' But I tell you, do not resist an evil person. If anyone slaps you on the right cheek, turn to them the other cheek also." The concept of turning the other cheek is a difficult one for police to grasp. Allowing a second slap after being slapped once is not in a police officer's DNA. But the slap that Jesus refers to is called a "smiting" in the King James Bible. A smiting does not involve physical violence. Even today, we use the expression "a slap in the face" to indicate an unexpected insult or putdown. Turning the other cheek does not mean we place ourselves or others in danger. Jesus was not throwing out the criminal justice system. Perpetrators can still be arrested and prosecuted for criminal acts. But Jesus does command us not to retaliate against those who insult us.

What shall we do then in the face of all these Golem makers? When Jesus was insulted and slandered, "He opened not his mouth" in protest (Isaiah 53:7 KJV).

You see, police must accept that there have been a lot of lies spread by the devil about God's sheepdogs. These lies are spread like a virus on social media. A lot of people drink this poison because they don't know any better. Jesus prayed, "Father, forgive them, for they do not know what they are doing" (Luke 23:34). To the Golem makers we must say, "In return for my love, they accuse me, but I pray for them" (Psalm 109:4 GW). Furthermore, 1 Peter 3:9 tells us, "Do not repay evil with evil or insult with insult. On the contrary, repay evil with blessing, because to this you were called so that you may inherit a blessing."

How can you reply to an insult with a blessing? Courtesy. Courtesy is a Christian superpower. This applies to all Christians in the face of attacks. Like police, when we are insulted, we can respond: "I'm sorry you feel that way" or "Have a good day." Calling people sir or ma'am in all situations demonstrates dignity for both the giver and the receiver. Also, saying *please* and *thank you* as part of your routine conversation never hurts. And don't forget the power of divine words like "Praise God" and "amen."

In the face of repeated attacks and accusations of the devil, the sheepdog endures. Jeff Wolf concludes his book *Blue Lies* by saying:

> As long as there are wolves who prey upon the sheep, there will always be sheepdogs willing to suit up, put their lives on the line, and endure the scrutiny, hatred, and scorn of the public. And because they are men and women of character, integrity, and honor, they will do it despite the malice of the anti-police, anti-law and order, Marxist mob. They will do it with love in their hearts, smiles on their faces, their uniforms pressed and their brass polished, knowing they do so with a righteous purpose and a valiant mission. They will serve while the unjust call for their prosecution and the riotous mob calls for

their murder, without retaliation, and without recourse. For, the police know that their presence is the only way the sheep can [survive] the wolf.

Tootsie Roll. Tootsie Roll. Tootsie Roll.

All of this is easy to say, but it can be very hard to do. It. Is. Just. So. Hard! Our human nature and our sheepdog spirit work against us when the situation calls for courtesy in the face of hateful insults and vicious verbal attacks. How can you train yourself to have such superhuman self-control in the face of vicious incitement and provocation?

Of course, the answer is prayer and immersing yourself in God's Word. "If the world hates you, keep in mind that it hated me first" (John 15:18). But there is an additional practical and powerful trick that I teach to our law enforcement officers nationwide. It is a great cop trick, but it really applies to everyone.

First, you must understand that the only thing in the universe you can control is yourself, right now. There is nothing else you can control. That is why faith is a critical component in all resiliency training worldwide. You must have a higher power to give these things to. Everything in the past is done; you must let go of it. Everything that anyone else does is outside your control. The only thing you can control is how you choose to respond.

If someone makes you lose your temper, then they have taken away from you the one thing you can control. But in reality, they didn't take it away from you. You *gave* it to them. It was the only thing you could control, and you gave it away to them. God's Word tells us, "A man without self-control is like a city broken into and left without walls" (Proverbs 25:28 ESV).

Let me give you a personal example. Since 1997 when I retired from the US Army, I have been on the road over two hundred days a year, training our police officers. I believe I might be the only police trainer to ever be "Peace Officer Standards and Training (POST) Certified," or the equivalent thereof, in all fifty states. Just by virtue of doing it for so long and so much, I am probably, by most standards, America's number one law enforcement trainer. (Praise God! All honor and glory to him!) Thus, I have been one of the primary targets of the individuals and organizations attacking our police officers. I have received hate mail and death threats that will curl your hair. I posted some of them as an article on my "Lt. Col. Dave Grossman" LinkedIn site if you are interested. Look at these letters and tell yourself that this is what our police officers deal with every day. Then say a prayer for our cops.

The people sending these attacks are trying to hurt me. If I let these things bother me, then they win. So how can you turn that into something positive?

Well, I have a particular brand of candy that I let myself have periodically. So when I receive an attack by mail, email, or in the media, I get a piece of candy. Remember, their goal is to hurt me with these attacks. I can picture them screaming in apoplectic outrage, "I told you what an evil person you are, and you get a chocolate-covered cherry?" That's right. So who wins now? Yes, I pray for them, and I try to do all the other things that we should do. But this is the trick that I use to create an environment in which I almost look forward to these attacks. "God gave us a spirit not of fear but of power and love and self-control" (2 Timothy 1:7 ESV).

I tell my law enforcement officers in my classes about this, and I tell them, "When someone gets in your face and says these hateful things to you, they want it to hurt you. And if it does, then they have succeeded, and you gave them power over the only thing you can control!" Thus, my advice to them is to have a bag of Tootsie Rolls in their police car. I suggest Tootsie Rolls because they don't melt in the heat or freeze too bad in the cold. They are individually wrapped and stay clean. And they give me happy memories of the Halloween candy I used to get when I was a kid. But you can choose any kind of candy you want. I tell my students:

> When someone gets in your face, you just smile politely and say to yourself, *Hey! Thanks to you, I'm gonna get a Tootsie Roll!* And when it gets really bad? Just grin and say to yourself, *Tootsie Roll. Tootsie Roll. Tootsie Roll.* Or, if your partner is starting to lose it? Yep: "Psst! Partner. Tootsie Roll!" And, yes, remember to pray for those who have done you wrong, when you get a chance.

Truly, God tells us, "Whoever is slow to anger is better than the mighty, and he who rules his spirit than he who takes a city" (Proverbs 16:32 ESV). With faith, godly self-control, some strategically placed Tootsie Rolls, and the tactical application of courtesy, police can take down Satan and defeat the Golem Effect.

Ultimate Underdogs: Martyrs of the Church

> The martyrs chained in prison cells
>   were still in heart and conscience free,
> and bless'd would be their children's fate
>   if they, like them, should die for thee!

My personal faith path has cut across traditions and denominations. I have had the honor to speak before a uniquely diverse body of Christian audiences across the decades. Like Puritan church leader Richard Baxter (1615–1691), I would like to say that "I am a CHRISTIAN, a MEER CHRISTIAN, of no other Religion." This is the original source for the title of C. S. Lewis' book *Mere Christianity*, representing Lewis' goal in that book, and it is most certainly the goal of this book.

After centuries of division, there is great joy in the current ecumenical Christian fellowship to be found in communities worldwide. And for me there is enormous pleasure in finding the "old that is strong" that "does not wither," and the "deep roots" that "are not touched by the frost," as J. R. R. Tolkien wrote in *The Fellowship of the Rings*.

In particular, the Catholic tradition, with their study and veneration of the martyrs of the church, has such amazing blessings to bestow upon the wider Christian body. From an evidence-based or logical, scholarly proof perspective, these martyrs are critical to the foundation and growth of God's church. And to my mind, the study of the church's martyrs is vastly more profitable than energy expended on eschatology.

We have said it before, and it is so very important: God could beat us over the head with his plan of salvation. If he wanted to, God could be in our face, undeniable, irrefutable, every day. But he doesn't want puppets, and he won't coerce us into loving him. "If you love something, set it free. If it comes back, it is yours." That is the spirit by which God loves us. God loves us, and he has given us free will. He has chosen to make salvation a matter of belief instead of overwhelming coercion. Trust rather than fear. Loving invitation rather than threats. Would we really want it to be any different?

God in his infinite love and wisdom knew that the death, burial, and resurrection of Jesus was sufficient for our salvation. "God so loved the world that he gave his one and only Son, that whoever believes in him shall not perish but have eternal life" (John 3:16). But for the world to embrace God's plan of salvation by faith, there had to be witnesses who would attest to the truth of this matter, unto the final and utmost extreme. By their testimony, innocent blood, and willing sacrifice, these martyrs became the ultimate underdogs upon which the greater Christian church was built.

We have already noted that eleven of the twelve disciples, and three of the four authors of the Gospels, were murdered for their faith. And men do not die for a lie. Some would claim (falsely) that there is not good historical evidence for this. But if we move one generation down from the original disciples, we have an enormous body of historical evidence for the second generation of the Christian church who were martyred for their faith. "They overcame him by the blood of the Lamb, and by the word of their testimony; and they loved not their lives unto the death" (Revelation 12:11 KJV).

In an article entitled "Evidence Based Faith," Erick Erickson recaps the historical evidence of these Christians who went to their deaths rather than renounce their faith. Clement (of Rome), whom Paul mentioned in the book of Philippians, was tied to an anchor and tossed into the sea by the Romans in AD 99. Ignatius, bishop of Antioch, was fed to wild beasts in the Circus Maximus in AD 108. Polycarp, bishop of Smyrna, was burned to death in AD 156 as local authorities begged him to recant Christ. This chain of commitment to Jesus has been passed along from generation to generation through relationship and discipleship. For instance, the apostle John was a disciple of Jesus Christ, Polycarp was a disciple of John, and Ignatius knew Polycarp. From person to person, generation to generation, the torch of faith in Christ has been passed along until it finally reached us. You and I are part of a long line of disciples, all leading back to Jesus Christ, the Master discipler, the very Son of God. From there the list of martyrs also comes, multiplied and amplified by the hundreds and thousands across the centuries.

Erickson addresses the skeptics who deny that Jesus even existed. "If he did not exist, then neither did the Greek philosopher Socrates. We have no writings from Socrates himself. We only know of his existence through the writings of other people. But no one would doubt Socrates existed." Indeed, there are more written eyewitness accounts of Jesus than there are of Socrates!

So, maybe Jesus' followers were all con men willing to die for the con. Maybe generations of con men followed them, and they all willingly died to keep the con going. Or maybe this skeptical perspective isn't true. In fact, the historical evidence for Jesus and the honesty and accuracy of his early disciples is so extensive that the burden of proof against it falls with the skeptic, not with the believer. Our faith is founded on fact, not on fantasy, which is just one reason that so many skeptics over the centuries put their trust in Jesus Christ and the New Testament writings that speak of him.

WARNORD Recap

Faith of the martyrs, we will love
　　both friend and foe in all our strife,
and preach thee, too, as love knows how,
　　by saving word and faithful life!

Erasmus rightly tells us that "Life can be sad, difficult and quick." It certainly was for these martyrs of the church. And, praise God, did they ever make their sacrifice count for something!

Ultimately, God built his church upon the amazing power of the ultimate underdog: his Son who was without sin and who died for our sins. Jesus led a life that was difficult and brief, about thirty-three years on this fallen world. But above all others, he—the King of martyrs—made it count.

Would we be willing to die for our faith? History is full of examples where Christians did just that. And if you actively search for them, you can find accounts of Christians around the world, right now, who are being murdered for their faith.

Consider Stephen, "a man full of faith and of the Holy Spirit" (Acts 6:5). Stephen rebuked the sinful Sanhedrin, a corrupt group of politicians, telling them, "You stiff-necked people! Your hearts and ears are still uncircumcised. You are just like your ancestors: You always resist the Holy Spirit!" (7:51). And how did the Sanhedrin respond to this correction? They dragged Stephen out of the city of Jerusalem and stoned him to death. Stephen is considered the first Christian martyr. Denouncing evil has always been a dangerous profession.

A 2022 JihadWatch.org article by Christine Douglass-Williams tells us that a "Record Breaking 360 Million Christians [were] Persecuted in 2021." The article goes on to state that "Almost 6,000 Christians were killed due to their religion." And all they had to do to avoid a horrible death was to simply stop worshiping Jesus, the Living Christ. Tootsie Rolls just don't hack it when it comes to facing death because of your faith. As we look in awe and amazement at such faith, we must recognize that God built his church upon the amazing power of the ultimate underdog.

No matter how bleak life may become, never doubt the power of God to deal with the problems that we face today. In his own sweet time, in *his* chosen way. "My flesh and my heart may fail, but God is the strength of my heart and my portion forever" (Psalm 73:26). A study of the martyrs of the church, and the triumphant majesty of God's empowering presence across the millennia, can make our current problems and challenges seem trivial.

My favorite hymn is "Once to Every Man and Nation" by James Russell Lowell. I try to weave the powerful words and concepts of that song into most of my books. And a portion of it is most definitely appropriate here.

> By the light of burning martyrs,
>> Christ, Thy bleeding feet we track,
> Toiling up new Calvaries ever
>> With the cross that turns not back.

Peace Prayer of Saint Francis

This prayer was widely distributed in both World War I and World War II. It is an excellent weapon for spiritual warfare. Attributed to St. Francis of Assisi, its origin is unknown, but it beautifully reflects his devotion to God. And it captures the concept of responding to hate with courtesy and facing persecution with peace.

> *Lord, make me an instrument of Your peace;*
>> *Where there is hatred, let me sow love;*

Where there is injury, pardon;
Where there is discord, harmony;
Where there is error, truth;
Where there is doubt, faith;
Where there is despair, hope;
Where there is darkness, light;
And where there is sadness, joy.

O Divine Master, Grant that I may not so much seek
To be consoled as to console;
To be understood as to understand;
To be loved as to love.
For it is in giving that we receive;
It is in pardoning that we are pardoned;
And it is in dying that we are born into eternal life.

—Francis of Assisi (1182–1226)

ORDER #21: Next Level Battle Prep

➤ When attacked in your life, how have you reacted?

   ○ Like an Underdog, rising above your accusers?

➤ Describe the Underdog Effect.

   ○ How does it defeat Satan and his minions?

➤ What are common triggers of hypervigilance (and the Golem Effect) that you must be prepared for?

    ○ How do you defend yourself?

➤ What is an Underdog's superpower?

    ○ Explain how you use it.

TWENTY-SECOND WARNING

THE WICKED DO NOT CONFESS OR SERVE CHRIST

Heartfelt regret brings repentance that leads to salvation, but impenitence is the unpardonable sin that brings death!

(Luther)

WARNORD #22

TWENTY-SECOND ORDER

REPENT YOUR WRONGS AND CHANGE YOUR WAYS

Repent and be clean, converted from sin, and reconciled to God. Those who do not admit their faults have the most to fear.

(Erasmus)

TWENTY-SECOND WARNING

THE WICKED DO NOT CONFESS OR SERVE CHRIST

Heartfelt regret brings repentance that leads to salvation, but impenitence is the unpardonable sin that brings death!

(Luther)

"Though your sins are like scarlet,
they shall be as white as snow;
though they are red as crimson,
they shall be like wool.
If you are willing and obedient,
you will eat the good things of the land;
but if you resist and rebel,
you will be devoured by the sword."
For the mouth of the Lᴏʀᴅ has spoken.
—Isaiah 1:18–20

"Come unto me, ye weary,
　　and I will give you rest."
O blessed voice of Jesus,
　　which comes to hearts oppressed!
It tells of benediction,
　　of pardon, grace, and peace,
of joy that hath no ending,
　　of love which cannot cease.

"Come unto me, dear children,
　　and I will give you light."
O loving voice of Jesus,
　　which comes to cheer the night!
Our hearts were filled with sadness,
　　and we had lost our way;
but morning brings us gladness,
　　and songs the break of day.

"Come unto me, ye fainting,
　　and I will give you life."
O peaceful voice of Jesus,
　　which comes to end our strife!
The foe is stern and eager,
　　the fight is fierce and long;
but thou hast made us mighty,
　　and stronger than the strong.

"And whosoever cometh
　　I will not cast him out."
O patient love of Jesus,

> which drives away our doubt;
> which calls us, very sinners,
>   unworthy though we be,
> of love so free and boundless,
>   to come, dear Lord, to thee!
>   –"Come unto Me, Ye Weary," by
>   W. Chatterton Dix (1873–1898)

God calls us, but he will not wait forever.

The wicked repeatedly reject God's call to repentance and redemption. The wicked hang on to their sinfulness and will not confess their sins. They take too much pleasure in sin and none in pleasing God. God does not seek to save anyone by threats and intimidation.

Our heavenly Father offers us to share in his glorious goodness and life. God's offer is open to everyone. But to those who would rather hang with Satan, then the Bible warns them, "It is a dreadful thing to fall into the hands of the living God" (Hebrews 10:31). Thus, Martin Luther issues his 22nd and final "Warning."

Fortunately—truly, infinitely, abundantly, and amazingly—our God is a loving God. Even though your sins are "red as crimson," the Lord is long suffering and forgiving, and he can make your sins disappear so you become "as white as snow" (Isaiah 1:18). The sacrifice has been made: the grace of the Lord is available through the blood of his Son, Jesus Christ. "By his wounds we are healed" (53:5).

God's call is the Spirit convicting you of your sins, giving you feelings of remorse and guilt. No person can say upon their death that they have not been given this gift of remorse and guilt (John 16:8–10).

Thus, we must define two important concepts here. First, what is impenitence? Second, what is the unpardonable sin?

Impenitent, Unpardonable?

The *KJV Dictionary* tells us that *impenitent* means "not penitent; not repenting of sin." It is one who refuses to repent, and it is very commonly used in this sense: "They died impenitent."

If you die impenitent, you are damned and doomed. You have passed up your final opportunity. The Lord Jesus said, "If you do not believe that I am He, you will indeed die in your sins" (John 8:24). Christ died for you, but you must do your part. You must accept and believe. "If you declare with your mouth, 'Jesus is Lord,' and believe in your heart that God raised him from the dead, you will be saved" (Romans 10:9).

What, then, is the "unpardonable sin"? In Mark 3:28–29 Jesus says, "Truly I tell you, people can be forgiven all their sins and every slander they utter, but whoever blasphemes against the Holy Spirit will never be forgiven; they are guilty of an eternal sin." The wonderful resource GotQuestions.org provides biblical answers to thousands of questions. It addresses *the very specific context of this verse*, with Jesus speaking directly to the Pharisees, who had witnessed the Son of God work a miracle and called it an act of Satan:

> The blasphemy of the Holy Spirit…cannot be
> duplicated today. Jesus Christ is not on earth…
> [and] no one can personally witness Jesus per-
> forming a miracle and then attribute that power
> to Satan instead of the Spirit.
>
> The unpardonable sin today is the state
> of continued unbelief…There is no pardon…for
> a person who rejects the Spirit's promptings to
> trust in Jesus Christ and then dies in unbelief.

Dr. Charles Stanley, who recently moved on, addressed this same topic: "The thought that a sin could be so bad that it is unforgivable sometimes leads people to fear that they may have committed it. That's why it is important to understand the context of this statement, which Jesus made to the Pharisees. Although they had seen compelling evidence that Jesus was the Messiah, the Pharisees refused to believe in Him." Dr. Stanley explains that the Pharisees even blasphemed the Holy Spirit by attributing to Satan the divine miracles that Christ performed. Then Stanley drew this conclusion: "If you are worried that you may have committed the unpardonable sin, then I can assure you that you haven't, because you are still feeling the conviction of the Spirit. God doesn't withhold salvation from a repentant sinner who comes to Him for forgiveness through faith in His Son. The only thing that makes sin unforgivable is a hard, unrepentant heart."

In an October 2014 blog post on the Ministry Matters website, Pastor Tom Fuerst added:

Guilt-trippy preachers and Sunday school
teachers may have used [this verse] to scare their
congregation and students. But Jesus wasn't refer-
encing your normal, everyday kind of sin here…

Jesus was talking about someone who
is so warped that their sense of good and evil,
justice and injustice, God and Satan are turned
upside down and they simply do not want to see
the world any other way.

Dr. Robert Stackpole of the John Paul II Institute of
Divine Mercy wrote, "A sin can only be 'unforgivable' when the
sinner refuses to seek forgiveness…We're talking about the sinner who remains in that spiritual condition to the bitter end."

Theologian and best-selling author, John MacArthur says:

The one who won't be forgiven is the one…who
gets full exposure to the truth, full exposure to
the gospel, full revelation and makes the final
conclusion…"It's not true, I reject Christ. It's a
deception."

…All manner of blasphemy can be forgiven except that final blasphemy that says with
full revelation, "I reject Christ."

MacArthur says, rather than take this rather obscure
verse out of context, it is far better "to remember Matthew
12:32 [which] says, 'You can speak a word against the Son of
Man and be forgiven.' We're all blasphemers of a sort who have

been forgiven if we've come to faith in Christ. Don't turn away. Get the full revelation and respond in full trust." As always, C. S. Lewis puts it so very well in his book *The Great Divorce*: "There are only two kinds of people in the end: those who say to God, 'Thy will be done,' and those to whom God says, in the end, 'Thy will be done.' All that are in Hell, choose it."

There is only one unpardonable sin, and Satan committed it when he knowingly and willingly rejected God, after having seen God and the Son in all their truth and goodness. When Satan rejected the Holy Spirit, the Spirit rejected him. The devil wants us all to believe that we have committed the unpardonable sin, just as he did. But that is more of his evil filth. Don't believe him. Satan is a liar. Only a believer who has the influence of the Holy Spirit can feel guilt and have these anguishing concerns. Meanwhile, the devil thinks nothing of his sins. No remorse. No regret. *That* is pure evil.

While there is life, there is hope. Eternal hope! For eternal life! Theologian and author Thomas J. Oord tells us (in his personal blog, ThomasJayOord.com), that "God *never* gives up calling us to love. God never gives up while we live in these bodies." It's not our place to judge who might be unredeemable and who is not; God is our judge, believer and unbeliever alike. Our mission is to treat all unbelievers as people who need Jesus Christ and call them to place their faith in him.

As Charles Spurgeon, called the "Prince of Preachers," tells us, our Commander's intent for our Great Commission and the ultimate goal of all spiritual warfare is to make disciples of all who are willing to come to Christ. In a sermon delivered at Exeter Hall on December 6, 1860, he said: "If sinners be damned, at least let them leap to Hell over our dead bodies. And if they perish, let them perish with our arms wrapped about their knees, imploring them to stay. If Hell must be filled, let it be filled in the teeth of our exertions, and let not one go unwarned and unprayed for."

> "And whosoever cometh
>   I will not cast him out."
> O patient love of Jesus,
>   which drives away our doubt;
> which calls us, very sinners,
>   unworthy though we be,
> of love so free and boundless,
>   to come, dear Lord, to thee!

WARNING #22: Next Level Battle Prep

➢   What is the unpardonable sin?

➢   What are the two meanings of "Thy will be done"?

TWENTY-SECOND ORDER

REPENT YOUR WRONGS AND CHANGE YOUR WAYS

Repent and be clean, converted from sin, and reconciled to God. Those who do not admit their faults have the most to fear.

(Erasmus)

He has delivered us from the power of darkness and conveyed us into the kingdom of the Son of His love, in whom we have redemption through His blood, the forgiveness of sins.
—Colossians 1:13–14 NKJV

You may be familiar with the "I Want You" poster used for recruiting during World War I and World War II. It depicts Uncle Sam pointing straight at the reader, with a stern look on his face, and then the caption, "I Want YOU for the U.S. Army.

Enlist Now!" There's a spiritual application here as well. As Chaplain Steve Sipe puts it, "The faith-based army of Spiritual Warriors that God is recruiting is an all-volunteer force!" And the army of God needs volunteers.

The artist for that famous poster was James Montgomery Flagg, one of America's leading illustrators. He studied in Europe and must have been aware of the work of the master Michelangelo Merisi da Caravaggio. In 1599, Caravaggio completed one of his greatest paintings, the *Calling of Saint Matthew*. The painting illustrates Matthew 9:9, when Jesus went into the custom house, observed Levi the tax-collector at his seat, and called to him, "Follow me."

In the painting, Christ points at Levi the tax-collector, and Levi points to himself with a look of shock on his face, as if to say, "Who? You can't mean me!" It is the literal "come to Jesus moment." Pope Francis has said that as a young man, he would often visit the *Calling of Saint Matthew* at the Contarelli Chapel in Rome and think to himself, "This is me, a sinner on whom the Lord has turned his gaze."

Now Levi, who would become Matthew, was a tax collector. His fellow Jews would have despised him not only as a Roman collaborator but also as a thief. You see, tax collectors had very little accountability during this time. Tax collectors had a well-deserved bad reputation for telling people they owed more than they did and then pocketing the difference. Tax collectors were just about as low as you could get.

It's hard to imagine what Levi thought when Jesus called him. Levi must have known who Jesus was. And Levi definitely knew himself, a sinner and scoundrel! After his call, Levi invited Jesus home for a feast, probably because he didn't know what else to do. On seeing this, the scribes and the Pharisees criticized Jesus for eating with Levi and his sinful friends. This prompted Jesus to answer, "I have not come to call the righteous, but sinners to repentance" (Luke 5:32).

It may seem amazing, but Levi left his wealthy but sordid life and became the apostle Matthew, the author of the first of the four Gospels. He would ultimately be martyred for his faith.

In selecting Levi the tax collector to be a disciple, Jesus was making a point, and the point is as powerful and valid as ever. That is, his invitation to come to him and follow him is open to everyone. We should not feel unqualified because of our job, lack of education, or our sinful past. All Jesus is looking for is sincere commitment: "Believe in the Lord Jesus, and you shall be saved" (Acts 16:31). Levi understood what the calling meant, and he obeyed the Lord unto death.

When Jesus points to you, don't delay or turn away. "Do not grieve the Holy Spirit of God, with whom you were sealed for the day of redemption" (Ephesians 4:30). When the Lord says, "I want you for my Christian Army," please, please: enlist *now*!

> "Come unto me, ye weary,
>   and I will give you rest."
> O blessed voice of Jesus,
>   which comes to hearts oppressed!
> It tells of benediction,
>   of pardon, grace, and peace,

of joy that hath no ending,
    of love which cannot cease.

The Weapon of Prayer

St. Alphonsus Maria de Liguori (1696–1787) said:

Prayer is, beyond doubt, the most powerful weapon...but we must really put ourselves into our prayer: it is not enough just to say the words, it must come from the heart. And also prayer needs to be continuous, we must pray no matter what kind of situation we find ourselves in: the warfare we are engaged in is on-going, so our prayer must be on-going also.

As we wrap up with the final order in the final WARNORD, we come full cycle to prayer. Do you remember your "Spiritual Warfare Equipment Issue" in *On Spiritual Combat*, based on the "Full Armor of God" in Ephesians 6? Do you recall what was the final and most powerful piece of equipment to be issued? It was your radio, the godly radio of prayer. It's rightly called the most powerful weapon in a Christian's arsenal.

In the movie *Saving Private Ryan*, the Army Ranger sniper Daniel Jackson offered a prayer prior to and during an engagement with the enemy. It was Psalm 25:2 (KJV):

O my God, I trust in Thee.

Let me not be ashamed;

Let not mine enemies triumph over me.

The Bible says, "Cast thy burden upon the LORD, and he shall sustain thee: he shall never suffer the righteous to be moved" (55:22 KJV). Indeed, courage is fear that has said its prayers: "I sought the LORD, and he heard me, and delivered me from all my fears" (34:4 KJV).

Note that in the movie, the other Rangers were always astonished at Jackson's calm discipline under fire. Did you ever wonder if Jackson's faith and prayers had something to do with his demeanor even while under fire?

Dr. Andrew Newberg, author of *How God Changes Your Brain*, has conducted brain scans on people with strong spiritual beliefs to see how their faith impacts their thinking and functioning. In one study, Dr. Newberg observed Franciscan nuns while they were in prayer. The nuns were doing a prayer called a centering prayer, repeating a particular phrase from the Bible, just like Private Jackson was doing. Dr. Newberg saw that the nuns activated their frontal lobes as they repeated the prayer, giving them focus while reducing anxiety.

You must choose a centering prayer for its personal content to have this focusing effect. Read the Bible and find a prayer that touches your heart. Fear has no foothold where God's love dwells. Psalms are always a good place to look. When you find a passage from the Bible that inspires your faith, write it down, repeat it, memorize it. Use the prayer when you wake up, before you go to work, before taking a dangerous mission, before you go home, before you go to sleep. Make this *your* passage and *your* prayer. Know that this is what we are commanded to do: "Pray continually, give thanks in all circumstances" (1 Thessalonians 5:17–18). Centering prayer is one great way to accomplish this divine command.

Courage Is Fear That Has Said Its Prayers

General George Patton is famous for ordering an Army Chaplain to say a prayer for good weather during the Third Army's approach to Bastogne. But Patton went beyond just having the chaplain pray. He had the prayer printed out and distributed throughout the Third Army so that the entire unit would join together in prayer. He turned his men and women into a prayer army.

That same chaplain, Monsignor James H. O'Neill, later wrote an account of what Patton told him on the morning of December 8, 1944. General Patton asked Chaplain O'Neill, "How much praying is being done in the Third Army?" Patton went on to explain why he asked:

> Chaplain, I am a strong believer in prayer. There
> are three ways that men get what they want;
> by planning, by working and by praying. Any
> great military operation takes careful planning
> or thinking. Then you must have well trained
> troops to carry it out: that's working. But between
> the plan and the operation there is always an

unknown. That unknown spells defeat or victory, success or failure. It is the reaction of the actors to the ordeal when it actually comes. Some people call that getting the breaks; I call it God.

Chaplain O'Neil said that General Patton talked about the Hebrew leader Gideon who defeated a much larger army with only three hundred soldiers. Afterward, General Patton ordered Chaplain O'Neil to call upon all the chaplains and the soldiers of the Third United States Army to focus their attention on the importance of prayer.

Chaplain O'Neil notes that, "On December 20,1944 [following several days of concerted prayer by the Third Army] the rains and the fogs ceased, and the fogs dissipated, to the consternation of the Germans and the delight of the American forecasters." He said the providential onset of perfect flying weather allowed US air power to support the American counterattack that relieved Bastogne and set the stage for winning the rest of the war.

General Patton later thanked Chaplain O'Neil: "Well, Padre, our prayers worked. I knew they would." Then he used his riding crop to crack Chaplain O'Neil on the side of his steel helmet. O'Neil said that was Patton's way of saying, "Well done."

"Come unto me, ye fainting,
   and I will give you life."
O peaceful voice of Jesus,
   which comes to end our strife!

The foe is stern and eager,
  the fight is fierce and long;
but thou hast made us mighty,
  and stronger than the strong.

Oh Lord, What Is My Mission?

There is a natural inclination to flee from evil. But all first responders and military who are servants of the Lord, and *all* sheepdogs under the authority of the Great Shepherd, are duty sworn and driven—driven and empowered by *love* and *empathy,* two of our superpowers—to run toward the sound of gunfire. To seek out disaster and save the victims:

- You should "save others by snatching them from the fire" (Jude 1:23).
- "Rescue the weak and needy; deliver them out of the hand of the wicked" (Psalm 82:4).
- "Rescue those being led away to death; hold back those staggering toward slaughter" (Proverbs 24:11).

This is a critical aspect of our overall mission. *This* is what sheepdogs live for. And prayer is the primary tool by which this is accomplished.

One last time: We. Cannot. Do. It. In our own strength. If we ask him, God will give us the will and the skill to say and do the right thing regardless of the earthly cost. Just as Jesus Christ did.

The war was won by Jesus Christ on the cross (John 3:16), but there are still battles raging. Until the Lord comes again, the devil has dominion over this earth. This world is still enemy occupied territory. Therefore, we are using guerilla warfare tactics against an evil enemy who is employing a brutal scorched-earth campaign. The strategic goal of the evil one is to cause as much destruction and suffering as possible (1 Peter 5:8) before he is permanently evicted and incarcerated (Revelation 20:10).

God created you on purpose and for a purpose: to protect the innocent from the murderer, the liar, the thief, and the sexually immoral; and to rescue the weak from the hand of the oppressor (Jeremiah 22:3). Christian courage to win this battle comes from the grace of God. Therefore, the faithful must be in constant prayer, asking God to en-*courage* us. And to empower us: "Praise the Lord and pass the ammunition!"

God needs *you* to be part of his human rescue mission (1 Peter 4:10–11). He calls it Operation Great Commission (Matthew 28:16–20). Christ is our general, and he doesn't want to leave one soul behind (1 Timothy 2:4).

> "Come unto me, dear children,
>   and I will give you light."
> O loving voice of Jesus,
>   which comes to cheer the night!
> Our hearts were filled with sadness,
>   and we had lost our way;
> but morning brings us gladness,
>   and songs the break of day.

WARNORD Recap

Luther tells us, "The wicked do not confess or serve Christ." Thus, Erasmus gives us one last critical order: "Repent and be clean, converted from sin, and reconciled to God." If you think you don't need God, then you are in big trouble! "Those who do not admit their faults have the most to fear."

Remember, there are only two "eternal" things you can ever do: to accept Christ as your Savior and to bring others to the knowledge of salvation. Take faith; you are saved by grace. Accept Jesus Christ as your Savior and march forward in service.

Remember, the most important prayer you will ever pray is the Sinner's Prayer:

Dear Lord Jesus, I know that I am a sinner, and I ask for your forgiveness. I believe you died for my sins and rose from the dead. I turn from my sins and invite you to come into my heart and life. I want to trust and follow you as my Lord and Savior. In your Name. Amen.

Jesus has promised: "I am with you always, to the very end of the age" (Matthew 28:20). He will be with you, beside you, behind you, and in front of you always, forever, as far as eternity extends. He will guide you, support you, equip you, never leaving you defenseless. So you can follow him and cooperate with him.

You can do this.

You and Jesus, together, you got this.
Onward, onward, Christian knight!
Onward to thy Hero's pilgrimage!
Onward faithful sheepdog, follow ye the Great Shepherd!

ORDER #22: *Next Level Battle Prep*

➤ What were the qualities of St. Matthew before he was called by Jesus?

  ○ How did Matthew respond when Jesus said, "Follow Me"?

➤ What was it like when Jesus said to you, "Follow Me"?

  ○ Do you know your godly assigned mission?
  ○ How do you receive your assignments?

Conclusion:
A Case Study in Spiritual Warfare

In 1979, three young second lieutenants, Jim Boyle, Jan Horvath, and Dave Grossman, graduated from Officer Candidate School (OCS) and the Infantry Officer Basic Course at Ft. Benning, Georgia, and we went forth to our first assignments as US Army officers. We had all been prior enlisted, coming up through the ranks as privates and young sergeants, and we had experienced the toxic impact of the drug dealers and drug users in the barracks.

Boyle and Horvath went to the 7th Infantry Division in Ft. Ord, California, where they became known as "Batman and Robin" and were rightfully feared by the druggies and dopers in their units. Young Lt. Grossman meanwhile went to the 9th Infantry Division in Ft. Lewis, Washington, where I became known as "Spiderman" because I would sometimes "body-jam" up the outside of the barracks buildings to climb into second and third floor windows to apprehend drug users.

In two different military bases, unbeknownst to each other, we followed almost identical paths. We each quietly went about our battle to drive the drug dealers and the drug users out of the barracks.

When the battalion shut down at the end of each day and during the weekends, according to military tradition—stretching back at least to the Romans—someone had to be left in charge. The battalion was entrusted to a lieutenant called the battalion staff officer (SDO), and each company was left under the authority of a sergeant who served as charge of quarters (CQ), all selected from a rotating roster. When serving as SDO, Boyle, Horvath, and Grossman would gather the company CQs and hunt for drug users in the barracks all night long. There was no war other than the Cold War going on, but we took our lives in our hands, night after night, fighting the rot from within.

I can't speak for Boyle and Horvath, but *I* was most definitely a "baby Christian." I was—and remain—far from perfect. Still, the Holy Spirit, the sacrificial example of Christ, and the love of God all worked within me and motivated me to stand up to the toxic drug culture.

One of my evaluation reports said that I had made "more drug busts than every other officer in the battalion, put together." Over seven hundred miles away in Ft. Ord, California, Boyle and Horvath were racking up a similar score.

In my book *On Killing,* I talk about how we take young men and women, we give them the tools and the skills to kill people, often we send them to get lots of experience at killing people, and then we bring them home. The critical question is: How do we make sure they do not use their killing skills on their own citizens? Any society that does not resolve this dilemma will be destroyed by their military veterans. And every military society has found the same solution: discipline, discipline, discipline. Thus, a lack of discipline among our military (like widespread breaking of the law and of regulations by doing drugs in the barracks) should be a cause for grave concern. (The same can be said for spiritual warfare! Remember, *our* disobedience and lack of discipline *grieves* the Holy Spirit.)

Company commanders from other units would ask me to train their lieutenants, and I was happy to do so. But the officers I trained just would not seek out the drug users. They were all good men. They didn't lack for knowledge. I think their deficiency may have been spiritual in nature.

Maybe those other lieutenants didn't understand (as Boyle, Horvath, and I did) the harm the drug users and drug dealers in the barracks were causing. Maybe they didn't comprehend the vital importance of discipline and the horrendous danger of widespread lawless behavior among our troops. Maybe they didn't know how the good soldiers living in the barracks had to fight daily, living in a kind of hell-on-earth, existing in a constant war zone if they didn't want to do drugs. Maybe they didn't realize that the drug users and drug dealers in our military also had an insidious, long-term cost. These druggies were unlikely to reenlist. But the good soldiers were disgusted and poisoned by the impact of these drug-using losers, and thus they were also less likely to reenlist. And these good soldiers were not likely to encourage their children to serve their nation in the years to come. It was a death spiral for our military and for our nation, as our politicians continued to demand that the military reflect the worst aspects of our culture and serve as a source of "social mobility" for the dregs of our society.

Mostly though, our fellow officers had been blinded by the world. Without God in their lives, without a spiritual compass, they didn't have the moral courage to do the hard right in the face of wrong.

We can see many of the 22 WARNORDs in our peers who did not actively hunt the drug dealers and the dope users. Let's use this as a case study and application of Luther's and Erasmus' 22 WARNORDS:

- They had no faith. (WARNORD #1)
- They doubted the Lord and every aspect of authority that flowed from above. (#2)
- They were self-centered, worrying about their safety. (#3)
- They resisted the Lord and the standards set by lawful authority. (#4)
- They were blinded by ambition and craved status, caring more about being popular with the troops than they cared about our military readiness. (#5 and #11)

- They had bought into false beliefs about drugs, and they were weak-minded and distracted, tricked, and tempted by the lies of the world. (#6, #7, #8, and #9)

- While there was no physical war going on, there was still a conflict for hearts and minds, and the drug users and the drug dealers were waging this war in the barracks. However, our peers were weak-minded, and they retreated from the heart of battle, fled from the devil, and deceived themselves. (#10, #12, #13, and #14)

- They said, "The drug culture is too strong" and didn't think they could make a difference. (#16)

- They felt no sorrow for the pain the good soldiers suffered, and they were not motivated by the drug dealers' conflict with the good soldiers. (#17 and #19)

- Most of all, they had no divine authority. They did not know God, and they did not truly serve Christ or, ultimately, their nation. (#20, #21, and #22)

Then Ronald Reagan was elected and began his term of office in 1981. He applied virtuous, honorable principles and solved the drug problem in the military within a year, using the urinalysis program and the expeditious discharges of bad troops. The battle against the drug dealers and the drug users in our Armed Forces continues to this very day, but never again would the drug users own the barracks.

I can tell you the story of many police officers, military officers, and non-commissioned officers who also confronted criminals with the same vigor, energy, and ingenuity. The story of Lieutenants Boyle, Horvath, and Grossman could be told ten-thousand times over.

The fight most of us will face is not like World War II, on some raging battlefield. The most insidious and essential conflict that we will face is the epic, eternal, *internal* battle, as we strive for righteousness and engage in daily spiritual warfare in our lives, struggling against rot and moral decay in a lost world.

And the answer for each of us, as we face our challenges in life, can be found in God's Word, and these 22 Warning Orders.

The Cold War: Eternal Vigilance

For a long time, America fought the Cold War: an endless battle to sustain readiness and virtuous behavior in the face of a monolithic, totalitarian communist evil. Our great achievement was fending off breakout warfare against communist regimes. Our greatest victory was that the Russians never came across a border we held, and political communism ultimately collapsed from within, destroyed by its own innate immorality and evil. You can make an argument that it was a victory unprecedented in the annals of history. A good portion of the world (NATO, SEATO, CENTO) under US leadership endeavored for generations to deter a war against the rest of the world.

Very few who serve in the armed forces across the centuries have engaged directly in bloody battles. Only a small minority of police officers have actually participated in gun battles with vicious criminals. Even for those who did engage in physical combat, it represented only a small portion of their lives. It is generally true that combat is 99 percent boredom and 1 percent sheer terror, and it can be in the 99 percent that the battle is ultimately won or lost.

Most sheepdogs have careers like Boyle, Horvath, and Grossman. Ours was mostly a struggle to deter a nuclear armed foe that had enslaved a good portion of the world while also fighting the rot from within our own ranks. It is likely that your personal battles will be similar.

Still, if we were to have failed in our duty, if but a single generation of our military or our law enforcement officers were to completely fail in this task of eternal vigilance, then our nation and our civilization would be doomed. And totalitarian states would immediately take the opportunity to conquer and destroy us. Truly, the price of freedom is eternal vigilance. All the WARNORDs in this book, all of Luther's and Erasmus' warnings and orders applied to us, and they apply to you, as we serve and fight our eternal spiritual battle against the rot and decay from within.

Also, never forget that in a democracy or a republic such as ours in America, *we* are the kings. Through our votes and our influence upon the political system, ultimately, *we* are the rulers. And if we do not use every bit of authority that we have to move our nation toward righteousness, then we are like the evil kings of old. If you wonder what they were like, read through 1 and 2 Kings and 1 and 2 Chronicles. These are honest, insightful accounts of a few good kings mixed among numerous bad and evil rulers. There you will also see the curses that God inflicted upon the bad kings for their evil steward-ship. Tragically, evil still afflicts nations and rulers, bringing curses upon us and our nations. As God's sheepdogs, we can use our authority to move our lands toward righteousness. We can and we must strive to do this.

A Personal Application

Look at just the first five WARNORDs and see how they apply to your personal spiritual battle as you strive to maintain and sustain your little part of our civilization. Consider again how they apply to you in your situation:

#1. Fight the wicked who have no faith by accepting God's great grace.

#2. Fight doubt by acting on your faith.

#3. Fight a selfish, self-centered world by analyzing your desires and bringing them under God's will.

#4. Fight the wicked who resist God by making Christ your only guide.

#5. Fight a world blinded by ambition by turning away from worldly things.

Now look at the summary of all these WARNORDs at the end of this book and apply them to your daily battle. Review them on a regular basis and apply them always. It might be valuable to go back through this book as a devotional, covering one WARNORD a day or even prayerfully applying one a week.

Si vis pacem, para bellum. "If you seek peace, prepare for war." The *pacem*, the "peace" we seek is peace with God, the only peace that truly matters. And we do indeed *parabellum*; we must "prepare for war." Spiritual warfare! The only war that truly matters, the battle for eternal souls.

Thus, we go forth, as our leader shouts, "Follow me! I will take the first bullet," and we engage in triumphant spiritual warfare, in God's holy power.

The eternal vigilance that makes it possible for our civilization to survive would be impossible without the Lord working within our peace officers, our first responders, our soldiers, sailors, airmen, and marines, and all those sheepdogs who serve the Great Shepherd. With Jesus as our Savior, we can literally "Charge hell with a squirt gun and emerge victorious!" says Rev. Wesley E. Blanton.

Remember, too, that it is good and right to pray for your nation. At the end of this book, take a look at another noble, old patriotic song written with America in mind and realize that it is a prayer.

> *O beautiful for spacious skies,*
>   *For amber waves of grain,*
> *For purple mountain majesties*
>   *Above the fruited plain!*
> *America! America!*

God shed His grace on thee
And crown thy good
with brotherhood
From sea to shining sea!

O beautiful for pilgrim feet,
Whose stern, impassioned stress
A thoroughfare for freedom beat
Across the wilderness!
America! America!
God mend thine every flaw,
Confirm thy soul
in self-control,
Thy liberty in law!

O beautiful for heroes proved
In liberating strife,
Who more than self their country loved
And mercy more than life!
America! America!
May God thy gold refine,
Till all success
be nobleness,
And every gain divine!

O beautiful for patriot dream
That sees beyond the years
Thine alabaster cities gleam
Undimmed by human tears!
America! America!

> *God shed His grace on thee*
> *And crown thy good*
> *with brotherhood*
> *From sea to shining sea!*

—"America the Beautiful," by Katharine Lee Bates
(1859–1929)

Each of us, in every task we are given, must do our utmost, with God's almighty hand upon us, to:

- Love God and love others as yourself (Mark 12:30–31). The Golden Rule is ever our "standing order" for guard duty (7:12).

- If you truly love people, then the greatest gift you can offer them is eternal salvation, and you will strive to fulfill the Great Commission and bring the gospel, the good news, to all corners of the world (Matthew 28:19).

- You can bring people to the knowledge of salvation by making your life a living witness, doing good deeds ceaselessly and tirelessly (Galatians 6:9).

- By giving all the honor and glory to God, you turn your works into God's works and become a powerful living witness (Revelation 4:11).

- Thrive! And live the life of love, joy, and peace that our loving Father wants to give you. And that love, shining out through you, can be the greatest witness of all, in a mighty reinforcing cycle of love and joy and salvation (Galatians 5:22).

- And then join your Father in heaven in an eternity of joy and peace that we can only faintly, vaguely comprehend here on this fallen world (Psalm 23:6).

One day the sheepdog will finally rest at the feet of the Great Shepherd, and we yearn to hear those words: "Well done, thou good and faithful servant."

Now may the God of peace, who through the blood of the eternal covenant brought back from the dead our Lord Jesus, that great Shepherd of the sheep, equip you with everything good for doing his will, and may he work in us what is pleasing to him, through Jesus Christ, to whom be glory for ever and ever. Amen...Grace be with you all.
—Hebrews 13:20–21, 25

Summary

WARNORD #1
FIRST WARNING

THE WICKED HAVE NO FAITH
The greatest wickedness is denying the Most High God.

FIRST ORDER

INCREASE YOUR FAITH BY ACCEPTING GOD'S GRACE
Even if the entire world appears mad.

─────────────── ✠ ───────────────

WARNORD #2
SECOND WARNING

THE WICKED DOUBT THE LORD

He who is not at one with God doubts and worries; they give up, thinking that God has forsaken them and has even become their enemy; they lay the blame for their ills on other men and become vindictive.

SECOND ORDER

ACT ON YOUR GOD-GIVEN FAITH
Even if you must undergo the loss of everything.

✠

WARNORD #3
THIRD WARNING

THE WICKED ARE SELF-CENTERED

The wicked…seek not God, nor cares for the things of God; they seek their own riches, their own glory…their own power, and, in a word, their own kingdom.

THIRD ORDER

ANALYZE YOUR DESIRES
Seek first the Kingdom of God and what God wants, then all your other needs will be met as well.

✠

WARNORD #4
FOURTH WARNING

THE WICKED RESIST THE LORD
The uncircumcised in heart and ears will always resist the
Holy Spirit.

FOURTH ORDER

MAKE CHRIST THE ONLY GUIDE AND GOAL
OF YOUR LIFE
Dedicate all your enthusiasm, all your effort, your leisure as
well as your business.

✠

WARNORD #5
FIFTH WARNING

THE WICKED ARE BLINDED BY AMBITION
Whatever man loves, that is his god. For he carries it in his
heart; he goes about with it night and day; he sleeps and wakes
with it, be it what it may—wealth or self, pleasure or renown.

FIFTH ORDER

TURN AWAY FROM WORLDLY THINGS
If you are greatly concerned with success,
you will be weak of spirit.

✠

WARNORD #6
SIXTH WARNING

THE WICKED SPREAD FALSE BELIEFS

The wicked are deluded by ideas hatched in their own brains. They blasphemy the truth with all kinds of falsehoods, calling evil good, and good evil; they put darkness for light, and light for darkness!

SIXTH ORDER

TRAIN YOUR MIND TO DISTINGUISH THE TRUE NATURE OF GOOD AND EVIL

Let your rule of government be determined by obedience to God, and the common good, by the example of Jesus Christ our Savior.

WARNORD #7
SEVENTH WARNING

THE WICKED ARE EASILY DISTRACTED

Some people hear the Word, but when the world brings them trouble, they quickly fall away.

SEVENTH ORDER

NEVER LET ANY FAILURE OR SETBACK TURN YOU AWAY FROM GOD

We are not perfect; this only means we should try harder.

WARNORD #8
EIGHTH WARNING

THE WICKED ARE EASILY TEMPTED BY SATAN
Satan reigns in us with full power, by temptation alone.

EIGHTH ORDER

FACE TEMPTATION WITH PRAYER,
NOT WITH WORRY OR EXCUSES
Begin to worry when you do not feel temptation, because that
is a sure sign that you cannot distinguish good from evil.

✠

WARNORD #9
NINTH WARNING

THE WICKED PRACTICE TRICKERY AND DECEPTION
The wicked seek their own gain through the other's loss and
forget the rule which says: "Do unto others that which you
wish they would do to you."

NINTH ORDER

ALWAYS BE PREPARED FOR AN ATTACK
Careful generals set guards even in times of peace.

✠

WARNORD #10
TENTH WARNING

THE WICKED FLEE FROM THE DEVIL

Submit yourselves, then, to God. Resist the devil and he will flee from you.

TENTH ORDER

SPIT, AS IT WERE, IN THE FACE OF DANGER

Keep a stirring Bible quotation with you for encouragement, so you may have courage through the Lord thy God.

WARNORD #11
ELEVENTH WARNING

THE WICKED CRAVE STATUS

If you become concerned with popularity and neglect your duty, it is easy enough to fall into sin.

ELEVENTH ORDER

GUARD AGAINST TWO DANGERS:
MORAL COWARDICE AND PERSONAL PRIDE

Dedicate all your effort and all your tribute to Jesus Christ our Savior.

WARNORD #12
TWELFTH WARNING

THE WICKED ARE WEAK-MINDED
The conscience of the wicked is shattered and confused and retains neither faith nor works.

TWELFTH ORDER

TURN YOUR WEAKNESS INTO STRENGTH
Delight in weaknesses, in insults, in hardships, in persecutions, and difficulties. Pray to Christ and say: "Lord, increase my faith."

WARNORD #13
THIRTEENTH WARNING

THE WICKED RETREAT FROM THE HEART OF BATTLE
The wicked flee and yet cannot escape.

THIRTEENTH ORDER

TREAT EACH BATTLE AS THOUGH IT WERE YOUR LAST
And you will finish, in the end, victorious!

WARNORD #14
FOURTEENTH WARNING

THE WICKED DECEIVE THEMSELVES

No one has sunk so deep into wickedness as those men who do many good works of their own.

FOURTEENTH ORDER

DON'T ASSUME THAT DOING GOOD ALLOWS YOU TO KEEP A FEW VICES

The enemy you ignore is the one who conquers you.

✠

WARNORD #15
FIFTEENTH WARNING

THE WICKED ARE EASILY PROVOKED

Man's heart and senses are inclined always to do evil, that is, to pride, disobedience, anger, and hatred.

FIFTEENTH ORDER

A GOOD KNIGHT WEIGHS HIS ALTERNATIVES CAREFULLY

The wrong way will often seem easier than the right way.

✠

WARNORD #16
SIXTEENTH WARNING

THE WICKED SAY "THE DEVIL IS TOO STRONG"
The devil convinces those weak in faith that all their good efforts are worthless and condemned, and one might as well remain a sinner.

SIXTEENTH ORDER

NEVER ADMIT DEFEAT EVEN IF YOU
HAVE BEEN WOUNDED
The good soldier's painful wounds spur him to gather his strength.

✠

WARNORD #17
SEVENTEENTH WARNING

THE WICKED CREATE CONFLICT AMONG THE
FAITHFUL
Sin doth corrupt and decay that which was well created, sowing the poison of dissension.

SEVENTEENTH ORDER

ALWAYS HAVE A PLAN OF ACTION
So when the time comes for battle, you will know what to do.

✠

WARNORD #18
EIGHTEENTH WARNING

THE WICKED ARE ENVIOUS OF OTHERS
The devil provokes jealousy, back-biting, vengeance, and all manner of angry works and words.

EIGHTEENTH ORDER

CALM YOUR PASSIONS BY SEEING HOW LITTLE THERE IS TO GAIN
We often worry and scheme about trifling matters of no real importance.

WARNORD #19
NINETEENTH WARNING

THE WICKED DO NOT FEEL SORROW FOR THE PAIN THEY CAUSE
The devil tempts us to bring shame and hurt on our mothers, fathers, wives, and children.

NINETEENTH ORDER

CONSIDER THE IMPACT ON YOUR FAMILY
"If I do what I am considering, would I want my family to know about it?"

WARNORD #20
TWENTIETH WARNING

THE WICKED HAVE NO DIVINE AUTHORITY
Evil is at its worse when the rule of man is preferred over the authority of God.

TWENTIETH ORDER

VIRTUE HAS ITS OWN AUTHORITY
Once a person has Christ in their heart, they would not exchange his authority for anything.

✠

WARNORD #21
TWENTY-FIRST WARNING

THE WICKED DO NOT KNOW GOD IN CHRIST
And if you do not know God, you cannot worship Him, praise Him, give Him thanks, nor serve Him.

TWENTY-FIRST ORDER

LIFE CAN BE SAD, DIFFICULT, AND QUICK: MAKE IT COUNT FOR SOMETHING
Since we do not know when death will come, dedicate yourself to Christ every day.

✠

WARNORD #22
TWENTY-SECOND WARNING

THE WICKED DO NOT CONFESS OR SERVE CHRIST
Heartfelt regret brings repentance that leads to salvation, but impenitence is the unpardonable sin that brings death!

TWENTY-SECOND ORDER

REPENT YOUR WRONGS AND CHANGE YOUR WAYS
Repent and be clean, converted from sin, and reconciled to God. Those who do not admit their faults have the most to fear.

Bibliography

Hymns

Alexander, Cecil F. "When Wounded Sore."

Barnes, F. D. "The Open Gate."

Bates, Katharine Lee. "America the Beautiful."

Berlin, Irving. "God Bless America."

Carter, M. "The Sacred Joy Which Virtue Brings."

Cowper, William. "God Moves in a Mysterious Way."

Crosby, Fanny J. "Let Us Work and Pray Together."

---------- "Never Lose the Golden Rule."

---------- "Rescue the Perishing."

Dix, W. Chatterton. "Come unto Me, Ye Weary."

Doane, George Washington. "Thou Art the Way, to Thee Alone."

Faber, Frederick William. "Faith of the Martyrs."

Francis, Samuel. "America (My Country, 'Tis of Thee)."

Herbertus, Petrus. "Faith Is a Living Power."

Hewitt, Eliza E. "Have We Laid Up Our Treasures in Heaven."

Lowell, James Russell. "Once to Every Man and Nation."

Luther, Martin. "A Mighty Fortress Is Our God."

Runyan, William M. "Word of God, O Sacred Treasure."

Sammis, John H. "Trust and Obey."

Schell, William Gallio. "Humility, Thou Secret Vale."

Solberg, C. K. "Amen, Be His Word and Spirit."

Townsend, Joseph L. "O Thou Rock of Our Salvation."

Unknown. "The Final Trump We Soon Shall Hear."

Valerius, Adrianus. "We Gather Together."

Van Dyke, Henry. "The Hymn of Joy."

Ware, Henry, "Happy the Home When God Is There.

Prayers and Poems

Bugenhagen, Johannes. "Pomeranian Agenda."

Dietrich, Veit. "Prayer for Steadfast Faith."

---------- "Prayer for the Coming of Jesus."

Francis of Assisi. "Peace Prayer."

Oatman, Johnson. "Standing like a Lighthouse."

Books, Articles, and Websites

Alexander, Cecil. "I Believe in the Holy Ghost." *Hymns for Little Children*. Toronto: H. Rowsell, 1859.

Amorth, Gabriele. "Facts about Satan and the Fallen Angels." *Catholic Exchange*, September 3, 2020. https://catholicexchange.com/facts-about-satan-and-the-fallen-angels-fr-gabriele-amorth/.

"Bass Reeves." Minnesota Churches of God Conference. September 25, 2017. https://mncogconference.org/articles/2017/9/9/bass-reeves.

Boggs, Johnny D. "Across the Old Southwest." *True West*. March 29, 2020. https://truewestmagazine.com/article/across-the-old-southwest/.

Bond, Michael. "How to Survive a Disaster." BBC. January 28, 2015. https://www.bbc.com/future/article/20150128-how-to-survive-a-disaster.

Bonhoeffer, Dietrich. *Ethics*. New York: The Macmillan Company, 1965.

---------- *Letters and Papers from Prison*. New York: Macmillan, 1972.

Bonhoeffer, Dietrich, and Reginald Fuller. *The Cost of Discipleship*. London: SCM Press, 1959.

Brady, Paul. *The Black Badge: Deputy United States Marshal Bass Reeves from Slave to Heroic Lawman*. Los Angeles: Milligan Books, 2005.

Brende, Joel, and Elmer McDonald. 1989. "Post-Traumatic Spiritual Alienation and Recovery in Vietnam Combat Veterans." *Spirituality Today*, 41 (3). www.domcentral.org/library/spir2day/894143brende.html.

Bunyan, John. *The Pilgrim's Progress*. Philadelphia: The John C. Winston Co., 1909.

Calhoun, Lawrence, and Richard Tedeschi. *Posttraumatic Growth in Clinical Practice*. New York: Routledge, 2012.

Calvin, John. "Commentary on Ephesians 4:30." *John Calvin's Commentary on the Bible*. 1840–57.

Campbell, Rebecca, and Tom Tremblay. "A Trauma Informed Approach to Law Enforcement First Response." https://www.youtube.com/watch?v=gtWD1XJrhNo&t=802s.

Chomsky, Noam. "Terror and Just Response." ZNet, July 2, 2002.

Collins, Jim. "The Stockdale Paradox." *From Good to Great: Why Some Companies Make the Leap…and Others Don't.* New York: HarperCollins, 2011. www.jimcollins.com/concepts/Stockdale-Concept.html.

Comey, James. "Statement on Orlando Mass Shooting." Press conference at FBI Headquarters, Washington, DC, June 13, 2016. https://www.americanrhetoric.com/speeches/jamescomeyorlandoshootings.htm.

Common Service Book of the Lutheran Church. Philadelphia: Board of Publication of the United Lutheran Church in America, 1918.

Davis, Marshall. "Courage As a Spiritual Practice." Spiritual Reflections by Marshall Davis, December 9, 2021. https://revmdavis.blogspot.com/2021/12/courage-as-spiritual-practice.html.

Delattre, Edwin. *Character and Cops: Ethics in Policing.* Washington, DC: AEI Press, 2011.

Dickens, Charles. *A Christmas Carol.* New York: Hodder and Stoughton, 1911.

Drushal, Mary Ellen. 1988. "Implementing Theory Z in the Church: Managing People as Jesus Did." *Ashland Theological Journal* 20 (1). https://biblicalstudies.org.uk/pdf/ashland_theological_journal/20-1_47.pdf.

Etheridge, Kristy. "After 'Unbroken': Billy Graham and Louis Zamperini." Billy Graham Evangelistic Association. December 22, 2014. https://billygraham.org/story/louis-zamperini-billy-graham-and-a-life-changing-decision-the-rest-of-the-unbroken-story.

Erasmus, Desiderius. *The Manual of a Christian Knight*. London: Methuen and Co., 1905.

Feder, Adriana, et al. 2008. "Posttraumatic Growth in Former Vietnam Prisoners of War." *Psychiatry* 71 (4). https://doi.org/10.1521/psyc.2008.71.4.359.

Fitzgerel, Noah. "Full Transcript of President Obama's Speech at Dallas Police Memorial." ABC News. July 12, 2016. https://abcnews.go.com/Politics/full-transcript-president-obamas-speech-dallas-police-memorial/story?id=40521153.

Freedom Resource Center. "Admiral Jim Stockdale." Accessed on April 16, 2023. www.freedomrc.org.

Fuerst, Tom. "Have You Committed the Unforgivable Sin?" Ministry Matters. October 20, 2014. www.ministrymatters.com.

Gates, Milo, ed. *The Campaign Prayer Book*. New York: Thomas Nelson & Sons, 1892.

Gladwell, Malcolm. *David and Goliath: Underdogs, Misfits, and the Art of Battling Giants*. New York: Little, Brown and Company, 2013.

Graham, Ruth. "This Is Your Brain on Faith." *U.S. Catholic*, June 10, 2014. https://uscatholic.org/articles/201406/this-is-your-brain-on-faith/.

Green, Susan. "Unforgivable Sin." St. Margaret's Church, Prestwich, Manchester, England. July 12, 2018. https://stmargaretsprestwich.com/2018/07/12/unforgivable-sin/.

Griffith, Howard. "Martin Luther's Doctrine of Temptation." *Reformed Faith and Practice* 4:3 (December 2019). https://journal.rts.edu/article/martin-luthers-doctrine-of-temptation/.

Groysberg, Boris, and Robin Abrahams. "What the Stockdale Paradox Tells Us about Crisis Leadership." Harvard Business School. August 17, 2020. https://hbswk.hbs.edu/item/what-the-stockdale-paradox-tells-us-about-crisis-leadership.

Gurnall, William. *Christian in Complete Armour.* London: William Tegg, 1862.

Harper, Anna, and Kenneth Pargament. "Trauma, Religion, and Spirituality: Pathways to Healing." In *Traumatic Stress and Long-term Recovery*, edited by K. E. Cherry, 349–64. New York: Springer International Publishing, 2015.

Harris, Jeanette, Joseph Currier, and Crystal Park. "Trauma, Faith and Meaning-Making." In *Psychology of Trauma*, edited by T. Van Leeuwen and M. Brouwer. New York: Nova Science Publishers, 2013, 135–50.

Hawks, Howard, dir. *Sergeant York*. 1941; Burbank, CA: Warner Bros. Pictures.

Heaney, Seamus. *Beowulf*. New York: Farrar, Straus, and Giroux, 1999.

"Humility in the Bible and 10 Tips for Teaching It to Kids." Gentle Christian Parenting, blog. July 24, 2020. https://gentlechristianparenting.com/humility.

Johnson, Sam. "I Spent Seven Years as a Vietnam POW: The 'Hanoi Hilton' Is No Trump Hotel." *POLITICO Magazine*. July 21, 2015. https://www.politico.com/magazine/story/2015/07/i-was-vietnam-pow-donald-trump-120436/.

Johnson, William. "Washington's Prayers." In *George Washington, the Christian*, 23–35. New York: The Abingdon Press, 1919. https://www.google.com/books/edition/George_Washington_the_Christian/FhgFAAAAYAAJ?hl=en&gbpv=1.

Kaufman, Scott Barry. "The Light Triad vs. Dark Triad of Personality." *Scientific American*. March 19, 2019. https://blogs.scientificamerican.com/beautiful-minds/the-light-triad-vs-dark-triad-of-personality/.

Kavussanu, Maria, Vassilis Barkoukis, Philip Hurst, Mariya Yukhymenko-Lescroart, Lida Skoufa, Andrea Chirico, Fabio Lucidi, and Christopher Ring. "A Psychological Intervention Reduces Doping Likelihood in British and Greek Athletes." *Psychology of Sport and Exercise* 57 (November 2021).

Keltie, Sir John Scott. *History of the Scottish Highlands: Vol. 5*. Edinburgh: Thomas C. Jack, Grange Publishing, 1887.

Klick, Jonathan, and Alexander Tabarrok. 2005. "Using Terror Alert Levels to Estimate the Effect of Police on Crime." *The Journal of Law and Economics* 48 (1): 267–79.

Kliegman, Aaron. "Eric Adams Wants NYC to Be 'Place of God' after Predecessor Targeted Religion throughout Pandemic." Fox News. March 17, 2023. https://www.foxnews.com/politics/eric-adams-wants-nyc-place-god-predecessor-targeted-religion-pandemic.

Leach, John. "Why People 'Freeze' in an Emergency: Temporal and Cognitive Constraints on Survival Responses." *Aviation, Space, and Environmental Medicine* 75:6 (2004). https://www.hptc-pro.com/wp-content/uploads/2014/01/Why-People-Freeze.pdf.

Learmonth, Eleanor, and Jenny Tabakoff. *No Mercy: True Stories of Disaster, Survival and Brutality*. Melbourne, Australia: Text Publishing, 2013.

Lewis, C. S. *The Four Loves*. New York: Harcourt, 1960.

---------- *The Great Divorce: A Dream*. London: HarperCollins, 2002.

---------- *The Last Battle*. New York: Macmillan, 1956.

---------- *Mere Christianity*. New York: Macmillan, 1960.

---------- *The Screwtape Letters*. London: Goeffrey Bles, 1952.

Linden, Magnus, and David Whetham. "'Dark triad': The Personality Profile That Is Linked to War Crimes." *The Print*. February 10, 2020. https://theprint.in/world/dark-triad-the-personality-profile-that-is-linked-to-war-crimes/361631/.

Linden, Magnus, Fredrik Björklund, Martin Bäckström, Deanna Messervey, and David Whetham. "A Latent Core of Dark Traits Explains Individual Differences in

Peacekeepers' Unethical Attitudes and Conduct." *Military Psychology* 31:9 (2019): 1–11.

Longenecker, Dwight. *Immortal Combat: Confronting the Heart of Darkness*. Manchester, NH: Sophia Institute Press, 2020.

---------- "The Un-Holy Trinity." Patheos. February 13, 2010. https://www.patheos.com/blogs/standingonmyhead/2010/02/the-un-holy-trinity.html.

Lopez, Anthony. "Why the Weak Sometimes Win and the Strong Never Learn." *Psychology Today*. March 13, 2019.

Luther, Martin. *The Bondage of the Will*. London: T. Bensley, 1823.

---------- *An Exhortation to Truly Good Works*. Martin Luther's Church Postil 1544. Accessed March 7, 2023. http://www.lutherdansk.dk/Web-sommerpostillen%20AM/Kirkepos.htm.

---------- "A Simple Way to Pray…for Master Peter the Barber." World Mission Prayer League. Accessed on March 7, 2023. https://wmpl.org/filed/resources/public/Literature/ASimpleWaytoPray.pdf.

---------- *A Treatise on Good Works*. Translated by M. Reu. Available at The Project Gutenberg. https://www.gutenberg.org/files/418/418-h/418-h.htm.

MacArthur, John. "The Unforgivable Sin." Grace to You. November 1, 2009. https://www.gty.org/library/sermons-library/41-16/the-unforgivable-sin.

MacCulloch, Diarmaid. *Christianity: The First Three Thousand Years*. New York: Penguin Publishing Group, 2010.

Magister, Sandro. "The Pope at Auschwitz: 'They Wanted to Kill God.'" Catholic Education Resource Center. May 29, 2006. https://catholiceducation.org/resources/the-pope-at-auschwitz-they-wanted-to-kill-god.

Morgan, Thaddeus. "Was the Real Lone Ranger a Black Man?" History. November 8, 2021. https://www.history.com/news/bass-reeves-real-lone-ranger-a-black-man.

Migliozzi, Anna. "The Attraction of Evil and the Destruction of Meaning." *International Journal of Psychoanalysis* 97:4 (2016): 1019–34.

Obama, Barack. "Full Transcript of President Obama's Speech at Dallas Police Memorial." ABC News. July 12, 2016. www.abcnews.go.com.

O'Neill, James H. "The True Story of 'The Patton Prayer.'" The Imaginative Conservative. March 24, 2022. https://theimaginativeconservative.org/2022/03/true-story-patton-prayer-james-hugh-o-neill.html.

Oord, Thomas Jay. "The Finally Impenitent." ThomasJayOord.com. December 1, 2019. https://thomasjayoord.com/index.php/blog/archives/the-finally-impenitent.

Park, Crystal L., Mary A. Mills, and Donald Edmondson. "PTSD as Meaning Violation: Testing a Cognitive Worldview Perspective." *Psychological Trauma: Theory, Research, Practice, and Policy* 4:1 (2012.): 66–73.

Pelikan, Jaroslav, ed. *Luther's Works, American Edition*. Vols. 1–30. St. Louis: Concordia, 1955–76.

Pisa, Nick. "Hitler and Stalin Were Possessed by the Devil, Says Vatican Exorcist." *Daily Mail*. August 28, 2006.

https://www.dailymail.co.uk/news/article-402602/Hitler-Stalin-possessed-Devil-says-Vatican-exorcist.html.

Plumb, Charlie. "Advice from a Prisoner of War (Charlie Plumb)." Beyond the Uniform. August 1, 2019. BTU #294. https://beyondtheuniform.org/blog/btu-294-advice-from-a-prisoner-of-war-charlie-plumb?rq=%23294.

"Poway Synagogue Shooter Inspired by Hitler, Unsealed Affidavit Shows." *Times of Israel*, June 18, 2019. https://www.timesofisrael.com/poway-synagogue-shooter-inspired-by-hitler-unsealed-affidavit-shows/.

"Praise the Lord and Pass the Ammunition!" National Museum of American History. Accessed on March 7, 2023. https://americanhistory.si.edu/collections/search/object/nmah_670902.

Prinzing, Michael, Patty Van Cappellen, and Barbara L Fredrickson. "More Than a Momentary Blip in the Universe? Investigating the Link between Religiousness and Perceived Meaning in Life." *Personality and Social Psychology Bulletin* 49:2 (2021): 180–96.

Reith, Charles. "Principles of British Policing." *A Short History of the British Police*. Oxford University Press, 1948.

Rogers, Adrian. *The Incredible Power of Kingdom Authority: Getting an Upper Hand on the Underworld*. Nashville, TN: B&H Publishing Group, 2002.

Rosalsky, Greg. "When You Add More Police to a City, What Happens?" National Public Radio, *Planet Money*. April 20, 2021. https://www.npr.

org/sections/money/2021/04/20/988769793/
when-you-add-more-police-to-a-city-what-happens.

Sale, Richard, dir. *Abandon Ship!* 1957; London, England:
Columbia Pictures.

Sandhu, Pritam Singh. "The Sinner's Prayer." South
Asian Christians. November 20, 2021. https://
southasianchristians.com/articles/team-sac-picks/
the-sinners-prayer/.

Sassoon, Siegfried. *Counter-Attack, and Other Poems.* New
York: E. P. Dutton & Co, 1919.

Simpson, Albert B. *Days of Heaven upon Earth: A Year Book
of Scripture Texts and Living Truths.* New York: Christian
Alliance Publishing Co., 1897.

---------- *In Step with the Spirit: Discovering the Dynamics of
the Deeper Life.* Chicago: Moody Bible Institute, 1998.

---------- *The Self Life and the Christ Life.* Harrisburg, PA:
Christian Publications, 1886.

---------- "A Solemn Covenant: The Dedication of Myself to
God." In *The Fourfold Gospel*, 22. Orlando, FL: Bridge
Logos, 2007.

Slane, Craig J. "Christ and the Spirit: Fleshing Out the Vision
of A. B. Simpson's Imitation of Christ." *Alliance Academic
Review* (1997). http://www.kneillfoster.com/aar/1997/
AAR1997-9.php.

Soldier's Prayer Book. Boston: Protestant Episcopal Prayer
Society. Circa 1863.

Souza, Raymond J. de. "Calling And Caravaggio." *Convivium*, September 21, 2017. https://www.convivium.ca/articles/calling-and-caravaggio/.

Spenser, Edmund. *The Faerie Queene*. New Haven: Yale University Press, 1981.

Spurgeon, Charles Haddon. "Grieving the Holy Spirit." *New Park Street Pulpit*, Volume 5. October 9, 1859. The Spurgeon Center. https://www.spurgeon.org/resource-library/sermons/grieving-the-holy-spirit/#flipbook/.

Stackpole, Robert. "Have I Committed the Unforgivable Sin?," The Divine Mercy, Marian Fathers of the Immaculate Conception. June 16, 2010. https://www.thedivinemercy.org/articles/have-i-committed-unforgivable-sin.

"The Stages of Recovery." Fort Behavioral Health. March 13, 2023. https://www.fortbehavioral.com/addiction-recovery-blog/the-stages-of-recovery.

Stanley, Charles. "What Is the Unpardonable Sin?" InTouchMinistries Devotional. iDisciple.org. https://www.idisciple.org/post/what-is-the-unpardonable-sin-2.

Stockdale, James, and Jim Collins. "Stockdale Paradox." *Model Thinkers*. Accessed on March 7, 2023. https://modelthinkers.com/mental-model/stockdale-paradox.

Stockdale, James B. *A Vietnam Experience: Ten Years of Reflection*. Stanford, CA: Hoover Press, 1984.

Taylor, Justin. "A Letter from Martin Luther on Spiritual Warfare." *The Gospel Coalition*. January 13, 2012. https://www.thegospelcoalition.org/blogs/

justin-taylor/a-letter-from-martin-luther-on-spiritual-warfare/.

Tocqueville, Alexis de. *Democracy in America*. New York: G. Dearborn & Co., 1838.

"U.S. Attorney, Law Enforcement Partners Announce Results of Child Exploitation Prevention Initiative: Dozens Charged as a Result of 'Operation Constant Vigilance.'" The FBI. May 3, 2011. https://archives.fbi.gov/archives/newhaven/press-releases/2011/u.s.-attorney-law-enforcement-partners-announce-results-of-child-exploitation-prevention-initiative.

U.S. Department of Defense. "Military Awards for Valor." Accessed on March 7, 2023. www.valor.defense.gov.

U.S. v. Holmes. U.S. Circuit Court for the Eastern District of Pennsylvania, 1842. www.cite.case.law/f-cas/26/360/.

Wallace, J. Werner. "Celebrate Christmas with Your Kids—They Already Believe in God." Fox News. December 19, 2021. https://www.foxnews.com/opinion/celebrate-christmas-kids-believe-god-j-warner-wallace.

---------- *Person of Interest: Why Jesus Still Matters*. Grand Rapids, MI: Zondervan, 2021.

Watson, Thomas. *The Christian Soldier, or Heaven Taken by Storm*. New York: Robert Moore, 1810.

"What Is the Unpardonable Sin/Unforgivable Sin?" GotQuestions. Accessed on March 7, 2023. www.gotquestions.org/unpardonable-sin.html.

Jeff Wolf (a.k.a. "CopRev" and author of the book *Blue Lies: The War on Justice and the Conspiracy to Weaken America's Cops*)

And finally, profound appreciation and gratitude to our wonderful editor, Bill Watkins, and our excellent copy editor, Caroline Rock.

About the Authors

Lt. Col. Dave Grossman, U.S. Army (Ret.), is an internationally recognized scholar, author, soldier, and speaker. He is one of the world's foremost experts in the field of human aggression, the roots of violence, and violent crime. He is an Army Ranger, a former West Point psychology professor, and a renowned trainer for military and law enforcement officers. His books (translated and published in eleven languages) include *On Killing, On Combat, On Spiritual Combat, On Hunting,* and *Assassination Generation.*

Sgt. Christopher Pascoe is retired from the Michigan State Police, where he served as a trooper and sergeant for thirty-one years. He was assigned to several posts, including the Michigan State Police Training Academy. He has made key contributions to the books *On Combat* and *Sheepdogs: Meet Our Nation's Warriors.* He is currently an adjunct professor of criminal justice at Washtenaw Community College and Eastern Michigan University and a guest instructor for newly promoted sergeants and supervisors.

Wolf, Jeff. *Blue Lies: The War on Justice and the Conspiracy to Weaken America's Cops*. Goshen, OH: Resurgence Publishing, 2021.

Yglesias, Matthew. "The Case for Hiring More Police Officers." *Vox*, February 13, 2019. https://www.vox.com/policy-and-politics/2019/2/13/18193661/hire-police-officers-crime-criminal-justice-reform-booker-harris.

Acknowledgments

Special thanks to our dedicated team of proofreaders and commentators known as the "alpha readers." Many small changes add up to a huge effect, and the culmination of all their contributions truly blessed this book. "As iron sharpens iron, so one person sharpens another" (Proverbs 27:17). May God bless all of you!

Leah Anaya

Gene Blanton

Andrew Bowell

Vicki Dorman

Joseph Giorgione

Gregory Guevara

David Kemp

Derrick Millett

Dr. Eric Murray, TeamTrainingAssociates.com

Keith Overby

Sequoia Palmquist

Steven Sipe

Mike Smock